Special Events

Best Practices in
Modern Event Management

Second Edition

Dr. Joe Jeff Goldblatt, CSEP

VAN NOSTRAND REINHOLD

I(T)P® A Division of International Thomson Publishing Inc.

New York • Albany • Bonn • Boston • Detroit • London • Madrid • Melbourne
Mexico City • Paris • San Francisco • Singapore • Tokyo • Toronto

Special thanks to Puff N Stuff Catering, Framboise Catering, Wildflowers Florist, The Thayer Hotel, The National Civil Rights Museum, and The Stone Ridge Library for their cooperation during the photographing of several of the color insert photos.

The author welcomes comments, ideas, and suggestions from readers. Send your messages via E-mail to: drevent@gwis2.circ.gwv.edu

First, the students, faculty, professional colleagues, family, and friends who have guided my journey into this new profession are to whom this volume is dedicated. Numerous in number, their unflagging support has enabled these pages to form from ideas to concepts to principles. My gratitude for these individuals and that of the Event Management profession is immeasurable.

Furturmore, those members of the Event Management family who are living with AIDS will hopefully benefit from these pages. A portion of all sales of this book will be donated to AIDS services within local communities. Together let us bring hope and good health as we continue to grow the profession of Event Management. To this cause, let this book and all of us be dedicated.

Contents

Foreword

The stakes have never been higher. Sponsors are more savvy. Audiences are more demanding. And, event producers and managers are held accountable by their clients to meet their financial and marketing goals more than ever before.

While special events as a social experience may have distant anthropological roots, special events as a discipline has only recently begun to emerge from a chaotic, primordial soup. During its stormy primeval era, event producers had only the tools of their own imagination, experience, and the oral history of a fragmented industry. Frequently, hard lessons were learned, many times followed by the extinction of both companies and careers.

Special events has evolved into a full-grown industry, an exciting new hybrid conceived through the convergence of marketing, promotion, entertainment, and the creative arts. For corporations, events have become an essential part of the marketing mix, touching consumers emotionally and with life-long impact in ways that traditional advertising, publicity, and promotion can not. Socially, events balance the powerful and rapid advancement of home-based entertainment alternatives which tend to isolate us, bringing us closer together to celebrate and commemorate.

For this hopeful species to have any future as an industry, it must constantly adapt to the ever-changing business environment. While today's event professional must be a producer and business strategist, a marketer and controller, a promoter and personnel manager, few received any academic training in the business of special events. With little training and no vast, scholarly body of knowledge from which to draw, most seasoned event professionals will candidly admit that there are missing links in their skill sets as managers and producers.

This book about the world's most exciting profession will help you unearth those missing links. If you are just starting in "the business," you have made available to yourself a valuable resource of knowledge and experience built over years, seen through the lens of today's business realities. If you are an experienced producer, you will find yourself nodding in confirmation of what you suspected was right all along, punctuated by frequent moments when your eyes open wide with the discovery of new concepts, philosophies, and paradigms.

Special events has never been more important to both business and the human condition, and there have never been better tools at your fingertips. So, before the lights go down and the curtain rises, reach out for the experience and expertise in these pages, and "break a leg."

Frank Supovitz
Vice President, Special Events
National Hockey League
New York, NY

Preface

Be careful what you wish for because it might come true.
—*Gertrude Whitby, 1890-1990*

As a boy I recall sitting in Aunt Gerts parlor in Texas and fiddling with her Edison phonograph. As I danced to the music from these scratchy recordings I told her my dreams. "One day I want to be in show business," I declared.

"Oh, you want to be an actor" she countered from the kitchen. "No, I want to produce events!" I shouted over the rousing melodies of John Philip Sousa's, "Stars and Stripes Forever." "What kind of events?" she asked. "Big ones" I boasted. "Fireworks, parades, and other celebrations," I roared. Wiping her hands on a dish towel she left the kitchen, lifted the needle on the Edison, turned to me, and in her wise way smiled and said, "Be careful what you wish for because it might come true."

Therefore, when an editor at Van Nostrand Reinhold telephoned my office at The George Washington University and asked me to write not one but two new editions to my first book I thought lovingly of my wise aunt. As the editor described her enthusiasm for the project because of the growth and positive future for the Event Management profession, I reviewed the text of my first book and realized that indeed everything I had wished for and so much more had come true.

In 1990 when that book was first published I wrote that it was my hope that special events would emerge as a respected profession. Only six years later this is happening in abundance. As the Founding Director for The Event Management Program at The George Washington University, I am surrounded by over 200 students who are professional meeting planners, exposition directors, festival managers, social event coordinators, fund raising specialists, event tourism consultants, corporate event managers, sport event directors, retail event managers, and just as many more titles representing the increasingly colorful quilt first defined as special events. But our program is not alone. Thousands more are enrolled in professional education programs at colleges, universities, trade associations, and other post secondary programs throughout the world. Through their efforts and yours they are earning respect for Event Management.

A Bright Future for Event Managers

The future of the Event Management profession is ripe with promise. This is due to several factors. First, the growth in two-income families has propelled the growth in the service industry. In record numbers, husbands and wives are turning to event managers to handle the details of their social life-cycle events. Second, the United States has become a nation of specialists. Those with specialized training such as Event Management are in demand by those individuals or organizations who require specific expertise. As the Event Management profession grows through education the individuals who are employed as event managers will be in greater demand. Finally, the Event Management profession incorporates multitasking skills that form a generic management base. For example, event managers must be marketing, human resource, and financial specialists to successfully produce effective events on a continuous basis. Those trained in this field are able to use these highly portable skills to succeed in other professions such as public relations or general business where Event Management may fall under the category of "other duties assigned." As the economy continues to be unpredictable and the labor force reinvents itself on a daily basis, event managers are well positioned to anticipate and even prosper from these changes. A 1995 article in *M & C Magazine* described how, due to lay-offs or downsizing, many traditional meeting planners were using their meeting planning skills in other fields to earn new income. Event managers are even better positioned as they are more broadly trained than meeting planners and this training and experience will enable them to succeed more quickly in locating a new position if required.

According to the Public Relations Society of America (PRSA), there are over 150,000 individuals who practice public relations. Event Management, according to PRSA, is one of the fastest growing and most important trends in this modern profession. Public relations is a discipline that grew out of journalism and psychology. Although well trained in writing and research, few of the current practitioners have Event Management training and this means new opportunities for trained event managers such as yourself.

Another profession related to communications is the 12,000 television and radio stations in the United States. According to the National Association of Broadcasters (NAB), the majority of these stations have an individual or individuals responsible for live station promotions. These events are usually managed by individuals with a marketing background with little to no logistics experience. Once again, this means opportunities for you in this expanding field.

In my own profession of higher education there are over 3,000 institutions and each produces numerous events ranging from convocation to commencement. Each university or college has at least one individual and in some cases many individuals who produce events full time and many more who are involved part time.

The Challenge of Change

The multitude of changes that took place in the special events community during the recession of the late 1980s and early 1990s could be grouped into three broad categories. First, the uncertain economic times had reduced spending for events and those firms that had concentrated on only producing mega or big ticket events were either out of business, merging, or slowly reinventing themselves. Second, the technological changes such as the rapid use of the facsimile, computer, modem, Internet, and other marvels of the modern age had placed greater stress on the special events community to accelerate delivery of ideas and the events themselves. Finally, competition had magnified as the special events field turned from a local business into a global one and through downsizing, literally hundreds and perhaps even thousands of former event professionals working for corporations and government agencies were now freelancing and competing with the more established firms.

These three trends—economic uncertainty, rapid technological advancement, and increased competition—had produced a major paradigm shift within the event industry. This shift occurred during the mid-1980s as the event industry was feeling overly confident and rapidly expanded. Now the industry was in an era of economic uncertainty, technological change, and escalating competition, and did not know how to cope or plan. This period, reflected by an uncharted course within and outside the industry, is where I began my research to provide the tools that would not only expand, but also sustain this industry and help it meet the challenges ahead.

The paradigm had shifted from an unformed group of professions known as special events into an emerging discipline encompassing many professions known as *Event Management.*

These professions are now required to prepare for the social, economic, and political challenges that confront established professions such as medicine, accounting, and law. Event Management has moved from infancy to adolescence and is now entering adulthood. In business terms, it has moved from birth to growth to maturity and now faces complacence which can be followed by decline or by reinvention and sustained growth through education and strategic planning. The latter is what this book aims to do with your commitment as a professional Event Manager.

How These Trends Affect You

The growth in the rapidly emerging discipline of Event Management has been unprecedented during the last forty years and has certainly accelerated during this decade. Those event managers who respond to challenging economic times with sound financial practices will produce consistently profitable events. Those event managers who anticipate and adapt emerging technologies to support their emerging discipline will most certainly produce more efficient and perhaps more profitable events. Those event managers who set quality standards and find the right market niche will help ensure that competition is kept in check. These three trends—economic uncertainty, rapid technological advancement, and increased competition—are *positive* signs for event managers and this is why this book is essential for your career and business. The first of these trends represents a unique opportunity to reinvent or perhaps for the first time actually define a profession. Second, these trends provide us with unparalleled technological innovations to produce more efficient, higher quality, and more profitable events. Finally, growing competition allows us to improve and focus on individual strengths through serving niche markets. These three trends and the paradigm shift they form provide you with an exciting platform from which to relaunch or build your career.

Under Construction: A Blueprint for the Professional Career

All careers are constantly under construction. However, the more successful careers, including Event Management, follow a general blueprint to match actions to the final product. Although some careers happen by accident, most are the result of a passion for a specific type of work, training, practice, professional networking, and that most ephemeral of experiences—timing.

My definition of a perfect job is to find something you like to do so much that you would do it for nothing. Once you have found this type of job the next challenge is to find someone to pay you to do it. Event Management is exactly this type of profession. This passion for helping people celebrate runs deep among serious event managers. Some even see their work as part ministry rather than solely a commercial profession.

Education: Your Unique Journey

To fully realize the potential of this paradigm shift you must begin your own unique journey. This book is the first step in a continuous educational process that you and millions of others are embarking on as businesses reinvent themselves at light speed. The changes identified in each field require skilled managers, marketers, and researchers with state-of-the-art and science tools. Only through continuous education can you make sure you remain sharp enough to make your dreams come true.

> Two woodsmen decided to engage in a competition to see who could be the first to chop down two mighty trees. At the appointed time one woodsman began to furiously chop, swinging the axe forcefully against the large tree. After several minutes the woodsman glanced over to the other woodsman and noticed that he was sitting against the tree cradling his axe. The first woodsman wiped the sweat from his brow and walked over to his challenger and asked why he was sitting down. "I am taking time to *sharpen* my axe," said the wise challenger. One hour later the first woodsman was still furiously wielding his axe as he heard the sound "timber!" and watched as the second woodsman felled his tree. Is there any doubt how the second woodsman won this competition?

Sharpening your skills through participation in professional organizations, attending educational programs, and networking with your peers is extremely important. This importance can be translated into bottom line results. According to the U.S. Bureau of the Census, the more you learn the more you will earn. This is reflected among event managers whose educational attainments are significantly better than the average public and perhaps as a result their incomes are significantly greater as well.

In a 1993 study of members of the International Special Events Society (ISES) the findings showed that event managers may earn between $25,000 and $75,000 as compared with a median U.S. salary of approximately $23,000. Correspondingly the majority of event managers has earned baccalaureate degrees and over 20 percent has earned graduate degrees as well. The baccalaureate diplomas ranged from advertising to zoology. However, nearly 25 percent have degrees in business administration, demonstrating the importance of a solid grounding in this discipline. Noticeably absent were degrees in Event Management. Through specialization in this profession you literally have the same opportunities that physicians, attorneys, accountants, and other professions enjoyed over one hundred years ago. The major difference is that these traditional professions were solely comprised of males and it required decades before women were admitted or given even marginal respect. By contrast, the Event Management profession is an equal opportunity career right from the beginning.

Global Opportunities

There are numerous global business opportunities for event managers. Traditionally, a client develops a close rapport with his or her event manager. Simultaneously, the event manager develops expertise into the client's organizational culture including the key individuals who comprise the decision-making process. Therefore, it is only natural that when an event that is held this year in New York is held the following year in New Mexico or even Norway the event manager will be asked to travel to that destination to maintain continuity. This important organizational or institutional memory is an important asset for event managers to develop.

Another asset that must be developed for the global marketplace is an understanding of the cultural, economic, and political nuances of each destination where the event is being held. Members of the International Congress and Convention Association (ICCA) told me that an event manager who wants to do business in Europe, Asia, or Latin America needs to spend significant time learning the business practices and cultures of each country. Learning the language is considerably easier than understanding why individuals in that country make certain decisions and how those decisions may be positively or negatively influenced by the actions of the event manager.

Event managers who are planning global careers should, according to the members of ICCA, speak and write one or more languages in addition to English. The most popular languages are French, Spanish, and German. As the Pacific Rim economy continues to develop, Japanese and Mandarin Chinese will be added to this list. Furthermore, it was suggested by ICCA members that global event managers must allow significant time to develop relationships with their global trading partners as these contacts develop slowly and cannot be rushed. The goal is to establish a long term partnership built on mutual trust.

Event Management: A Multidisciplinary Profession

The most interesting finding of the ISES study was that only 50 percent of the event managers work time was invested in the management of events. This explains the multidisciplinary nature of this emerging discipline. Whether you currently are an administrative assistant or the CEO, chances are that at some time you have had to organize a meeting or other event. You probably used transferable management skills to accomplish this project. However, you soon realized that specialized training was also needed to produce an effective event. Many of the students who apply for admission to the Event Management program tell me that although managing events was but one of their job responsibilities it was the one they most enjoyed. Therefore, they are seeking further training in this profession to improve their chances for long-term success doing something they truly enjoy. In learning these highly portable skill sets they are simultaneously increasing their opportunities for long-term career success in many other professions as well.

As I counsel these students I realize that this emerging discipline identified in this book as the profession of Event Management is part of a much larger movement. Millions of career professionals and those just starting their careers are in search of work that is meaningful, financially rewarding, and yes, fun. With the elimination of long term security in most jobs workers are now in search of a career path that satisfies deeper longings in addition to financial compensation. They are turning to Event Management because it allows them to combine people, travel, creativity, and the tangible reward of seeing a project through completion into a satisfying and rewarding career. In their eyes I see the excitement of new, real opportunities and feel their determination to succeed in this profession. Through your efforts and thousands of others, humankinds oldest tradition is being rapidly transformed into a modern profession known as Event Management.

Wise, old Aunt Gert was right. Be careful what you wish for because it might come true. Mine did and so will yours as you turn your dreams into plans by using this book to grow your career and enjoy boundless success.

Acknowledgments

Event managers assemble quality teams to produce consistently effective events. The team that assembled to produce this volume has over 25,000 years of experience in this profession. Their scholarship and professional experiences have ensured that this text reflects a broad cross section of the luminaries in Event Management. If you were fortunate enough to engage each one as a consultant for one day you would have invested over one million dollars in fees. As I interviewed these individuals for the first edition and now this second edition I am impressed with their generosity in freely sharing their secrets of success with others.

The form of this manuscript required a master's touch. Fortunately for me the author, and you the reader, my longtime associate Dylan Aramian has supplied that touch. Her good taste, common sense, and commitment to quality is reflected in every line and for this I am most grateful.

The editorial team at Van Nostrand Reinhold—made certain that my creative instincts would be given solid form through logical application and thereby ensure that you receive a tool that is both efficient and practical. This team is certainly part of the extended family of Event Management professionals as reflected by their enthusiasm and devotion to this project.

Finally, and most importantly, Nancy, Max, and Sam, my beloved family, granted me the priceless gift of time allowing me to do what I enjoy—helping to sustain and expand this profession. Although this debt cannot be repaid I hope that this volume reflects adequately the love and support of my family that enabled me to conduct this work. As an Event Management family we enjoy celebrating and this book most certainly reflects that spirit fostered in our home.

As you run your fingers over the names of the *Event Management* professionals listed below, remember that every time you see the term Event Management, their talent, industriousness, and devotion is behind every letter. They are truly the authors of this new profession.

Richard Aaron, CSEP

Craig Aramian

Dylan Aramian

Rusty Aramian

Karen R. Baker

Ayhan V. Baker

Angelo Bonita

Janna Bowman

Terry L. Brady

William Burdette

Jeff & Sheila Campbell

Melissa A. Campbell

Robert J. Caskey

Kimberley P. Collins

Alice Conway, CSEP

John J. Daly, Jr., CSEP

Dr. Lisa Delpy

Paul Demos

Andrea Dixon

Ashleigh A. Dockery

Gene Donati

Arnold S. Ehrlich

Robert Estrin

Burt Ferrini

David Fowler

Andrea C. Frank

Dr. Douglas Frechtling

Jack Frost

Amy L. Galton

Dr. James Gelatt

Leon Gendin

Dr. Donald Getz

Michelle L. Glemser

Max B. Goldblatt (deceased)

Max D. Goldblatt

Rosa deBlanc Goldblatt

Sam D. Goldblatt

Audrey Gordon

Sharon Group, CAE

Stedman Graham

J. Robert Graves

Dr. Joseph A. Greenberg

Jeffrey Hamberger, Esquire

Chris Hargrove

Earl C. Hargrove, Jr.

Dr. Donald E. Hawkins

Hill Herwood

Tanya M. Headley

Treb Heining

Linda Higgison

Denise Hitchcock, APR

Sir Thomas Ingilby

Klaus Inkamp, CSEP

Jewell Jackson

Robert F. Jani

Dana L. Jarvis

Felice M. Jones

Lu Kleppinger

William K. Knight

Leah Lahasky

Xujie Liu

Barnett Lipton

Laurie Lowe

Kristin M. Lundy

Darwin Lynner (deceased)

Nancy R. Lynner

Ruth C. Lynner

Stephen J. Masten

Sarah K. May

Linda McFarlin

Erin McGee

Cynthia R. McDowell

Carol McKibben, CSEP

Mona Meretsky, CSEP

Freddie J. Meynell

Terrance L. Morris

Anne Morton

Jack Morton

Mark Murray

Kari Nestande

Lucia Nevai

Harry D. Oppenheimer

Gabriel Ornelas

Jerold Panas

Dr. Salvatore Paratore

Roger de Pilkington

Edwin Phelps

Barbara Pomerance

Dr. Catherine Price

Kristan L. Quackenbush

Dr. Paul O. Radde

Judith J. Reddington

Tiffany Rippe, CMP, CSEP

Ambassador Selwa S. Roosevelt

Marc Rose, CSEP

Cantor Arnold H. Saltzman

Lisa B. Shafran

Professor Patti Shock

Steve Schwartz

Sharon Siegel

Kathleen W. Siegfried

Rita Bloom Smith, CSEP

Dr. Valene Smith

Professor Sheryl Spivack

Traci L. Silk Punke

Julie Sistrunk

James H. Steeg

Wayne Stetson

Anne E. Stine

Frank Supovitz

Diaka N. Tartt

Arden A. Tellini

Tamara L. Thomason

Raymond B. Thompson

Barbara Tober

Mary Toups

Stephen Joel Trachtenberg

Donald Trump

Edith Turner

Victor Turner

Jon Ukman

Lesa Ukman

Joseph A. Van Eron

Darnyse L. Werts

Dr. Susan Weston

Gertrude Whitby

Carter & Ernestine Wheelock

Anita L. Wiler

Guion Williams

Dr. Peggy Williams

Dan Witkowski

Dr. Brunetta Wolfman

Nancy C. Yim

Suk Kyu Yoon

Jennifer S. Ziehl

Howard Zusel

Introduction to Event Management

From Special Events to Event Management

To prepare for the future one must value and thoroughly understand the past. The term "special events" may have first been used at what is often described as the "happiest place on earth." In 1955 when Walt Disney opened Disneyland in Anaheim, California, he turned to one of his imagineers, Robert Jani, and asked him to help solve a big problem. Each day at 5:00 P.M. thousands of people, in fact almost 90 percent of the guests, would leave the park. The problem with this mass exodus was that Walt's happiest place on earth remained open until 10:00 P.M. That meant he had to support a payroll of thousands of workers, utilities, and other expenses for five hours each day with no income.

To correct this problem, Robert Jani, then director of public relations for Disneyland, and later the owner of one of the most successful Event Management production companies in the world, Robert F. Jani Productions, proposed the creation of a nightly parade that he dubbed the "Main Street Electric Parade." Dozens of floats with thousands of miniature lights would nightly glide down Main Street delighting thousands of guests who remained to enjoy the spectacle. This technique is used today in all Disney parks with perhaps the best example at Epcot where a major spectacular is staged every night. According to the producers this spectacle results in millions of dollars of increased spending annually.

One of the members of the media turned to Robert Jani during the early days of the Main Street Electric Parade and asked, "What do you call that program?" Jani replied, "A special event."

"A special event, what's that?" the reporter asked while scratching his head. Jani thoughtfully answered with what may be the simplest and best definition of a special event.

> *"A special event is that which is different from a normal day of living."*
> —ROBERT JANI, 1955

According to Jani, nowhere on earth does a parade appear on main street every night of the year. Only at Disneyland where special events are researched, designed, planned, managed, coordinated, and evaluated does this seemingly spontaneous program take place every night. Jani, who would later produce National Football League Super Bowl half-time spectaculars as well as the legendary Radio City Music Hall Christmas Show, among many other unique events, was a man whose motto was "dream big dreams and aim high."

ANTHROPOLOGICAL BEGINNINGS

Some thirty-five years later in the first edition of this book I defined special events as:

> *"A unique moment in time celebrated with ceremony and ritual to satisfy specific needs."*

My definition emerged from that of anthropologist Victor Turner who wrote that "every human society celebrates with ceremony and ritual its joys, sorrows, and triumphs." According to Turner and other researchers I had studied in my exploration of anthropology, ceremony and ritual were important factors in the design, planning, management, and coordination of special events.

Five years later after interviewing nearly 150 experts in special Event Management for my first book I discovered that while special events represents many professions one individual is always at the helm of this large vessel. That person is the *event manager.*

Growth Opportunities

Only four decades ago, when an orchestra was needed to provide music for a wedding or social event, one consulted with an orchestra leader. Very often the orchestra leader would provide references for additional talent to enhance the event. Mike Lanin, president of Howard Lanin Productions of New York City, tells the story of a meeting his father, Howard Lanin, the renowned society maestro, had with a client in Philadelphia during the late 1920s. Having already asked Lanin to provide music for her daughter's coming-out party being held at the Bellvue-Stratford, the client asked that he provide decor as well. When Lanin asked how much the client would like to spend, the client replied, "Just make it lovely, Howard—just make it lovely." Lanin immediately realized that to make this huge ballroom "lovely" might require an investment of five figures. With inflation, the cost of such an undertaking today would well exceed six figures. But Lanin was fortunate to have earned his client's total trust. Without further discussion, the orchestra leader and decorator went to work. Few clients of any era would offer such an unlimited budget. But more and more often, special events professionals such as the Lanin's are being asked to provide more diversified services. And while orchestra leaders may have been comfortable recommending decorations and other services and products for social events three decades ago, they and others with specific areas of expertise found that, when it came to events designed for advertising and public relations opportunities, they required specialized assistance.

Public relations is a proud ancestor of the celebrations industry. Less than fifty years ago, the modern profession of public relations and advertising became an accepted tool in American commerce. When a corporation wished to introduce a new product, increase sales, or motivate its employees, its corporate leaders turned to public relations and advertising professionals to design a plan. Today the celebrations industry includes tens of thousands of hard-working professionals who, for the first time in the industry's history, are truly working together to offer their clients the excellent services and products they deserve. As an example of the growth of Event Management in the public relations field, consider this comment from the first person in the United States to receive a master's degree in public relations, Professor Carol Hills of Boston University: "My students are extremely interested in events. They recognize that public relations and events are inseparable. Event Management is certainly a growth area in public relations practice."

According to the International Council of Shopping Centers (ICSC) in New York, marketing directors who produce events for local and regional shopping centers can earn in the high five figures. Marketing professionals have recognized the need for specialized training and the benefits of certification within their industry. Events help attract and influence consumers to purchase specific products and services from small retail stores up to major regional shopping centers with hundreds of shops. In this age of entrepreneurism, the creation of new business is far greater than the growth of established firms. With each new business created, there is a new opportunity to celebrate through a grand opening or other special event. There are over one million new businesses created annually in the United States that may require an event manager to produce an opening celebration.

The *Event Manager* is the person responsible for *researching, designing, planning, coor-*

dinating, and *evaluating* events. You will learn about each of these phases in the pages to come. However, the logical question one may ask is: What is the Event Management profession?

Event Management Profession

Event Management is the profession that requires public assembly for the purpose of *celebration, education, marketing,* and *reunion.* Each of these overarching activities is encompassed by the profession of Event Management. While it can be argued that Event Management, like tourism, is actually comprised of many industries, increasingly as data is gathered and scientific tests are conducted it becomes more apparent that Event Management represents a unique body of knowledge.

According to experts in the field of professional certification, all professions are represented by three unique characteristics. First, the profession must have a unique body of knowledge. Second, the profession typically has voluntary standards that often result in certification. Third, the profession has an accepted code of conduct or ethics. The profession of Event Management meets each of these qualifications.

Let us explore further the definition of Event Management. The term *public assembly* means events managed by professionals who typically bring people together for a purpose. While an individual can most certainly hold an event by himself or herself, arguably, it will not have the same complexities of an event with 10 or 10,000 people. Therefore, the size and type of the group will determine the level of skills required by the professional event manager.

The next key word is *purpose.* In daily lives events take place spontaneously and, as a result, are sometimes not orderly, effective, or on schedule. However, professional event managers begin with a purpose in mind and direct all activities toward achieving this specific purpose. Event managers are purposeful about their work.

The third and final key component is the four overarching activities that represent these purposes—*celebration, education, marketing,* and *reunion.*

CELEBRATION

This activity is characterized by festivity ranging from fairs and festivals to social life-cycle events. Although the term "celebration" can also be applied to education, marketing, and reunion events it serves to encompass all aspects of human life where events are held for the purpose of celebration.

When one hears the word "celebration" the image of fireworks or other festivities typically is conjured. In fact, the word celebration is derived from the Latin word "celebrare" that means to "honor." Another commonly accepted definition is "to perform" as in a ritual. Therefore, celebrations usually refer to official or festive functions such as parades, civic events, festivals, religious observances, political events, bar and bas mitz-vahs, weddings, anniversaries, and other events tied to the person's or organization's life cycle or of historical importance.

EDUCATION

From the first event in kindergarten or preschool to meetings and conferences where many adults receive continuing education throughout their entire adult life, educational events mark, deliver, test, and support growth for all human beings. This growth may be social such as the high school prom or it may be professional such as a certification program. Regardless of the purpose, a public assembly is either primarily or secondarily educationally related.

The term "educate" is also derived from Latin; the term "educere" means to "lead out." Through education events, event managers lead out new ideas, emotions, and actions that improve society.

Examples of education events include convocation, commencement, alumni events, training at a corporation, meetings and conferences with specific educational content, and a fairly new activity known as *edutainment*. Edutainment results from the use of entertainment devices (such as singers and dancers) to present educational con-cepts. Through entertainment guests may know, comprehend, apply (through audience participation), analyze, and even evaluate specific subject matter. It may be used to lead out new ideas to improve productivity.

MARKETING

Event marketing, according to *Advertising Age,* is now an intrinsic part of any marketing plan. Along with advertising, public relations, and promotions, events serve to create awareness and persuade prospects to purchase goods and services. These events may be private such as the launch of a new automobile before dealers or public as in Microsoft's Windows '95® program. Retailers have historically used events to drive sales, and now other types of businesses are realizing that face-to-face events are an effective method to satisfy sales goals. The appearance of soap opera stars at a shopping center is but one example of many types of promotions used to attract customers to promote sales.

REUNION

When human beings reunite for the purposes of remembrance, rekindling friendship, or simply rebonding as a group they are conducting a reunion activity. Reunion activ-ities are present in all of the Event Management subfields because once the initial event is successful there may be a desire to reunite. The reunion activity is so symbolic in the American system that President Bill Clinton used this theme for his inaugural activ-ities.

Event Management Subfields

The desire and need to celebrate is one of those unique characteristics that makes us human. The humorist Will Rogers is reported to have said, "Man is the only animal that blushes . . . or needs to!" Human beings are the only animals that celebrate and this not only separates us from the lower forms but perhaps raises us to a transcendent or even spiritual level. The growth in the following Event Management subfields certainly reflects this extraordinary capability of celebration to transform humans and entire industries.

As noted earlier, anthropology historically has recognized a four-field approach to this established discipline. However, the profession of Event Management is encompassed by many specialized fields. Among these are *advertising, attractions, broadcasting, civic, corporate, exposition, fairs, festivals, government, hospitality, meetings, museums, retail,* and *tourism.* Event managers may specialize in any of these fields; however, rarely does the event manager labor in more than a few of these specializations. For example, a director of Event Management for the zoological society may plan events for the zoo and some of those events may involve retail promotions. Therefore, a knowledge of education and marketing as well as administration and risk management is important.

These subfields are not scientifically categorized as there are many linkages between them. However, the following list provides an overview into the possibilities for event managers as they seek to chart their future course of study. Once trained in the fundamentals of Event Management, event managers must specialize or concentrate their studies in one or two event subfields. By concentrating in two areas event managers are further protected from a downturn in a specific market segment as they have been trained in two different subfields. For example, if association meeting planners suddenly realized that they were no longer in demand due to outsourcing, being cross-trained in corporate event management they may be able to smoothly transition to this new field. Use the following list of subfields as a guide to focus your market or future employment options.

CIVIC EVENTS

Beginning with the U.S. bicentennial celebration in 1976 and continuing with the individual centennial, sesquicentennial, and bicentennials of hundreds of towns and cities, America has created more events than at any other time in the history of the republic. In both Europe and Asia, celebration is rooted in long-standing religious, cultural, and ritual traditions. The young nation America has not only blended the traditions of other cultures but has created its own unique events such as the annual Doo-Dah Parade in Pasadena, California. In this event anyone and everyone can participate and they do. There is a riding lawn mower brigade, a precision briefcase squad, and other equally unusual entries. As America matures, its celebrations will continue to develop into authentic made-in-the-U.S.A. events.

EXPOSITIONS

Closely related to fairs and festivals is the exposition. Although divided into two categories of public and private, the exposition has historically been the place where retailers meet wholesalers or suppliers introduce their goods and services to buyers. Some marketing analysts have suggested that it is the most cost-effective way to achieve sales as people who enter the exposition booth are more qualified to buy than a typical sales suspect. Furthermore, the exposition booth allows, as do all events, a multisensory experience. This experience influences customers to make a positive buying decision. A major shift in this field has been to turn the trade show or exposition into a multisensory, live event with educational and entertainment programs being offered in the various booths. And this field like many others is growing. Although some smaller trade shows have consolidated with larger ones there are just as many or perhaps more shows being created each year. This spells opportunity for savvy event marketers who wish to benefit from this lucrative field.

FAIRS AND FESTIVALS

Just as people assembled in the marketplace in ancient days to conduct business, commercial as well as religious influences have factored into the development of today's festivals, fairs, and public events. Whether a religious festival in India or a music festival in the United States, each is a public community event symbolized by a kaleidoscope of experiences that finds meaning through the lives of the participants. This kaleidoscope is comprised of performances, arts and crafts demonstrations, and other media that bring meaning to the lives of the participants and spectators.

These festivals and fairs have shown tremendous growth as small and large towns seek tourism dollars through these short-term events. Some communities use these events to boost tourism during the slow or off-season and others focus primarily on weekends to appeal to leisure travelers. Regardless of the reason, fairs (often not-for-profit but with commercial opportunities) and festivals (primarily not-for-profit events) provide unlimited opportunities for organizations to celebrate their culture while providing deep meaning for those who participate and attend.

HALLMARK EVENTS

The growth of the Olympic Games is but one example of how hallmark events have grown in both size and volume during the past decade. From America's Cup to Hands Across America to the centennial celebration of the Statue of Liberty, the 1980s were a period of sustained growth for these megaevents. While television certainly helped propel this growth, the positive impact of tourism dollars has largely driven the development of these events. Ironically, the World's Fair movement appears to have ebbed perhaps due to the fact that the inventions that previous World's Fairs showcased (space travel, computers, teleconferencing) have become commonplace and there is no need to offer any further predictions because these supposedly future happenings actually occur before the fair opens. This provides an opportunity to reinvent, revive, and perhaps sustain, this hallmark event.

HOSPITALITY

In the hospitality industry hotels throughout the world are expanding their business interests from merely renting rooms and selling food and beverages to actually planning events. Nashville's Opryland Hotel may have been the first to create a department for special events as a profit center for the corporation. They were followed by Hyatt Hotels Regency Productions, and now other major hotel chains, such as Marriott, are also exploring ways to move from fulfilling to actually planning and profiting from events.

MEETINGS AND CONFERENCES

The Convention Liaison Council, an organization that represents over two dozen organizations in the meeting, conference, and exposition industries, stated in 1995 that the annual contribution to the U.S. economy by these industries is over fifty billion dollars. Since the widespread use of the jet airplane in the 1950s, meetings and conferences have multiplied by the thousands as attendees jet in and out of cities for three- and four-day events. These events are primarily educational seminars that provide networking opportunities for both association members as well as corporate employees. Whether a corporate or association event, the globalization of the economy has produced significant growth in international meetings and as a result event managers are now constantly traveling both domestically and internationally.

RETAIL EVENTS

From the earliest days of the markets of ancient times sellers have used promotions and events to attract buyers and drive sales. The paradigm has shifted in this subindustry from the early 1960s and 1970s when retailers depended on single-day events to attract thousands of consumers to their stores. Soap opera stars, sports celebrities, and even live cartoon characters during a Saturday appearance could increase traffic and in some cases sales as well. Today retailers are much more savvy and rely on marketing research to design long-range promotional events that use an integrated approach combining a live event with advertising, publicity, and promotions. They are discovering that cause marketing such as aligning the product with a worthy charity or important social issue (for example, education) is a better way to build a loyal customer base and improve sales. This shift from short-term quick events to long-term integrated event marketing is a major change in this subindustry.

SOCIAL LIFE-CYCLE EVENTS

Bar and bas mitzvahs, weddings, golden wedding anniversaries, and other events that mark the passage of time with a milestone celebration are growing for two important reasons. As the age of Americans rises due to improvements in healthcare there will be many more opportunities to celebrate. Only a few years ago a fiftieth wedding anniversary was a rare event. Today most retail greeting card stores sell golden anniversary greeting cards as but just one symbol of the growth of these events.

In the wedding industry it is not uncommon to host an event that lasts three or more days including the actual ceremony. This is due to the great distances families must travel to get together for these celebrations. It may also be due to the fast-paced world in which we live and that often prevents families and friends from uniting for these milestones. Whatever the reason, social life-cycle events are growing in both length of days and size of budgets.

Funeral directors report that business is literally booming. Coupled with the increase in number of older U.S. citizens is the fact that many people are not affiliated with churches or synagogues. Therefore, at the time of death a neutral location is required for the final event. Most funeral chapels in the United States were constructed in the 1950s and now require expansion to accommodate the shift in population. New funeral homes are being constructed and older funeral homes are being expanded.

In the first edition of this book I predicted that in the not too distant future funerals may be held in hotels in order to provide the guests with overnight accommodations as well as to provide a location for social events. Now I predict that in some large metropolitan areas funeral home construction will be coupled with zoning decisions regarding hotel and motel accommodations to provide a total package for out-of-town guests. With the collapse of the traditional family of the 1950s and the proclivity Americans have for relocation it is not unreasonable to assume that weddings, funerals, and reunions are those events central to our lives for reconnecting with family and friends. Perhaps one growth opportunity for future event managers will be to design a total life-cycle event environment providing services including accommodations for these important events in a resort or leisure setting.

Social life-cycle events have always been important. While conducting focus group research at a local nursing home, a ninety-seven-year-old woman told me, "When you get to be my age you forget almost everything. What you do remember are the important things, your daughter's wedding, your fiftieth wedding anniversary, and other milestones that make life so meaningful." Increasingly due to limited time availability, individuals are turning to event managers like you to organize these important milestone events.

SPORT EVENTS

One example of the growth in popularity in professional sports is the rapid development of sports hall of fame and museum complexes throughout the United States. The 1994 World Cup soccer craze throughout the United States generated excitement, visibility, and in some cases, significant revenue for numerous destinations. Before, during, or following the big game, events are used to attract, capture, and motivate spectators regardless of the game's outcome to keep supporting their favorite team. In fact, the line has been blurred between sport and entertainment largely due to the proliferation of events such as pre-game giveaways, post-game fireworks and musical shows, and even promotions such as trivia contests during the game.

Tourism

Since the U.S. bicentennial in 1976 when literally thousands of communities throughout the United States created celebrations, event tourism has become an important phenomena. According to a study I conducted in 1994, those communities that do not have the facilities to attract the largest conventions increasingly are turning to event tourism as a means of putting heads in beds during the off-seasons and weekends. Whether it is in the form of arts and crafts shows, historical reenactments, music festivals, or other events that last anywhere from one to ten days, America is celebrating more than ever before and profiting from event tourism. From tax payers to political leaders to business leaders, more and more stakeholders are becoming invested in event tourism.

Stakeholders

Stakeholders are individuals or organizations who invested in your event. For example, the stakeholders of a festival may include the board of directors, the political officials, the municipal staff, the participants (craftspeople), the utility companies, and others. The event manager must scan the event environment to identify both internal as well as external stakeholders. An internal stakeholder may be a member of the board, the professional staff of the organization, a guest, or other closely related individual. External stakeholders may include the media, municipal officials, city agencies, or others.

A stakeholder does not have to invest money in the event to be considered for this role. Their emotional, political, or even personal interest in your cause is evidence of their investment in your event.

The Event Management Profession Model

From defining the profession, to identifying the principal activities conducted within this profession, to listing some of the subfields where event managers work, this is not intended to be a comprehensive analysis. Rather it is a framework within which you can begin to see a pattern emerge. This pattern is reflected in Figure 1-1. This model depicts the linkages between the definition, the activities, the subfields, and stakeholders. It will be useful to you as you begin or continue your studies in Event Management as it provides a theoretical framework supporting the organization of this profession.

Figure 1-1
The Goldblatt Model for the Event Management Profession

THE PROFESSION

Event Management

The function that requires public assembly for the purpose of
celebration, education, marketing, and reunion.

THE PROFESSIONAL TITLE

Event Manager

The individual responsible for researching, designing, planning,
coordinating, and evaluating an event.

SUBFIELD SPECIALIZATIONS

Examples of Subfields: Civic Events, Expositions, Fairs and Festivals,
Hallmark Events, Hospitality, Meetings and Conferences, Retail Events,
Social Life-cycle Events, Sport Events, and Tourism.

STAKEHOLDERS

Individuals or organizations who are financially, politically,
emotionally, or personally invested in the event.

How to Use This Book to Grow Your Career

Now that Event Management is emerging as a professional career it is essential that you carefully manage your growth to sustain your development for many years to come. There are numerous challenges in developing any professional career, albeit medicine, law, or Event Management. Identifying these challenges and developing a strategic plan to address these challenges is the most effective way to build long-term success. The four primary challenges professional event managers encounter are time, finance, technology, and human resources. They are the four pillars upon which you will reconstruct or construct a successful career (see Figure 1-2). This chapter will help you transform these challenges into opportunities for professional growth as well as better understand the emerging resources available in this new profession.

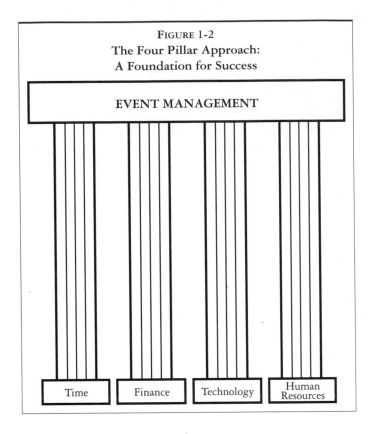

FIGURE 1-2
The Four Pillar Approach:
A Foundation for Success

EVENT MANAGEMENT

Time | Finance | Technology | Human Resources

MASTERING YOURSELF

The first person to be managed is you. Your ability to organize, prioritize, supervise, and delegate to others is secondary to first being able to manage your time and professional resources efficiently and effectively. Once you are sufficiently well managed you will find managing others is much easier. Managing yourself essentially involves setting personal and professional goals and then devising a strategic plan to achieve them. This involves making choices. For example, you may want to spend more time with your family and that will determine what field of Event Management you elect to specialize in. Certain fields will rob you of time with your family and friends, especially as you are building your career, while others will allow you to work a semiregular schedule. Association or corporate meeting planning may require that you work 9:00 A.M. to 5:00 P.M. for forty weeks of the year and 7:00 A.M. to 10:00 P.M. or later during the convention preparation and production. Hospitality Event Management positions, by contrast, may require long hours every day for weeks on end. After all, the primary resource of the event manager is time. It is the one commodity that once invested is gone forever. Setting personal and professional goals has a direct correlation to the type of work you will perform as an event manager. Hopefully, the fruits of your labors will represent an excellent return on your investment.

MASTERING TIME MANAGEMENT

Your return on your investment is in direct proportion to your ability to efficiently manage your time. This is so important that it bears further explanation. If you only have eight hours to produce an event that normally requires twelve or more hours, you can either lose money or make money by how you plan and use the time available. For example, you may ask yourself what resources can be consolidated, what meetings combined, and what tasks delegated to allow you to remain focused on your eight-hour deadline. Or you can hire extra labor, purchase additional resources, schedule more meetings, and try to handle all the details yourself. The choice is yours. These principles of time management are first applied in your daily life. How you spend your time performing everyday activities directly influences how you achieve your goals during your Event Management career.

One key element in effective time management is the ability to use your time effectively by distinguishing between what is urgent and what is important. Urgency is often the result of poor research and planning. Importance, however, results from a knowledge of priorities of time, resources, and the overarching goals of the event. I recognized this principle upon selling my business when for the first time in my adult life I was able to distinguish between my personal and professional time. Too often the event manager—one who usually loves what he or she is doing for a living (thereby distinguishing this individual from most of the working population of the world)—combines personal and professional time to their detriment. In my own experience, I carefully analyzed the capacity for personal and professional time each week and learned that only 168 hours are available. Of these hours 56 are invested in sleeping and 21 in eating, leaving 91 hours for work and personal commitments. For nearly 15 years I had used between 70 and 80 of these valuable hours for work-related activities leaving only 10 or so per week for my family and myself. With this analysis complete I set about matching my time to my new goals.

One of the reasons I sold my business was to spend more time with my family and improve myself both mentally and physically. Therefore, I realized that by working smarter instead of longer I could accomplish in fifty hours the tasks it had formerly taken me 25 percent more time to do. This new plan would allow me to spend additional time with my family and work toward achieving other personal goals I had set.

Effective time management must begin with setting personal and professional priorities especially as this profession is one with a high degree of burnout. Finding a healthy balance between the worlds of work, family, leisure, recreation, and spiritual pursuits is essential to your long-term success as an event manager. This book will not only help you find this balance but also show you how to carefully integrate time man-

WAR STORY

The opening of the Donald J. Trump Taj Mahal Casino Resort in Atlantic City, New Jersey, presented significant time management challenges. The entire event took place in the front driveway of the casino. This required closing the entrance to erect scaffolding, position lasers, hang lights, and make other important technical preparations. However, nothing is more important to running a casino than making sure the gamblers have easy unrestricted access to the facilities. A time line was carefully constructed that allowed the erection of the scaffolding to take place between midnight and 10:00 A.M. Rehearsals were also conducted during this time. By carefully considering the event goals (producing profit for the casino) the time required for installation was adjusted to satisfy the needs of all parties including the client.

Lesson Learned

Determine the event goals and then match all time bands to support these elements.

agement principles into every aspect of your Event Management professional career. This integration of time management principles will ultimately allow you more hours for recreation, leisure, and self-improvement, while providing increased earnings with fewer working hours. Figure 1-3, Best Practices for Event Time Management, will help you develop an effective system suitable for your personal and professional style.

MASTERING FINANCE

Becoming a wise and disciplined money manager is another pillar upon which you can construct a long-term career in Event Management. During your Event Management career you will be required to read and interpret spreadsheets filled with financial data. You cannot entrust this to others. Instead, you must be able to understand their interpretations of this data and then make judgments based upon your final analysis. Many event managers are uncomfortable with accounting. When interviewing students for admission to the Event Management program at The George Washington University, I noted that over 90 percent described that they are not comfortable with their financial or accounting skills.

Sharon Siegel, executive vice-president of Deco Productions of Miami, Florida, has

FIGURE 1-3
Best Practices for Event Time Management

1. Budget your time and relate this budget directly to your financial and personal priorities. As an example, if you value your family life, budget a prescribed period of time to be with your family each week.

2. Determine by an analysis of your overhead what your time is worth hourly. Remind yourself of the value of your time by placing a small sign with this amount on it near your telephone and condense extraneous phone calls and other activities that are not profit-producing.

3. Make a list of tasks to complete the next day before you leave the office or go to bed. Include all telephone calls to be made in this list and carry it with you for ready reference. In the age of cellular communications you can return calls from anywhere. As each task is completed triumphantly cross it off. Uncompleted tasks should be moved to the next day's list.

4. Determine whether meetings are essential and the best method for communicating information. Many meetings may be conducted via telephone conference call rather than in person. Other meetings may be canceled and the information communicated through memoranda, newsletters, or even video or audio recordings.

5. When receiving telephone calls determine if you are the most appropriate person to respond to the caller. If you are not the most appropriate person direct the caller to the best source. As one example, when individuals contact you for information about the Event Management industry refer them immediately to the International Special Events Society (1-800-688-ISES). Tell them if they have additional questions you will be pleased to answer them after they contact ISES.

6. Upon opening mail or reading facsimiles handle each item only once. Respond to casual correspondence by writing a note on the document and returning it with your business card. Not only is this efficient but it is also good for the environment. Respond to business documents upon receipt by setting aside a prescribed time of day to handle this important task.

7. Have your mail sent to you through an overnight service when traveling for more than three business days. This allows you to respond in a timely manner.

8. Prepare a written agenda for every meeting no matter how brief. Distribute the agenda in advance and see that each item includes a time for discussion. When appropriate ask the meeting participants to prepare a written summary of their contributions and deliver them to you prior to the start of the meeting. This will assist you in better preparing for the contributions of the meeting participants.

9. Establish a comprehensive calendar that includes the contact name, address, and telephone number of individuals with whom you are meeting. Use computer software contact information programs to take this information on the road with you.

10. Delegate nonessential tasks to capable assistants. The only true way to multiply your creativity is to clone yourself. A well-trained, well-rewarded administrative assistant will enhance your productivity and even allow you to occasionally take some well-deserved time off.

owned her company for several years and well understands the importance of prudent financial management. "Watching your overhead is extremely important," says Sharon, "especially if you are constructing and storing props." Siegel, former owner of Celebrations, merged her company with an entertainment firm and provides full-service destination management services including design and fabrication of decorations. To help control overhead, her firm is located in the same building as her husband's large party rental operation. Not only does this protect the bottom line but it improves gross income through referral business generated through the party rental operation.

Sound financial practices allow savvy event managers to better control future events by collecting and analyzing the right information through which to make wise decisions. This book will show you many ways in which you may become more comfortable with accounting and as a result help you greatly improve your profitability to ensure a long, prosperous future in this profession. Figure 1-4, Best Practices for Event Management Financial Success, will assist you with establishing your own framework for long-term profitability.

MASTERING TECHNOLOGY

New advances from the fax machine as well as new technologies from integrated systems digital networks (ISDN) to the Internet (see side bar) and E-mail are transforming the way in which event managers conduct business. As but one example, most resumes that I review describe computer skills and software literacy. While this is a basic requirement for most administrative jobs it is surprising that many event managers are still somewhat intimidated by the computer age.

Overcoming this intimidation through the selection of proper tools to solve daily challenges is an essential priority for modern event managers. These basic tools may include software programs for word processing, financial management, and database management.

Word processing skills allow the event manager to easily and efficiently produce well-written proposals, agreements, production schedules, and other important documents for daily business. Many successful event managers incorporate desktop publishing software with word processing tools to produce well-illustrated proposals and other promotional materials.

We have previously discussed the importance of prudent financial management. Financial spreadsheet software allows modern event managers to quickly, efficiently, and accurately process hundreds of monthly journal entries and determine instantly profit or loss information from individual events. These same software systems also allow you to produce detailed financial reports to satisfy tax authorities as well as to provide you with a well-documented history of income and expense. Most importantly, the use of electronic financial management tools will enable you to determine instantly your cash flow position to further ensure that at the end of the month you have enough income to cover your bills and produce retained earnings for your organization.

FIGURE 1-4
Best Practices for Event Management Financial Success

1. Set realistic short- and long-term financial goals.

2. Seek professional counsel.

3. Identify and use efficient technology.

4. Systematically review your financial health.

5. Control overhead and build wealth.

Learning to use these systems is relatively simple and most event managers report that they are impressed with the ease and efficiency of this technology as compared to the days of pencil or pen entries in financial journals. There are numerous brand names available for purchase and I encourage you to determine at the outset your financial management needs and then select software that will cost-effectively meet those needs now and for the immediate future.

Database systems will allow you to compile huge amounts of information ranging from vendor to prospective client to guest lists and organize this information for easy retrieval. Event managers coordinate hundreds of resources per year and the ability to store, organize, and retrieve this information quickly and cost efficiently as well as securely is extremely important for business operations and improved earnings.

There are numerous software systems available and many that may be customized to fit the individual needs of your organization. However, event managers may fail to recognize the time required to initially enter the data and the discipline required to continue to add to the original database in a systematic manner. According to Dan Mummaw, event manager from Lansing, Michigan, effectively using information technology requires commitment from the entire team. "We asked everyone in the office to pitch in and help us build the database. It was difficult at first and some people actually left the organization but in the final result we are a more effective and profitable organization," says Mummaw.

Information technology whether for human, financial, or organizational purposes is the critical link between an average organization soon in decline or a great Event Management firm with expansive growth potential. Figure 1-5, Best Practices for Event Management Technology, provides an approach for acquiring the right technology to match your needs.

MASTERING HUMAN RESOURCE SKILLS

Empowering people is one of the most important human resource skills the event manager must master. Thousands of decisions must be made to produce successful events and the event manager cannot make all of them. Instead, he or she must hire the right people and then empower them to make a range of important decisions.

FIGURE 1-5
Best Practices for Event Management Technology

1. Identify the technology needs within your organization.

2. Review and select appropriate technology.

3. Establish a schedule for implementation.

4. Provide adequate training for all personnel.

5. Systematically review needs and adapt with new technology.

NAVIGATING THE INTERNET FOR EVENT MANAGEMENT SUCCESS

Nearly fifty million individuals are currently using the Internet to satisfy their information, marketing, and other personal and professional needs. It is predicted that this number will rise to over one billion by the year 2000. Will the Internet reduce or eliminate the need for public assembly? On the contrary, futurists such as Alvin Toffler and William Hallal predict that this unprecedented information technology will increase the desire for public assembly as hundreds of millions of people assemble virtually and find common interests that require public assembly to fully satiate their needs.

The Internet is a complex network of millions of computers that sends and receives information globally. Initially conceived by the Department of Defense Advanced Research Projects Agency, the Internet was installed as a highly-stable network with no single point of origin. Initially, only the government, university scientists, and technical people used the Internet to share information due to its inherently technical interface. With the invention of the *browser,* a software program that allows the ability to view parts of the Internet graphically (known as the World Wide Web), the Internet is now the fastest growing communications device in the world. Not since the invention of the printing press has communications been so rapidly transformed.

To use the Internet you will need to identify a local access server such as one of the online subscription services (America Online, CompuServe, Prodigy) or one of hundreds of local access firms. Once you are admitted to cyber (meaning "to steer") space you may easily navigate between thousands of sites (or *home pages*) using search engines which allow you to search for information that has been indexed.

In the Event Management profession there are hundreds of home pages on the Internet system (see the Appendix for some examples). When viewing sites with a browser on the World Wide Web, using the point and click method it is easy and fun. Many of the pages contain *hyperlinks,* which are a way to access more information. After you click your mouse on a highlighted key word *(hypertext)* in a home page a related home page appears.

One of the easiest and fastest ways to conduct research is through the Internet system. For example, the event manager who desires to identify sources for entertainment may either review a variety of home pages related to this subject or visit a *chat room*—a live link across the Internet—to query other individuals who are interested in the same subject.

ISES members use an electronic bulletin board system not on the Internet to post services they need when developing proposals or researching other destinations. The bulletin board is similar to a chat room in that it allows the participants to communicate asynchronously. By comparison a chat room is a synchronous conversation in real time.

If you can wait a day or two to retrieve the information you require, the bulletin board may be a viable option. However, if you need the information now you will want to go directly to the chat room or home page.

Regardless of what service you use, the Internet system is the event manager's most dynamic tool in transforming tomorrow's events through unlimited education and research. Get connected, log on, navigate, and surf the event management superhighway to find greater success.

The empowerment of event staff and volunteers is contrasted with the primary reason for failure by most Event Management concerns. According to informal interviews with dozens of Event Management entrepreneurs the greatest challenge is not creativity but instead financial administration. Perhaps this is why in many companies the chief financial officer (CFO) is one of the best compensated at the executive level.

As event managers become more educated in finance, human resource management, and other business skills they are actually demonstrating entrepreneurial skills to their present employers. Many employers actually reward entrepreneurs (or as they are commonly referred to as *intrapreneurs*) as they exhibit the skills needed to autonomously manage a complex competitive environment.

Therefore, one of the benefits of mastering skills in Event Management is the ability to learn how to effectively run your own business to improve your performance as an employee. In addition, you may also be improving your opportunity to one day own and operate your own successful Event Management consulting practice. Managing your financial affairs requires education, professional counsel, and discipline.

THERE IS NO SUBSTITUTE FOR PERFORMANCE

Harold Gineen, former chairman of ITT when meeting with his team and listening to their assurances of improving profits, would invoke the most sacred of all Event Management business principles when he said gravely, "There is no substitute for performance." Four pillars of long-term success in Event Management—time, financial, technology, and human resource management—must be applied in order to achieve consistent success. Setting benchmarks to measure your achievements will help you use these pillars to build a rock solid foundation for your Event Management career. According to Sharon Siegel and many of her colleagues, all event managers are ultimately only measured by their last performances. Steadily applying these best practices will help ensure many stellar event performances to come.

Challenges and Opportunities

Three important challenges await you in developing a long, prosperous professional career in Event Management. Each of these challenges is interrelated to the other. The environment in which business is developed, the rapid changes in available resources, and the requirement for continuous education forms a dynamic triangle that will either support your climb or entrap you while limiting your success. You will find that your ability to master each of these challenges dramatically affects your success ratio throughout your career.

BUSINESS DEVELOPMENT

Every organization faces increased competition as the world economy becomes smaller and you find that you no longer compete in a local market. Performing a competitive analysis in your market area is an important step in determining who your present and future competition is and how you will differentiate yourself to promote profitability. One way to do this is to thoughtfully consider your organization's unique qualities. After you have identified these qualities compare them to the perception your current and future customers have of other organizations. Are you really all that different from your competitors? If you have not identified your unique differentiating qualities you may need to adjust the services or products you provide to achieve this important step. Figure 1-6 provides a guide to best practices in competitive advantage analysis.

Whether you are the owner, manager, or employee, maintaining a competitive advantage in Event Management is the secret to success in long-term business development. Combine this technique with constantly reviewing the trade and general business literature as well as information about general emerging trends to constantly maintain your most competitive position.

Relationship marketing is increasingly important since the development of affinity programs by retailers in the 1950s. For the past half-decade modern organizations are just now learning what buyers and sellers in ancient markets knew hundreds of years ago. All sales are based on relationships. Implied in that relationship is the reality that the buyer and seller like, respect, and trust one another. The higher the price the more important this process becomes. Therefore, event managers must use events to further this important process.

According to *Advertising Age* and other major chroniclers of global marketing relationships, relationship marketing is the fastest segment in the entire marketing profession. The event manager must invest the same time larger organizations do to understand how to use events to build solid relationships that promote loyalty, word of mouth endorsement, and other important attributes of a strong customer and client relationship.

RESOURCE DEVELOPMENT

As more and more organizations create their own "Web" pages on the World Wide Web consumers will be increasingly exposed to infinite resources for Event Management.

FIGURE 1-6
Best Practices in Competitive Advantage Analysis

1. Audit your organization's unique competitive advantage—quality, product offering, price, location, trained and experienced employees, reputation, safety, and so on.

2. Survey your current and prospective customers to determine their perception of your unique attributes as compared to competing organizations.

3. Anonymously call and visit your competitors and take notes on how they compare to your unique competitive advantage.

4. Share this information with your staff and adjust your mission and vision to promote greater business development.

5. Systematically review your position every business quarter to determine how you are doing and adjust your plan when necessary.

Your challenge is to select those resources that fit your market demand and cultivate them to ensure the highest consistent quality. One of the reasons brand names have grown in importance is due to the consumers' desire for dependability and reliability. Positioning yourself and your organization as a high-quality, dependable, and reliable service through your careful selection of product offerings will further ensure your long-term success. Whether you are selecting vendors or determining what quality of paper upon which to print your new brochure, every decision will reflect your taste and more importantly that of your customers. Determine early on through research who you are serving and then select those resources to match their needs, wants, desires, and expectations. Figure 1-7 demonstrates how this may be accomplished.

LIFELONG LEARNING: A USER'S GUIDE

If the 1950s were the age of innocence in Event Management then the 1990s and well into the new millennium may be described as "the renaissance." You are part of an era of unprecedented learning and expansion of knowledge in the field of Event Management. This book will serve as your primer to direct you to additional resources to ensure that you stay ahead rather than behind the learning curve in this rapidly changing and expanding profession. One way to do this is to establish learning benchmarks for yourself throughout your career. Attending one or two annual industry conferences, participating in local chapter activities, or setting aside time each day to read relevant literature (see books, periodicals in Appendix) about the profession will certainly help you stay current. Perhaps the best proven way to learn anything is to teach some-

---

FIGURE 1-7
Best Practices in Resource Development

1. Identify through research the market(s) you are serving.

2. Establish a database to collect information abut the needs, wants, desires, and expectations of your customers.

3. Regularly review new products (some event managers set aside a specific day each month to see new vendors) and determine if they meet the standards set by your customers.

4. Match the needs, wants, desires, and expectations to every business development decision. For example, do your customers prefer to do business with you in the evening? If so, stay open late one night per week.

5. Regularly audit your internal procedures to make certain you are developing new business by positioning your products and services as quality, dependable, and reliable resources for your customers.

one else what you have learned. Collecting information that can later be shared with your professional colleagues is an excellent way to develop the habit of life-long learning. Figure 1-8, Best Practices to Lifelong Learning, further illustrates this point.

When you carefully audit the business environment, select resources that demonstrate your quality, dependability, and reliability, and engage in a program of lifelong learning, you will be far ahead of your current and future competitors. This book will help you best understand the profession of Event Management as both an art and a science requiring not only your creativity but also your exacting reasoning ability. However, any book is only a catalyst for future exploration of a field of study. As a result of using this book to promote your future growth you will have established the rigor required to become a scholar of Event Management and an authority in your own organization. To maintain your position, you will not only need to return to this book as a central reference but begin a comprehensive file of additional educational resources. This book provides several appendix resources from which you may assemble this base of knowledge. Upon completing this book use the Appendix to further enlarge your comprehension of the profession by contacting the organizations listed to request educational materials to improve and sustain your practice. After all, doctors, lawyers, and accountants as well as numerous other established professions require continuous education to meet licensing or certification standards. Our profession must aspire to this same level of competence. This will occur through your use of this book and commitment to future educational opportunities.

FIGURE 1-8
Best Practices to Lifelong Learning

1. Budget time and finances to support continuing education on an annual basis.

2. Require or encourage your employees to engage in continuous Event Management education by subsidizing their training. Ask them to contribute by purchasing books that are related to the course work.

3. Establish a study group to prepare for the Certified Special Events Professional (CSEP) examination.

4. Set aside a specific time each week for professional reading. Collect relevant information and then highlight, clip, circulate, or file this information at this time.

5. Attend industry conferences and expositions to expose yourself to new ideas on an annual basis. Remember that upon returning to your organization you will be required to teach what you have learned to others. Therefore, become a scholar of your profession.

WAR STORY

While attending an industry conference I discovered a new technology that instantly created an animated character who communicated important business topics for a corporate audience. When Xerox Team Excellence asked me to produce its event and develop a theme that matched its new digitized logo design I turned to the vendor I had met through the industry conference (Interactive Personalities of Minneapolis, Indiana) and together we created "Chip"—the animated digitized logo. Through continuing education I not only met a new vendor but I also learned how to effectively use this technology to achieve the exact results required by the client.

Lesson Learned

Attend industry conferences in search of specific solutions. As a bonus, you may take home more than you initially were in search of.

Getting Focused

Although ISES has identified nearly two dozen professions within the events industry you must soon decide how you will focus your studies. After reading the preface and this chapter you should be able to comprehend the macroprofession of Event Management through the brief descriptions of the many subfields. Now is the time to begin to focus your studies on one or two specific subfields such as tourism, meetings, festivals, reunions, social life-cycle Event Management. To assist you with this effort fifteen Event Management Positions have been selected along with a description of the background or experience typically required for each. Use Figure 1-9 as a tool to get focused and select the one or two areas where you wish to concentrate your studies.

Did you note the similarities in background and experience in each of the positions? The key to your success in this business (or any other for that matter) is a thorough grounding organization, negotiation, finance, and marketing. Human relations experience is also essential as is the related volunteer coordination skill. Increasing in importance is your ability to design, conduct, and analyze research. Throughout this book each of these skills will be discussed in detail. However, you must now begin to focus on how you will apply these skills to your particular career pursuits.

FIGURE 1-9

Fifteen Event Management Positions and Background and Experience Typically Required

Event Management Positions	Background and Experience Typically Required
Attraction Event Manager	Organization, marketing, logistical, human relations, financial, negotiation.
Catering Director	Food and beverage coordination, organization, financial, supervisory, sales, negotiation.
Civic Event Manager	Organization, legal and regulatory research ability, human relations, financial, marketing, logistical, negotiation.
Convention Service Manager	Organization, supervisory, financial, logistical, human relations, negotiation.
Family Reunion Manager	Human relations, marketing, financial, organization, supervisory, negotiation.
Festival Event Manager	Organization, financial, marketing, volunteer coordination, supervisory, entertainment, cultural arts, negotiation.
Fund-Raising Event Manager	Research, fund-raising, proposal writing, marketing, human relations, volunteer coordination, financial.
Political Event Manager	Affiliation with a cause or political party, volunteer coordination, financial, marketing, human relations, fund-raising.
Public Relations Event Manager	Writing, organization, research, financial, marketing, human relations, logistical, negotiation.
Retail Event Manager	Marketing, advertising, organization, financial, human relations, public relations, logistical, negotiation.
School Reunion Event Manager	Research, organization, financial, marketing, negotiation, volunteer coordination.
Social Life-Cycle Event Manager	Human relations, counseling, organization, financial, negotiation.
Sport Event Manager	General knowledge of sport, organization, financial, marketing, negotiation, volunteer coordination, supervisory.
Tourism Event Manager	Organization, political savvy, financial, marketing, research.
University/College Event Manager	Organization, financial, supervisory, marketing, logistical, human relations, negotiation.

Event Management is a profession that provides skills for use in a variety of related disciplines. Grounded in the science of management, you will also learn skills in psychology, sociology, and even anthropology as you further develop your career. As you move from one subfield to another these foundational skills will serve you well. They are the portable elements of this curriculum that you may take with you and apply to a variety of different types of events.

Using This Book to Accelerate Professional Growth

There are opportunities for growth on every page of this book. To cultivate and ensure your growth will require personal and professional discipline. Set aside a period of time each day to study this book. Remove all distractions such as the telephone, interruptions from staff, and other auditory and visual noise. Make a sign for your door that states "Do Not Disturb" and then spend twenty minutes intensely concentrating on your studies. Research has shown that the average person cannot concentrate as well after twenty minutes. Therefore, set your alarm for twenty minutes and when the alarm sounds get up, walk around, exercise for five or ten minutes, and then return to your studies for another twenty-minute period. Allow two twenty-minute periods per day with breaks. This will require that you set aside one hour per day for professional Event Management education.

Within one month you will complete your studies if you only use Monday through Friday for this activity. Instead of setting a goal to finish, why not instead use these days to further enrich your knowledge base by keeping a reading log to document other learning opportunities?

SELF-EDUCATION: THE READING LOG

Each chapter of this book represents the sum of many years of professional reading by this author. Therefore, as you approach a new chapter look for related writings in industry trade and professional journals as well as general media such as the daily newspaper. As you identify these readings save them for your study time. When you complete your two twenty-minute study periods give yourself a bonus by reading the related reading and then noting in your reading log the title, author, date, and a short description. Developing this habit during your study period will begin a lifelong process that will richly reward you throughout your career. Make certain you develop a filing system for these readings for future reference and use the reading log as a classification system for easy reference.

BENCHMARK CHECKLISTS

Self-improvement is the goal of every successful person. It is a continuous process. To ensure continuous self-improvement and business improvement requires utilizing an old tradition in a new context. The term *benchmarking* was first used by Xerox Corporation to describe the way its corporate leaders reinvented its organization to compete more effectively. This process was so successful that Xerox won the most coveted award in corporate America—the Malcom Baldrige Award for Quality. The principles of benchmarking are simple; however, the application requires commitment and discipline.

Benchmarking is a management process where you study similar organizations to determine what systems they are using that can become quality benchmarks for your own organization. Once you have identified these benchmarks your organization's goal is to meet or exceed these standards within a specified period of time.

The checklists throughout this book are your benchmarks. They are the result of twenty-five years of study of successful individuals and organizations in the profession of Event Management. Your goals should be to develop the rigor to meet or exceed these standards during your Event Management career.

War Stories

Famed Event Manager Barnett Lipton, the man who successfully orchestrated 88 grand pianos onto the field for the 1988 Super Bowl Half Time Show, is a fan of a little tome entitled *The Art of War* by the Chinese philosopher Sun Szu. According to Lipton, the best practices of effective Event Management are contained between the covers of this small book. Szu describes in philosophical depth the importance of planning, strategy, and preparation in combat. Lipton uses the "war" metaphor for the organization of most events including the mega ones for which he has been responsible. It is a good metaphor. In fact, in some event settings I have heard the term "war room" used to describe the central office or primary management area. Most will agree that planning, strategy, and preparation are the key ingredients to successful events.

By now you have already experienced two "War Stories." Each of these stories is true. In fact, this entire book is based upon hundreds of war stories from which polices, procedures, practices, and later principles of conduct were formed into checklists. As you read these "War Stories" determine what lesson you can apply from the particular event. Have you had similar experiences? How did you resolve them? Is there a better solution? These questions and more should be prompted as a result of your study of these war stories.

The Appendix

This important part of the book is designed to provide you with extensive resources in one location to use throughout your professional life. Review these listings and determine what gaps you currently have in your operations, marketing, or other areas and use these resources to begin to ensure closure. Furthermore, as Event Management is an emerging discipline and rapidly expanding profession you may notice gaps in the Appendix that you can fill. Please send me your resources at the E-mail address listed on the copyright page of this book and you will be duly acknowledged in the next edition.

The Main Event

After you have completed each chapter you will discover "The Main Event" section—a review of the most salient points of each chapter. Carefully review "The Main Event" to reinforce the key points of each chapter.

Role and Scope

This book's role is to expand the knowledge base in the emerging discipline of Event Management. The scope of its task is to provide concrete techniques to immediately improve your practice as an event manager. Your career needs will determine ultimately how you use this book to improve your business. However, if you are sincerely interested in expanding the knowledge base in Event Management through your pursuit your practice will improve in equal proportion to your level of commitment. This is so important it bears repeating. **If you are interested in expanding the body of knowledge in Event Management your skills will improve in equal proportion to your level of commitment.**

Therefore, as in most professions, the harder you work, the more you will learn. And as is also true in all professions, the more you learn, the more you will earn. I encourage you to become a scholar of this fascinating profession and as suggested earlier read this book as though some day, somewhere, you will be requested to teach others. I challenge you to achieve mastery through these pages so that those you will influence will leave this profession even better prepared for those who will follow.

I, like you, am a student of this profession. There are new learning opportunities every day. Over a decade ago, I stood outside a hospital nursery window gazing lovingly on our newborn son Sammy. Only a few hours earlier, I had telephoned my cousin Carola in New Orleans at one o'clock in the morning to announce his birth and, choking back tears, to tell her and the family that he would be named for my uncle, her father who had recently died. Celebrating this new life together, we laughed out loud about the "curse" that might come with my son's name. Would he be as funny, charming, irascible, and generous as my Uncle Sam? His potential was limitless. Confucius declared several thousand years ago that "we are cursed to live in interesting times indeed." Like Sammy, regardless of what road you take in the infinitely fascinating Event Management profession, you can be assured of finding opportunity in very interesting times. In the closing lines of his best-seller, *Megatrends,* John Naisbitt exalted the world he had spent years analyzing: "My God, what a fantastic time in which to be alive." The future that you and your colleagues will create will carry the curse of Confucius, the joy of Naisbitt, and the final assurance of the French poet Paul Valery, who wrote, "The trouble with the future is it no longer is what it used to be." Your future is secure in knowing that overall there are 150 million new births annually in the world and, therefore, just as many events (and many more) to manage.

NEXT ON THE AGENDA

The overarching skill of an effective event manager is the series of abilities encompassed in the competency of administration. Chapter 2 will carefully prepare you to successfully research, design, plan, coordinate, and evaluate every event every time.

PART I

Administration

Catering professionals review the production schedule prepared by the event manager to ensure a smooth event operation. *(Photo courtesy of J. Gerard Smith)*

Exciting food presentation is the event manager's opportunity to tease and titillate the guest. *(Photo courtesy of J. Gerard Smith)*

The centerpiece provides not only decor, but also focus to unify the event table.
(Photo courtesy of J. Gerard Smith)

An attractive environment can be created with the use of tasteful centerpieces.
(Photo courtesy of J. Gerard Smith)

Using radios (walkie-talkies) the event manager is able to communicate with several departments and receive immediate updates on the progress of the event.
(Photo courtesy of J. Gerard Smith)

Video production is essential for events that require broadcast, documentation, or improved communication through video magnification. *(Photo courtesy of J. Gerard Smith)*

The electronic portable generator is a critical back-up tool and should be used in pairs when the generator is the primary source of power. *(Photo courtesy of J. Gerard Smith)*

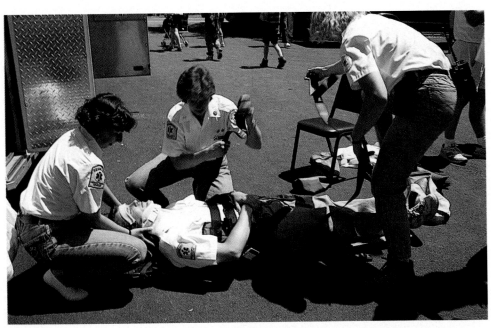

Knowledgeable event emergency medical technicians or paramedics are used as the first responder for injuries and illnesses at your event. Emergency drills ensure rapid response and consistent quality practice. *(Photo courtesy of J. Gerard Smith)*

Tents not only provide durable and portable temporary shelter but also shout "celebrate" to welcome guests from near and far. *(Photo courtesy of J. Gerard Smith)*

Retail events, such as holiday celebrations, provide event managers with numerous opportunities to raise spirits and increase sales. *(Photo courtesy of J. Gerard Smith)*

The use of props and fabrics helps transform a vast space into an intimate themed environment at moderate cost. *(Photo courtesy of J. Gerard Smith)*

Balloon arches identify the entrance and provide an inexpensive large scale decor solution. *(Photo courtesy of J. Gerard Smith)*

The epergne centerpiece allows the guests to make eye contact while enjoying the visual spectacle that graces the center of the table. *(Photo courtesy of J. Gerard Smith)*

The use of a double buffet with matching theme decor enables the guests to converse with one another and alleviates crowding. *(Photo courtesy of J. Gerard Smith)*

Modern party rental specialists provide much more than tables and chairs. From marquees to dance floors and everything in between, the event manager often need only contact the local party rental specialist. *(Photo courtesy of J. Gerard Smith)*

The modern wedding often takes place in nontraditional environments. This allows the event manager to use his or her creativity to transform these spaces into a romantic setting. *(Photo courtesy of J. Gerard Smith)*

The Five Critical Stages
for All Successful Events

All successful events have five critical stages in common to ensure their consistent effectiveness. These five phases or steps of successful Event Management are *research, design, planning, coordination,* and *evaluation.* In this chapter we will explore each of these phases in order to enable you to produce successful events every time. See Figure 2.1.

Research

Excellent research reduces risk. The better research you conduct prior to the event the more likely you are to produce an event that matches the planned outcomes of the organizers or stakeholders. For many years public relations professionals and other marketing experts have realized the value of using research to pinpoint the needs, wants, desires, and expectations of prospective customers. Government leaders regularly conduct feasibility studies prior to authorizing capital investments. These feasibility studies include exhaustive research. An event is a product that is placed before the public with the reasonable expectation that they will attend. Therefore, it is imperative that you conduct careful and accurate consumer research to reduce risk of nonattendance.

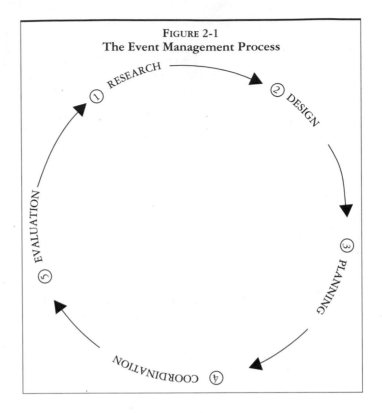

FIGURE 2-1
The Event Management Process

I have interviewed hundreds of leading Event Management professionals and they have confided that more time must be devoted to research and evaluation of events. According to these experts, if more time were devoted to these phases of the Event Management production process then ultimately less time and expense would be needed to complete the intervening steps.

The three types of research that are used for pre-event research are quantitative, qualitative, or a combination or hybrid of both. Matching the research type to the event is important and is determined by the goals of the research, the time allowed for conducting the research, and the funds available.

MARKET RESEARCH TECHNIQUES

Before bringing a new product or service to market the inventor or manufacturer will conduct market research to determine the needs, wants, desires, and expectations of the target market. Whether your event is a new product or pre-existing product, market research is required to determine how to obtain the very best position in a sometimes crowded marketplace. Typically qualitative and, in most cases, focus group research is used for this purpose.

Market research will help you determine the target or primary market as well as these secondary and tertiary markets for your event. Market research will also enable you to study the service levels expected by your guests as well as the perceptions by your internal stakeholders of the services currently being delivered. By studying your market in depth you are able to spot emerging trends, develop new service delivery systems, and solve minor problems before they become major catastrophes.

One example of this is the event manager who discovered through research that her attendees could not register for the upcoming convention during normal business hours due to workplace regulations. Therefore, she invested in an answering service for six months prior to the meeting to accept registrations between the hours of 5:00 P.M. and 8:00 A.M. This new service was a major success and registrations markedly increased for the conference.

QUANTITATIVE VS. QUALITATIVE

Quantitative Pre-Event Research

Event managers primarily use quantitative research to determine demographic information such as gender, age, income, and other pertinent facts about the future market for the event. This research is relatively inexpensive to conduct and easy to tabulate and analyze with computers. Figure 2-2 provides a model of a typical quantitative pre-event research survey.

Whether you use a written survey, an "in person" interview, or telephone interview method of construction, the research survey is of prime importance. To achieve the greatest possible response, offer a reward such as "enclose your business card and we will share the research findings with you" or offer an immediate incentive such as enclosing a one dollar bill.

Questions may be developed in two different styles. Question 4 uses a *Likert Scale* to allow the respondent to select the response that precisely states his or her opinion. Question 5 uses a *Semantic Differential Scale* to allow the respondent to respond by selecting a continuum between two opposing adjectives. The number that the respondent circles indicates the likelihood of attending or not attending your event.

Qualitative Pre-Event Research

Market research consultants rely on qualitative research to probe for hidden meanings in quantitative studies. Qualitative research tells the research organization what is beneath the numbers in quantitative research and therefore is an important step in the research process. This type of research may take the form of a focus group, participant/observer research, or a case study. Selecting the proper methodology is dependent on your goals, the time available, and the funding.

The *focus group* is typically comprised of eight to twelve individuals of similar background and experience who assemble for the purpose of discussion. A trained facilitator leads the group through specific questions that will provide clues to the goals or outcomes desired from the research. A focus group may be one hour in length although

---

FIGURE 2-2
Quantitative Pre-Event Survey Model

The following survey will enable the organizers of XYZ event to determine the feasibility of producing the following event. Your participation is important in this effort. Answer all questions by checking the appropriate box. Return this survey by January 1, 1997.

1. Gender?   ☐ Male   ☐ Female

2. Age?   ☐ Under 25   ☐ 26-34   ☐ 35-44   ☐ 45-60   ☐ 61 and over

3. Income?   ☐ Under $24,999   ☐ $25,000-34,999   ☐ Over $35,000

4. If the event were held during the summer I would: *(Likert Scale)*
   ☐ Not Attend   ☐ Maybe Attend   ☐ No Opinion   ☐ Probably Attend   ☐ Positively Attend

5. If the event were held during the fall I would: *(Semantic Differential Scale)*
   Not Attend   ☐ 1   ☐ 2   ☐ 3   ☐ 4   ☐ 5   Positively Attend

6. If you checked number 1 above please describe your reasons for nonattendance in the space below: *(Open-ended question)*

_____

_____

_____

Return this survey by January 1, 1997 to:

The Event Management Program
The George Washington University
2100 Pennsylvania Ave. NW Suite 250
Washington, DC 20037

To receive a *free copy* of the survey results please include your business card.

---

in most cases they last between ninety minutes and two hours. In some instances, a room with a one-way mirror is used to allow the other stakeholders to observe the participants for subtle changes in body language, facial reactions, and other gestures that may reveal information in addition to their verbal opinion. The focus group is audiotaped and the tapes are later transcribed and analyzed to identify areas of agreement or discord.

The *participant/observer* style of qualitative research involves placing the researcher in a host community to participate in and observe the culture of those being studied. For example, if you desire to determine whether or not a certain destination is appropriate for relocation of your event you may wish to visit, participate, and observe for an extended period of time before making your decision. Interviews with key informants are essential to this research.

The third type of qualitative research is entitled the *case study*. In this style a preexisting event is singled out as a specific case to be studied in depth. The event may be studied from a historical context or the stakeholders may be interviewed to determine how personality, skill, and other factors drive the success of the event. The case study enables the event researcher to draw conclusions based upon the research gleaned from a comparable event.

Cost

Qualitative research is generally more expensive than quantitative research due to the time that is involved in probing for deeper, more meaningful answers than only digits. The cost of training interviewers, the interviewer's time, the time for analyzing the data, and other costs contribute to this investment.

Although the cost is greater, many event managers require both qualitative and quantitative studies to validate their assumptions or effectively research their markets.

Combined Research

In most cases event managers use a combination of quantitative and qualitative research to make decisions about future events. This combined research allows the event manager to find out large volumes of information in a cost-efficient manner using the quantitative method and then probe for hidden meanings and subtle feelings using the qualitative approach.

Effective quantitative research has elements of qualitative research included to increase the validity of the questions. Event managers should use a small focus group or team of experts to review the questions before conducting the survey. These experts can confirm that the question is understandable and valid for the research being conducted.

Figure 2-3 provides a simple way for event managers to determine what research methodology is most effective for their purpose.

The goals and required outcomes of the research combined with the time frame and funding available ultimately will determine the best method for your pre-event research. Regardless of the type of research you conduct it is important that you take care to produce valid and reliable information.

VALIDITY AND RELIABILITY: PRODUCING CREDIBLE PRE-EVENT RESEARCH

All research must be defended. Your stakeholders will ask you bluntly, "How do you know that you know?" If your research has high validity and reliability you can pro-

---

FIGURE 2-3
Selecting the Appropriate Pre-Event Research Method

Goal	Method
Collect gender, age, and income data	Written survey
Collect attitudes and opinions	Focus group
Examine culture of community	Participant/observer
Identify comparable characteristics	Case study
Collect demographic and psychographic data	Combined methods

vide greater assurance that your work is truthful. Validity primarily confirms that your research measures what it purports to measure. For example, if you are trying to determine if senior citizens will attend your event then you must include senior citizens in your sample of respondents to ensure validity. Furthermore, the questions you pose to these seniors must be understandable by them to ensure that their responses are truthful and accurate.

Reliability helps prove that your research will remain truthful and accurate over time. For example, if you were to conduct the same study with another group of senior citizens would the answers be significantly different? If the answer is "yes" then your data may not be reliable. Designing a collection instrument that has high validity and reliability is a challenging and time-consuming task. You may wish to contact a university or college marketing, psychology, or sociology department for assistance by an experienced researcher in developing your instrument. Often a senior level undergraduate student or graduate student may be assigned to help you develop the instrument and collect and analyze the data for college credit. The participation of the university or college will add credibility to your findings.

Interpreting and Communicating Research Findings

Designing and collecting pre-event research is only the beginning of this important phase. Once you have carefully analyzed the data and identified the implications of your research as well as provided some recommendations based upon your study it is necessary that you present the information to your stakeholders. The way that you do this will determine the level of influence you wield with the stakeholders.

If the stakeholders are academics or others who have a research background, using tables or a written narrative may suffice. However, if, as is most often the case, the stakeholders are unsophisticated with regard to research, you may instead wish to use graphs, charts, and other visual tools to illustrate your findings. To paraphrase Confucius, "One picture is certainly worth a thousand numerals." Figure 2-4 describes how to effectively present your pre-event research findings.

Distributing a well-produced written narrative with copies of the information you

---

Figure 2-4
Effectively Presenting Your Pre-Event Research Findings

1. Determine your audience and customize your presentation to their personal communication learning style.

2. Describe the purpose and importance of the research.

3. Explain how the research was collected and describe any limitations.

4. Reveal your findings and emphasize the key points.

5. Invite questions.

are presenting (such as graphs from slides) will be helpful to the stakeholders as they will require more time for independent study before posing intelligent questions. In the written narrative include a section describing the steps you have taken to produce research that demonstrates high validity and reliability and list any independent organizations (such as a university or college) that reviewed your study prior to completion.

Communicating your research findings is an essential phase in the research process. Carefully prepare, rehearse, and then thoughtfully and confidently reveal your data. Summarize your presentation by demonstrating how the findings support the goals and objectives of your research plan.

THE FIVE W'S = HOW TO PRODUCE CONSISTENTLY EFFECTIVE EVENTS

Too often students will ask me "what event" they should produce for a class project instead of *"Why"* they should produce the event in the first place. Following the economically rocky early 1990s, corporations, associations, governments, and other organizations began to carefully analyze why a meeting or event should occur. This solid reasoning should be applied to every event decision.

The first step is to ask *"Why"* must we hold this event? There must be not one but a series of compelling reasons that confirm the importance and viability of holding the event.

The second step is to ask *"Who"* will be the stakeholders for this event? Remember stakeholders are both internal and external parties. Internal stakeholders may be your board of directors, committee members, staff, elected leaders, guests, or others. External stakeholders may be the media, politicians, bureaucrats, or others who will be investing in your event. Conducting solid research will help you determine the level of commitment of each of these parties and better help you define "who" this event is being produced for.

The third step is to determine *"When"* this event is being held. You must ask yourself if the research through evaluation time frame is appropriate for the size of this event. If this window of time is not appropriate you may need to rethink your plans and either shift the dates or streamline your operations. "When" may also determine where the event may be held.

The fourth step involves determining *"Where"* the event will be held. Once you have selected a site as you will discover in this chapter your work becomes either easier or more challenging. Therefore, this decision must be made as early as possible as it affects many other decisions.

The fifth and final "W" is to determine from the information gleaned thus far *"What"* is the event product you are developing and presenting. Matching the event product to the needs, wants, desires, and expectations of your guests while satisfying the internal requirements of your organization is no simple task. "What" must be carefully and critically analyzed to make certain the why, who, when, and where are synergized in this answer.

Once these five questions have been thoroughly answered it is necessary to turn your deliberations to *"How"* will our organization allocate scarce resources to produce maximum benefit for the stakeholders. The *SWOT* analysis provides a comprehensive tool for ensuring that you systematically review each step.

SWOT Analysis: Finding the Strengths, Weaknesses, Opportunities, and Threats

Before you begin planning your event customarily a SWOT analysis must be systematically implemented to secure your decision making. The SWOT analysis assists you with identifying the internal and external variables that may prevent your event from achieving maximum success.

Strengths and Weaknesses

The strengths and weaknesses of an event are primarily considerations that can be spotted before the event actually takes place. Typical strengths and weaknesses found in many events are shown in Figure 2-5.

The strengths and weaknesses may be uncovered through a focus group or individual interviews with your major stakeholders. Obviously if the weaknesses outnumber the strengths and there is no reasonable way to eliminate the weaknesses and increase the strengths within the event planning period you may wish to postpone or cancel the event.

Opportunities and Threats

These two key factors generally present themselves either during the event or after it has occurred. However, during the research process they should be seriously considered as they may spell potential disaster for your event.

Opportunities are those activities that may be of benefit to your event without significant investment by your organization. One example is selecting a year to hold your

---

Figure 2-5
Event Strengths and Weaknesses

Strengths	Weaknesses
Strong funding	Weak funding
Good potential for sponsors	No potential for sponsors
Well-trained staff	Poorly-trained staffed
Many volunteers	Few volunteers
Good media relations	Poor media relations
Excellent site	Weak site

event that coincides with your community's or industry's 100th anniversary. Your event may benefit from additional funding, publicity, and other important resources simply by aligning yourself with this hallmark event.

Threats are those activities that prevent you from maximizing the potential of your event. The most obvious threat is weather; however, political threats may be just as devastating. The local political leaders must buy into your civic event to ensure cooperation with all agencies. Political in-fighting may quickly destroy your planning. A modern threat is that of terrorism. The threat of violence erupting at your event may preclude individuals from attending.

Figure 2-6 describes typical opportunities and threats for your event.

You will note that although strengths and weakness are often related, opportunities and threats need not be. Once again, your goal is to identify more opportunities than threats in making a decision to proceed with your event planning. All threats should be carefully considered and experts should be consulted to determine ways that threats may be contained, reduced, or eliminated.

The SWOT analysis is a major strategic planning tool during the research phase. Using the SWOT analysis the event manager can not only scan the internal and external event environment but can proceed to the next step that involves analyses of the weaknesses and threats and provide solutions to improve the event planning process.

The research phase of the event administration process is perhaps the most critical. During this period you will determine through empirical research whether you have both the internal and external resources essential to make a decision to produce an effective event. Your ability to select the appropriate research methodology, design the instrument, collect, analyze, interpret, and present the data will ultimately determine whether or not your event has significant foundation for future success. The first pillar of the Event Management process—research—rests squarely in the center of the other four supporting columns. Although each is equal in importance, future success of the event depends on how well you conduct the research phase.

Figure 2-6
Event Opportunities and Threats

Opportunities	Threats
Civic anniversary	Hurricanes and tornadoes
Chamber of Commerce promotion	Political in-fighting
Celebrity appearance	Violence from terrorism
Align with environmental cause	Alcoholic consumption
Tie-in with media	Site in bad neighborhood

FIGURE 2-7 The SWOT Analysis		
S = Strengths		
1. Strong funding 2. Well-trained staff 3. Event well respected by media	Internal Internal External	**Existing Conditions**
W = Weaknesses		
1. Weak funding 2. Few human resources 3. Poor public relations history	Internal Internal External	
O = Opportunities		
1. Simultaneous celebration of a congruent event. 2. Timing of event is congruent with future budget allocation.	External Internal	**Future/Predictive Conditions**
T = Threats		
1. Weather 2. New board of directors will lead this event.	External Internal	

Design: A Blueprint for Success

Having thoroughly researched your event and determined that it is viable, time may now be allotted to use the right side of the brain—the creative capacity—to create a general blueprint for your ideas. There are numerous ways to begin this process, but it is important to remember that the very best event designers are constantly visiting the library, attending movies and plays, visiting art galleries, and reviewing periodicals to maintain their inspiration. This continuous research for new ideas will further strengthen the activities you propose for your event.

BRAINSTORMING AND MIND MAPPING

Too often in volunteer-driven organizations the very best ideas are never allowed to surface. This occurs because well-meaning volunteers (and some not so well-meaning volunteers) tell their colleagues that "this will never work" or "this is impossible at this time." Although their opinions are certainly valid, the process of shooting down ideas before they are allowed to be fully developed is a tragic occurrence in many organizations. Creativity must be encouraged and supported by event managers because ultimately the product you will offer is a creative act. Creativity is an essential ingredient in every Event Management process.

Therefore, when beginning the design phase of this Event Management process conduct a meeting where creative individuals are encouraged to brainstorm about the various elements of the event. The event manager is the facilitator of this meeting and in addition to various creative stakeholders you may choose to invite other creative individuals from the worlds of theater, dance, music, art, literature, and other fields. At the outset of the meeting use a flip chart to lay out the ground rules for the discussion. In large bold letters write out "Rule Number 1: There are no bad ideas." "Rule Number 2: Go back and reread Rule Number 1."

You may wish to begin the session with an activity that will stimulate creativity. One activity I've used is to place an object in the center of the table and invite the participants to describe what it might become. For example, a shoe box might become a tomb, a rocket, or a small dwelling. As each person offers their ideas the others should be encouraged to be supportive.

After this initial activity you should encourage teamwork by repeating the first activity and encouraging each member to build upon the first person's initial idea. If the first person described the box as a tomb the next person might suggest inside is a famous event manager and the next person would offer that at night legend has it that the sound of fireworks exploding inside the tomb can be heard. The teamwork process is not only important for creativity but will serve you well throughout the entire Event Management process.

Once you have completed these initial warm-up activities the members should be given simple suggestions regarding the "why" of the event. From these suggestions they should be encouraged to provide creative ideas for "who, when, where, what, and how." As the facilitator, if one member (or more than one member) tends to dominate the discussion ask him or her to summarize and then say "thank you" as you quickly move on to others to solicit their ideas. Use the flip chart to list all of the initial ideas and do not try to establish categories or provide any other organizational structure.

Mind mapping allows the event manager to begin to pull together the random ideas and establish linkages that will later lead to logical decision making. Using the flip chart, ask each member of the group to revisit their earlier ideas and begin to link them to the four W's and ultimately help you see how the event should be developed. Write why, who, when, where, what, and how in the center of a circle on a separate page of the flip chart. From this circle draw spokes that terminate in another circle. Leave the circles at the end of each spoke empty. The ideas of your team members will fill these circles and they will begin to establish linkages between the goal (why, who, when, where, what, and how) and the creative method.

Figure 2-8 demonstrates an example of a successful event mind mapping activity.

Mind mapping is an effective way to synthesize the various ideas suggested by the group members and begin to construct an *event philosophy*. The event philosophy will determine the financial, cultural, social, and other important aspects of the event. For example, if the organization sponsoring the event is not-for-profit the financial philosophy will not support charging high fees to produce a disproportionate amount of funds or the tax status may be challenged. Mind mapping allows you to carefully sift through the ideas and show how they support the goals of the event. In doing this an event philosophy begins to emerge. Those ideas that do not have a strong linkage or support the philosophy should be placed on a separate sheet of flip chart paper for future use. Remember Rule Number 1?

THE CREATIVE PROCESS IN EVENT MANAGEMENT

Special events require individuals with the ability to move easily between the left and right quadrants of the cerebellum. The right side of the brain is responsible for creative, spontaneous thinking while the left side of the brain handles the more logical aspects of our lives. Event managers must be both right and left brained to be able to function effectively. Therefore, if you have determined that one side of your brain is less strong than the other you must take steps to correct this in order to achieve maximum success in Event Management.

The majority of this text is concerned with logical, reasoning activities. Therefore, assuming that one of the aspects of Event Management that you find attractive is the creative opportunities afforded in this profession, I will provide some insight into ways to develop your creativity to the highest possible level. Remember that developing creativity is a continuous process. The reason some corporations put their advertising accounts out for review to other agencies periodically is to be sure that the current agency is working at its highest possible creative level. As an event manager, you too must strive for constant review of your creative powers to make certain you are in high gear.

Figure 2-9 offers a series of tips for continuously developing your creativity.

Perhaps the best way to continually stretch your creativity is to surround yourself with highly-creative people. Whether you are in a position to hire creativity or must seek creative types through groups outside of the office you must find the innovators in order to practice innovation.

MAKING THE PERFECT MATCH THROUGH NEEDS ASSESSMENT AND ANALYSIS

Once you have satisfactorily completed the brainstorming and mind mapping activities it is time to make certain that your creative ideas perfectly match the goals and objectives of your event. This is accomplished through a *needs assessment and analysis.*

The needs assessment and analysis enables you to create an event that closely satisfies the needs of your stakeholders. You actually began this process by asking "why and who." Now it is time to take it one giant step forward and actually survey the stakeholders to determine if your creative solutions will satisfy their needs. To accomplish

FIGURE 2-8
The Event Management Needs Assessment

WHY?	+	WHO?	+	WHEN?	+	WHERE?	+	WHAT?
What is the compelling reason for this event? Why must this event be held?		Who will benefit from this event? Who will they want to attend?		When will the event be held? Is the date and time flexible or subject to change?		What is the best destination, location, and venue?		What elements and resources are required to satisfy the needs identified above?

= HOW?

Given answers to the five W's, how do you effectively research, design, plan, coordinate, and evaluate this event?

FIGURE 2-9
Creativity Continuing Education

1. Visit one art gallery each month.

2. Attend a live performance of opera, theater, or dance each month.

3. Continuously read great works of literature.

4. Enroll in a music, dance, literature, visual arts, acting class, or discussion group.

5. Apply what you are discovering in each of these fields to your profession of Event Management.

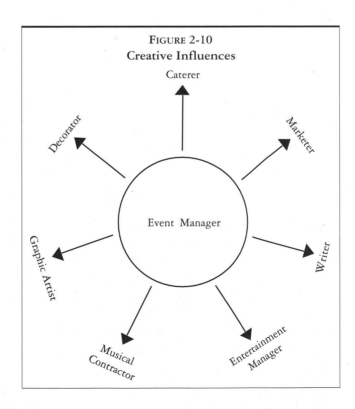

FIGURE 2-10
Creative Influences

this part of the design phase develop your ideas into a series of questions and query the key constituents for your event and determine if the various elements you have created—from advertising to decor, from catering to entertainment, and everything in between—meet their expectations. Once you are confident that you have adequately assessed the needs of the stakeholders and confirmed that you have through analysis determined how to satiate these needs, you are well prepared to confirm the final feasibility of your event design.

Is It Feasible?

Feasibility simply means that you have objectively looked at the event design to determine if what you propose is feasible given the resources available. This is the final checkpoint before actual planning begins and therefore must be given adequate time for review. Municipalities often engage professional engineers or other consultants to conduct lengthy feasibility studies before approving new construction or other capital expenditures. Although you may not need a battery of consultants, it is important for you to thoroughly review all previous steps in determining the feasibility of your event plan.

The three basic resources that will be required are financial, human, and political. Each of these resources may have varying degrees of importance depending on the nature of the event. For example, a for-profit or large hallmark event will require significant financial investment to succeed. On the other hand, a not-for-profit event will rely on an army of volunteers and therefore the human element is more important. A civic event will require greater political resources to accomplish. Therefore, when assessing and analyzing feasibility first determine in what proportions the resources will be required for the event. You may wish to weigh each of the resources to help prepare your analysis.

Financial Considerations   You will want to know if sufficient financial resources are available to sustain development and implementation of the event. Furthermore, you must consider what will happen if the event loses money. How will the creditors be paid? You will also want to know what resources you can count on for an immediate infusion of cash should the event require this to continue development. Finally, you must carefully analyze the cash flow projections for the event to determine how much time is to be allowed between payables and receivables.

The Human Dimension   Human beings are the most complex of all mammals. In assessing the feasibility of your event you must not only know where your human resources will come from but also how they will be rewarded (financially or through intangibles such as awards and recognition). Most importantly you must know how they will work together as an efficient event team.

Politics as Usual   The increasingly important role of government leaders in event oversight must be viewed with a practiced eye. Politicians see events as both good (opportunities for publicity, constituent communications, and economic impact) and bad (drain on municipal services and potential for disaster). When designing civic events it is particularly important that you understand and enlist the support of politicians and their bureaucratic ministers to ensure smooth cooperation for your event. Furthermore, for all events it is essential that you carefully research the permit process to determine if the event you have designed is feasible according to the code within the jurisdiction where the event will be held.

The Approval Process

The research and design phases add to your event history once the event is approved. The approval process may be as simple as an acceptance by your client or as complex as requiring dozens of signatures from various city agencies that will interact with the event. Regardless of the simplicity or complexity of this step you should view it as an important milestone that once crossed assures you that your plan has been reviewed and deemed reasonable, feasible, and has a high likelihood-to-succeed ratio. All roads lead to official approval whether in the form of a contract or individual permits from each agency. Without official approval your event remains a dream. The process for turning your dreams into workable plans requires careful research, thoughtful design, and finally critical analysis. This could be called "the planning to plan phase" because it involves so many complex steps related to the next phase. However, once the approval is granted you are on your way to the next important phase: the actual planning period.

Planning Effective Events

The planning period is typically the longest period of time in the event management process. This historically has been due to disorganization. Disorganization is best characterized by frequent changes resulting from substitutions, additions, or even deletions due to poor research and design. Ideally, the better job you do in the research and design area the simpler and briefer the planning period will become. Since events are planned by human beings for other human beings this theory is fraught with exceptions. However, your goal should be to develop a smooth planning process due to your careful research and design procedures.

The planning phase involves using the time/space/tempo laws to determine how to best use your immediate resources. These three basic laws will affect every decision you make; how well you make use of them will govern the final outcome of the event.

TIMING

The law of timing refers to how much time you have in which to act or react. The first question many event managers first ask the client is, "When would you like to schedule the event?" The answer to that question tells you how much time you have to prepare. Often that timetable may seem incredibly short.

W A R   S T O R Y

A man telephoned my office and asked if I could deliver an elephant to his wife for their fiftieth wedding anniversary. "When do you need it?" I asked. "Tomorrow!" he declared. I immediately told him I would go to work, and in short order I contacted an elephant trainer and arranged a full-grown Asian elephant to be delivered by tractor trailer to the woman's front door. The man, dutifully impressed, asked, "Can I have two elephants next time?" What the man did not realize was that in order to fulfill the agreement five employees worked around the clock. No other event could be sold or serviced during this time period. I estimated that for the elephant delivery the lost business opportunity was nearly five times the estimated profit. Or we lost five times as much as we earned during this event.

Lesson Learned

Do not set up unrealistic time expectations. Before committing to any agreement analyze how this event will impact your scarce resources. An event that drains your resources is not one that will sustain your long-term career goals.

The length of time available for planning and for the actual production will dramatically affect the cost and sometimes the success of the event. Equally important, as you discovered in the introduction, is how you use your time. The Greek philosopher Theophrastus said, "Time is the most valuable thing a human can spend."

Mona Meretsky, president of COMCOR, a Fort Lauderdale corporate events firm, notes that, when budgeting her time to prepare a final cost estimate for the client, she realizes that the time she invests will exceed the number of billable client hours because she is a perfectionist. She will "take as much time as is required for each event to make certain that the details are attended to. It pays off in the long run. I've never had a corporate client not come back." Budgeting your time, as shown by Meretsky, is not an exact science but rather a dynamic experience that must be governed by the importance of each event.

When budgeting your time for a proposed event, some independent event managers estimate the amount of time necessary for pre-event client meetings, site inspections, meetings with vendors, ongoing communications and contract preparation, actual event time from time to arrival through departure, and post-event billable time. You may wish to allocate your billable time to follow the five phases of the event process—research, design, planning, coordination, and evaluation.

You can only estimate the time involved in these tasks and therefore must add a contingency time factor to each phase. Mona Meretsky believes that using a ten percent contingency factor will help you cover that extra time required but not originally projected.

Like Mona Meretsky, Audrey Gordon, sole proprietor of Audrey Gordon Parties of Chicago, admits that her actual time often exceeds her projected time. "A bar mitzvah could, if necessary, be planned in one eight-hour day. The worst case scenario is days of planning, as people usually change their minds often."

By paying careful attention to the research and design phase you will be able to budget your time more precisely. This is particularly true for the event itself. This part of planning involves when to arrive for a particular event, when to cue the appropriate musician or performer, when to take breaks, and of course when to stop. Planning the timing of an event is as important as managing your planning time.

Mona Meretsky says, "I request that my personnel is set up for our events one hour in advance. In Florida guests often arrive early, and we must be ready when they are."

Audrey Gordon, owner of a one-person firm, must rely on legions of vendors to produce her social life-cycle events. Her planning must be careful and precise even to the point of listing what song is to be played at a specific time. The net result of her exhaustive preparation is that the guest is able to relax and enjoy the event, as every element happens logically, sequentially, and on time.

The moment the client approves the date of the event, the event manager must begin assessing how the planning period will affect their other business operations. Therefore, the law of timing sometimes requires that when an unreasonable time frame is allotted for professionally producing an event the event manager must decline to accept the opportunity. The ultimate factor that will govern every decision regarding timing is made when you ask yourself, "Given this amount of time can I produce an event that displays the quality and professionalism I am known for without losing other equal or possibly larger opportunities?" Your answer will determine whether the light turns green, fades to yellow, or becomes red.

SPACE

The law of space refers to both the physical space where the event will be held and the space of time between critical decisions pertaining to the event. The relationship of timing to space is one that is constant throughout the entire event process.

In the 1988 Super Bowl Half Time Show in Jack Murphy Stadium, Radio City Music Hall Productions designed an elaborate half time show featuring eighty-eight grand pianos. Suddenly, without warning, the day before the actual production the producer was instructed that his set-up time for the production was reduced to only a few minutes. Further complicating matters, the groundskeepers at the stadium raised seri-

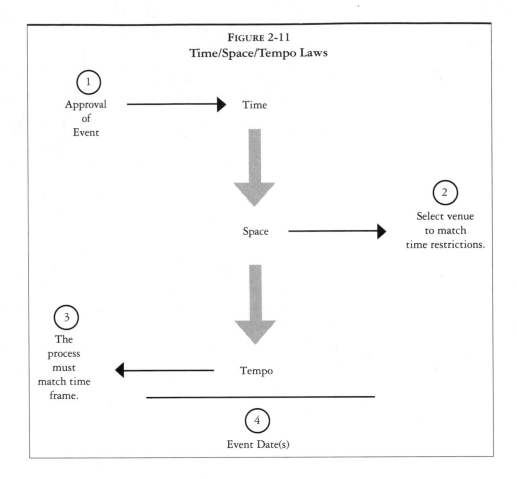

FIGURE 2-11
Time/Space/Tempo Laws

① Approval of Event ⟶ Time

② Select venue to match time restrictions.

Space ⟶

③ The process must match time frame. ⟵ Tempo

④ Event Date(s)

ous concerns that the movement of the pianos onto the field would affect the sacred turf where the second half of the game would be played. In this example and numerous others the actual physical space governs the time required for various other elements of the event.

When selecting a *venue* for your event the location and physical resources present will significantly impact the time that must be further invested. If you select a historic mansion with elaborate permanent decor, less time will be required to decorate this site. By comparison if you select a four-wall venue such as hotel or convention center (where you are literally renting the four walls), significant time and expense must be invested to create a proper atmosphere for the event.

Burt Ferrini, event manager at Northeastern University in Chicago, recognizes the importance of space. As the manager for the commencement exercises, Ferrini must coordinate thousands of individuals in a space most are not familiar with. Furthermore, he must ensure that the event runs precisely on time. "I prepare individual schedules for each group of participants and then after rehearsing them individually I blend them together in a master schedule. Breaking the large event down into component parts and then reassembling it on the day of the event helps ensure a smooth ceremony."

When considering the space for your event some event managers prepare an elaborate checklist to carefully review each and every element. Your checklist should reflect the goals and objectives of the event and not merely replicate a form you have copied for convenience. One of the primary considerations when selecting the space is the age and type of guest who will be attending. Older guests may not be able to tolerate extreme temperatures and this may preclude you from selecting solely an outdoor venue. For events with young children you may or may not wish to select a site in a busy urban setting. Go back to the research and needs assessment phase and review why this event is important and who are the stakeholders. Then select a venue specifically to match their needs, wants, and expectations.

The terms *ingress* and *egress* are important concepts when first reviewing the potential venue. Ingress defines the entrances or access to the venue and egress refers to the exits or evacuation routes. When considering ingress and egress you must consider not only people, including those with disabilities, but also vehicles, props, possibly animals, and indeed any element that must enter or exit the site. You must also keep in mind the window of time available for the ingress or egress as this will determine the number of portals (doors) that may need to be available for this purpose.

Parking, public transportation, and other forms of transportation including taxis, limousines, and tour busses must also be considered when analyzing the site. These considerations should include the number of parking spaces, including those for the disabled, the availability and security/safety of public transportation, and the time required to dispatch a taxi.

Figure 2-12 is a good beginning for you to be able to develop a customized site inspection checklist.

The Site Inspection

Perhaps the most important activity involving space is the site inspection. Using a comprehensive, customized checklist will make this task efficient and thorough. It will also allow you to delegate this task to others if you are not able to travel to the site yourself. Always carry a retractable tape measure, instant camera, notepad, and pencil on such an inspection.

Upon arrival, note the ingress to the parking facilities for up to one mile away. What will be the estimated travel time in heavy to moderate traffic, and are there alternative routes if the main artery is blocked by an accident or construction? Determine where the parking area will be for your official and VIP vehicles. Find out if special identification is required for those vehicles to park in these preapproved areas. Measure the height of the loading dock (if available) from the driveway to make certain your vehi-

---

FIGURE 2-12
Site Inspection Checklist Criteria

Amenities

1. Ability to display banner in prominent location.

2. Limousines for VIPs.

3. Upgrades to suites available.

4. Concierge or VIP floors.

5. Room deliveries for entire group upon request.

6. In-room television service for special announcements.

7. Personal letter from venue manager delivered to room.

8. Complimentary parking for staff or VIPs.

9. Complimentary coffee in lobby.

10. Complimentary office services for staff such as photocopying.

Americans with Disabilities Act

1. Venue has been modified and is in compliance.

2. New venue built in compliance with act.

3. Modifications are publicized and well communicated.

Capacity

1. Fire marshall approved capacity of venue for seating.

2. Capacity of venue for parking.

3. Capacity for exposition booths.

4. Capacity for storage.

5. Capacity for truck and vehicle marshaling.

6. Capacity for pre-event functions such as receptions.

7. Capacity for other functions.

8. Capacity for public areas of venue such as lobbies.

9. Size and number of men's and women's rest rooms.

Catering

1. Full-service, venue-specific catering operation.

2. Twenty-four-hour room service.

3. Variety of food outlets.

4. Concession capability.

5. Creative, tasteful food presentation.

FIGURE 2-12
Site Inspection Checklist Criteria *(continued)*

Equipment

1. Amount of rope (running feet) and stanchions available.

2. Height, width, and colors available for inventory of pipe and drape.

3. Height, width, and skirting colors available for platforms for staging.

4. Regulations for use and lift availability for aerial work.

5. Adequate number of tables, chairs, stairs, and other equipment.

Financial

1. Complimentary room ratio.

2. Guarantee policy.

3. Daily review of folio.

4. Complimentary reception or other services to increase value.

5. Function room complimentary rental policy.

Location/Proximity

1. Location of venue from nearest airport.

2. Distance to nearest trauma facility.

3. Distance to nearest fire/rescue facility.

4. Distance to shopping.

5. Distance to recreational activities.

Medical/First Aid

1. Number of staff trained in CPR, Heimlich maneuver, and other first aid.

2. Designated first-aid area.

3. Ambulance service.

Portals

1. Size and number of exterior portals.

2. Size and number of interior portals including elevators.

3. Ingress and egress to portals.

Registration

1. Sufficient well-trained personnel for check in.

2. Ability to provide express check-in for VIPs.

3. Ability to distribute event materials at check in.

4. Ability to display group event name on badges or buttons to promote recognition.

5. Effective directory or other signs for easy recognition.

(Figure continued on next page)

FIGURE 2-12
Site Inspection Checklist Criteria *(continued)*

Registration

1. Sufficient well-trained personnel for check in.

2. Ability to provide express check-in for VIPs.

3. Ability to distribute event materials at check in.

4. Ability to display group event name on badges or buttons to promote recognition.

5. Effective directory or other signs for easy recognition.

Regulations

1. Designation of a civil defense venue to be used in emergencies.

2. Pre-existing prohibitive substance regulations.

3. Other regulations that impede your ability to do business.

4. Fire code requirements with regard to material composition for scenery and other decoration.

5. Local fire officials' requirements for permission to use open flame or pyrotechnic devices.

6. Requirement regarding the use of live gasoline-powered motors.

7. Policy regarding live-trained animals.

Safety and Security

1. Exterior and interior walkways are well lit.

2. Venue has full-time security team.

3. Communications system in elevators is in working order.

4. Venue has positive relationship with law enforcement agencies.

5. Venue has positive relationship with private security agencies.

6. Fire sprinklers controlled per zone or building-wide. Individual zone can be shut off, with a fire marshall in attendance, for a brief effect such as pyrotechnics.

7. Alarm system initially silent or it immediately announces a fire emergency.

8. Condition of all floors (including the dance floors).

Sleeping Rooms

1. Sufficient number of singles, doubles, suites, and other required inventory.

2. Rooms in safe, clean, working order.

3. Amenities such as coffee makers and hair dryers available upon request.

4. Well-publicized fire emergency plan.

5. Balcony or exterior doors properly secured.

FIGURE 2-12
Site Inspection Checklist Criteria (*continued*)

Utilities

1. Electrical power capacity.

2. Power distribution.

3. Working on-site reserve generator (and a backup) for use in the event of a power failure.

4. Responsible person for operation of electrical apparatus.

5. Sources for water.

6. Alternative water source in case of disruption of service.

7. Separate billing for electricity or water.

Weight

1. Pounds per square foot for which venue is rated.

2. Elevator weight capacity.

3. Stress weight for items that are suspended such as lighting, scenic, projection, and audio devices.

cles can deliver directly onto the dock. This knowledge alone may save you thousands of dollars in additional labor charges.

Ask the venue officials to show you the entrance door for your personnel and the walking route to the pre-event waiting area (dressing rooms, green rooms, and briefing rooms). Write these instructions down and read them back to the official. Note who supplied these instructions as they will later be given to your personnel, and should there be a problem, you must be able to refer back to your original source for clarification.

Measure the square footage of the waiting area and determine how many persons can be accommodated when official furnishings are included. Locate the rest rooms and note if they are adequate or require upgrading, for example, bringing in nicer amenities such as specialty soaps, toilettes, perfumes, full-length mirrors, and fresh flowers.

Ask the venue official to lead you from the waiting area to the location of the actual event. Thoroughly examine the event site from the perspective of the spectator or participant. Most important, can the spectator see and hear comfortably? Sit in the seat of the spectator farthest from the staging area. Determine how the person with the most obstructed view can best see and hear.

When possible ask the venue official to supply you with a floor plan or diagram of the site. Use this site diagram as a general blueprint and then confirm and verify by using your measuring device to measure random locations. Note any variances for later adjustment on the final diagram.

Finally, before you leave the venue sit in one of the chairs your spectator will occupy for a minimum of fifteen minutes. Determine if it is comfortable for your guests. If not, ask if alternate seating is available and at what cost.

Developing the Diagram

Transferring the results of the site inspection to a final, carefully produced diagram at one time was a major labor-consuming operation. Today, however, using modern computer tools such as computer-assisted design and drafting (CADD) systems this task has been simplified. For those event managers who are uncomfortable with computers a manual system has been developed involving scale cutouts of magnets that correspond to the typical inventory of most venues (chairs, tables, platforms, pianos, and so on) and once assembled the final product may be photocopied for distribution.

Before beginning the process of developing the diagram, audit all internal and external stakeholders and create a listing of every element that must be depicted on the diagram. These elements may range from decor to catering tents and from first-aid centers to parking locations. You will later use this checklist to cross-check the diagram and make certain every element has been included.

After the first draft diagram has been developed it must be distributed to stakeholders for a first review. Ask the stakeholders to review the diagram for accuracy and return it within a fixed amount of time with any additions, deletions, or changes.

Finally, after you have received comprehensive input from the stakeholders prepare a final copy for review by officials who must grant final approval for the event. These officials may include the fire marshall, transportation authorities, or others responsible for enforcing laws and regulations.

Once you have constructed a final, approved diagram you have made the giant step forward from dream to idea to final plan. The third and final law of Event Management planning ensures that you effectively implement your plan.

TEMPO

The final law of event planning is concerned with the rate or tempo at which events take place both during production planning and during the event itself. From the moment the client approves your agreement or authorizes you to proceed with planning to the final meeting, you must be aware of the projected rate at which events will happen. Improved technology such as fax and on-line services has dramatically accelerated the process and subsequently the demands of clients to "do it now." However, now is often not as efficient as later. When the event manager is pressured to deliver a product before it is fully developed, the results may be less than exemplary. Therefore, as you manage the rate at which tasks will be completed and events will occur, it is important to consider if each action is being performed at the best time. "Maybe" is not an acceptable response. To determine if this is the best moment for this task to be handled, ask yourself if you have sufficient information and resources to implement it. If not, try to delay the action until you are better prepared.

Establishing the proper tempo is not an exact science. Rather, like a conductor of an orchestra you must allow your personal taste, energy, and experience to guide you as you speed up or slow down the tempo as required. Analyzing the event site and estimating the time required for the project, the event manager is better able to set the tempo or schedule for the setup, production, and removal of the equipment. Without this advance analysis, the event manager becomes an orchestra conductor without benefit of a score, a musician without benefit of a maestro.

Understanding the needs of the guests also helps establish and adjust the tempo during the event. If the guest is primarily concerned with networking, a leisurely time frame should be followed to allow for plenty of interaction. For example, while the transition from cocktails to dinner may be brisk when the program is more important than networking, the transition may be slowed when the emphasis is on the connections the audience members make among themselves.

Paul Demos, longtime director of catering at the Chicago Hilton and Towers Hotel, matches the type of service to the needs of the guests. "The number of courses, whether wine is served, the dress style of the guests," according to Demos, all govern the ultimate tempo of the event and type of service required.

These three basic laws, as old as human creation itself, govern the planning of all events. To become an expert event manager you must master your ability to manage time in the most minute segments. You must develop the vision to perceive the strengths, weaknesses, opportunities, and threats of every space. Finally, you must be able to analyze the needs of your guests to set the tempos that will ensure a memorable event.

THE GAP ANALYSIS

Too often event managers proceed by rote memory to produce an event in a style with which they are most familiar. In doing this they often overlook critical gaps in the logical progression of event elements. Identifying these gaps and providing recommendations for closure is the primary purpose of the *Gap Analysis*.

This planning tool involves taking a long, hard look at the event elements and identifying significant gaps in the planning that could weaken the overall progression of the plan. One example is the event manager who has scheduled an outdoor event in September in Miami Beach, Florida. September is the prime month in the hurricane season. The event manager has created a wide gap in his or her plan that must be closed to strengthen the overall event. Therefore, finding a secure indoor location in case of a weather emergency would be a good beginning toward closing this gap.

Use a critical friend—a person whose expertise about the particular event is known to you—to review your plan and specifically search for gaps in your logical thinking. Once you have identified the gaps look for opportunities to close them.

By implementing the findings from the SWOT and Gap Analysis, you are able to begin executing your plan. This execution phase is known as coordination.

Coordination: Executing the Plan

As the light turns green the tempo accelerates and you are now faced with coordinating the minute-by-minute activities of the event itself. I was once asked, "What does it take to be a competent event manager?" "The ability to make good decisions," I swiftly answered. After reading the introduction you realize that it requires much more than good decision-making ability; however, it is also true that during the course of coordinating an event you will be required to make not dozens but hundreds of decisions. Your ability to use your professional training and experience to make the correct decision will affect the outcome of the entire event. While it is true that event managers should maintain a positive attitude and see problems as challenges in search of the right solution, it is also important that you apply critical analysis to every challenge that comes your way. Figure 2-13 provides you with a simple but effective way to make these decisions.

AUTHORITY VS. RESPONSIBILITY

One of the challenges in event coordination is making certain that the person who has the responsibility for implementing certain elements also has the authority to make the decision regarding those elements. Without the authority to implement policy, responsibility becomes weak. Make certain you have the authority before you accept the responsibility and consequently grant those you supervise the authority required to accomplish their responsibilities.

Event managers are leaders who through example motivate others. Managers often merely control problems and therefore do not promote growth in people. Leaders, how-

---

FIGURE 2-13
Event Coordination Decision-Making Methods

1. Collect all of the information. Most problems have many sides to review.

2. Consider the pros and cons of your decision in terms of who will be affected.

3. Consider the financial implications of your decision.

4. Consider the moral and ethical implications of your decision.

5. Make the decision and do not look back.

ever, help the people they lead to find solutions to the challenges they face. Leading people so they are able to make the correct decision themselves is one of the most important roles you play as an event manager.

MACROEVENT VS. MICROEVENT MANAGEMENT

When coordinating the event too often the event manager attempts to micromanage the details of every single element. This compounds your time constraints and frustrates your staff and volunteers. Instead of micromanaging, the effective event manager will carefully select the most competent individuals to manage various aspects and then grant them the authority to carry out their responsibilities. The appropriate role for the event manager is that of a macroinfluencer or team leader who is available to coach, correct, and provide a strategic direction for all team members.

Event managers basically coordinate people and things. People are the most complex and usually most irreplaceable resources and therefore must be given careful consideration. Whether you are coordinating full-time or permanent part-time staff or vol-

WAR STORY

Standing backstage at the John F. Kennedy Center for the Performing Arts I started to interfere with my event coordinator's management of the Salute to First Lady Barbara Bush during the presidential inaugural celebration. One of the acts was running late and I was ready to ring down the curtain. I began to step forward to say "do it my way" when my assistant touched my elbow and calmly said, "He knows what to do." Although I knew that, I also felt responsible to rush in and try to immediately solve the problem. Had I done so, the event coordinator would not have found the solution himself. Within seconds, the situation was under control and the audience was on their feet singing "God Bless America." I shook my event coordinator's hand and congratulated him for a job well done—without my interference.

Lesson Learned

Think before you interfere. Usually the solution is nearby and by allowing your team members to discover it themselves they learn to analyze and solve problems effectively.

unteers, training, orientation, empowerment, and evaluation are important tools to produce long-term Event Management success.

Evaluate: The Link to the Next Event

The Event Management process, as shown in Figure 2-14, is a dynamic spiral that is literally without end. The first phase—research—is connected with the last—evaluation. In this phase you will ask, "What is it we wish to evaluate and how will we best accomplish this?"

Events may be evaluated by each component part of the Event Management process or through a general comprehensive review of all phases. It is up to you and your stakeholders to decide what information you require to improve your planning and then implement effective strategies to accomplish this phase.

Perhaps the most common form of event evaluation is the written survey. Usually the survey is conducted immediately following the event to collect the satisfaction level of the participants and spectators. As with any evaluation method there are pros and cons to this immediate feedback. One bias is the immediate nature of the feedback that prohibits the respondent from digesting the total event experience before providing his or her feedback.

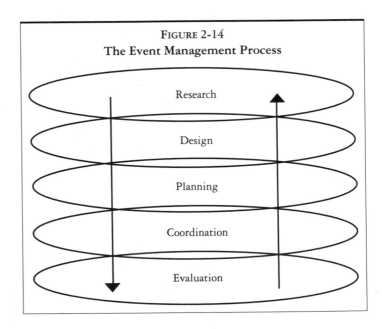

FIGURE 2-14
The Event Management Process

Research

Design

Planning

Coordination

Evaluation

Another form of evaluation is the use of monitors. A monitor is a trained individual who will observe an element of the event and provide both written and verbal feedback to the event manager. The event monitor usually has a checklist or survey to complete and will then offer additional comments as required. The benefit of this type of evaluation is that it permits a trained, experienced event staff member or volunteer to objectively observe the event while it is taking place and provide instructive comments.

The third form of event evaluation is the telephone or mail survey conducted after the event. In this evaluation the event manager surveys the spectators and participants after the event either through a mail or telephone survey. By waiting a few days after the event to collect this data the event manager is able to glean from the respondents how their attitudes have changed and developed after some time has passed since they participated in the event.

A new form of evaluation and one that is growing in popularity is the pre- and post-event survey. This evaluation allows the event manager to determine the respondents' knowledge, opinions, and other important information both before and after their attendance at the event. This is especially helpful when trying to match expectations to reality. For example, the event guest may state upon entering the event that they expect, based on the advertising and public relations, to enjoy nonstop entertainment. However, upon completing the exit interview they register disappointment because of the gaps in the programming. This type of evaluation helps the event organizers close the gaps between over-promising and under-delivering certain aspects of the event.

Regardless of the form of evaluation you use, it is critical that you do not wait until the end of the event to find out how you are doing. If you were to attend any banquet where I am responsible for the event you might be surprised to see me wandering from table to table and asking the guests how they are enjoying their dinner. In doing this I am able to uncover gaps in the execution of the plan. One guest might admit "I ordered vegetarian and was served meat." I am able to immediately correct this error. If I had waited until the man had filled out an evaluation form it would have been too late.

Take the temperature of your guests hourly to make certain you are on target with meeting your goals and objectives. By doing this you are able to immediately reset your course and ensure that together you will arrive at the same destination—a successful event.

This Event Management process is the conceptual framework for every effective event. The process is dynamic and will require selectivity by the event manager to determine where to begin and how to proceed to best accomplish his or her objectives. One event may be past the research stage when the event manager is merely retained to coordinate the elements. Still another may be midway through the planning phase. The effective event manager will immediately recognize that the event process cannot be complete or totally effective unless each of these phases is carefully considered. It matters not where you begin the process. It is essential that every phase be considered, visited, and understood.

Communications: The Tie That Binds

Event Management is a profession whose success or failure ratio often depends on the ability of individuals to effectively communicate with one another. It does not matter whether this communication is oral, written, electronic, or all three. What is important is that event managers become practiced communicators in order to maintain clear communications with all stakeholders.

Often both visual and auditory noise will provide a barrier to open communication. Visual noise includes those visual distractions that take place when you are trying to communicate with others. Auditory noise may be music, traffic, or other distractions that interfere with others' ability to hear and concentrate on what you are saying.

Remove all noise before trying to communicate with others. Find a quiet place to meet, remove visual distractions, and then verify and confirm that those you are communicating with comprehend what you are sharing.

Written communications are essential not only for record keeping but also for purposes of mass distribution. It is impossible to verbally repeat to one thousand people an event update without distortion. Remember the children's game "gossip"? Use memorandums, briefing statements, bulletins, and other documents to communicate effectively to one or many others. The memorandums should include an "Action Required" statement to enable the reader to know how best to respond and in what time frame.

Bulletins must be sporadic or you run the risk of becoming the person who cried wolf once too often and now are ignored by everyone. Newsletters are a particularly effective tool for communications; however, use caution as they are extremely labor intensive.

Perhaps one of the best ways to communicate is through a meeting. When scheduling a meeting make certain you prepare an agenda in advance that lists the items for discussion. Distribute this document in advance of the meeting to those who will attend and ask them to comment. This will help them prepare for the meeting. Use the agenda to guide the meeting and as the leader serve as a facilitator for discussion. Using a flip chart will help you capture ideas and at the same time stick to the agenda. One extremely effective device is to assign the meeting participants prework so they come to the meeting prepared and ready to make specific contributions.

Alternative communication techniques include producing audiotapes and videotapes as well as using teleconferencing through compressed video (telephone lines). Since the average person commutes twenty or more minutes twice daily to the office this is an excellent time to put your meeting or information on audiotape, add a little music, and share your ideas. The major drawback to this alternative is that the communication is one way. Videotapes also allow you to creatively express your thoughts with photos, interviews, and music and to show the tape before a large group of people creating excitement in numbers. Two-way video using existing telephone lines and a compressed system is an effective way to present data, visuals, and some person-to-person interaction. It is also relatively inexpensive compared to traditional satellite uplink/downlink technology.

The use of computer on-line chat rooms has grown in popularity due to the rapid expansion of the Internet technologies. When using chat rooms avoid personal issues and conduct your postings in a businesslike manner. Personal issues may be addressed through other mediums such as telephone calls. Chat rooms are excellent information exchange opportunities and you will find that your colleagues will perennially provide you with new resources for producing better events.

Synergy: Linking Administration, Coordination, Marketing, and Risk Management

The Walt Disney Company is the only organization of its size with an executive board position titled Vice-president for Synergy. Due to the diversity in the Disney product line (theme parks, retail stores, movies, recordings, sport, television) the leaders of this successful organization believe that one person must be responsible for ensuring that there is synergy between all aspects of the business operation.

Up to one year in advance, before Disney rolls out a new movie, the retail stores are developing new products, the theme parks are planning new live shows, and the other aspects of this corporation are also preparing for joint promotion and distribution of this new product. This kind of synergy allocates Disney's scarce resources in the most efficient manner.

Your event also has scarce resources. These resources include your ability to administrate, coordinate, market, and manage the risk for the event. You must carefully and thoroughly link these four competencies together throughout the event process in order to efficiently produce the very best and most profitable event product.

The administration process of the event serves as the foundation for the resources you will select and manage during the coordination process. Poor administration will later undermine your ability to coordinate the event. Strong coordination will result in better marketing results. Unless your operations people are aware that today's tickets are discounted all the advertising in the world will be wasted. The link between coordination and marketing, and for that matter administration, is vital. Finally, legal, ethical, and risk management issues form a strong river current that runs through every decision you make in Event Management. If your marketing team leader overpromotes or inaccurately promotes the event, he or she will place those who must coordinate event operations at a great disadvantage. Subsequent chapters will introduce each of these competencies in detail but at this early stage it is important for you to recognize the connection between each one. Together they weave a strong tapestry that will shield you from future harm and provide a rich understanding of how each member of your team must work together productively.

THE MAIN EVENT

There are five critical phases for all successful events. These are research, design, planning, coordination, and evaluation. Although you may begin the event process during any phase it is important that all phases be visited and understood. Successful event managers understand the linkage between the basic Event Management competencies known as administration, coordination, marketing, and risk management. These four competencies form the core for most events and when linked synergistically ensure a strong, reliable, professional product. This is the best possible environment within which to produce your event.

NEXT ON THE AGENDA

Event design involves the five senses. In Chapter 3 you will learn how to develop the total event environment in order to create exciting first and lasting final impressions.

Designing the Event Environment

Like a playwright who molds his or her play to create a setting that a theater's limited confines can accommodate, so event managers face a similar challenge each time they are called upon to create an environment. Whether the site is a palatial mansion or a suburban park, the challenges remain the same. How can the site be adapted to meet the needs of our guests? Ballrooms with their four bare walls, department stores filled with products, and even main streets upon which parades are staged offer the same problems and opportunities as those confronting playwrights and set designers.

When creating an environment, the special events professional must once again return to the basic needs of the guests. The final design must satisfy these needs to become successful. Lighting, space, movement, decor, acoustics, and even such seemingly mundane concerns as rest rooms all affect the comfort of the guests and so play vital roles in creating a successful environment.

Five Card Draw: Playing Five Senses

When attempting to satisfy the needs of your guests, remember that the five senses are most powerful tools. Like five winning cards in the event manager's hand, combining the five senses—tactile, smell, taste, visual, and auditory—to satiate the needs of guests is the primary consideration when designing the event environment. The olfactory system creates instant emotional and creative reactions within your guests. How many times have you walked into a room, noticed a familiar smell, and suddenly experienced déjà vu? Event Management pioneer Jack Morton says that smell is the most powerful sense because of the memories it produces. In fact, smell may be generally the strongest sense in terms of generating emotional response, however, this will vary among individual guests. Therefore, as the event manager you must actively seek to employ in your environmental design elements that will impact all of the senses.

When designing a "Gone with the Wind" banquet you may erect a backdrop that immediately conjures memories of Tara, play music from the famous movie's theme, and even have Rhett and Scarlett look-a-likes at the door to greet and touch your guests. However, that magnolia centerpiece on the table is sadly missing one element. When you add a light scent of Jungle Gardenia perfume suddenly the event becomes a total sensory experience.

Just as some guests are sensitive to certain stimuli such as smell or auditory, other guests have a primary sense that they rely upon. Due to the influence of television many baby boomers may rely primarily on their visual sense. When designing the environment this is important to recognize when you are trying to quickly communicate your message. Use the senses as instruments to tune the imagination of your guests. Be careful to avoid playing sharp or flat notes by overdoing it. Find the perfect sensory melody and your guests will become creatively and emotionally involved in your event.

Figure 3-1 will enable you to survey your guests to determine their level of sensitivity as well as their primary sensual stimuli in order to create an effective event sensory environment.

FIGURE 3-1
The Sensory Audit and Plan

1. Use a focus group to determine the primary sensory stimuli of your guests.

2. Identify any oversensitivity or even allergies your guests may have that could be irritated by certain sensory elements.

3. Use the draft diagram of the event environment to identify and isolate the location of certain sensory experiences.

4. Share this design tool with typical guests and solicit their attitudes and opinions.

5. Audit the venue to determine the pre-existing sensory environment and what modifications you will be required to implement.

SOUNDSCAPING

To communicate with the guests at an event, you must design a sound system and effects that are unique and powerful enough to capture their attention. Do not confuse powerful with loud, however. Poignant background music at a small social event has as much power as a booming rock beat at a retail promotion. As with other components of event production, successful use of sound requires gauging and meeting the needs of the audience.

Sound by itself is a most powerful sensation. When asked which of her senses she would like to have returned to her, the late Helen Keller, blind and deaf since birth, explained that the ability to hear is more important than the ability to see. The eyes can deceive, but the way in which others speak and the thoughts they share reveal much about personality and intentions. Sound unlocks our imagination and allows us to visualize images buried in our subconscious. When planning the sound design for your event, many questions need to be considered. What is to be the dominant sensory element for the event? Sound may be the dominant sensory element for your event; for example, if live music or extensive speeches are the major component of your event, your investment in quality sound production may be paramount.

How will sound help support, reinforce, or expand the guests' perceptions of the event? Consider the theme of your event and devise ways in which sound can be used to convey that theme to the guests. For example, if you are planning a Polynesian theme event, the use of recorded island-type music at the entrance will help communicate that theme.

Are the architectural conditions in the venue optimal for sound reproduction? This question is most important, considering the number of new sites being created every day. The majority of these sites was not designed for optimum sound reproduction, and the event planner or sound designer must therefore consider how to improve the sound conditions in the venue. In the five special events markets, sound design, like lighting, is growing tremendously. In the social market, not only are live bands used more than ever, but with the addition of new electronic instruments, the repertoire of a small live band can be increased manyfold. Moreover, the rise of the disc jockey format and the more frequent use of videotape requires that the sound quality must be better than ever before. As the sophistication of the audio components available to the average consumer has increased, the sound systems for retail events have had to improve in quality as well to match the sound many guests can experience in their living rooms. Whether it be a fashion show or a visit with Santa, excellent sound is required to give the event credibility and value in the eyes (or ears) of the guest. Millions of dollars worth of merchandise may be on display, but if the sound system is poor, the guest perceives less value and is less inclined to buy.

Meetings and convention events also place more importance on sound reproduction for their programs. Gone are the days when a meeting planner was content to use the hotel house speakers for live music. Today many musical groups carry their own speakers, mixing boards, and operators.

VISUAL CUES

Baby boomers and subsequent generations, raised in front of televisions, may require strong visual elements to assist them with experiencing your event. This includes using proper signs to orient the guest and provide clear direction. Additional visual elements that must be considered are the proper and repetitive use of the key design element such as the *logo*. The logo is the graphic symbol of the organization sponsoring the event. Not only must this symbol be accurately represented but it must always appear in the same manner to benefit from repetitive viewing and establish consistency to promote retention.

WAR STORY

A magnificent fiftieth anniversary banquet was set for members of the Institute of Food Technology in a luxurious museum when the event manager noticed the band rolling in their speakers. Upon close inspection the event manager noted that amidst the decorator's splendor the band had placed chipped, bruised, dented, and unsafe-looking speakers. Furthermore, upon conducting a sound check he noticed that due to the domed ceiling the sound bounced throughout the room and the speakers would be inaudible to many of the 300 guests. Using resources from the museum's audiovisual inventory, the event manager added perimeter speakers to direct the sound to those dead areas of the room. After sending his assistant to a local hardware store, the event manager used black paint and black fabric to disguise the battered speakers just in time for the first musical notes to sound as the guests came streaming into the event.

Lesson Learned

Inspect equipment in advance or specify the condition in the contract. Conduct a sound check during the preliminary site inspection at the venue. Stand in several areas of the room and clap your hands to identify dead spots, see if the sound is clear, or bounces in many directions.

TOUCH

Whether you are considering the cloth that will dress the banquet table, the napkins, or the printed program, touch will immediately convey the quality of the event environment. To establish this sense use several different textures and while wearing a blindfold touch the various elements to determine what feelings are promoted. When handling the cloth do you feel as though you are attending a royal gala or a country picnic? When holding the program are you a guest of the king or the court jester? Use this blindfold test to help you narrow down your choices and effectively select the right fabric, paper, or other product to properly communicate the precise sense of touch you desire.

SMELL

Earlier we discussed the use of a perfume such as Jungle Gardenia to stimulate the sense of memory through smell. Remember that throughout the event environment a series of smells may be present that will either create the correct environment or confuse and irritate the guest. When conducting the site inspection note if the public areas are overdeodorized. This smell is often a clue that these chemicals are being used to mask a foul smell. Instead, you may wish to look for venues whose aromas are natural and the result of history, people, and of course, natural products such as plants and flowers.

Some individuals are extremely sensitive to strong odors. Therefore, when using the sense of smell do not overdo it. Instead, establish neutral areas where the smell of a scented candle, flowers, or food odors is not present to provide the nose with a respite from this stimulation. However, establishing individual areas where the strong aroma of pizza baking or chocolate melting is also important to both attract and convey the proper atmosphere. You may, for example, wish to incorporate the smell of barbecue into your western-themed event or pine trees into your Christmas wonderland. Again, when establishing these areas of smell try and isolate them so that the guests can return to neutral zone and not feel overwhelmed by this sense.

TASTE

The final sense of taste will be discussed in great detail in Chapter 7; however, the event manager must realize that the catering team members play a critical role in establishing a strong sensory feeling for the event. Carefully consult in advance with the catering team and determine the goals and objectives of the food presentation and then determine how best to proceed with combining the other four senses with the sense of taste to create a total olfactory experience for the guests. Keep in mind the age, culture, and lifestyle of your guests. Older guests may not be as sensitive to taste while still other guests may require spicier food combinations to engage the sense of taste. The taste sense historically has been linked with a strong sensual experience. Play the taste card for all it is worth and you will transform the guests from spectators to fully-engaged participants who will long remember the succulent event you have designed.

BLENDING, MIXING, AND MATCHING FOR FULL EFFECT

Make certain that you carefully select those event design sensory elements that will support the goals and objectives of the event. Do not confuse or irritate the guests by layering too many different senses in an effort to be creative. Rather, design the sensory experience as you would select paint for a canvas. Determine in advance what you hope to achieve or communicate and then use the five senses as powerful tools to help you accomplish your goals.

BELLS AND WHISTLES: AMENITIES THAT MAKE THE DIFFERENCE

Once you have established the atmosphere for your event environment and satisfied the basic needs of all guests, you have the opportunity to embellish or enhance their experience by adding a few well-chosen amenities. An amenity is best defined as a feature that increases attractiveness or value. In today's added value-driven business environ-

WAR STORY

An event manager reported that during a demonstration on how to use pepper gas to disarm an assailant the first five rows of the audience began coughing loudly and fled the room clutching their necks. The event manager went directly to the speaker and asked, "What happened?" The security expert replied, "Nothing. I never released the pepper gas. I have done this demonstration dozens of times without a problem." After a little further investigation by the local police it was determined that during the program a large glass jar of pepper was dropped in the adjoining kitchen and the heating, ventilation, and air-conditioning system sucked the pepper into the meeting room causing the guests to rapidly ingest this painful substance. Later, when told of the actual culprit, the guests found it humorous.

Lesson Learned

Check the heating, ventilation, and air-conditioning systems of the venue to determine how smells are conveyed throughout the environment. The scent from a candle or smoke from a barbecue pit can cause discomfort unless these systems are properly regulated.

ment amenities are more important that ever before. These amenities may range from advertising specialty items given as gifts at the beginning or the end of the event, interactive elements such as virtual environments, and even child care.

A popular way to stretch the budget is to transform the guests into decor elements. This is accomplished by distributing glow-in-the-dark novelty items such as necklaces, pins, or even swizzle sticks. As the guests enter the darkened event environment suddenly their glowing presence creates exciting visual stimuli. Firms such as Liquid Light in Los Angeles, California specialize in customizing these items with the slogans, logo, or name of the sponsoring organization.

Another effective amenity that is growing in popularity is the virtual event environment. Using virtual reality software the guests are able to experience many different environments at the same time. Wearing specially constructed goggles the guest is visually propelled to the top of a skyscraper where he or she does battle with evil demons or may stroll casually through a virtual trade show environment visually pausing to inspect a variety of different booths. These systems have become integral to the success of high-tech industries and are gaining in importance in assisting the guests with maximizing their time while at an event by providing the opportunity to visit several different environments in a short time period.

Whether glow-in-the-dark jewelry or virtual reality software, the needs, wants, and desires of the guests must be consistently evaluated to determine if the communications media you are using is effective and efficient. Using feedback from specific populations will help you rapidly achieve this purpose.

Identifying the Needs of Your Guests

Once you have gathered all of the quantitative data from the site inspection it is time to carefully analyze your findings and determine what implications emerge for your event environment design. Most important considerations include the legal, regulatory, and risk management issues that are uncovered during the site inspection.

If the venue is not in full compliance with the Americans with Disabilities Act you may need to make certain modifications in your design. For example, a large quasi-government corporation asked me to create a tropical theme including a small bridge at the entrance where guests would stroll over a pond containing live goldfish. In creating this design we factored in the need to provide full and equal access for disabled guests and therefore ramped both ends of the bridge to satisfy this need.

According to Ross Weiland's writing in the January 1995 issue of *Successful Meetings* magazine, the event industry must be more sensitive to the rights of the disabled. It is not only the moral and ethical importance that must be considered, it is a matter of federal law.

The statute states:

Title III-Sec. 302 a) General rule. No individual shall be discriminated against on the basis of disability in the full and equal enjoyment of the goods, services, facilities, privileges, advantages, or accommodations of any place of public accommodation.

As a result of this historic legislation, wheelchair ramps, braille menus and signs, sign language interpreters, and other elements have become commonplace at events. Event managers are responsible for complying with this law.

Figure 3-2 provides a comprehensive checklist for incorporating the Americans with Disabilities Act into your event environmental design.

LISTENING TO SPECIAL NEEDS

After seeking written feedback from your prospective guests regarding their special needs it is important to take one additional step to fully meet their expectations. You may wish to invite individuals with special needs to conduct their own site inspection of your proposed venue and become part of the planning team. Individuals in wheelchairs, older guests with limited mobility, and the visually and hearing impaired can provide you with important information to improve your total event environment. Local orga-

---

FIGURE 3-2
The Americans with Disabilities Act Event Design Checklist

1. Survey your guests in advance of the event to determine what accommodations will be required.

2. Include the following language on all brochures or other offerings: "If you require special accommodations please describe below."

3. Survey the venue to determine what gaps must be closed prior to your event.

4. Establish wheelchair seating positions.

5. Maintain a clear line of sight for guests using sign language interpreters.

6. Work with disabled speakers to provide access to the podium.

7. Provide audiotranscription services of the stage action for the visually disabled.

8. Select venues with, or provide handrails for, guests with physical infirmities.

9. Provide tables with appropriate height for wheelchair users.

10. Contact the U.S. Department of Justice if you have additional questions about designing an event environment that meets the compliance regulations. Telephone the Americans with Disabilities Act information line at (800) 514-0301.

11. Train your staff to better meet the needs of people with disabilities.

nizations such as Easter Seals or the Muscular Dystrophy Association can refer you to individuals who will volunteer to offer their advice and counsel during your planning stage. Listen carefully to their suggestions and incorporate where feasible. Your goal is to produce an event environment that is accessible and effective for everyone.

THE IMPLICATIONS OF SIZE, WEIGHT, AND VOLUME

Let us assume that your design requires massive scenery and the ingress to your venue is a standard width and height door. How do you squeeze the elephant through the keyhole? The answer is, of course, very carefully. Seriously, make certain that your design elements can be broken down into small units. Using component parts for the construction process will enable you to design individual elements that will easily fit through most doorways.

Weight is an important consideration as many venues were not built with this factor in mind. Before bringing in elements that have extraordinary weight check with the facility engineer to review the construction standards used in the venue and then determine if the stress factor is sufficient to accommodate your design. Furthermore, shifting weight can cause serious problems for certain venues. Therefore, if you are using a stage platform and simply placing a heavy prop you may not experience any problems. However, if on this same platform you are showcasing fifty aerobic dancers performing high-energy routines the platforms may not be sufficiently reinforced to handle this shifting weight. In addition to reviewing the stress weight that the area can accommodate with the engineer or other expert, conduct independent tests yourself by actually walking across the stage or examining the undergirdings to ensure that what goes up will not come down.

The final consideration is volume. The fire marshall determines the number of persons that can be safely accommodated in the venue. You, however, greatly influence this number by the seating configuration, the amount of decor, and other technical elements that you include in the final event environment. Less equals more. Typically the less design elements you incorporate the more people you can accommodate. Therefore, when creating your total event design first determine the number of people you must accommodate. Subtract the amount of square feet required for the guests and the remainder will determine the volume of elements that contribute to the event environment. See Figure 3-3 for an example. Do not do this in reverse. Some event managers first create a lavish design only later to find out that the number of guests will not allow them to install this design.

SECURING THE ENVIRONMENT

Just as the fire marshall is responsible for determining occupancy, the police and local security officials will determine how to secure the environment to reduce the possibility of theft or personal injury. When considering the theme and other important design elements remember that people will be walking under, over, and within this environ-

---

FIGURE 3-3

Calculating and Sizing the Event Environment

First: Identify the total number of persons and multiply the square feet (or meters) required for each person:

Example:
  50 couples
$\times$ 10 square feet per couple

$\overline{}$

$=$ 500 square feet

Next: Subtract the total amount of square feet required for the couples from the total space available.

Example:
  1,000 square feet available for dance floor
$-$ 500 square feet required by couples

$\overline{}$

$=$ 500 square feet available for props, tables, chairs, and other equipment.

---

ment and their safety must be paramount in your planning. Providing adequate lighting for traversing the event environment, securing cables and other technical components with tape or ramps, and event posting notices of "Use Caution" or "Watch Your Step" are important considerations when designing both beautiful as well as safe event environments.

Theft, sadly, is a major concern in designing the event environment. Do not make it easy for individuals to remove items from the event environment. Secure perimeter doors with guards or provide bag check stations at the entrance to discourage unscrupulous individuals from easily lifting valuable event elements. This is especially important when designing expositions where millions of dollars of merchandise may be on display for long periods of time. Furthermore, do not allow event participants to store merchandise or personal goods such as purses in public areas. Instead, provide a secure area for these elements to ensure a watchful eye.

TRANSPORTATION AND PARKING FACTORS

The venue may or may not provide easy vehicle ingress. Therefore, well in advance you must locate the proper door for load in of your equipment, the times the dock is available for your deliveries, and other critical factors that will govern your ability to transport your equipment and park your vehicles. Other considerations for transportation include the approved routes for trucks and other vehicles. In some jurisdictions, such as Washington, D.C., truck and large vehicular traffic is strictly regulated. Once again, inquire well in advance with both transportation as well as venue officials to determine the most efficient route.

Whether you are parking your vehicles in a marshaling facility or on the street considerations must be taken for security as well as easy access. Some venues may not be located in the safest of neighborhoods and therefore securing your vehicles as well as providing safe and fast access to these vehicles is of prime importance. Well lit, fenced-in areas are best for parking; however, the proximity of the vehicles to the loading area of the venue is the prime concern.

You may think that transportation and parking has little to do with creating the proper event environment but these two considerations should be given significant attention. Many events have started late or suffered in quality due to late or lost vehicles and inefficient load in operations. Remember, you may design the most incredible event environment, but until it is shipped, loaded in, and installed properly, it is only your idea. Proper transportation and installation will turn your idea into a dynamic event environment.

Manage the Event Environment and They Will Come Back

Understanding the basic needs of the guest is of paramount importance, especially when you are working with a smaller budget than you would like. In circumstances where the budget is severely restricted, there are ways, using your imagination, to stretch limited funds. Use your budget to enhance the beginning and the end, as this is what the guest will most remember. Following are some considerations for managing the design of an event environment.

ENTRANCES AND RECEPTION AREAS
The event manager must immediately establish the theme of the event with environmental design. The use of proper signs, bearing the group's name or logo, and appropriate decor will reassure guests that they are in the right place. Consider the arrival process from the guests' point of view. They received the invitation some time ago and probably did not bring it with them to the event. Therefore, they are relying on memory to guide them to the right building and the right room. Once they have located parking, they ask the attendant to direct them to XYZ event. The attendant is rushed, having to park several hundred cars for perhaps as many as six different functions, and cannot recall the exact location of the affair. Should the guests stumble upon your site and not recognize it because the logo is absent or the entrance does not communicate the theme of the party, they will become confused and lost. Providing your own personnel in costume or professional wardrobe will help guests locate your event, as will

proper signage. Upon arrival, guests should have an "Ah-ha!" experience, knowing they have arrived at the right place at the right time. You can offer your guests an "Ah-ha!" experience and create a positive impression by properly designing the reception area at which they are greeted. When guests must wait in long lines, they often begin to resent the event or its hosts. You must plan for these delays and offer solutions.

Figures 3-4, 3-5, 3-6, and 3-7 demonstrate how to place greeters, or "damage control" hosts, to handle problems in the reception area. In Figure 3-4, the guests have begun to form a second row at the reception table. When this occurs, your greeters should immediately invite the second-row guests to step forward to the additional tables set behind the primary tables. Having extra tables available will be perceived by your guests as an added courtesy and will help ease heavy arrival times. Note that the guests at the primary tables enter between them so as not to conflict with the guests at the additional tables.

Figure 3-5 shows a solution to the problem of guests arriving without an invita-

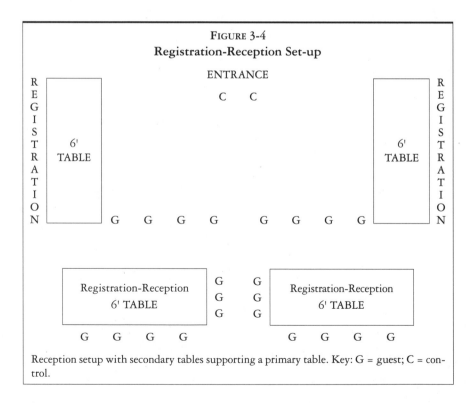

FIGURE 3-4
Registration-Reception Set-up

Reception setup with secondary tables supporting a primary table. Key: G = guest; C = control.

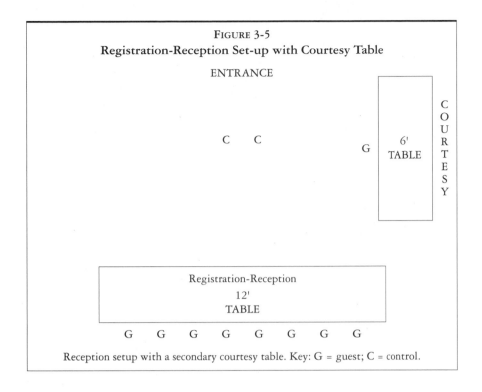

FIGURE 3-5
Registration-Reception Set-up with Courtesy Table

ENTRANCE

C   C

G   6'
TABLE

C
O
U
R
T
E
S
Y

Registration-Reception
12'
TABLE

G   G   G   G   G   G   G   G

Reception setup with a secondary courtesy table. Key: G = guest; C = control.

tion, when their names do not appear on the list of invitees. To avoid embarrassment and delay, the guest is invited to step forward to the courtesy table, conveniently isolated from the general crowd flow. There the problem can be quietly and courteously resolved, or the guest may be ushered out a back door without disrupting the event.

The scenario depicted in Figure 3-6 is one every experienced event planner has known. During heavy arrival time, such as the second half hour of a one-hour cocktail party preceding the main event, long lines of guests are forming while those staffing the reception tables are trying to greet arrivals quickly and efficiently and keep the line moving. Professional greeters can make the guests' wait less annoying. Their job is simply to greet the guests in line, quietly thank them for coming, and answer any questions they may have while waiting. Often professional performers, such as strolling mimes, clowns, jugglers, or magicians, may be used in this area to entertain, thereby distracting guests while they wait in line.

When you expect long lines over a brief period, the best arrangement is a variation of Figure 3-4. By using two additional courtesy tables, positioned at an angle as

```
┌─────────────────────────────────────────────────────────────────────────────┐
│                                                                               │
│                              FIGURE 3-6                                        │
│                  Registration-Reception Set-up with Greeters                  │
│                                                                               │
│                                 ENTRANCE                                       │
│                                                                               │
│                                 C     C                                        │
│                                                                               │
│                                                                               │
│           ┌─────┐   G    G                    G    G   ┌─────┐                 │
│           │     │   G    G                    G    G   │     │                 │
│           │     │   G    G                    G    G   │     │                 │
│           │     │   G    G                    G    G   │     │                 │
│           │     │   G    G                    G    G   │     │                 │
│           │     │   G    G                    G    G   │     │                 │
│           │     │   G    G         P          G    G   │     │                 │
│           │     │   G    G                    G    G   │     │                 │
│           │ 12' │   G    G                    G    G   │ 12' │                 │
│           │TABLE│   G    G                    G    G   │TABLE│                 │
│           │     │   G    G                    G    G   │     │                 │
│           │     │   G    G         P          G    G   │     │                 │
│           │     │                                      │     │                 │
│           │     │                                      │     │                 │
│           │     │                                      │     │                 │
│           └─────┘                                      └─────┘                 │
│                                                                               │
│   Reception setup integrating the professional greeter into the flow of guest traffic. Key: G = │
│   guest; C = control; P = professional greeter.                               │
│                                                                               │
└─────────────────────────────────────────────────────────────────────────────┘
```

shown in Figure 3-7 you may alleviate crowding. The reception setup integrating the professional greeter into the flow of guest traffic further insures the ease and comfort of your guests.

In Figure 3-7, you can keep the guests moving forward and handle disputes at the same time. The hosts and hostesses at these courtesy tables should be trained to resolve disputes quickly and know when to refer the guest to a supervisor for further assistance. Most disputes can be simply remedied, requiring no more than preparation of a name badge, a payment, or other minor business. If handled at the primary table, such tasks become cumbersome. Experienced planners know that the floor plan for the reception

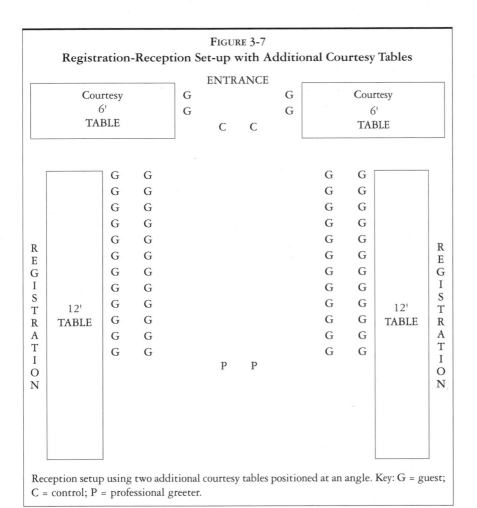

FIGURE 3-7

Registration-Reception Set-up with Additional Courtesy Tables

Reception setup using two additional courtesy tables positioned at an angle. Key: G = guest; C = control; P = professional greeter.

area should facilitate guest arrivals and is critical to the success of the event. The way in which the guest is first received at an event determines all future perceptions he or she will have about the event program you have designed. Take time to plan this area carefully to ensure an efficient and gracious reception.

FUNCTION AREAS

The reception area may create the first impression, but the main function area will determine the effectiveness of your overall design. This is the area in which the guest will spend the most time, and this is the area where your principle message must be com-

---

Figure 3-8
Traditional Theater- or Classroom-Style Set-up

STAGE

_____   _____

_____   _____

_____   _____

_____   _____

_____   _____

_____   _____

_____   _____

_____   _____

_____   _____

municated to the guest in a memorable manner. Traditional space designs are currently being rethought by meeting planners as well as psychologists to develop a more productive environment. Dr. Paul Radde is a psychologist who has pioneered the development of physical space planning for conferences that provides a more optimum environment in which to learn. Dr. Radde has, often to the chagrin of various hotel set-up crews, determined that speakers prefer and often deliver a better talk when there is no center aisle. In the traditional theater- or classroom-style setup shown in Figure 3-8, all of the speaker's energy escapes through the center aisle. When this lane is filled with live bodies, the speaker's interaction is increased, as is the human connection among the audience members themselves.

Figure 3-9 demonstrates the optimum setup, complete with wide aisles on each side to allow for proper egress. With this setting, each row should be at least six inches farther apart than in Figure 3-8 to allow for more efficient egress.

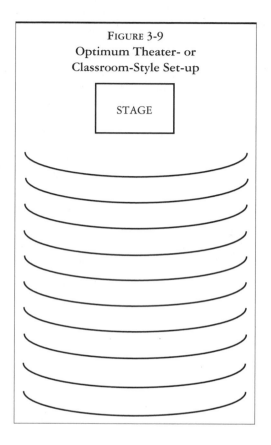

FIGURE 3-9
Optimum Theater- or
Classroom-Style Set-up

STAGE

Some fire marshals prohibit the arrangement in Figure 3-9 because some audience members will be seated too far from an aisle. An excellent alternative is shown in Figure 3-10, in which the front two rows are solid, with side aisles beginning behind row two.

Perhaps the best adaptation is found in Figure 3-11. In this arrangement all rows except the first five are sealed, and the center aisle is easily reached by latecomers in the rear of the auditorium. Planning an effective seating arrangement is only the beginning. Masking tape or rope on stanchions can be used to seal the back rows, as shown in Figure 3-11, encouraging guests to fill in the front rows first.

Once filled with guests, the tape is removed. After thirty years of watching audiences head for the back rows, I experimented a few years ago with this method to find out if I could control seating habits without inconveniencing the audience unduly. Much to my delight, several audience members have thanked me for this subtle suggestion to move up front. Without this direction the audience becomes confused and retreats to old habits.

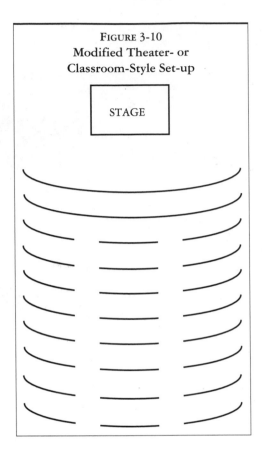

FIGURE 3-10
Modified Theater- or
Classroom-Style Set-up

STAGE

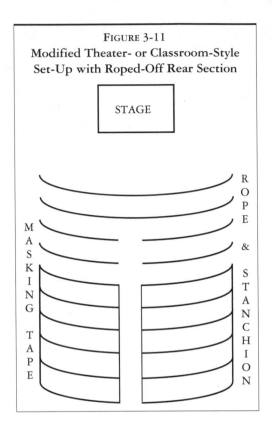

FIGURE 3-11
Modified Theater- or Classroom-Style
Set-Up with Roped-Off Rear Section

STAGE

Interestingly, once a guest claims a seat, he or she will return to it throughout the event. However, unless I have predetermined that they will sit up front by making the back rows unavailable, all of the coaxing and bribing (I once placed dollar bills under front-row seats) will not move the audience from the back-row comfort zone.

INNOVATIVE SITES

The purpose of creatively designing your environment is to provide a dynamic atmosphere within which your guest may experience the event. Decorator Terry Brady knows all too well how important such an atmosphere can be, as he once staged a banquet in a tractor trailer. The guests were escorted up the steps and dined inside an actual tractor trailer decorated by the Brady Company's team of artists. The goal of this creative design was to surprise and intrigue guests, who were picked up in limousines and brought to this isolated and inelegant site. Inside the tractor trailer, they found luxurious decor, complete with chandeliers, tapestries, and fine linens. Brady recalls that the total tab for the forty guests, including catering, service, and decor, was roughly $16,000. Not every client will allocate upwards of $400 per person for an event. Nonetheless, the event planner is increasingly faced with the challenge of finding innovative, creative environments in which to stage their events. Curators of museums and public buildings in record numbers throughout the United States have begun setting fees and offering their buildings to groups that wish to host a reception or meeting in a novel atmosphere. With these new opportunities for use of public space come increased challenges for decorators, who must now cope with the increased demand for atmospheric props in place of flats, banners, murals, and other more traditional scenic devices. Figure 3-12 is just a sampling of ideas for unusual sites in which to hold special events. The possibilities for exciting, innovative, and offbeat event sites are infinite. It is important, however, that your selection be logical and practical in terms of location, parking, setup, budget, and use of space.

One important book is entitled "Places" and lists hundreds of event sites throughout the world. The publication may be obtained by telephoning (212) 737-7536. A local or regional monograph is entitled "Perfect Places" by Lynn Broadwell and Jan Brenner. In this northern California-based publication venues ranging from historic homes to modern museums are described with careful attention to both aesthetic and logistical detail. This publication may be obtained by calling (510) 525-3379. A companion book by Broadwell is entitled "Here Comes the Guide" and focuses on sites for weddings. According to Lynn Broadwell's writing in "ISES Gold," "Twenty years ago event sites were a rare commodity. What's changed? Everything."

Figure 3-12 provides you with a comprehensive listing of prospective event sites. Use this listing to brainstorm with your event stakeholders to determine the best venue for your next event.

Wherever you turn, you will find new products and new services available to help you transform an environment for a creative special event. Many unusual products can be found at gift shows (trade shows featuring new and unusual gift items), antique stores and shows, flea markets, used and classic clothing stores, hotel close-out sales, and other businesses selling off their stock. The ISES world wide resource directory contains additional groups and organizations that can help you create an environment for your next special event.

AMENITIES AND FURNISHINGS

The possibilities for linens, silverware, glassware, centerpieces, and even costumes for your servers are greater in the profession today than ever before. Sites, sources, and suppliers for these items can be found in journals, such as *Event World, Special Events* magazine, and various industry newsletters. See the Appendix for dozens of additional resources.

FIGURE 3-12
Event Sites

In Transit

Aircraft Carrier
Blimp
The Concorde
Concorde SST
Cruise Ship
Double-Decker Bus
Hot-Air Balloon
Monorail
Moving Railroad Train

Orient Express
Paddle Wheel Steam Boat
Roller Coaster
Space Shuttle
Stationary Caboose
Subway Platform
Tractor Trailer
Trolley
Yacht

Design by Mother Nature

Apple Orchard
Arboretum
Botanical Center
Caverns
Central Park
Christmas Tree Farm
Dude Ranch
Formal Garden

Greenhouse
Meadow
National Forest
Pasture
Rose Garden
Summer Camp
Underneath a Waterfall

Music, Music, Music

Estate of Deceased Music Star
Gazebo or Bandshell in a Park
Grand Ole Opry Stage
Opera House

Recording Studio
Symphony Hall
Television Set of "American Bandstand"

On Stage

Circus Center Ring
Circus Museum
Comedy Nightclub
Community Theater
Famous Actors Dressing Room

Professional Theater—Lobby, Backstage, On-stage
Theater Green Room
Theatrical Museum

At the Movies

Any Movie Theater
Drive-In Movie
Estate of a Deceased Film Star
Former Movie or Television Location (Such as the Bridge in Madison County or Southfork Ranch in Dallas)

Former Movie Set (Such as Universal Studios Back Lot or Granada Studios Tour)
Historic Movie Theater
Radio City Music Hall

Food, Glorious Food

Apple Orchard
Bottling Plant
Cannery
Cornfield

Distillery
The Kitchen of a Bakery
Vineyard

FIGURE 3-12
Events Sites (continued)

Infamous

Alcatraz

Former Speakeasy

Homes of Famous Outlaws (Now, Often
  Museums)

Microbrewery

Nightclub

Saloon in a Ghost Town

Stately

Castle

Cathedral

Convent

Mansion

Monastery

The Child in You

Amusement Park

Carousel

Children's Museum

Children's Theater

Clown Alley at a Circus

Fairgrounds

Laser Tag Center

Puppet Theater

Virtual Reality Center

Wild Places

Animal Shelter

Aviary

Local Animal Farm or Ranch

Pet Kennel

Stable

Wild Animal Park

Zoo

In Scholarly Pursuits

University/College Dining Hall

University/College Library

University/College Private Dining Facility
  (President's Dining Room)

University/College Theater, Meeting Room,
  Chapel

In Glass Cases

Aquarium

Art Museum

Aviation Museum

Historical Society Museum

Medical Museum

Natural History Museum

Planetarium

Potter's Studio

Science Museum

Sculpture Museum

Textile Museum

Behind the Scenes

Aircraft Hanger

Baseball Dugout

Current Embassy

Diplomatic Reception Rooms at the U.S.
  Department of State

Empty Swimming Pool

Football Locker Room

Former Embassy

Movie Sound Stage

Presidential Library

Television Studio

(Figure continued on next page)

Figure 3-12
Events Sites *(continued)*

The Winner Is You

Basketball Court	Home Plate on a Baseball Diamond
The Fifty-Yard Line of a Football Field	Racetrack
Full Swimming Pool	Roller Rink
Hockey Rink	Former Olympic Games Venue

Ghoulish and Ghastly

Abandoned Hospital Morgue	Funeral Home
Abandoned Hospital Operating Room	Mausoleum
Cemetery	Tombstone Manufacturer

Highly Scientific

Computer Laboratory	General Science Laboratory

Edible Centerpieces and Displays

The centuries-old European custom of including elaborately designed food displays as part of the decor is finally becoming popular—indeed, in some regions, de rigueur—in the United States. This important area of setting design can range from fancy carved crudités for the hors d'oeuvre to elaborate centerpieces carved from thick, dark chocolate. Today's special events professionals are as concerned with the aesthetic appeal of the food selections as they are with taste. In fact, food presentation has become an art form in the United States, one in which annual competitions are held in areas ranging from ice sculpture and sugar works to chocolate and pastry design. When incorporating food into your overall design, remember that, ultimately, most food is intended to be eaten. The display must be accessible to the guests and still look appealing after guests are served. If possible, a server should offer the first guests who visit the display a serving of the decorated or carved item. This will help encourage other guests to partake by themselves. You may wish to prepare two versions of the item: one for show on an elevated, lighted platform and one for serving, placed within reach of the guests. This will allow every guest to appreciate the work of your culinary artists throughout the event.

Decorating the Environment

The decorating profession has undergone a rapid transformation since the days when Howard Lanin's client told him to "just make it lovely." Today making it lovely involves a specialized professional in touch with the latest styles and products with which to

WAR STORY

My firm produced the opening of Warner LeRoy's famous Potomac Restaurant in Washington, D.C. LeRoy is a famous showman-restauranteur who is best known for his celebration-theme restaurants, such as New York City's Tavern on the Green. For the opening of the Potomac, we created a series of food parades, featuring actors and actresses wearing elaborate costumes from ice shows and circuses and carrying oversized food displays, culminating with a chocolate mold of the U.S. Capitol. This final course was entitled "Capitol Meltdown": When the servers poured a special sauce over each serving, it sizzled, bubbled, and melted into a rich and creamy chocolate dessert. As the Capitol melted, fireworks exploded overhead as a live 50-member band performed "The Stars and Stripes Forever." Warner LeRoy later wrote to applaud our efforts, saying, "You exceeded my expectations."

Lesson Learned

First the eye must become excited to stimulate the palate. Use creative methods to tease the eye and other senses with food and beverage.

---

create specific environments that will satisfy guests' individual needs. Today's designers are creating more profound, if only temporary, works of art to frame special events. Sixty years ago special events were most often held either in private rooms, private clubs, churches, public sites, or hotels. Modern decorators are faced with the challenge of turning almost any conceivable space into a suitable environment for a special event. From football fields to tractor trailers, today's decorators must display more imagination, creativity, and skill than ever before to keep pace with changing styles and trends. The designer/decorator's craft is one of transformation. Turning a polo field into a castle, a ballroom into the land of Oz, or a black tent into an extraterrestrial fantasy, decorators transport guests from the ordinary to the extraordinary by creating a world of fantasy.

Regional customs and geographic location may determine to some extent what types of products are used for some events. Very often, for example, a client in Florida will request a mariachi theme, and a client from the Southwest will desire a Polynesian holiday. But expanded delivery services, which allow suppliers to express-mail almost any-thing overnight, have enabled designers and decorators to obtain almost any product for a special event, regardless of location.

One challenge decorators face is designing an environment that will satisfy both primary and secondary audiences. Creating designs and products that will translate to television, film, and still photography is becoming increasingly important. Consequently, when formulating design ideas, consider both the primary and secondary audiences—who will view this event and in what format? Perhaps the design will be detailed in such a way that it will show well in close-up photography. Many stock decor items avail-able in today's events marketplace did not exist sixty years ago. Synthetic fibers and plastics have become increasingly sophisticated, enabling the fabrication of countless imaginative pieces. Even as these lines are written, products continue to be developed, providing greater selection at lower cost. Trying to describe all the products and tech-niques available to the event practitioner is impossible. The following discussions will introduce you to some of the more popular products and the imaginative ways that some innovative special events planners use them. Their continual exploration of new ways to satisfy clients' needs is the ultimate key to creative design.

Interactive Decor

Today's guests want to be more than just spectators at a special event—after all, movies and television provide plenty of opportunities to watch fantastic special effects and see gorgeous set designs and wonderful performances. To provide more than just a passive viewing experience, the event designer must create an environment that allows the guests to participate—to be actors in the decorator's dream world.

In Atlanta, I experimented with this idea of interactive decor with an audience of prestigious and somewhat jaded professional catering executives. The challenge was to show these hospitality professionals something new working, as always, within a spe-cific budget. The theme of the banquet was "Starship NACE" (National Association of Catering Executives). As the guests entered the foyer, they passed between two twenty-five-inch color television monitors that featured a close-up view of an extraterrestrial's face. As each guest passed, the alien greeted him or her by name and offered a warm welcome to the event. I stood in the shadows, out of sight, and watched the guests' reac-tions—they suddenly stopped and laughed, clearly baffled by how an image on a screen could recognize and greet them. In actuality, an actor was hidden in a side room. As each guest stepped into the reception area, a technician using a two-way radio revealed the name to the actor, who in turn announced the name on television. Fog machines were set a few feet beyond the television monitors; just as the guests were recovering from one experience, they would receive a small blast of dry chemical fog to surprise them again. Throughout the cocktail reception, a prerecorded endless-loop cassette tape featuring space sounds and a professional narrator making preboarding announcements was played. When the time came to open the ballroom doors for dinner, four astronauts dressed in white jumpsuits, with NACE embroidered on their breast pockets, and blue and white space helmets, also featuring the NACE emblem, appeared in front of each door. As the doors were slowly opened, more fog seeped from the ballroom into the cocktail area. The guests entered the ballroom via a tunnel constructed of black pipe and drape and hundreds of miniature white lights. They tiptoed over a moonscape atmosphere, created by thousands of Styrofoam peanuts covered by ground cloth. Walking through that tunnel, the guests were entering another world. Once inside the ballroom, a robot welcomed the guests from the dance floor and instructed them to "be seated quickly, as the starship would be departing soon." Also Sprach Zarathustra, the music used in the movie 2001: A Space Odyssey, played in the background, and the sound effects of sonic blasts were added, projected through four different speakers to create a true sense of surround sound. One-dimensional scenic pieces of planets were hung from the walls, and miniature strobe lights created the effect of starlight.

Later chapters explore how the use of video and live action helped to provide constant interaction for the guests attending this event. At this point it is sufficient to understand the importance of creating a design that will meet the needs of the guests. Today any site can be transformed through decor, using a variety of products and techniques. Regardless of the site and the decoration details, however, the designer's objective remains the same: satisfying the guests. To accomplish this goal, the designer must involve the guests in the event as much as possible through their senses, their activities, and their emotions. Site design can facilitate such involvement, as the "Starship NACE" event demonstrates.

In another example of interactive decor, my firm was involved in designing a theme event entitled "A Dickens of a Christmas," in which the streets of Victorian London were recreated to bring the feeling of Charles Dickens' England to a hotel exhibit room. Since one of Dickens' best-known tales is A Christmas Carol, we decided to employ a winter setting and scattered artificial snow throughout the hall. I was delighted to see the usually staid guests kicking the snow throughout the room as they traveled down each lane, participating actively in the setting. We also included a group of street urchins (actually professional boys and girls with extensive Broadway credits), who were instructed to attempt to steal food from the lavish buffets throughout the room. Each time they snatched a scone, the waiters would grab them and say, "All right, if you want to eat, you must sing for your supper!" The children then proceeded to sing a ten-minute medley of holiday carols. The guests reacted first with surprise when the waiter reprimanded the children and then, within seconds, became emotionally involved as the adorable and talented children sang for their supper. A life-sized puppet of Ebenezer Scrooge was also used. As guests wandered by his house (a display piece), he popped his head out and shouted, "You're standing on my kumquats! Get out of my garden now! Bah, humbug!" The guests, of course, loved this Christmas nemesis. Those who were recognized by the puppeteer were called by name, much to their delight and the delight of their friends. Mr. Scrooge created gales of laughter, once again emotionally stimulating the guests.

The potential for effective design is truly greater than ever. To succeed, the guest must be involved sensuously, physically, and emotionally. The Bible tells us that "there is nothing new under the sun." My friend, Cavett Robert, chairman emeritus of the National Speakers Association, has said, "Much that is described as 'new' is actually old wine in new bottles." These maxims apply to the decor industry, as with every advancement of new technology, the basic principles of satisfying the guest's sensual, physical, and emotional needs remain unchanged.

INSIDE THE WORLD OF EVENT DESIGN

Hargrove, Inc., of Lanham, Maryland, was founded in the late 1930s by Earl Hargrove, Sr. Hargrove specialized in what was then called "window trimming," decorating store windows of retail establishments in the Washington, D.C., area to promote sales. With the advent of television, Hargrove's clients began to funnel their advertising dollars into the new medium, and his business soured. When his son, Earl Jr., returned home from a stint in the Marine Corps in the late 1940s, he joined his father's company. Earl Jr., wanted to pursue the new and lucrative field of convention and trade show display and exposition decorating, but his father wanted to remain solely in the specialty decorating market. Although they separated for a time, Earl Jr., pursuing the convention market and Earl Sr., struggling in the specialty decorating market, they eventually rejoined forces. Their longevity in the Washington, D.C., events arena is best symbolized by their association with the national Christmas tree located beside the White House.

In 1949 Earl Hargrove, Jr., placed the star high atop the tree; in that same year, he and his father renewed their business partnership, and a new brilliance in special events decor began. Today that partnership includes many more members of the Hargrove family, a talented team of employees, and a large warehouse-studio filled with thousands of props, scenic items, and parade floats. When Earl Hargrove, Jr., began in partnership with his father, he discovered the lucrative market for Washington social events. He recalls receiving an order to decorate a country club in the early 1950s for which the total bill was $350. Times certainly have changed, both in terms of budget and available products with which to decorate. Today a third-generation Hargrove, Chris, directs a sales team that provides decor for major casinos, corporations, and associations as well as private individuals who seek decor for their bar and bas mitzvahs, weddings, and other celebrations. Chris believes his mission in the social-event field is to bring the client's theme to life through decor. Doing so today, however, is trickier than in past years, in part because of more stringent fire regulations. According to Chris, "Three states have particularly tough fire laws governing interior decor, and others are following. Every product we use must be flameproofed, which in the balloon industry, for example, is very difficult to accomplish, largely due to high manufacturer's costs." When

Earl Jr., began with his father, the available materials were paper, cloth, and wood. Today he and Chris enjoy many more options, including foam, fiberglass, a wide selection of flameproofed fabrics, and a full range of plastics, to mention only a few. Forty years ago, the guest was content to merely view the decoration. Today, Chris is challenged to give the guest a feeling of participation and interaction with the element of the decor.

He designs sets for themed events using devices such as "time tunnels," which the guests walk through to enter the main event, or three-dimensional props that the guests may touch. Both Hargroves agree that a successful decorator must offer a full range of services and products to be successful. Hargrove, Inc., will rent out a single prop or create an entirely new themed event. This diversity has proven successful for over forty years. The Hargroves, along with other professional decorators, suggest that, while there are millions of new decorating ideas for special events, not all of them are practical. Therefore, it is always important to consider the following when choosing decorations. See Figure 3-13 for a decor checklist.

Parades and Float Design

Starting with the original Cherry Blossom parade in Washington, D.C., the Hargrove artists have been recognized as leaders in the U.S. float design and construction industry. Many nationally known parades, including the annual Miss America parade in Atlantic City and the 1987 We The People parade in Philadelphia, celebrating the

---

FIGURE 3-13
Decor Checklist

1. What will the venue (site, building) allow in terms of interior/exterior decor?

2. What are the policies regarding installation? What are the policies or laws of the local municipality regarding decorating materials?

3. What is the purpose of the decor?

4. Are you conveying a specific theme?

5. Is there a specific message?

6. What period or style are you attempting to represent?

7. What are the demographics and psychographics of your attendees?

8. Are they spectators or participants?

9. What are the budgetary guidelines for the decor?

10. How long will it be in use?

11. Which existing scenic pieces can be modified to fit your theme or convey your message?

bicentennial of the U.S. Constitution, have featured Hargrove floats. Designing, building, transporting, and operating floats can be a costly enterprise. But the rewards for the sponsor, in terms of publicity, can be priceless, provided the right steps are taken. The questions in Figure 3-14 should be addressed before contracting to design a float.

When asked why he continues to pursue this extremely labor-intensive sector of the decorating profession, Earl explains, as usual, with a story: "A few years ago, I was in Atlantic City with the Miss America Parade, and a man in the convention pipe-and-drape industry saw me watching my floats go down the boardwalk. He said, 'Earl, why don't you get out of the float business and just concentrate on the convention draping part?' That's where the profits are.' Well, I didn't answer him, but I knew at that moment how different our company is from all the others. This guy was the unhappiest guy in the world. He didn't really love what he did. On the other hand, we do what we love to do, and I hope it shows in our work."

Parade floats are a perfect example of the need to consider the ultimate viewership of your design. Corporations sponsor floats in an effort to develop positive publicity and influence consumers to buy their products and services. Since only a few parades are televised nationally, most floats need only ensure that the sponsor's theme is conveyed to the live audience viewing the event. Many floats include people—pageant queens, actors, actresses, costumed characters, and celebrities—in their design. When planning the float design, it is essential to consider their place in the display. The wardrobe color of the person riding on the float, for example, will affect the total look

---

FIGURE 3-14
Parade Float Checklist

1. What does the parade committee or organization allow in terms of size, materials, and thematic design?

2. Under what meteorological conditions and in what climate will the float be used? (Some float builders specialize in designs suitable for particular climates.)

3. Will the float appear on television?

4. What investment will the sponsor make?

5. What constraints are imposed by the parade itself regarding construction, size, weight, materials, and themes? (For example, spatial constraints may limit a float's dimensions.)

6. What message does the sponsor wish to convey?

7. Where will the floats be stored prior to the parade?

8. What is the physical environment of the parade route?

of the float and therefore is an important design concern. Additionally, the lighting at the time of the parade will determine to some extent which colors and materials will best convey your message.

As I noted above, it is essential to review the parade organization's requirements for parade floats before making any design choices. In most cases it will be appropriate to feature the float sponsor's name prominently in the design. The manner in which you incorporate the sponsor's name or logo into the float design will affect the integrity of the display itself. Be careful to make the sponsor's name and/or logo a cohesive part of the design whenever possible, rather than merely tacking a loose sign on the side as though it were an afterthought. Your ability to incorporate the sponsor's message into your final design in a seamless manner will determine the effectiveness of the float in the eyes of both the viewer and the sponsor. Whether it's themed decor for social events or major parade floats for the Philadelphia Thanksgiving Day parade, the Hargrove family, starting with their late founder, Earl Sr., continues today with another powerful father-and-son team—Earl Jr., and Earl III (Chris)—to bring new innovations to the art and science of decor. They are serious businessmen concerned with profit and growth, but they are guided ultimately by the feeling that they bring a special magic to special events. The Hargroves still ensure the placement of the star high atop the national Christmas tree; perhaps this is a symbol of the bright, shining influence their art has shone upon the special events universe.

Say It With Flowers

A major floral decorator on the East Coast, Angelo Bonita, of Floral Events Unlimited by Angelo Bonita, is fond of describing his work for social and corporate events as "combining floral, food, and props to create 'still lifes.'" His family once owned a nursery business in Pennsylvania when he was young, and Angelo became an expert, not only in how best to grow plants, but also in the wide range of possibilities in floral design. At a recent conference of special events professionals, he predicted the following trends regarding event decor. "Clients and their planners will place a new emphasis on casual elegance and that American style: originality."

Flowers are usually more costly than stock rental pieces because of their perishable nature. According to some designers, the markup for floral is often four times the cost. If the cost of the floral centerpiece is $20, the designer will sell it to the client for $80 to recover his or her labor, materials, and overhead costs, plus retain a margin of profit.

John Daly, CSEP, president of John Daly, Inc., of California, began his successful design firm with floral products. He suggests that when designing vertical centerpieces the following guidelines should be observed: "The centerpiece height should not exceed fourteen inches unless it is loose and airy, therefore see-through, over the fourteen-inch mark. This, of course, does not apply to the epergne arrangement. An epergne is a flower holder, such as a candelabra or mirrored stand, that raises the flowers from the table.

W A R   S T O R Y

Ambassador Selwa Roosevelt, Chief of Protocol during the Reagan Administration, reminded me of how important it is to know the purpose of an event before designing its decor. She told of her surprise—upon entering a room in which a luncheon hosted by the secretary of state was to be held—at finding Secretary Shultz removing the centerpiece from his table. The elaborate vertical centerpiece was obstructing his ability to make eye contact with his guest and therefore inhibited communication. Can a proper centerpiece help ensure world peace? This instance certainly suggests an improper one might prevent it!

Lesson Learned

Proper decor enhances communication, serving as an effective catalyst for a successful event.

When using the epergne, the base of the floral arrangement should begin at least twenty-four inches above table height."

Daly believes that event design has truly matured into both a fine art and science because of the new materials available and the speed at which they can be obtained. Today a wider range of floral products is available because of the advances in transportation and shipping. With the advent of overnight delivery systems, Daly can have virtually any product he wishes for any event in any location. As designer for events in Seoul, Korea, and on the Virgin Islands, this advantage has increased his ability to use fresh and exciting ideas in many far-off event sites.

It's a Balloon

Balloon decor can range from a simple balloon arch to more elaborate designs, such as three-dimensional shapes or swags of balloons, intertwined with miniature lights, hung from the ceiling. Balloons can create special effects, such as drops, releases, and explosions.

Balloon drops involve dropping balloons over the audience from nets or bags suspended from the ceiling. Releases include setting helium-filled balloons free outdoors from nets, bags, or boxes, all commercially available. Explosions might include popping clear balloons filled with confetti, or popping balloons mounted on a wall display to reveal a message underneath.

From centerpieces to massive walls of balloons, such as the U.S. flag displays that Treb Heining created for the city of Philadelphia, balloon art has become an established part of the special events industry. Organizations such as the National Association of Balloon Artists (NABA) and Pioneers Balloon Company's The Balloon Network are working to educate both balloon professionals and their clients to the uses of this art form as well as to ensure greater responsibility in employing it.

Howard Zusel, owner of A-1 Entertainment of Chicago, Illinois, has staged enormous corporate theme events for tens of thousands of guests. Zusel stocks a large inventory of amusement- or carnival-type props and equipment. From popcorn poppers to moon bounce equipment, Zusel's firm is one of the leading purveyors of these products in the Chicago area. For corporate events, Zusel works closely with the corporation to create a workable floor plan or site plan. Each of his props and amusement devices is positioned to attract and engage the guest. Because of his total understanding of the components of a successful event, Zusel's firm also provides themed entertainment to bring the props to life. All personnel is properly uniformed and neatly groomed to meet and serve the guests. Zusel annually dispenses hundreds of thousands of balloons; in the carnival and amusement business, they are a basic decor item. Balloon design is not, however, limited to carnival or amusement themes. In fact, while the balloon may be rooted in this tradition, it has "taken off," enjoying the soaring acceptance and prominence in the decor industry. Balloon art has become an integral part of event decor largely because of the innovations of Treb Heining of California. From creating an enormous birthday cake for a tenth-anniversary celebration at a shopping mall to supervising the balloon effects for the opening and closing ceremonies of the Los Angeles Olympic games, Heining has been at the forefront of his profession for many years. He began by selling balloons at Disneyland in Anaheim, California, and later began to use the same products for decoration at both social and corporate events. He has designed the massive balloon drops for the Republican National Conventions, incorporating the balloon-holding nets in the decor prior to the actual drop.

In recent years there has been much discussion regarding the effect of balloon releases on the environment. Marine biologists have determined that wind currents cause balloons to drift out over bodies of water, where they lose velocity and eventually fall into the waters below. They are concerned that sea animals may ingest these products and become ill or die. While there is presently no conclusive evidence that balloon releases have harmed marine animals, what goes up must eventually come down, and both the balloon professional and his client must act responsibly. Electric power companies in some jurisdictions throughout the United States have reported incidences where foil balloons have become entangled in power lines following a release, causing power failures due to the conductivity of the metallic balloon. All of the balloon professionals disapprove of foil balloon releases as well as releases where a hard object is included in or on the balloon itself. While it is impossible to regulate a balloon's final destination after a release, it is possible to design and stage releases that will not adversely affect the environment. A tethered release—where the balloons are released on long tethers and not allowed to float freely—may be one alternative. In some jurisdictions the Federal Aviation Administration requests notice of balloon releases in order to advise pilots in the area.

Tents: Beyond Shelter Is Decor

One example of a new adaptation of a classic environment is in the tenting industry. Developments in materials and workmanship in this industry have multiplied the design possibilities of tents. Only three decades ago, the standard tent available for a special event was a drab olive U.S. Army tarpaulin. Flooring was rarely considered, and lighting was most elementary. Today, however, thanks to major innovators such as Harry Oppenheimer, C.E.O. of HDO Productions, the tenting industry has truly come of age. Oppenheimer sees his services as "essentially solving a space problem. For that special occasion, such as a fiftieth anniversary, you don't have to build a family room to accommodate your guests. You can rent a tent with all of the same comforts of a family room." Oppenheimer believes the successful tenting professional prepares for the unforeseen, imagining the structure in snow, wind, rain, and perhaps hail. Most professionals in the tenting industry will not only carefully inspect the ground surface but will also bore beneath the surface to check for underground cables and pipes that might be disturbed by the tent installation. When Oppenheimer receives an inquiry for tenting from a prospective client, he first dispatches an account executive from his firm to meet with the client in person and view the site. Once the site has been inspected, the account executive is better prepared to make specific recommendations to the individual client. HDO Productions uses a computer network to track the client's order. The computer will first tell HDO if equipment and labor are available to install the tent on the date requested. The computer then lists the number of employees needed for the installation as well as prints the load sheet for the event.

Today's tent fabrics are more likely to be synthetic than muslin. Synthetics provide a stronger structure that is easier to maintain and aesthetically more pleasing. Oppenheimer particularly likes such innovations as the Parawing tent structure which can be used indoors as well as outdoors in venues that need aesthetic enhancement to mask unfinished portions or obnoxious views. The addition of lighting to these sail-like images will make the event even more aesthetically pleasing. Heating, air conditioning, and flooring are also now available for tented environments. Each of these important elements can help ensure the success of your tented event. A competent tenting contractor will survey your installation area and determine if flooring is advisable, or perhaps essential, because of uneven topography. Listen carefully to his or her recommendations. I had the misfortune of watching three thousand women remove their fancy dress shoes as they sank ankle deep in mud under a tent. The client refused to invest in flooring, although the additional cost was quite minimal. A pouring rain arrived just before the guests stepped under the canopy and flooded the public areas of the tent. It is a wonder the client did not have to replace three thousand pairs of ruined shoes. From wooden floors to Astroturf, your tent contractor can recommend the most cost-efficient ground surface for your event. In some instances the location for the tent may require grading or other excavation to prepare the land for the effective installation. This preliminary evaluation and recommendation is conducted by many tent contractors at no charge in order to prepare a proper bid for an event.

Heating or air conditioning can increase the comfort of your guests, thus helping increase attendance at your tented event. Once again, your tent contractor will assist you in determining whether to add these elements and what the cost will be. If you elect to air-condition or heat your tent, make certain the engineer in charge of the temperature controls remains on-site during the entire event. The temperature in the tent will rise as it fills with guests, and the heating or air conditioning therefore must be adjusted throughout the event to ensure comfort. When you use a tent, you not only take responsibility for ensuring the comfort and safety of your guests, but in some jurisdictions you are actually erecting a temporary structure that requires a special permit. Check with local authorities.

A tent provides a special aesthetic appeal; like balloons bobbing in the air, white tent tops seemingly touching the clouds signal event to your arriving guests. Few forms of decor make as immediate and dramatic an impression as a tent does. With a competent tent contractor, the problems you might anticipate are easily manageable, and the possibilities for an innovative event, year-round, are limitless.

Decor Costs

When hiring a design professional for an event, expect to cover not only the cost of labor, delivery, and the actual product, but also the consultation fee of the designer. In some cases this consultation fee may be included in the final bid for the job. If you are soliciting many different proposals, it is best to outline your budget range for the project to the prospective designers up front. This openness may dictate the selection of products for your event. Labor is a major component of design charges because the designer-decorator's craft is so time consuming.

The complexity of the design will affect costs, as will the amount of time available for installation. The longer the time allowed for installation, the fewer persons required. I have seen decor budgets double when less than one hour was allotted for installation of a major set. Allow enough time for the designers to do their work from the very beginning, alleviating the need for last-minute extra labor to complete the job. While many variables are involved in pricing decor, a typical margin of profit above the direct cost of materials and labor is 40 percent. This amount does not include the general overhead associated with running a business, including insurance, rent, promotion, vehicles, and the like. Therefore, today's designer must be very careful when quoting prices to ensure that his or her costs are adequately recovered, additionally allowing for a profit in order to grow. When purchasing design services, remember that each designer possesses a unique talent that may be priceless to your particular event. This perception of value may, in your estimation, overrule the pricing formulas described above.

Themed Events

The theme party or theme event originated from the masquerade where guests would dress in elaborate costumes to hide their identity. From these masquerade events a variety of themes was born. Today it is typical to attend western, Asian, European, south and central American themed events as often themes are derived from destinations or regions of the country or world.

Robin Kring, author of *Party Creations Book of Theme Design* says that "theme development and implementation are really very easy. Themes can be built on just about any item you can think of."

Themes usually are derived from one of three sources. First, the destination will strongly influence the theme. When guests travel to San Francisco they want to enjoy a taste of the city by the bay rather than a Texas hoedown. The second source is popular culture including books, movies, and television. Whether the theme is a classic *(Gone with the Wind)* or topical *(Toy Story)*, the idea is usually derived from popular culture. The third and final source is historical and current events. Themes reflecting the Civil War, World War II, or the landing of a man on the moon as well as the collapse of the Berlin Wall have strong historical or current significance and may be used to develop themes. The following list of themes in Figure 3-15 and recommended elements further illustrates this point.

FIGURE 3-15
Themes from Popular Culture, History, and Current Events

Theme	Audience	Elements
The Wild Wild West	All ages, very popular with men.	**Decor:** Hay bales, western-style bar, western jail set for photos, saloon with swinging doors. **Entertainment:** Gun slingers, lariat act, whip act, knife-throwing act, medicine man magic show, western band, western dancers, fiddle ensemble, harmonica act, strolling guitarist, cowboy singer on live horse, steer, and trainer. **Food and beverage:** Barbecue, hamburgers, biscuits, baked beans, rattlesnake, fowl, fresh pies.

FIGURE 3-15
Themes from Popular Culture, History, and Current Events *(continued)*

Theme	Audience	Elements
South of the Border	All ages, international guests, events held in states or bordering Mexico.	**Decor:** Small bridge over the Rio Grande river, customs officials and signs at the entrance, bright yellow lighting inside entrance, carts with vendors in Mexican attire selling novelties, cacti, colorful blankets of southwestern design, umbrella tables with tequila logo on top. **Entertainment:** Mariachi musician, flamenco and folk dancers, folk artists weaving baskets and other handicrafts. **Food and beverage:** Tacos, fajitas, refried beans, rice, chili, tamales, guacamole, margaritas.
The New Millennium	Younger guests, men and women, businessmen and businesswomen, scientists, engineers, scholars.	**Decor:** Large video projection screens projecting star pattern at entryway followed by a darkened tunnel with thousands of miniature lights and space like sound effects. Dance floor covered in light fog with pulsing lights. Internet stations on personal computers set throughout the room. **Entertainment:** Robots, actors in astronaut costumes, actors in alien costumes, high-tech band performing space-associated music. **Food and beverage:** Space food preset at each setting with freeze-dried ice cream, jelly beans representing various vitamins.
Mardi Gras	Younger guests, especially appropriate for New Orleans events.	**Decor:** Two large paper mache heads or floats frame the entrance, one doubloon given to each guest to exchange for a drink, purple, green, gold balloons, exterior facades of Bourbon Street landmarks. **Entertainment:** Quick sketch artists, jazz band including second line parade, Mardi Gras revelers throwing beads. **Food and beverage:** Mufalata sandwiches, seafood including crawfish and oysters, gumbos, red beans and rice, shrimp Creole, biscuits, po' boy sandwiches, snowballs, king cakes, hurricane-style drinks.
River Boat	All ages, especially older audiences.	**Decor:** Small gangplank bridge leading to doorway. Life preserver over doorway with name of event displayed. Inside main function room is casino, theater, long bar, colorful pennants, and flags. **Entertainment:** Dixieland jazz band, banjo players, close-up magicians masquerading as gamblers. **Food and beverage:** Southern cuisine including ribs, pork, fried chicken, grits, mint juleps, bourbon served in souvenir shot glasses.

(Figure continued on next page)

	FIGURE 3-15	
	Themes from Popular Culture, History, and Current Events *(continued)*	
Theme	**Audience**	**Elements**
Paris Nights	All ages, especially younger audiences.	**Decor:** Entryway marquee with chaser lights representing a Paris night club, in the center of the room a three-dimensional replica of the Eiffel Tower outlined in miniature lights, ficus trees on the perimeter with miniature lights, backdrops or sets of typical Parisian facades including the Louvre, the Follies Bergere, and the Comedie Francaise. **Entertainment:** Quick sketch artists, cancan dancers, cafe orchestra, chanteuse. **Food and beverage:** Crepes, cheeses, pastries, wines, champagne.
Hooray for Hollywood	All ages.	**Decor:** Sign announcing "The Hollywood Palladium," red carpet with rope and stanchion on either side, follow spotlights sweeping the carpet, inside the function room film props such as directors' chairs, cameras, lights, backdrops, a wind machine, and other props. **Entertainment:** A team of young male and female fans screaming as the guests arrive, a recording studio for instant sing-alongs, improvisational movie set area with instant replay, photo area with guests wearing wardrobe from famous movies. **Food and beverage:** Menu items from Hollywood.
Broadway Bash	All ages.	**Decor:** Large entrance sign proclaiming "Opening Night Starring" the name of the guests. Fake ticket booth distributing programs. Guests enter through stage door and actually walk on to the stage. **Entertainment:** Actors portraying ticket sellers, takers, stage doorman, actors. Broadway orchestra in pit performing selections from top Broadway shows. Musical comedy performers performing popular Broadway songs, photos taken with Broadway look alikes. **Food and beverage:** New York cuisine including Coney Island frankfurters, New York Strip steak, Manhattan Clam chowder.

An important consideration when planning theme parties is to understand the history of the group. Themes can be overused and it is important that you rotate themes to maintain the element of surprise. When planning theme parties use Figure 3-16 as a guide.

The answers to these questions will provide you with ample instructions to begin your planning of a terrific themed event. The list of themes in Figure 3-15 is by no

FIGURE 3-15
Themes from Popular Culture, History, and Current Events (continued)

Theme	Audience	Elements
Rock Around the Clock	Younger audiences, baby boomers.	Decor: Giant jukebox facade serves as entranceway. Interior transformed into gymnasium complete with basketball hoops at each end of dance floor and school name and logo on dance floor. Bright ribbon in the school colors swagged from the ceiling. Mirror ball for lighting effect. Entertainment: 1950s, 1960s, 1970s rock 'n' roll. Hula hoop contest, servers on roller blades, a phone booth stuffing contest and a '57 Chevy for photos. Food and beverage: Beer, pizza, hot dogs, hamburgers, malts, French fries, cherry Cokes.
Dickens of a Christmas	All ages.	Decor: Entryway with Covent Garden design, fake snow scattered throughout, cemetery area with the tombstones of Marley and famous British writers, facades of London landmarks including the Tower of London, Big Ben, and Parliament. Entertainment: A team of strolling urchins sings for their supper, a Salvation Army worker plays harp, Father Christmas poses for photos, a woman strolls selling live geese in cages. Food and beverage: Cider, ale, beer, wassail, holiday punch.
Rave Party	Generation X, teenager.	Decor: Fencing, salvage, industrial equipment. Entertainment: Punk rock band, DJ with lighting effects. Food and Beverage: Fast food.

FIGURE 3-16
Theme Party Checklist

When planning a theme party, ask your client:

1. What is the history of your theme parties? What did you do last year?

2. What is the purpose or reason for this event?

3. Is there a specific theme you wish to communicate?

4. To convey the theme, is food and beverage, decor, or entertainment most important for your group's tasks?

5. Remembering that first and last impressions are most important what do you want the guests to most remember from this event?

means exhaustive. However, it does reflect a sample of the top themes in current use in American events. When selecting a theme make sure you are certain the theme can be easily and effectively communicated through decor, entertainment, food and beverage, and of course, invitation and program design.

BIG THEME SUCCESS WITH SMALL BUDGETS

Even the slightest budget can enjoy big results through a carefully planned theme event. First, you must decide what elements are the most important because it is not likely that you will be able to equally fund everything you desire. If your guests are gourmets obviously the largest percentage of the budget will be dedicated to food and beverage. On the other hand, if they are creative, fun loving individuals who are only slightly interested in the menu you will want to shift your dollars to decor and entertainment. Make certain that the first impression (entrance area) is well decorated as this not only sets the tone for the event but also is often the most photographed area. Next, include a series of surprises such as a dessert parade or the arrival of a guest celebrity as your auctioneer, to keep your guests on the edge of their seats.

Finally, share your resources with others. Check with the director of catering at the hotel and find out if other groups are meeting in the hotel before, during, or following your stay. Ask for permission to contact their event manager and determine if you can produce the same event and split the costs for decor and entertainment. You will find that you can afford 50 percent more by allocating your scarce resources in this manner.

TRENDS IN THEME EVENTS

Interactive events are transforming couch potatoes into fully participatory guests. David Peters of Absolute Amusements in Florida annually produces hundreds of interactive events ranging from The Team Excellence Olympics for Xerox Corporation to school picnics. Peters features unusual interactive equipment such as Sumo Wrestling (where the participants wear giant foam rubber suits), the Velcro® wall (where the participants wear Velcro®-covered jump suits and jump and land in various positions on a large wall covered with Velcro®), and virtual surfing (where surfers stand on boards attached to electronic terminals and they see themselves on a large video monitor as they roll, slide, and sometimes tumble into the virtual ocean).

When designing interactive events keep in mind the safety conditions of the participants. Alcohol will of course increase the margin of risk for a guest. Some event managers require guests to sign hold harmless and waivers to acknowledge the risk involved with the activity.

Your event environment is the opportunity to explore dozens of opportunities in decor, entertainment, and other elements to make every moment unique and memorable. Every event manager has essentially this same opportunity. But understanding how the various pieces fit together to solve the puzzle that is the event environment, you provide a finished picture that will be remembered by your guests for years to come.

WAR STORY

A sponsor of the Olympic Games asked me to produce a Winter Olympic Games Carnival for their top engineers. To create immediate excitement we stretched white linoleum in the middle of the room and bathed it in ice blue light. We then placed hockey goals at both ends. As the guests entered they were given inflatable hockey sticks and Styrofoam pucks, told to remove their shoes, and hit the ice! This activity was a major success as the players pretended to glide across the ice and send their puck flying into the goal.

Lesson Learned

Always anticipate the outcome of any activity or decor idea. Find ways through sound research to contain or reduce the risk and create a controlled environment where safe fun can be enjoyed by all.

Your ability to design, balance, and mold this collage will be rewarded by the guests' total immersion into the environment leaving an indelible impression for many years. Remember, this is one reason you are so valuable. You are the artist and scientist who creates and plans this unique moment in time.

Sustainable-Event Management: Conserving the Environment

When I addressed The Nature Conservancy, a major U.S. environmental research and educational organization that focuses on environmental issues, I was impressed with how these leaders use events to communicate the important message of conservation. You can use every event as an opportunity to stress environmental sensitivity. Whether implementing a recycling plan or selecting products that do not harm the ecosystem, the event manager has an implied responsibility through sustainable event planning to produce events that are environmentally sensitive.

ENVIRONMENTAL SENSITIVITY

This sensitivity is important for two major reasons. First, it is the right thing to do. When allocating scarce resources for your event remember that no resource is as scarce as the environment in which we live, work, and play. Second, clients are increasingly requesting that every event meet or exceed certain environmental standards. Major corporations have been criticized by their customers for not demonstrating enough sensitivity to the environment. Therefore, when these same corporations retain you to manage their event they want you to reflect their renewed commitment to environmental concerns.

The best way to accomplish this is to clearly define the organization's environmental policy and then incorporate these policies into your event environment design and operations. Event sponsors who practice recycling in all likelihood will want recycling bins at the event they sponsor. Event sponsors who do not use foam products for disposable serving utensils will not want you to specify these items in your catering orders. Meet with the key environmental policy person for the organization sponsoring your event and determine with their help how to incorporate their policies within your event environment.

Why not create your own environmental policies? To ensure that events enjoy sustainable growth it is important for you to establish your own environmental policies that will demonstrate to prospective event sponsors your knowledge and sensitivity regarding these issues. These policies need not be repressive. However, they must be consistent. Do not alter your policies to merely satisfy the budget considerations for the event. Instead, seek creative solutions such as finding a sponsor for the recycling station to make certain your environmental ideals are well protected at every event.

RECYCLE YOUR SUCCESS

In the exposition event field a growing trend is the recycling of leftover materials such as paper, pens, pencils, and other reusable supplies to local schools. Usually these items end up in the dumpster when only a few blocks from the venue there may be a school with children who cannot afford these basic supplies. You may wish to incorporate this program in your agreements to inform your sponsor of your policy of recycling your success to help others.

Many event sponsors recycle leftover food products to local homeless shelters or food distribution agencies. This assures your guests that you are committed to sharing the success of your banquet with those less fortunate. Some venues require the recipients to sign a hold harmless form; however, regardless of the legal technicality, this opportunity to feed others should be seized for every event.

Still another way to recycle your success is to build into your event a project to benefit a local organization. Some event organizers provide a day before or after the event to cleanup a local playground, paint a school, or perform some other community service using the skills of the attendees at the event. To arrange this activity contact the volunteer center in the local community. The office of the mayor is a good place to start to locate the local volunteer coordinating organization. Tell the office what resources you are bringing to their destination and then apply your success to help others.

THE MAIN EVENT

1. The five senses are used to fully establish the event environment.

2. Create sensory areas and also identify some neutral zones.

3. Comprehend and use the Americans with Disabilities Act to create accessible environments for all guests.

4. Themed events may come from three sources. First, destinations themselves suggest ideas. Next, popular culture such as movies, books, or television constantly produce themes. Finally, historical or current events help mark significant moments in time through theme design.

5. Big budgets do not always guarantee successful themed events. Instead, select the most important elements to your guests, add a surprise or two, and keep them on the edge of their seats by demonstrating your creativity.

6. Produce *sustainable* events by establishing and complying with environmental policies and practices.

NEXT ON THE AGENDA

Sound financial methods will sustain your event management practice for years to come. Even if you are uncomfortable with accounting or other financial techniques you must be able to guard the bottom line. Chapter 4 provides you with the skills to not only stand guard but to easily improve your profitability through careful projection of expense and revenue.

Financial Techniques
for Consistent Success

The most common deficiency I have identified in all event managers relates to the area of financial management. Event managers by nature rely on the right side of the brain and often ignore the important logical thinking abilities that help ensure long-term success. Regardless if you use the services of a professional bookkeeper and/or accountant, knowledge of financial management is essential to the practice of modern Event Management. This knowledge is not difficult to master and with the development of modern software systems it is actually simple and many say fun to practice. Whether or not you enjoy financial management is not the issue. Few people enjoy studying for and taking their drivers' license exams. However, can you imagine what the streets would be like without this base line of knowledge? Wrecks, death, and destruction everywhere might result from this lack of rigor. Financial ignorance can just as easily wreck a creative, successful Event Management business and destroy one's reputation as well as produce serious legal implications. This chapter is essential if you are planning not only to make money but to keep it as well. Additionally, as your business ages along with you, this chapter will help you learn how to work a little less and earn a little more.

Budgeting

The event budget is the most important tool you will use to manage the financial decisions within your Event Management business. Each event represents a separate budget. Your daily business operations also require an annual budget to keep track of your proposed spending and projected earnings. Each event budget also represents the financial philosophy of the event. If your event is a charitable endeavor your financial philosophy will be markedly different than if it is a commercial venture. First, determine what the financial philosophy of your event is before you begin the budget process.

A budget represents the income and expenses of your organization or the individual event. An event budget is based upon the following factors:

1. The financial history of previous identical or similar events.

2. The general economy and your forecast for the future.

3. The income expenses you reasonably believe you can expect with the resources available.

FINANCIAL HISTORY

The best financial history is that which occurs over a three-year period. In some cases it is not possible to construct a precise history and the event manager must rely upon what is known at the time the budget is prepared. In still other cases the event manager will have to rely upon other events of similar size and scope to develop the budget because his or her event is a first-time venture and no history exists. Not only is it important to base your budget on history, it is equally important that you develop controls to begin collecting financial data on the event budget you are currently preparing. This data will become the next event's historic information and help you construct a better budget.

THE GENERAL ECONOMY

The economy is chaotic, unpredictable, and some economists would add, a disaster waiting to happen. You, however, must not be a victim to these predictions but instead use general economic data to assist you with the development of your budget. Reams of secondary data are available about the local, state, and national economy from offices of economic development as well as the U.S. Department of Commerce. No event takes place in a vacuum. Whether you are managing the International Special Olympics in New Haven, Connecticut, or the local food and wine festival your event's success will be affected by the general economy. Indicators of strong economic health usually include low unemployment, a steady rate of inflation, and healthy retail sales. Other indicators include new home building activity, new industry, and capital investments by local, state, or federal government. Before locking in your final budget consult with an economist from a local college or university, a representative from the local office of economic development, or even the editor of the business section of your local newspaper and ask for their opinion on the health of the economy.

REASONABLE PROJECTED INCOME

The Greek word for logos or logic means to act reasonably. A budget based on certain logical assumptions of projections of income is one that is within reason. To logically project revenue based on the resources available, market research as well as a general knowledge of the economy must be considered. For example, if your city festival is being held this year on the local payday from the area's largest industry, does that mean that you can reasonably expect spending will be increased for your event? The only way to test this theory is with research. You may wish to contact other events of similar size and scope and evaluate their experience with similar circumstances. Furthermore, you may wish to survey some of the workers to determine if they are more likely to attend the event this year and if so will they be inclined to increase their spending due to the coincidence of their payday and event date. Making reasonable assumptions about projected revenue is one of the most important decisions you must handle as you begin the budgeting process. Gather all of the facts, seek objective opinions and counsel, and then conservatively project the revenue you hope to achieve.

W A R   S T O R Y

Based on a recent fund-raising event the organizers of a second fund-raising event deduced that they could raise $10,000 in less than six weeks from sponsorship. The previous event's organizers had sent a facsimile request to 100 prospective sponsors and received $20,000 in actual sponsor dollars within a three-week period. Using this precedent, the organizers of the second event based their income projection on raising $10,000 through sponsorship. A few days before the event the organizers had still not raised the $10,000 and realized that instead of delivering $5,000 in net proceeds to the selected charity they would be delivering $1,400.

Lesson Learned

When projecting income make certain you are comparing apples to apples. The first event dealt with security issues and the sponsors were people who could directly benefit, including insurance companies. The second event was to benefit a children's charity and it was difficult to convince sponsors to participate within the short time frame.

TYPICAL INCOME CATEGORIES

Due to the wide range of events represented by the subfields within the Event Management profession it is difficult to categorically list every type of income. However, there are some general items that most budgets include. Figure 4-1 lists these items.

EXPENSES

When preparing your budget, the first thing you will note under the expense category is how many more items are listed as compared to income. My late father-in-law, a successful businessman, once told me, "The income comes in through one or two doors, but the expense can leak out of many doors." In the strange economic times of the mid-1990s organizations are placing greater emphasis on monitoring expenses because it is easier to control costs than to project revenue. My father-in-law also reminded me that Benjamin Franklin observed some 200 years ago, "A penny saved is a penny earned." Developing solid, predictable expense categories is critical to sound financial management. These expense items often come from historical data or comparing your event to others of similar size and scope. The actual amount budgeted for each expense line item is what you and your advisors believe to be reasonable based upon the information known at the time the budget is prepared. Therefore, the more you know, the more precise your budgeting for expenses. This is another reason why record keeping is so vital to the success of your financial management operations. Figure 4-2 will enable you to understand the general expense categories for most events.

STRUCTURING ACCOUNT CODES

Each income or expense item must have a corresponding account code. Accounts are those general budget categories where items of similar type and impact on the over-

---

FIGURE 4-1
General Event Income Items

Advertising revenues
Concession sales
Donations
Exhibit or exposition booth rental fees
Gifts in kind (actual fair market financial value)
Grants and contracts
Interest income from investments
Merchandise sales
Registration fees
Special events ticket sales
Sponsorship fees
Vendor commissions (hotels)

FIGURE 4-2
General Event Expense Items

Accounting	Complimentary registrations or admission	Materials shipping/freight fees	Signs
Advertising			Site office furniture rental
Advertising specialties	Consultants	Miscellaneous or other	Site office supplies
Audiovisual equipment rental	Decor	Percentage of administrative overhead	Site rental
Audiovisual labor	Entertainment		Site telephone expense
Automobile mileage reimbursements	Evaluations	Permits	Sound equipment rental
	Food and beverage	Photocopying	Sound labor
Automobile rental	Guest transportation	Photography	Speakers' fees and/or honoraria
Awards and recognition	Gratuities	Postage	
Brochure and other collateral design	Insurance	Proceedings editing, design, and printing	Speakers' travel
	Legal counsel		Staff travel
Brochure and other collateral mailing	Licenses	Public relations	Videography
	Lighting equipment rental	Registration contract labor	Volunteer appreciation activities and gifts
Brochure and other collateral mechanical preparation	Lighting labor	Registration materials	
	Local, state, provincial, and federal taxes	Research	
Brochure and other collateral printing		Risk management corrections	

---

all budget are grouped together for more efficient analysis. For example, in the administration category the following items would appear.

Decor

Insurance

Site telephone expenses

Under the account category staff/volunteers the following items would be grouped together.

Volunteer appreciation activities and gifts

Staff accommodations

Volunteer accommodations

Each account code has a numerical listing to make it easy to find individual entries. The general categories start with the 100 series. For example, administration would be 100, marketing would be 500, and so on. Each individual item would have a separate sequential numerical listing as shown in Figure 4-3.

FINDING AND SUPERVISING AN ACCOUNTANT

Contact your local chamber of commerce to obtain a referral for an accountant who may be familiar with event budgets or service type businesses. Once you have prepared a draft budget seek the counsel of the accountant to review your budget and help you

---

FIGURE 4-3
Typical Event Expense Account Codes

100 **Administrative**
500 Marketing
501 Advertising
502 Advertising specialties
503 Brochure and other collateral design
504 Brochure and other collateral mechanical preparation
505 Brochure and other collateral mailing
506 Brochure and other collateral printing
507 Public relations

---

with establishing the various line items and account codes. Your accountant will be able to interpret the tax codes for you to make certain that your accounts match the terms and requirements for the local, state, provincial, and federal tax authorities.

Make certain you discuss billing and fees with your accountant. You may retain the accountant to handle specific operations or to coordinate all of your financial procedures. Obviously the cost will greatly fluctuate based upon the amount of tasks you ask the accountant to perform. Using accounting software may help you reduce your costs and provide you with better, faster information.

ACCOUNTING SOFTWARE

Since the invention of the spreadsheet program for computers accounting has never been the same. Commercial software packages such as Quicken™ have allowed small businesspeople to quickly, accurately, and cost effectively record their journal entries. What once required many hours with a pencil and eraser has, thanks to modern computer science, been reduced to a fraction of the time.

Using commercial software, while time efficient, does require certain additional safeguards. First, make certain you always backup your data on a floppy diskette and store this information in a safe, fireproof location. Next, regularly send a copy of your data to your accountant so that he or she can prepare your monthly, quarterly, and annual financial reports. Finally, consult with your accountant to determine the best type of software to invest in because to a large extent you will be partners and you should be using software that will allow you to effectively communicate on a regular basis.

Producing Profit

The financial purpose of every for-profit business is to produce a fair net profit. The term profit means the earnings over and above all expenses. Not-for-profit organizations do not, for obvious reasons, use the term profit. Instead, they refer to this excess of income over expense as retained earnings. In fact the earnings are not retained for long as they are required by the tax code to reinvest them in their business operations rather than distribute them to shareholders as some for-profit businesses do.

Producing a fair net profit is both challenging and possible for Event Management businesses. The challenge is that event managers must work with a wide range of clients and it is difficult to carefully budget for each event to ensure a net profit. There are too many variables to ensure that this happens every time. However, if the business is to remain healthy at year end, a net profit must result from the business activities.

While there is no average for net profit, let us consider for the purposes of discussion that your financial goal is to achieve an annual net profit of 15 percent. To do this you must carefully guard all fixed overhead expenses.

FIXED OVERHEAD EXPENSES

Fixed overhead expenses are those predictable items such as rent, salaries, insurance, telephone, and other standard operating expenses required to support the Event Management business. The better you are able to achieve a lower cost of sale the greater net profit you will achieve. To lower your cost of operations it is imperative that you try to reduce your fixed overhead expenses. Many Event Management firms have suffered great losses or have even gone out of business entirely because they tried to expand too rapidly. Expansion brings increased cost of sales and increased cost of sales means you must produce much greater income. Due to the volatility of the world economy as we discussed earlier, this is not always possible. Once you have firmly cut your fixed overhead expenses to a level that allows you to maintain quality but at the same time produce a fair net profit you must turn your attention to *variable or direct expenses.*

VARIABLE EXPENSES

Variable expenses are more difficult to predict because often they are purchased last minute from vendors and the prices may fluctuate. Variable or direct expenses include audiovisual rentals and labor, registration materials, proceedings design and printing, and other items with a total cost that is reliant upon the final number ordered and your ability to negotiate a fair price. Due to last minute registrations and an increase in walk-up guests for a variety of events it is extremely difficult to wait until the last minute to order certain items. Printing as well as advance notice for audiovisual equipment rental and labor requires a sufficient window of time to deliver a quality product. This means that your ability to use historical data to project the volume of items you will need or to order less with an option to rapidly obtain additional supplies will greatly help you reduce your variable or direct expenses. In addition, your ability to carefully negotiate the best deal for your event organization will also have tremendous impact on these items.

NET PROFIT VERSUS GROSS PROFIT

Event managers endeavor to produce a fair net profit. The difference between net profit and gross profit is the percentage of fixed overhead expenses that were dedicated to producing a specific event. Figure 4-4 depicts how you calculate the true net profit of the event.

Fixed overhead expenses dedicated to the individual event include a percentage of staff salaries and benefits, a percentage of the office expense, and other shared expenses. This percentage will fluctuate but by using time sheets you can easily calculate the staff time directed to the event and the other expenses such as rent, insurance, and telephone may be given a percentage based on the time recorded from the time sheets. For example, if a specific event requires 200 staff hours from a total of 400 available you may assume that during that period the fixed operating expenses should be assigned at the rate of 50 percent. Therefore, if during that period salaries, rent, phone, and insurance are valued at $50,000 the amount assigned is $25,000 as shown in Figure 4-4.

Your event financial goal is to achieve a fair net profit for each and every event. To do this you must reduce fixed overhead expenses to under 30 percent of the cost of every event operation. This allows 70 percent for direct expenses. The better you project, negotiate, and order the goods and services reflected in these items, the greater net profit or retained earnings your organization will enjoy.

Cutting Costs

Your ability as an event manager to rapidly cut costs to ensure consistent profits is one that will serve you well throughout your career. To decide which costs may be cut without sacrificing the integrity of the entire event, you must begin with the budgeting process by prioritizing expenses. Seek counsel from your stakeholders and honestly explain that in the worst case scenario if certain items must be cut from the budget what would they like to preserve and which should go to ensure a profit. Although this is a difficult decision process it is wise to make such decisions free from internal and

---

FIGURE 4-4
Achieving Net Profit

	$100,000	Income
−	$70,000	Direct Expenses
=	$30,000	Gross Profit
−	$25,000	Fixed Overhead
=	$5,000	Net Profit

external pressures during the final days of the Event Management process. Typically these costs are associated with variable or direct expenses. Therefore, the expenditure is not made until later in the Event Management process. Cutting your event's costs is one way to help improve your cash flow.

Ensuring Positive Event Cash Flow

Cash flow is the liquidity that allows you to pay your bills, including salaries, in a timely manner. When this liquidity is gone your reputation may not be far behind. To ensure a positive event cash flow two measures are necessary. First, you must prearrange with your vendors payment terms and conditions that will allow you to collect the adequate revenues to honor these obligations. Second, you must diligently collect those funds that are due and payable to you in a timely manner in order to meet your obligations to your vendors.

Payables are those financial accounts that you have established with vendors. These are funds that are due and payable according to the agreements you have arranged with individual vendors. Receivables are those funds due to your event organization by a certain date. Aging receivables are simply those funds that were not collected at the time they were due.

WAR STORY

"Hello, yes I am calling to inquire about the check for $45,000 that is due today. Can you please tell me the status of that payment?" said the weary event manager to his client. "Oh, yes, that check is being cut right now and we are going to drop it in the mail today," answered the client optimistically. "Don't mail it," said the event manager, knowingly, "I will come get it now."

Lesson Learned

Collecting receivables is one of your most important business activities. Even the best clients are not as anxious to release the funds as you are to receive them. Do not let receivables age. Go get them when due. Once they are in your possession they are earning interest income in your account. Make your receivables work for you and not against you by paying close attention to this important Event Management principle.

Figure 4-5 provides simple techniques for collecting Event Management receivables.

One of the challenges with the value of Event Management services is that there is often rapid depreciation as soon as the curtain rises. Consider this scenario. Your client has invested $50,000 with your firm to produce a gala awards dinner. Midway through the dinner the client's spouse notices a cigarette burn in the tablecloth. Later he or she comments on "skimpy" floral arrangement. Finally, he or she complains loudly about the inferior music and food. Before long the client locates you and wants to discuss the bill. Ironically, only three hours earlier the client walked through the ballroom and told you effusively how beautiful everything looked. Buyers of Event Management services and products are not usually experts in your profession. That is why they have retained you. Because the purchase of Event Management services and products is sometimes an emotional decision the buyer may be easily influenced by others. *The only leverage you have as the professional provider of these services is to collect your full fee as soon as possible because the value of your performance will rapidly deflate otherwise.* The old maxim "people only value what they pay for" is absolutely true in this profession as well as medicine and other established professions. And by the way, physicians have a tough time collecting as well and most have established policies of requiring payment at the time services are rendered.

Effective management of accounts receivable is only half of the equation needed for solid cash flow. The second half requires that you become knowledgeable about typical accounts payable agreements and learn to negotiate for the best possible payment terms.

Accounts Payable: Finding the Best Terms

When establishing relationships with vendors it is important that you learn as much as possible about the size, scope, and nature of their business. You will want to know if they own or lease their equipment. You will also want to know when they may have

---

FIGURE 4-5
Collecting Event Management Receivables

1. Log on your calendar the day the receivable is due.

2. Telephone early in the morning to ask when your payment will be processed.

3. If possible, arrange to pick it up.

4. If not possible to pick it up, offer to provide an express-mail service.

5. Courteously, but firmly request payment until received.

periods of slow business. Their "off season" can produce favorable terms and perhaps discounts for your event. You will also want to know if the vendor could benefit from exposure through your event. Some event managers have a stringent rule about not letting vendors promote themselves directly to their clients. However, it is my belief that these hard and fast rules may prevent you from providing your client with the products and services your vendor may be able to offer. In one example a video production company telephoned me after a major corporate event and asked permission to contact the corporate headquarters to provide their services directly. Not only did I encourage them to do so, I wrote letters to my client and others on their behalf. As a result of this courtesy and flexibility this firm will work with me on price in the future for other clients who I may serve. Therefore, beware the dangerous word "always" as it may cause you to provide less service than possible.

The key to negotiating excellent terms with vendors is first to establish professional friendships and conduct business in an atmosphere of mutual respect. The more you know about your professional partners (vendors) and the more they know about you, the easier it is to do business. There are typical accounts payable customs and traditions in the Event Management profession; however, your ability to make friends and provide assistance to your vendors will alter these customs to your benefit.

TYPICAL ACCOUNTS PAYABLE CUSTOMS

One accounts payable custom is for the vendor to require a deposit of 50 percent of the final contracted cost as a deposit and receive the full balance plus any additional agreed upon charges immediately following the event. Entertainment vendors, especially those representing major celebrities, are even more stringent. They may require full payment in the form of a certified check prior to the first performance as a guarantee.

Another accounts payable custom is for the vendor to require a small deposit (as low as 10 percent) and then invoice you for the balance due net ten or thirty days after the event. The final custom allows you to pay on account your balance. In this custom typically you are a regular, good customer of the vendor and they are allowing you to pay off the balance monthly or within a reasonable amount of time without interest, late charges, or other penalties.

The final custom is for the vendor to extend credit to your organization allowing you to authorize purchases and be invoiced at a later date by the vendor. This is the best scenario as you are able to negotiate credit terms well in advance. Although most accounts are due within thirty days of the date of the invoice I have heard of some arrangements where the vendor will extend credit for sixty or even ninety days to maintain the account. It is up to you to negotiate the best possible terms.

NEGOTIATING ACCOUNTS PAYABLE

Always negotiate from a position of strength. Strength in the area of accounts payable means that you have collected as much information as possible about the vendor with

WAR STORY

A convention and visitors bureau asked me to moderate a panel comprised of professional meeting planners who were addressing their prospective vendors on the subject of "How to Best Sell to Us." I knew I was in trouble when the first meeting planner stood up and lambasted the vendors by saying, "Don't call me. I am too busy to talk to you. Besides, I don't even know you." The second meeting planner joined this litany by announcing, "Don't mail to me. I have no place to store your promotional materials so I put them in the round file." This routine continued as three more meeting planners spoke for what seemed like an eternity. As the last planner sat down I realized it was time to turn to the audience for questions. Hands shot up from throughout the audience and the adversarial relationship was worsened when the first vendor said, "You don't return our calls, you trash our mailings. How am I going to reach you?" The next vendor accused the planners of ignoring them at social functions that the vendors actually sponsor. As the moderator I remembered that my job was to inject moderation into these testy proceedings. Turning to both warring tribes I said, "We have lost sight of the most important person. This person is the one who built the hotels where you work, is responsible for your salaries, raises, and promotions at the organizations for whom you plan meetings, provides the fuel for the jets that allow you to hold your events, and whose support, loyalty, and patronage enable us to work in an industry most of us love. That person is the guest. The most important person in our industry. Our relationship with each other is important but our mutual relationship with the guest is the most important aspect of this discussion. Let us not forget this for if we do our guests will reject us and all of us will suffer together. It is far easier and more important to find ways to work together to serve the guest than to perpetuate this adversarial atmosphere."

Lesson Learned

There is an undercurrent of misunderstanding resulting from poor communications in the Event Management industry. Remove these barriers by learning as much as possible about your professional partner's needs and expectations.

whom you need to negotiate. The answers to the questions in Figure 4-6 will enable you to negotiate favorable terms for your accounts payable.

Once you have the answers to these questions it is time to ask your vendor for more favorable terms. To do this you will need to provide your vendor with documentation about your own business health. Testimonials from recent clients, a list of accounts receivable, and other financial data will also help you create a favorable impression. Once you have established your credibility with the vendor ask for the most favorable terms. You might ask for credit and ninety days. The vendor may counter with thirty days and you then agree on sixty days. Do not play hardball. Remember, this same vendor will be servicing your clients, and maintaining their goodwill is of supreme importance. However, you have a responsibility to your event organization to negotiate the most favorable terms and must remain firm in your pursuit of what you believe to be a fair agreement.

Your vendor may ask for a trial period of time after which he or she may extend better terms once you have demonstrated your ability to consistently meet your obligations and provide the benefits your vendor expects. I cannot emphasize enough how important your relationships with your vendors are in the full spectrum of your event operations. The following war story is typical of many businesses in the Event Management profession.

CONTROLLING PURCHASES

The most common device for approving purchases is called the purchase order. No purchase should be authorized without an approved purchase order. This form specifies the

---

FIGURE 4-6
Learning About Your Vendor

1. How important is your business to this vendor?

2. What time period is your business most needed?

3. Are your clients the types of organizations your vendor would like to do business with? How well funded/capitalized is your vendor?

4. How does your vendor market his or her services and products? How sophisticated are your vendor's business operations?

5. What are your vendor's standard and customary accounts payable terms?

6. Most importantly, are there other clients of this vendor you can speak with to determine what types of terms they are receiving?

W A R   S T O R Y

Monday morning the stock market plunged to its lowest level and by Tuesday I knew we were in trouble. Many of our New York clients were stockbrokers and corporations and they were calling every five minutes to ask for their deposits to be returned because they were cancelling their holiday parties. Within twenty-four hours our healthy Event Management firm had become ill and unless steps were taken would collapse from lack of business. First, we explained to the staff the problems that we were facing and told the salespeople that they would be paid by commission rather than both salary and commission. Although this did not go over very well, other firms were releasing their employees and we agreed to retain our loyal staff and continue paying their benefits. Next, I sequestered myself in my office for an entire day and telephoned all of our vendors and explained to each that for the first time in nine years we could not meet our obligations on time. I told them I did not know when we could pay the balance but would send as much as possible each month until the balance was paid. I was shocked when the first vendor I called, a small costume company owner said, "Joe, your business is important to me. Don't worry. Let me know if you need help." Nine years of paying our bills on time and dealing fairly and honestly had produced an atmosphere where time and understanding was now readily available. Within six months things were back to normal and we learned a most valuable lesson.

Lesson Learned

Immediately notify vendors of late payments. Do not wait for collection notices. Work with vendors to ensure that they can count on your business and know that you will honor your financial obligations. These relationships are golden. Had the vendors cutoff their supplies our business would not have survived. Not only did it survive, but it thrived and two years later was sold to a larger firm. One of the reasons the purchaser bought our business was because of the excellent relations with suppliers/vendors.

product or service approved for purchase, the number of units, the price per unit, and the total amount due including taxes and deliveries. The type of shipping and date and time of arrival should also be clearly specified. It should also state the payment terms. Instruct all of your vendors by letter that you will only be responsible for purchases preceded by a valid purchase order. On each purchase order include the following statement:

"Vendor may not substitute or alter this order without the written permission of the purchaser."

This statement helps you avoid the creative vendor who is out of red tablecloths and believes you will accept blue instead at the same price. Finally, the purchase order must have a signature line that grants approval and the date of the approval. The purchase order is the most important tool you have to control your purchases and therefore monitor those numerous doors where expenses leak and potentially drain your event economic engine.

Common Event Financial Challenges and Solutions

The Event Management profession is a business and not unlike other businesses there are common problems and solutions. When Event Management business owners assemble for annual meetings and conferences they can be heard discussing many of these same challenges year after year. As one wag said, "The problems don't change, the solutions only become more difficult." Perhaps by reviewing Figure 4-7 you will be able to anticipate some of these challenges and thereby take measures to avoid them entirely.

FIGURE 4-7
Common Financial Challenges and Solutions

Challenge: Negotiating employees' salaries and benefits.

Solution: Collect information from ISES or from firms in similar market areas. Use this information to determine a market basket figure from which you can negotiate up or down based on the potential value of the employee to your firm.

Challenge: Proper compensation for Event Management salespeople.

Solution: Three methods are customary. First and most prevalent is a draw versus commission. This approach requires that you provide the salesperson with a small stipend until his or her commissions have equaled this amount. After he or she has equaled the amount of the draw the stipend stops and the salesperson receives only sales commissions. The second approach is straight commission. In this case usually the salesperson has existing accounts and is immediately earning commissions. Typical commissions range between 3 and 7 percent of the gross sale. Therefore, a salesperson who produces $500,000 in gross revenue will earn $35,000. The final custom is to offer the salesperson a salary plus bonuses based on sales productivity. This bonus is typically awarded after the salesperson reaches a certain threshold in sales such as one million dollars.

(Figure continued on next page)

FIGURE 4-7
Common Financial Challenges and Solutions *(continued)*

A typical bonus is 1 or 2 percent of sales. A salesperson earning a salary of $50,000 could earn an additional $20,000 based on a 2-percent bonus on one million dollars in sales.

Straight salary as compensation is the least desirable because it provides no financial incentive and salespeople are typically driven by financial incentives. Whatever arrangement you agree upon do not change it for one year. You will need one year of financial data upon which to base your review and future course of action.

Challenge: Client is slow to pay balance of account.

Solution: Inquire as to how you can help expedite payment. Can you pick up the check? Is there a problem and could the client pay the largest portion now and the rest later? Are other vendors being paid? Does the client have a history of slow payment? What leverage do you have? Can you suspend services until the balance is paid or payment on account is made? Could you speak with one of the owners or principals and solve this problem? Can you find a creative solution like the one Andy Stefanovich of Opus Event Marketing, Richmond, Virginia, found? Andy had his dog send the collection notice complete with begging for food and a paw print.

Challenge: Out of cash.

Solution: With prudent management of accounts payable and receivable this problem should not occur. Assuming that a business emergency has caused this unfortunate situation you must immediately contact vendors and notify them of your intent to pay. Then notify all past due accounts receivable and accelerate collection. Reduce or stop spending with regard to fixed overhead. Next, contact your lenders to access a line of credit based upon your receivables until you have sufficient cash to meet your expenses.

Challenge: Vendor promotes himself or herself to your client directly.

Solution: Do you have written policies and procedures outlining what is and what is not permissible by your vendor? Realistically, how will their promotion injure your business? Can you negotiate with your vendor to receive a commission from any future sales to this client since you were the first contact?

Challenge: Employee is terminated, starts own business, and takes your clients.

Solution: Does the employment agreement forbid this practice? Assuming that it does you can have your attorney send a cease and desist letter. This rarely helps because the client has no constraints on who they do business with. Either way you lose. Instead, suggest to the former employee that he or she may wish to provide you with a commission on the first sale he or she makes with your former client as a courtesy for providing the first introduction. This way you can release the client and also receive some compensation for your effort in first identifying the account. If the former employee refuses to provide you with a commission chances are his or her bad business ethics will eventually alienate him or her from enough industry colleagues that it will limit the amount of sales he or she is able to achieve and significantly reduce the level of services received from vendors who are suspicious of his or her behavior.

These common challenges and typical solutions should serve as a guide or framework to guide your decision making. Although most of the solutions in modern business still rely on common sense I have noticed that there is nothing so uncommon in today's business environment than common sense. You will want to test each of these solutions with your business advisors (attorney, accountant, mentor) before implementing it to make certain that it addresses your particular problem and provides the most logical solution. There is no such thing as a general solution for a specific problem. All business problems are specific in nature and you must seek a solution that addresses your precise problem.

Typical Event Budgets

The following sample budgets will serve as a guide as you develop your own financial plans for various events. Each budget has the same structure; however, you will note that in the case of not-for-profit organizations the term "profit" has been substituted with the term "retained earnings." Use these budgets as a model as you endeavor to create consistently effective financial management systems for your organization.

The Bottom Line

Your budget is a general guide to the income and expense projected for your event. It may be adjusted as necessary provided you can justify these changes and receive approval from your stakeholders. For example, if your revenue projections are way ahead of schedule your variable costs will also increase proportionately. Use the budget as a valuable tool that may be sharpened as needed to improve your percentage of retained earnings.

Awards Banquet	
Income	
100 Registrations	
101 Pre-registrations	25,000
102 Regular registrations	50,000
103 Door sales	5000
Subtotal	$80,000
200 Marketing	
201 Sponsorships	15,000
202 Advertising	10,000
203 Merchandise	5000
Subtotal	$30,000
300 Investments	
301 Interest income	1000
Subtotal	$1000
400 Donations	
401 Grants	5000
402 Individual gifts	10,000
403 Corporate gifts	25,000
Subtotal	$40,000
Total income	**$151,000**

(Figure continued on next page)

Awards Banquet *(continued)*

Expenses

100 Administration (Fixed expense)	
101 Site office furniture rental	1000
102 Site office supplies	1000
103 Site rental	3000
104 Site telephone expense	1000
Subtotal	$6000
200 Printing (Fixed expense)	
201 Design	3000
202 Printing	5000
203 Binding	1000
Subtotal	$9000
300 Entertainment (Fixed expense)	
301 Talent fees	10,000
302 Travel and accommodations	1000
303 Sound	2000
304 Lights	2000
Subtotal	$15,000
400 Food and beverage (Variable expense)	
401 300 dinners @ $50	15,000*
402 Open bar for one hour	3000*
403 Ice sculpture	500
Subtotal	$18,500

*Note: Includes taxes and gratuities.

500 Transportation (Variable expense)	
501 Staff travel	1000
502 Valet parking	750
Subtotal	$1750
600 Insurance (Fixed expense)	
601 Cancellation	1000
602 Host liability	500
Subtotal	$1500
Total expenses	**$51,750**
Total variable expense	**$29,250**
Total projected income	**$151,000**
Total projected expense	**$51,750**
Gross retained earnings	$99,250
Percentage of fixed overhead	$25,000
Net retained earnings (reinvestment)	**$74,250**

Music Festival

Income

100 Ticket sales	
101 Regular advance	50,000
102 Student advance	25,000
103 Regular door sales	100,000
104 Student door sales	50,000
103 Group sales	25,000
Subtotal	$250,000
200 Marketing	
201 Sponsorships	50,000
202 Advertising	25,000
203 Merchandise	30,000
Subtotal	$105,000
300 Investments	
301 Interest income	3000
Subtotal	$3000
400 Donations	
401 Grants	10,000
402 Individual gifts	0
403 Corporate gifts	25,000
Subtotal	$35,000
Total income	**$393,000**

Expenses

100 Administration (Fixed expense)	
101 Site office furniture rental	500
102 Site office supplies	500
103 Site rental	10,000
104 Site telephone expense	1500
Subtotal	$12,500
200 Printing (Fixed expense)	
201 Design	1000
202 Printing	5000
Subtotal	$6000
300 Entertainment (Fixed expense)	
301 Talent fees	50,000
302 Travel and accommodations	5000
303 Sound	5000
304 Lights	5000
Subtotal	$65,000

(Figure continued on next page)

Music Festival *(continued)*

Expenses *(continued)*

400 Transportation and Parking (Variable expense)	
401 Staff travel	500
402 Parking lot rental	3000
Subtotal	$3500
600 Insurance (Fixed expense)	
601 Cancellation	1000
602 Host liability	500
603 Comprehensive general liability	2000
604 Pyrotechnics rider	1000
Subtotal	$4500
Total expenses	**$51,750**
Total variable expense	**$29,250**
Total projected income	$393,000
Total projected expense	$91,500
Gross retained earnings	**$301,500**
Percentage of fixed overhead	**$150,000**
Net retained earnings (reinvestment)	**$151,500**

Conference and Exposition

Income

100 Registration	
101 Early bird discount	100,000
102 Regular	50,000
103 On site	25,000
104 Spouse/partner	10,000
105 Special events	15,000
Subtotal	$200,000
200 Marketing	
201 Sponsorships	10,000
202 Advertising	15,000
203 Merchandise	10,000
Subtotal	$35,000
300 Investments	
301 Interest income	1000
Subtotal	$1000

Conference and Exposition *(continued)*

Income *(continued)*

400 Donations	
401 Grants	5000
Subtotal	**$5000**
500 Exposition	
501 200 booths @ $1500	300,000
502 50 tabletops @ $500	25,000
Subtotal	**$325,000**
Total income	**$566,000**

Expenses

100 Administration (Fixed expense)	
101 Site office furniture rental	1500
102 Site office supplies	500
103 Site rental	30,000
104 Site telephone expense	1500
Subtotal	**$33,500**
200 Printing (Fixed expense)	
201 Design	2000
202 Printing	10,000
Subtotal	**$12,000**
300 Postage (Fixed expense)	
301 Hold this date	1000
302 Brochure	5000
303 Miscellaneous	500
Subtotal	**$6500**
400 Entertainment (Fixed expense)	
401 Talent fees	5000
402 Travel and accommodations	500
403 Sound	0
404 Lights	0
Subtotal	**$5500**
500 Transportation and accommodations	
501 Staff travel	1500
502 Staff accommodations	1500
Subtotal	**$3000**

(Figure continued on next page)

Conference and Exposition *(continued)*

Expenses *(continued)*

600 Insurance (Fixed expense)	
601 Cancellation	3000
602 Comprehensive general liability	2000
Subtotal	$5000
700 Speakers (Variable expense)	
701 Honoraria	10,000
702 Travel	3000
703 Accommodations	1000
704 Complimentary registrations	3000
705 Per diem	1000
Subtotal	$18,000
800 Audiovisual (Variable expense)	
801 Rentals (general sessions)	25,000
802 Labor (general sessions)	10,000
803 Rentals (Breakouts)	2000
804 Labor (Breakouts)	1000
805 Prerecorded modules	5000
Subtotal	$43,000
900 Exposition (Variable expense)	
901 Pipe and drape	10,000
902 Aisle carpet	20,000
903 Signs	5000
Subtotal	$35,000
Total projected income	**$566,000**
Total projected expense	**$161,500**
Gross retained earnings	$404,500
Percentage of fixed overhead	$199,000
Net retained earnings (reinvestment)	**$205,500**

Although most event managers find that financial matters are the least interesting aspect of their role and scope of their jobs, you now understand that to sustain long-term success it is critical that you firmly control this important management area. The better you become at watching the bottom line the more resources that will become available to you for other more creative activities.

THE MAIN EVENT

1. Always establish a working budget and seek counsel from your accountant and stakeholders before final implementation.

2. Firmly control accounts payable and accounts receivable.

3. Establish a purchase order system to control costs.

4. Diligently collect accounts receivable.

5. Constantly refine and sharpen the budget to improve your financial planning.

NEXT ON THE AGENDA

Event Management is a profession whose greatest natural resource is people. In Chapter 5 you will learn how to recruit, train, retain, reward full- and part-time staff and volunteers, and help them find the motivation within to improve the overall quality of your events.

Quality Event Leadership for Staff and Volunteers

The most effective event managers are not merely managers, rather, they are dynamic leaders whose ability to motivate, inspire others, and achieve their goals are admired by their followers. The difference between management and leadership is perhaps best characterized by this simple but effective definition. *Managers control problems whereas leaders motivate others to find ways to achieve goals.* In a study in Australia, the number one quality sought by employers or event managers was the ability to lead others. Your goal is to become an event leader whose team members will respect, admire, and follow to achieve mutual goals.

Motivation is critical to the successful Event Management operation. Event team members often work long hours for many consecutive days. Burnout is a reality in this sometimes grinding occupation. It is essential that your event team members find the motivation within themselves to be able to push on during trying circumstances always focusing on achieving your mutual goals. To accomplish this daunting task the event manager must first provide both staff and volunteers with valid reasons for wanting to achieve the goals. Second, the event manager must provide staff and volunteers with the tools to achieve the goals. Finally, the event manager must provide the staff and volunteers with coaching and support to help them overcome adversity and rise above the challenges they may encounter. Perhaps most importantly, the event manager must serve as cheerleader or mentor and when appropriate celebrate publicly the success of the individual members as well as the entire team.

Setting Mutual Goals for Major Motivation

The first task is actually the easiest. Once you have conducted your feasibility study and have determined what the goals and objectives of the event will be, then survey your team members and ask them to interpret these goals from a personal perspective. What does it mean to your concessions leader to "achieve sales of 5 percent or greater than last year?" Perhaps the concession leader will be able to list this accomplishment on his or her resume, if there is commission involved he or she will profit financially, or perhaps promotion could result from his or her accomplishment. The old maxim— people only do what they are rewarded for—is absolutely true when it comes to personal motivation. Meet with each individual team leader and ask them to interpret the event's goals and objectives on a personal level and then ask each leader to simultaneously meet with their colleagues and repeat this process.

After identifying the reasons for buying into the larger event goals, ask each person to list these goals and prominently post them in a place they will notice them everyday. Perhaps the bathroom mirror, by the bed, or near the telephone would be effective locations. These personal goals/motivations must become burned into the human consciousness so that everyone of your team members is pulling as hard as possible due to their personal stake in the event.

There is a story of a college professor leading a tour in a train station. His bewildered students could not understand why he brought them to the tracks to watch a train depart. The wise professor asked the students, "What do you see?" One student shyly answered, "A locomotive and twenty cars." The professor then asked, "What else do you see"? Another student proudly said, "The train is leaving the station!" The professor gathered the students close and pointed to the locomotive and said, "The engine is now doing all the work. In a matter of moments the cars will gather momentum and do their part to increase the overall velocity of the train. First, one person pulls. That's what I am doing by asking you questions. Later, others push. That is what you must now do to benefit from this course. Start pushing." The astonished students nodded silently and then almost in unison began asking questions as they followed the professor out of the station.

You must develop this same sort of momentum with your team members. Encourage them to share with you their dreams, goals, and aspirations. Where possible, provide a work atmosphere that will help them achieve these objectives.

Finding the Right Tools

Winston Churchill during World War II wrote to President Franklin Delano Roosevelt and said, "Mr. President, give us the tools and we will finish the job." Churchill was referring to the tools needed to overcome German oppression. You must find and provide the proper tools for your staff and volunteers to win their war as well.

To identify what type of tools your team members will require hold a series of small group meetings and discuss what hardware (desks, files, and office supplies) will be needed as well as what software (training) will best enable them to efficiently and effectively achieve their goals. Once you have identified these tools then ask each person to remove any item from their list that is not absolutely essential at this time. Then ask each team member to place an asterisk by those items that could be shared with others thereby reducing your overall cost. After you have reduced this list to the most efficient resources ask the team members to study this final list for forty-eight hours and then return their final list to you with any further changes to make certain you have not overlooked any essential resource.

The Event Manager as Coach

A winning coach not only develops strategy but adjusts the plan when necessary to help win the game. You are the head coach for your event team and in this role you must listen effectively to problems, concerns, challenges, and conflicts and provide assistance to remove these obstacles. These conflicts may be personal or they may be relational; however, as the coach or mentor to your team members you must be available to listen, process, and then react. Interpersonal conflicts are perhaps the most difficult and may undermine the entire event team's effectiveness. Therefore, when listening to these problems realize that unless they are addressed quickly and completely they could cause bigger problems further down the line.

The best way to handle interpersonal conflicts is to first find out the source of the problem and interview all parties. These problems are rarely the result of one person's actions. Next, suggest a cooling-off period so the staff or volunteers involved can return to the discussion in a more objective frame of mind. Finally, bring the parties together to discuss solutions. Usually this will effectively handle the problem. However, in those rare instances when the problem continues and may undermine the organization you must consider either transferring the individuals involved to other areas or in the worst case scenario releasing them from the event team.

Establishing clear policies and procedures for each work area is the best proactive way to avoid or contain problems. However, within these policies and procedures there will always be gray areas that may require arbitration. To remain neutral in these discussions you may wish to ask an outside expert such as a marketing, legal, or accounting colleague to help arbitrate the conflict that is not covered in your policies and procedures. These professionals will be familiar with many other similar businesses and events and will be able to bring a global as well as objective presence to this resolution process.

As the coach-mentor you must constantly keep your ear to the grapevine to head off any negative dissension and provide your team members with gentle but firm direction to help them remain focused on their goals. Human beings are complex animals who may easily become distracted or depressed unless you are there to remind them that they are making a positive contribution to the overall goals of the event.

Celebrating Your Success

The effective event leader looks for opportunities to celebrate the individual, and success experienced by your organization. Registration way ahead of last year? Break out the champagne! Mary confirmed that $10,000 sponsorship? Blow up the balloons and cut the cake that reads "Way to Go Mary!" Your team has won an award for your recent event? Celebrate with dinner and dancing for the entire team. Your team will readily recognize that every good deed can get rewarded if you take the time to notice and mark the occasion.

You may wish to appoint one person from your organization as the internal event specialist in charge of these celebrations so you can readily delegate these tasks and be assured that each one is handled by a capable individual. Too often event employees are like the shoemakers' children in that their managers plan wonderful events for others but scrimp on their own behalf. Your internal events should be models for all external events and your team should feel proud to not only be part of your celebration but to have made a positive contribution to the event. This is especially true of volunteers who work long hours for no financial remuneration.

Volunteer Coordination

Volunteers are the life blood of many events. Without volunteers these events would cease to exist. In fact, the vast majority of events is entirely volunteer-driven. The profile of the volunteer has changed dramatically during the past two decades and it is important that the event manager recognize this change.

The emergence of the two-income family has meant that half of the volunteer force in the United States (women) is no longer available to work as full-time volunteers. Furthermore, since many individuals have more than one job and must carefully balance school, children's activities, and other commitments with their volunteer responsibilities it is increasingly difficult to attract volunteers to assist with events.

Effectively recruiting, training, coordinating, and rewarding volunteers is a vital part of many Event Management operations. Although challenging, the following recommendations will help you streamline this critical function.

RECRUITMENT

Many event managers are now turning to corporate America to recruit legions of volunteers for their events. First, the corporation is asked to serve as an event sponsor and as part of its sponsorship the corporation may provide key executives to give advice and counsel or a team of 100 volunteers or more to manage the beverage booths, games, or other aspects of the event. A good source for volunteer leadership through corporations is the office of public affairs, public relations, or human resources. Toni McMahon, executive director of the Arts Council of Fairfax County and producer of the International Children's Festival, goes right to the top. "I start with the chief executive officer. If I can get this person to buy into the event others will surely follow," says Toni. Her track record speaks for itself with literally dozens of major corporations providing hundreds of volunteers for this annual event.

Other sources for volunteers are civic and fraternal organizations. Part of the mission of these organizations is community service so they will be receptive to your needs. Another related organization is schools, both public and private. In many school districts across the United States high school students are required to complete a minimum number of community service hours in order to graduate. And don't overlook colleges and universities. Many institutions of higher learning have dozens of student organizations that also have a service mission and may be willing to participate in your event.

The key to attracting these groups is the WIFM principle. WIFM means "What's in it for me?" When you contact these organizations learn a little bit about their needs and then use the objectives of your event to help them fulfill their needs. The service aspect is a natural. Ron Thomas, CEO of the Tennessee Walking Horse National Celebration, coordinates dozens of community organizations such as the Kiwanis who provide concessions for his event. Their activity is the major fund-raising aspect of their organization each year. They know exactly what's in it for them: cash. This cash enables them to do good work all year long. Determine what's in it for them and you will quickly find volunteers standing in line to help your event succeed.

TRAINING

All volunteers must be trained. This training need not be time-consuming but it must be comprehensive. One way to reduce the amount of time required is to publish a handbook for volunteers that summarizes the policies and procedures of the event. Training may take the form of a social gathering such as an orientation or it can be formalized instruction in the field at the actual event site. It does not matter how you deliver this training as every group of volunteers will require a different method in order to help them learn. However, what is important is that you test for mastery to make certain they are learning and applying the skills you are imparting. Testing for mastery can be done through a written exam, observation, or a combination of both.

COORDINATION

The on-site management of volunteers entails coordinating their job performance to ensure you are accomplishing the goals of the event. Depending on the skill level of the volunteers you must assign team leaders or supervisors in sufficient number to oversee their performance. Remember that the coordination of volunteers involves coaching and mentoring. Make certain your team leaders or supervisors are skilled in these areas.

REWARDING GOOD PERFORMANCE

Don't wait until the end of the event to say thank you. Some organizations publish volunteer newsletters while others host holiday parties to thank their volunteers for their help during the annual summer festival. Giving volunteers early, frequent, and constant recognition is a critical component in developing a strong and loyal volunteer team. You may wish to create an annual contest for Volunteer of the Year or some other such recognition to encourage good-natured competition among your team. Make certain that you carefully research with your volunteers how to effectively recognize and reward their service to the event.

Leadership Styles

In classes at The George Washington University I use a leadership exercise to dramatically convey the three different leadership styles found among event managers. I divide the class into three groups and give each team a set of popsicle sticks. I then instruct each group to construct an event site using the popsicle sticks. One group will do this using a democratic approach, the other with autocratic principles, and the third with a laissez-faire approach.

The democratic group easily and efficiently arranges the popsicle sticks in a pleasing formation and their conversations, discussions, and decision making flows smoothly. The arrangement of the popsicle sticks is a dramatic representation of the effectiveness of their process.

The autocratic group can barely decide how to place their popsicle sticks due to dissension and arguments regarding turf. This group is too busy battling among one another to accomplish the goals required by the event.

Finally, the laissez-faire group constantly arranges and rearranges their popsicle sticks as without clear direction or facilitation they have trouble achieving consensus and their popsicle sticks demonstrate this confusion.

Each of these event leadership styles has an important role to play in the Event Management process. Your ability to navigate among these styles and use the one that is appropriate at the right time is essential to achieve success.

DEMOCRATIC STYLE

Typically this leadership style is used during the early stages of the event process. It is an excellent approach for facilitating discussions, conducting focus groups, and building consensus as you assemble your stakeholders. It is also effective as you move from the design phase into the coordination phase. Before you can coordinate your team members' efforts you must first demonstrate that you are willing to listen and that you are able to function as a good facilitator. These two skills—listening and facilitation—are hallmarks of democratic event leadership.

AUTOCRATIC STYLE

When the fire marshall tells you to evacuate the event site you should not use the democratic approach. The democratic event leadership style has one major drawback: it takes time to reach consensus. When an emergency evacuation is required there is no time or any reason to try and reach consensus. Instead you must use the autocratic approach and give the order to evacuate. Then you must supervise carefully to make certain your instructions are being followed. The autocratic approach should be used sparingly. It is impossible, for example, to force volunteers and increasing staff members to do things they do not wish to do. Therefore, the autocratic approach should only be used when time is of the essence.

LAISSEZ-FAIRE STYLE

This approach is least used in Event Management because it requires a team with skills equal in level and therefore the event manager does not have to facilitate to ensure that goals are being achieved. It is rare that an event organization has a team with skills at a similar level. Most event organizations are comprised of many people with a variety of different skills and even commitment levels. Therefore, it is impossible for the event manager to sit back and let the group decide for themselves how to proceed. Beware the laissez-faire event manager. He or she may be unskilled and is trying to transfer his or her incompetence to the entire event team.

When you are faced with this scenario move quickly to empower others on the team to assist this individual with facilitation decision making to ensure that the event goals and objectives are being met.

The most common way to reduce large amounts of complex information about the event to a manageable communications process is through published policies and procedures. All events of substance have such a document and it helps drive the decision making of the event.

Less than twenty-four hours before the opening of the Trump Taj Mahal Resort and Casino I assembled all of the major vendors in my hotel room for a situation analysis report of the event. For seven days heavy rains and fierce winds had battered the technical equipment we attempted to set up in the parking lot. Due to this catastrophic weather it would be impossible to rehearse this evening so we would be forced to run the final production without confirming and seeing how the effects worked under darkness or actual performance conditions. The vendors realized that we had two options. The first option was to wait and see how the weather would develop during the course of the next day and then make a decision at 10:00 A.M. whether to reschedule or cancel. The second option was to decide tonight to move the production in a modified version inside the Mark Etess Arena. The vendors were leaning toward the latter option when I asked each individual to report on the condition of their equipment. Each person stated that their equipment was in good working order. I then asked each person to assess his ability to perform the production without a performance conditions rehearsal. Once again they all reported in the affirmative. As a democratic leader I used this information to make a decision and then asked the vendors to confirm my decision. They did so. The following evening the sky cleared and millions of people witnessed a uniquely spectacular corporate event. And no one knew until now that we considered moving it indoors or that the talented technicians who performed this spectacular did so without the benefit of rehearsal.

Lesson Learned

Use the democratic leadership style to achieve group consensus. Only with group consensus can you effectively achieve your event goals and objectives.

Developing Policies, Procedures, and Practices

Everyone benefits from well-written policies and procedures. First, the internal stakeholders benefit from having a clear process through which to make decisions. Second, the external stakeholders benefit from using a tool to help them understand the organization and the decision-making process of the event team. Finally, the guests themselves benefit. Although they may never see a copy of the policies and procedures in the event of a life-threatening emergency thanks to this document lives may be saved.

This document is used in a variety of ways. It may be given to all full-time staff and volunteers as a reference tool. It may be distributed to members of the board of directors to guide the development of future policies. Most importantly, it may be used by the event manager to implement the board's policies through carefully developed procedures.

Policies are conceived and approved by the sponsoring organization's trustees. Typically this is the owner of the event such as a private businessperson, corporate board of directors, or the trustees of a not-for-profit group. The policies that are developed and approved reflect the vision and mission of the organization as well as comply with local, state, provincial, and federal laws.

Procedures are the implementation tactics for policy. Policy may be broad, overarching rules of conduct whereas procedures are the regulations that administrators or event managers use to implement policy. Both policies and procedures are essential to produce and sustain successful events.

Creating Policies, Procedures, and Practices

Many events have well-crafted policies and procedures that can serve as a model for your organization. Contact another event organization of similar size and scope and ask them to share a copy of their policies and procedures. In addition, ask them how they most effectively communicate these policies and procedures to their stakeholders.

Carefully review your vision and mission statement and use your event strategic plan as a litmus test for every policy and procedure you create. Appoint experts in a variety of different event fields including volunteer coordination, risk management, sponsorship, and others to help you review and create the final draft of your policies and procedures.

Convene a focus group comprised of typical event stakeholders to make certain that what you have written can be easily and effectively implemented. Next, survey a wider group to sample their opinion. This group should include external stakeholders such as government, police, fire, and other officials.

Make certain that your policies and procedures are fully in compliance with the local, state, provincial, and federal laws. Retain an attorney to review your document to insure compliance. Your document may be beautifully written but unless it is in full compliance with all laws it will be of no value.

Finally, regularly evaluate and revise your policies and procedures. Laws change, events mature, and other changes require that your policies, procedures, and practices document be revisited annually to look for gaps and provide updates to close these gaps.

One example of this is the massive revisions that were required following the implementation of the Americans with Disabilities Act.

Figure 5-1 provides a brief example of a typical event policy and procedure.

Effective Leadership

Your ability to demonstrate effective event leadership will ultimately transform the people on your team. In Figure 5-2 a selection of typical event challenges and solutions is listed. The third column allows you to note the opportunity that is created as a result of helping your team identify the right solution. Use this exercise to identify new ways to motivate your team to achieve even greater success through your event.

As you can see from this brief example the faster you empower your event team to find their own solutions they will not only create new opportunities for themselves but more importantly enable the event to rapidly achieve the goals and objectives desired by the stakeholders. Every great event leader is a teacher. According to Bob Jani, the key to becoming a successful event manager is the ability to lead and delegate. He

---

FIGURE 5-1
Typical Event Policies, Procedures, and Practices

I. **Media Conferences**

Media conferences will be held prior to the annual event and at other times as required. (**POLICY**)

A. The event manager will schedule the media conference with staff. (**PROCEDURE**)

  1. The public relations coordinator will implement the media conference. (**PRACTICE**)

B. Participants will include but not be limited to credentialed members of the media, members of the board of trustees, and invited guests.

  1. Credentials will be required for admission to the media conference.

  2. The public relations coordinator will issue these credentials.

C. The chair of the board of trustees will serve as the official spokesperson for the event organization at all media conferences. In the absence of the chair, the event manager will serve in this position.

  1. The official spokesperson will prepare in advance a copy of his or her written remarks and distribute for comment to the board.

  2. An audiorecording will be made of each media conference.

    a. The public relations coordinator will be responsible for recording the media conference and providing a written transcription.

FIGURE 5-2
Typical Event Challenges, Solutions, and Opportunities

Challenge	Solution	Opportunity
	Example:	
Underfunded	Sponsorship	Promotions, commissions
Short time frame	Prioritize elements	_____
Untrained volunteers	Training	_____
Understaffed	Volunteers	_____
Uncooperative government	Use political influence agency	_____
Celebrity cancels	Replace or show video	_____
Limited parking	Use satellite lots and bussing	_____

believed that when the event manager can transfer his or her skills completely to others, he or she has been successful. Indeed Bob Jani hoped that had been his contribution to the event management industry. "Perhaps other peoples' lives were enriched because we had an opportunity to work, to learn, to experience together. Hopefully there's nothing that I've spent energy and time on that wasn't worthwhile at the time I was spending it. Your attitudes change, of course, as you mature and become older. You become a little more discerning, perhaps about where you spend your time," said Jani who added, "I really think I have been playing teacher for the last thirty years because I try to make an educational exercise out of every event. In a way I've been conducting school for over thirty years."

The first assembly of the event team is not unlike the convocation of a new school year. It is your opportunity to play teacher, mentor, coach, and most importantly, leader as you help others to find the motivation to achieve your event's goals.

THE MAIN EVENT

1. Event leadership enables your team members to find the motivation to continue achieving the event goals and objectives.

2. You cannot motivate others; they must motivate themselves by identifying clear personal goals and objectives.

3. Volunteers are the lifeblood of most events. Recruiting, training, coordinating, and rewarding are critical to the success of this activity.

4. The three styles of event leadership are democratic, autocratic, and laissez-faire. Each style may be used during the course of the event.

5. Policies, procedures, and practices serve as a blueprint for event decision making.

NEXT ON THE AGENDA

Now that you have successfully completed Part One, Administration, you are prepared to master the second major competency in Event Management: Coordination. In Part Two you will master the skills to coordinate a variety of events. Now turn to Chapter 6 and get started by learning how to use the time line and production schedule to chart your course for producing effective events.

PART II

Coordination

The Time Line
and Production Schedule

If policies and procedures provide a rationale and regulation for day-to-day event decision making then the time line and production schedule serve as the map that ensures that you will safely arrive at your destination. The policies, procedures, and practices comprise the rules of the road, but without the production schedule you may never find the right road or navigate so poorly that your event is hopelessly lost before you even begin.

The production schedule is sometimes referred to as the *resume* or *event order* by event managers. It has also been referred to as the *itinerary* by travel and tourism event managers. In fact, it is the *schedule* that logically and completely describes all of the elements that will be *produced* for the event and therefore it is best termed a *time line production schedule.* The *time line* is the sequential listing of tasks that takes place before and following the event. The *production schedule* is the detailed listing of tasks with specific start and stop times occurring from set up through load out of the event.

Improving Event Performance

Hundreds or perhaps thousands of elements must be coordinated to produce a fool-proof event. Just as a coach carefully writes down his or her plays and shares these plans with the team the event manager must also reduce his or her plans to writing and communicate these details with the event stakeholders. Using the time line-production schedule will improve your event performance in many ways. A few of these are listed in Figure 6-1 to enable you to better understand the benefits of this planning tool.

Many of the competencies we have discussed in previous chapters including history, communication, and logical and reasonable thinking are incorporated in the production schedule process. However, the most important reason for implementing the time line-production schedule into your planning process is that it absolutely improves event performance.

This is accomplished through improved communications. Each and every member of your event team is able to refer to the time line-production schedule and determine quickly and efficiently what is supposed to happen at what time. For this reason alone, it is a most valuable tool and should be used from the research period through the final evaluation.

Improving Financial Effectiveness

One area that governs all other areas of the event is financial management. The production schedule allows you, in spreadsheet fashion, to see how you are allocating your scarce event resources in the most efficient manner. Once you have assembled all of the details in logical sequence you can carefully review to see if there are any duplications or ways in which resources may be reallocated for greater cost savings. For example, if you notice that the installation is scheduled for Sunday at 7:00 A.M. and that will result in paying time and one half to your crews you can try and rearrange your Friday activities to schedule the setup within the straight time rate.

Every single element on the production schedule impacts your event financially.

FIGURE 6-1
Benefits of Using the Time Line-Production Schedule

1. Requires the event manager to systematically and logically schedule every element involved in the event.

2. Provides a unique comprehensive communications tool for the other team members to use.

3. Enables external stakeholders such as police, fire, security, and medical to stay informed regarding event operations.

4. Is easily distributed to internal and external stakeholders via computer modem for quick updates.

5. Provides an accurate historical accounting of the entire event.

WAR STORY

I sent a production schedule to the hotel in Denver, Colorado, telling them that I was going to use a fog machine to create a space age environment in the ballroom for a 9:00 A.M. Sunday event. After carefully reviewing the production schedule and seeing the fog highlighted with an accompanying request to disable the smoke detectors I received a telephone call from the director of catering. "What kind of fog do you use?" she asked politely. I quickly checked with the vendor and read to her the contents of the formula. She seemed pleased and due to the submission of the production schedule I assumed that all systems were GO. On Sunday morning we conducted a rehearsal and placed the president of the organization in a space suit complete with helmet and he stood in the center of a platform. The fog was turned on, a few lights were added, and the effect was accomplished. At 9:00 A.M. the doors to the ballroom opened and the guests slowly entered apparently mesmerized by the fog, lights, space age music, and astronaut. As the guests took their seats the president moved to the lectern and removed his helmet. The audience immediately applauded because they recognized their leader. He leaned into the microphone and said, "Good morning ladies and gentlemen and welcome to your future!" At that precise moment the doors burst open and twenty-nine members of the Denver Fire Department marched into the ballroom wearing yellow rain slickers and gas masks, and carrying six foot axes. Surprisingly the audience did not panic. Instead they stood and applauded at what they assumed to be actors. The fire chief was noticeably agitated by this demonstration and used his megaphone to announce: "You are to evacuate this ballroom immediately." Now the audience really cheered and some even hugged the nearest fireman. Once again, the fire chief did not seem pleased and he began looking for the source of the smoke. He turned his attention to the lectern where a small stream of smoke continued to emit from the fog machine. The chief raised his axe and charged toward the lectern as the president turned to me in horror and asked, "Now what do I do?" I stepped out from backstage and met the chief at the fog machine and waiving the production schedule said, "Chief, it's a fog machine. Everyone knows but you." The fire chief shook his head

(War Story continued on next page)

W A R   S T O R Y   *(continued)*

from side to side and mumbled out loud, "Why don't they ever tell us about these things?" He then led his men out the back door and once again the audience stood and cheered.

Lesson Learned

Make certain the production schedule is distributed to all critical parties well in advance of the event. Verify and confirm that these parties have received, read, and approved your event operations prior to the production.

Therefore, when looking at this schedule you should constantly look for ways to best allocate your event resources in the most cost-efficient manner.

Creating the Production Schedule

There are three important resources to incorporate when creating your draft document. First, you must check with key informants to be certain you have incorporated all critical information. Second, you will want to explain the production schedule at an upcoming group meeting to receive feedback from the entire group. Finally, you must recheck the timing, function, and assignment to check for gaps and make certain your production schedule is logical.

KEY INFORMANTS

Ask the senior members of your team to assist you with constructing the draft production schedule. Instruct each team member to create an individualized production schedule reflecting the operations of their individual department. Once you have received all of the schedules combine them into one integrated instrument. After you have integrated all of the schedules distribute the draft document to the same key informants and ask them to check your work for accuracy and see if there are any additions, subtractions, or changes. Figure 6-2 describes a list of typical key informants to assist you in preparing and reviewing the production schedule.

GROUP MEETINGS

Transfer the production schedule to an overhead transparency and use the next team meeting as an opportunity to explain this document. Slowly and carefully walk through

---

FIGURE 6-2
Typical Event Key Informants

1. Admissions coordinator	12. Legal advisor
2. Assistant event manager	13. Lighting coordinator
3. Advertising coordinator	14. Medical coordinator
4. Audio-visual coordinator	15. Police
5. Caterer	16. Public relations
6. Decorator	17. Registration coordinator
7. Entertainment coordinator	18. Risk management coordinator
8. Exposition coordinator	19. Safety coordinator
9. Facility management	20. Security coordinator
10. Fire department	21. Transportation coordinator
11. Food and beverage coordinator	22. Ushering coordinator

---

each step of the schedule pausing occasionally to ask if there are any questions. Solicit feedback from the group on how to best depict the schedule as well as ways to consolidate operations and improve efficiency.

TESTING, TIMING, FUNCTION, AND ASSIGNMENT

The production schedule is a table comprised of six columns. These columns allow you to enter the various key components or elements of the event in logical sequence. It is critical that you test your production schedule by seeking input from critical friends who have produced similar events of the same size and scope. Similar to a budget, the time line-production schedule is a projection of how things should happen based on the knowledge available to you at this time. Figure 6-3 shows a typical event production schedule table. You may adapt this model for your own needs. Make certain the time line-production schedule includes the five phases of Event Management—research, design, planning, coordination, and evaluation.

Implementation

After you have completed the production schedule you must circulate a series of drafts to key constituents to ensure that approvals are received before issuing the final document. Always attach a cover memorandum instruction for each reader on how to analyze the production schedule and describe the kind of input you are seeking. For exam-

FIGURE 6-3					
Model Event Production Schedule					
Date	Start	Activity/Venue	Persons	Stop	Note
Planning Phase:					
10/15	1:00 P.M. EST	Pre-event team meeting/main con-ference room	Goldblatt & team leaders	3:00 P.M. EST	Catering
Coordination Phase:					
10/16	8:00 A.M. EST	Install stage, lights, sound/Ballroom C	Tech crews	4:00 P.M. EST	Clear area for installation

ple, you may ask one reader to proof for typographical errors while another is to concentrate on validating the timing for the various activities. Each key constituent should have a specific role to play relevant to their level of expertise. However, each constituent should review the entire plan to check for overall gaps as well as their own particular area of expertise.

Timing the Release

When working with celebrities or very important persons (VIPs) the timing of the release of the production schedule grows in importance. The production schedule should not be a public document. It is not a press release addendum. Rather, it is a confidential planning tool that is for internal use only. However, once it is published you run the risk of information leaking to external constituencies. Therefore, precautions must be taken.

You may wish to list the VIPs with a pseudonym or leave out his or her movements entirely in earlier versions of the schedule. Usually VIPs do not confirm their participation until a few days before the event and this is for security reasons. Check with your security advisors and especially the head of security for the VIP to determine when best to include the movements (if at all) on the production schedule.

Monitoring the Schedule

Appoint several capable individuals to serve as monitors and oversee various stages of implementation of the production schedule. They should have a copy of the schedule and in the notes section list any variances from the published schedule. If, for example, the event is late in starting this should be noted with the actual start time. If the event runs overtime this should also be noted with the actual stop time. This kind of information is extremely important when planning future events and budgeting adequate time to the various elements you will use.

The monitor should turn in his or her copy of the production schedule with the notes included immediately after completing his or her assignment. Figure 6-4 demonstrates typical notes that your monitor may insert.

Things Change

About the only thing you can count on today is that things will change and sometimes far too rapidly to update the production schedule. When a change must be made quickly, use a printed bulletin headlined "CHANGE NOTICE" to ensure that every member of your team is aware and able to adjust their schedule to accept this change. Figure 6-5 depicts a typical change notice.

FIGURE 6-4
Typical Monitor Notes

Date	Start	Activity/Venue	Persons	Stop	Note
10/15	1:00 P.M. EST	Pre-event team meeting/main conference room	Goldblatt & team leaders	3:00 P.M. EST	Catering **Actual start: 1:15 P.M. Actual stop: 3:30 P.M. Catering 15 minutes late.**
10/16	8:00 A.M. EST	Install stage, lights, sound/Ballroom C	Tech crews	4:00 P.M. EST	Clear area for installation

---

FIGURE 6-5
Typical Change Notice

CHANGE NOTICE
Distribution: All event staff and volunteers.

Change: The opening ceremony previously scheduled to start at 10:00 A.M. on May 15, 1996, has been changed. **The new start time is 10:15 A.M.** The reason for this change is the television feed has been moved and the new time is the actual start of the broadcast.

Summary: Note time changes for opening ceremony.

Previous time: May 15, 10:00 A.M.

New time: May 15, <u>10:15 A.M.</u>

W A R   S T O R Y

The domino theory certainly applies to Event Management. Unless you anticipate change and work with it you will be overcome by its implications. When
a corporation retained my firm to plan a reception at a local hotel they of course
signed the contract and initialed the start time for the event. Despite all good
intentions they arrived one hour early. One of my team members ran breathlessly
up three flights of stairs to the ballroom and while panting said, "They're here!"
From the whites of his eyes I did not question for a moment who he was describing but instead hurried into the lounge and slipped the pianist fifty dollars all
the while dragging him by the arm to play the piano on the bandstand as we tried
to play catch up. As the 300 guests began to ascend the staircase I distributed
the costumes the actors would later wear to the banquet servers and they did double duty until things were better under control. Finally, I wiped the perspira-
tion from my brow, stood at the door, gritted my teeth, and said to the meeting planner, "Good evening and welcome." Later, slowly and carefully we incorporated the original elements into the event and the evening actually was
extremely successful as things started slowly and began to build to a climax. Of
course the slowness was from the guests' perspective, which is all that matters.

Lesson Learned

The time line-production schedule is a valuable tool for informing both internal and external stakeholders. Share your schedule with clients as one more way
to inform them about the critical timing elements of your event.

Using the Time Line-Production Schedule
to Manage Change

One of the most useful aspects of the production schedule is its ability to assist you in
managing change. As literally hundreds of decisions must be made on a daily basis, the
production schedule provides a solid framework for decision making.

Perhaps your celebrity has been delayed in another city and will be arriving late
for your function. A quick glance at the production schedule allows you to make the

necessary adjustments and see how these adjustments are affecting other elements of the event. In addition, sharing a common document with your team members you can solicit their input before making the adjustments to ensure that you are in concert with one another.

Using integrated system design network (ISDN) technology you will be able to send the most complex production schedule using fiber optics and involve as many people as necessary in your review and decision-making process. As each of you sits in front of your computer terminal sharing the same document you will be able to make minute or major changes and immediately see and discuss the ramifications of your decisions. In a world fraught with accelerated change this will be a major advancement in the Event Management process.

The Resume Versus the Production Schedule

Meeting event managers traditionally use the term "resume" in place of production schedule. The resume is comprised of not only the time, venue, task, and person responsible but also detailed information regarding room setups, audiovisual, and other components of the meeting. A typical resume is shown in Figure 6-6.

The deficiencies in the resume shown above include the absence of a contact person or person responsible for this function and a cell for notes regarding the actual start and stop times for the event. Although the resume is widely used in the meeting Event Management field it has some gaps that you must be aware of. When deciding which tool to use for your event first share your template or model with the venue that will be responsible for handling most of the meeting event logistics. Confirm and verify that the tool you propose to use will be accepted and used by their staff prior to implementation.

Evaluation

The best way to evaluate the use of the production schedule is to ask the key stakeholders if the process was effective. Did the schedule help you understand the big and little

---

FIGURE 6-6
Resume

Date	Time	Function	Location	Setup	Attendance	Catering	A/V
Friday	10:00 A.M.– 12 M. (noon)	Board meeting	Room 102	Hollow square	20	Coffee, Juice	Overhead

picture of the event? Was the production schedule useful in keeping track of start and stop times? Were there any deficiencies in the time line-production schedule? How could the schedule be improved next time?

A quantitative way to monitor the use of the schedule is to review the notes section and look for wide gaps between the scheduled start and stop times and the actual times. Carefully study those elements of the event where the gaps were inordinately wide and seek solutions in your planning for next time.

Remember that the production schedule is similar to a budget in that it is a broad project management tool with history that may be used to improve the overall planning process. Make certain you are diligent about reviewing the final schedule and comparing your projected elements with the final event. From this process improvements will be made and your production scheduling process will become more scientific in the future.

THE MAIN EVENT

1. Use the time line-production schedule to organize, time, coordinate, and evaluate your event.

2. Seek input from your stakeholders before issuing the final copy of the time line-production schedule.

3. Time the release of the schedule to support security needs.

4. Monitor the actual versus the projected time and look for gaps.

5. Evaluate the time line-production schedule to improve the process for next time.

NEXT ON THE AGENDA

Historically events have been linked with food and beverage. Feasting has traditionally been an integral part of human celebration and in Chapter 7 you will learn how to transform feeding people into a total event focused around the art of catering.

Effective Catering Techniques

Food, beverage, and celebration are inextricably connected. From social life-cycle events to giant hallmark events such as the Olympic Games or Super Bowl, the relationship between food and frivolity has been a close one. This is not to suggest that it is not serious business as well.

The event catering field has grown in even greater proportions than other segments of the overall industry. With this growth has come significant challenges. These challenges have come from the relatively easy entry most people have into this field. The television series "Kate and Allie" served as a stereotypical example but made a valid point as two women moved from making fruit baskets to producing full-scale catered dinners out of their home kitchen. While there are no official statistics on how many individuals have entered the catering profession I am confident that if they were published, they would be astonishing. It seems the only regulation imposed is by the local health department. The sheer numbers of individuals who have entered the event catering business in recent years make it impossible to adequately control this field.

Therefore, while growth has increased due to demand (two-income families reliant on caterers and other food providers) problems have accompanied this growth. Among these problems are uneven food quality and service as well as immature business skills which often result in difficult business relations with fellow event professionals.

On the positive side of this complex field, much of the creativity, not to mention the actual business that is generated in Event Management, stems from catering professionals. This may result from the basic human need to be fed. I am convinced, however, that this is also part of what trends expert Faith Popcorn calls our "egonomic society." Popcorn maintains that individuals will spend whatever it takes to satisfy the ego. Perhaps the best example of this is the fast growth in the coffee or espresso bar industry. As one coffee vendor told me, "I may charge three dollars for a product that you could make at home for pennies but I offer you instant self-esteem, relaxation, energy, and renewal. What other product provides that much at such a low cost?"

To fully understand the modern catering field the event manager must recognize two distinct features that distinguish catering from other professions. First, traditional food operations are confined to fixed locations and provide a relatively fixed menu to a known market. Caterers, by contrast, may inhabit a temporary location that may or may not be unusual and challenging. Second, although all food professionals must work with certain time constraints, the caterer must serve his or her product within a specified period of time working closely with the band leader, decorator, and entertainment coordinator as well as the event manager. On a moment's notice the caterer may have to adjust his or her food service due to other factors such as late seating, the early end of a performance, and other elements too numerous to name.

A Temporal Art

Event caterers are usually one of three business types and each is defined by location. First, the caterer may be an institutional caterer commonly described as an "in-house" or on-premise caterer who may or may not have permanent kitchens and offices at the event venue. This caterer may limit the choices for the event manager but can provide greater security with being familiar with the idiosyncrasies of the venue.

The second business type is the traditional off-premise caterer whose clients engage him or her to cater meals at a temporary location. The location or venue may or may not have permanent kitchen facilities. However, the off-premise caterer is responsible for providing the necessary equipment and services to create an atmosphere of permanence in this temporary locale.

The third and final type of event caterer is the concessionaire. This individual may use a mobile kitchen or concession trailer to dispense his or her product or may work in a fixed venue from a permanent or temporary concession area. In some venues the in-house catering operation simultaneously operates all concession activities as well.

Obviously, there is significant variation in these event catering business operations. However, generally, when contracting caterers the three types will include on-premise, off-premise, and concessions. A growing trend in an effort to boost revenues is for on-premise caterers to begin catering off-premise in private homes and even other venues.

Although the on-premise caterer provides the lion share of major event catering operations the off-premise caterer may actually feed the broadest possible constituency. The off-premise caterer must have the ability to establish a temporary kitchen in a tent, an aircraft hangar, or even in a jewelry store. This type of caterer works closely with party rental specialists to ensure that he or she can provide the appropriate equipment on a moment's notice. Furthermore, the off-premise caterer must establish adequate resources for utilities, deliveries, waste disposal, and other critical elements of any catering operation. Finally, the off-premise caterer must stay abreast of local health and sanitation regulations to ensure that he or she is in compliance regardless of the event's location.

In actuality, although many off-premise caterers may boast of their ability to provide their services uniformly in any location in most major metropolitan areas, this is limited to relatively few in number. When you add multiple events on the same date this number shrinks dramatically.

As the on-premise caterer continues to expand off-premise he or she is learning that the rigor of the temporary location is much greater than the fixed or permanent venue. Some on-premise caterers have ceased off-premise operations for this very purpose. They quickly discover that on- and off-premise are two very different catering skills and when trying to conquer both worlds one inevitably suffers.

Location, Location, Location

Of the five W's in Event Management "Where" is perhaps most critical to the on- and off-premise caterer for a variety of reasons. First, the caterer must comply with specific health department codes and regulations that will govern where he or she may operate. Second, food and beverage preparation is time dependent and the distance between the food preparation area and the serving location can determine a whole range of quality and service issues. What happens if hot food becomes cool or even cold during transit? How will the guests feel about slow food delivery? Finally, what utilities, equipment, and other resources are available to the caterer to successfully prepare, serve, remove, and clean up?

The location of the event is therefore a critical consideration for the off-premise caterer. However, the on-premise caterer must also be sensitive to these issues as even the most routine event can suffer from logistical problems. As one example, what happens in the convention center when the caterer must serve 1,000 guests on the ground floor and the kitchen is located on the second floor and the elevator stops working? Or perhaps the event manager has asked the caterer to serve the meal in an unusual location such as in a tent in the parking lot. Does the caterer have the necessary equipment and additional labor to successfully accomplish this task? These questions and many more must be considered well in advance of establishing the location for the catered meal.

Equipment

Obviously tables, chairs, china, silver, and other standard equipment will be required to serve a quality meal. However, the event manager must ensure that the caterer has access to the appropriate style and quantity to match the needs of the event.

Some caterers own a sufficient inventory of rental equipment while others have close relationships with party and general rental dealers to provide these items. The event manager must inspect the equipment to ensure that the caterer has not only sufficient quantity but that the quality is appropriate for the event.

When considering quantity remember that the caterer may have multiple events on the same date. Make certain that additional inventory is available in case your guest list increases suddenly at the last moment. Furthermore, make certain that if the quantity of items is increased the inventory will remain high quality.

Beyond china and silver some caterers also maintain a healthy inventory of tables, chairs, linens, and other serving utensils such as chafing dishes, props, and other elements that will provide you with a cohesive look. Some caterers stock unusual items from a specific historic period or feature items that reflect their style of catering. A caterer who primarily services the social life-cycle market may provide latticework props and gingham linens while the caterer who works in the corporate event market may provide white linens and more traditional china and silver. The event manager must select a caterer who has existing equipment and experience that matches the goals and objectives of the specific event.

Utilities

As the caterer plugs in the coffee urn suddenly the music from the band comes to a screeching halt. The puzzled guests look confused while standing on the dance floor but both the event manager and catering director know that what has happened is an overloaded circuit caused by the coffee urn. The event manager must audit the caterer's

WAR STORY

A large convention center spent considerable effort patching things up with a large group that had a most unusual dining experience. The caterer had contracted to serve 5,000 people and promptly ran out of dishes and serving utensils. As each guest would lay their fork down the server would quickly remove it, rush it to the kitchen, rinse it, and recirculate it to the next hungry diner. As a result of this confusion many of the guests were never fed, others only had a bite, and most were miserable. The inability of the caterer to provide enough equipment to professionally serve the meal created national publicity and robbed the caterer of the goodwill of this client and perhaps future ones as well.

Lesson Learned

Meet well in advance with the caterer and describe in writing your food and beverage needs. Confirm that the caterer has sufficient experience and inventory to serve your group. Check references with groups of similar size and type. There is no need to go into the pantry and count the spoons. However, determine if the caterer owns sufficient equipment, will rent, or use a combination approach to ensure delivery of a quality product to your guests.

utility needs as well as the other vendors' to determine if the venue can support these requirements.

In addition to electricity the caterer will require water. The proximity of the water will also be an important factor as costs may increase if water must be transported from a great distance. The third and final requirement for all catering operations is waste management. The caterer must have a system for disposing of waste materials. The event manager must ensure that the caterer has the necessary resources to perform professionally.

Time Constraints

Time is of the essence in most catering operations for a variety of reasons. First, the caterer must prepare and deliver his or her product within a reasonable amount of time to ensure freshness and quality. Second, the caterer must carefully orchestrate the delivery of his or her product within a complex setting in which multiple activities are being staged. For example, a dinner dance may require that the caterer serve various courses between dance sets. At some events the caterer must provide his or her entire service within a short time frame to ensure that all servers are out of the function room in time for speeches or other aspects of the program.

Service Styles

The term service refers to the method used for serving the catered meal. In the United States the three most popular forms of service are the seated banquet, the standing or seated buffet, or the standing reception where food items are passed by servers to guests. Each of these service types helps satisfy specific goals and objectives. Figure 7-1 provides a simple guide on when to employ a specific type of service.

W A R   S T O R Y

One thousand guests sat down to eat their preset salads and fifteen minutes later their meals had not been touched. Looking at my watch I realized that we had allotted only one hour for the entire meal service and that the major name entertainer would go on late unless the guests started eating immediately. The lateness of the performance could result in guests leaving before the show and/or additional charges from the union stagehand labor for overtime. After consulting with the banquet captain I went to the offstage microphone and announced, "Ladies and gentlemen, please enjoy your salad, our program will begin in seven minutes." Suddenly a clatter of forks was heard that was earth shattering. The salads were rapidly consumed and we were back on schedule. The banquet captain later asked me if I could provide that announcement for other groups to ensure that she could serve the meals on time.

Lesson Learned

Guests require a proper cue to begin eating. Either an invocation, welcome, announcement, or even "bon appetit" must be given to ensure that the meal will begin and subsequently end on time.

FIGURE 7-1
Event Service Styles and When to Use Them

Event	Service Styles
Brief networking breakfast	Standing buffet
Breakfast with speaker	Seated buffet
Breakfast with speaker, program	Seated banquet
Brief networking luncheon	Standing buffet
Luncheon with speaker	Seated buffet
Luncheon with speaker, program	Seated banquet
Brief cocktail reception	Passed items
Extended cocktail reception	Standing buffet or individual stations
Brief dinner	Standing buffet or individual stations
Dinner with speaker, program	Seated banquet
Formal dinner	French service

In addition to these service styles the exposition is an important location to carefully orchestrate effective catering. Exposition managers know that food and beverage serve as a strong attraction and increase traffic multifold in the exposition hall. One of the more popular methods is to provide the guests with an apron (usually donated by a sponsor and imprinted with their logo) and then distribute pocket sandwiches. With this technique the guests can walk, talk, shop, and eat. It is a very efficient way to provide food service for guests at the exposition and resembles one giant walking picnic.

The picnic style is also a popular technique for corporate and reunion events. Although this is a difficult style in terms of service, it is extremely popular among guests who want to sit together as one large group. This style is also popular with Octoberfest events as it resembles the German beer hall.

English and Russian services, while not as popular in the United States, are two styles that may be implemented for the right occasion. The English style involves serving each table from a moving cart. Russian service requires that the server use silver platters from which he or she places each course onto the guest's plate. Both styles of service may be requested but make certain the caterer is properly equipped and schooled to produce an effective result.

Logistical Considerations

Proper and efficient guest flow as well as effective methods for ensuring the timely delivery of food and beverage are essential considerations for the catered event. The event caterer may have substantial experience working in a permanent venue but when asked to provide services off-premise he or she may not be aware of the additional rigor required to survive in the jungle. To survive and thrive one must know the basic laws of the event jungle. Figure 7-2 outlines these important considerations.

Your catering event professional will suggest other ideas to help you accomplish your goals and objectives. However, remember that you must prioritize the event's goals and objectives and catering may or may not be high on the list. Therefore, it is impor-

---

FIGURE 7-2
Logistics Laws for Effective Catered Events

1. Determine in advance the goals and objectives of the catered event and match the logistical requirements to these objectives. For example, a brief networking event should use fewer chairs and tables to allow the guests time to mix and mingle with numerous individuals.

2. Determine the ages and types of guests and match the requirements to their needs. For example, if the guests are older more chairs may be needed to provide additional comfort during an extended reception.

3. Identify the food preparation and other staging areas and ensure that there is a clear passageway to the consumption area. Check the floors to make sure they are free of debris and allow the service staff to move quickly.

4. Whenever possible use a double buffet style for this type of service. The double buffet not only serves twice as many guests but also allows the guests to further interact with one another as they receive their food.

5. Do not place food stations in areas that are difficult to replenish. Large crowds of guests may prevent service personnel from efficiently replenishing food stations.

6. When passing food items place a few servers at the entryway in order that guests visibly notice that food is available. It is easy for servers to disappear in a large crowd and this technique ensures that most guests will see and consume at least one of the food items being offered.

7. Use lighting to highlight buffets, carving, and other stations. Soft, well-focused lighting directs the guests' eyes to the food and makes it easier to find as well as more appetizing.

8. Use servers at the entryway to pass drinks rapidly to guests as they enter, or open the bars at the furthest distance from the entrance first. Smaller events with ample time may benefit from passing drinks; however, larger events where the guests must be served quickly may benefit from the bar stag-

ing scenario. Once the distant bars begin to experience lines of ten or more persons, open succeeding bars working your way toward the entryway.

9. Instruct the bar captain to close all bars promptly at the appointed time. Use servers to line up at the entryway to assist in directing guests into the main function room.

10. Provide return tables to accept glassware as guests transition into the next event. Carefully staff these areas to avoid too many glasses accumulating.

11. Request that servers distribute any welcome gifts or programs during the set-up period and be staged in each dining station to assist with seating. Servers should be requested to offer chairs to guests without hesitation to expedite seating.

12. Use an invocation, moment of silence, or a simple "bon appetit" to cue guests to begin the meal.

13. The following service times should typically be used for catered events.
    Cocktail reception: Thirty minutes to one hour.
    Seated banquet: One to two hours.
    Preset salad consumption and clearing: fifteen to twenty minutes.
    Entree delivery, consumption, and clearing: twenty to forty minutes.
    Dessert delivery, consumption, and clearing: fifteen to twenty minutes.
    Coffee and tea service: ten to fifteen minutes.

14. Make certain all service personnel have exited the function room prior to speeches or the program. If this is not possible, make certain front tables have been served and that servers only continue service as quietly as possible in back of the function area.

15. Request that servers stand at exit doors and bid guests good-bye and distribute any parting gifts from host/hostess.

tant to maintain balance as you decide where to focus your emphasis during specific periods of the event.

Once you have identified the event's goals and objectives you will match the service style to make certain your guests' needs are satisfied. After the basic needs are satisfied it is time to add some magic to turn the ordinary catered affair into an extraordinary special event. Here are some proven methods for accomplishing this goal.

Catering Ideas

THE LIVING BUFFET

Effect

As guests browse along a seemingly normal buffet table they are startled as the head of lettuce suddenly starts talking to the cauliflower and the cauliflower turns to the guest for advice on how to handle the unruly lettuce.

Method

Using a standard buffet table cut two twenty-four inch holes in the top. The holes should be located approximately twelve to eighteen inches apart and away from the front edge of the table. Place two actors in head pieces that carefully resemble lettuce and cauliflower under the table with their heads penetrating the hole. It is best if the head piece covers their eyes or they keep their heads slightly bowed until time to speak. Elaborately garnish all of the area around the fake lettuce and cauliflower. Use theatrical lighting to soften the light on this area of the buffet.

Reaction

Guests will shriek with delight and the talking lettuce and cauliflower will become one of the best memories of your catered event.

Bonus

Write a brief script between the lettuce and cauliflower where they engage in a heated discussion about health and nutrition. Have the actors turn to the guests to ask their opinions.

THE HUMAN BUFFET TABLE

Effect

A beautiful woman or man supports an entire buffet upon his or her garment.

Method

Place a male or female actor in the center of two buffet tables. The buffet should be slightly elevated on platforms so that the edge of the table is at eye level. Construct a costume for the female and male that appears to support the entire buffet. The woman may wear a long dress and the skirt may be supported with matching fabric used to skirt swag the front edge of the buffet table (see Figures 7-3 and 7-4) or the male may wear a colorful tailcoat and his tails are extended with matching fabric to drape the tables. Place bright light on the actors in colors to complement their costumes and slightly softer light on the buffet tables. Match the lighting for the actors' wardrobe with softer lighting in matching colors on the buffet skirting.

Reaction
Guests will ooh and ahhh as your elegant actors wave and invite them to dine.

Bonus
Direct the actors to freeze and come to life periodically. This will create an ongoing activity for the guests to observe and enjoy.

FIGURE 7-3

OLD BLACK MAGIC

Effect

Thirty servers enter once the guests are seated. Each server is carrying a silver tray with two top hats. Suddenly the entire room begins to glow in the dark.

Method

Purchase sixty black plastic top hats. Fill each top hat with twenty glow-in-the-dark bracelets and sticks. Line the waiters up outside the function room service entrance. Upon a cue from yourself instruct the servers to enter as you play music such as "Old Black Magic" or "Magic to Do." As the servers arrive at the tables and place their hats in the center, quickly turn off the lights. Instruct the servers to place their trays under their arms, clap their hands, and distribute the glow-in-the-dark pieces from inside the hats to the guests.

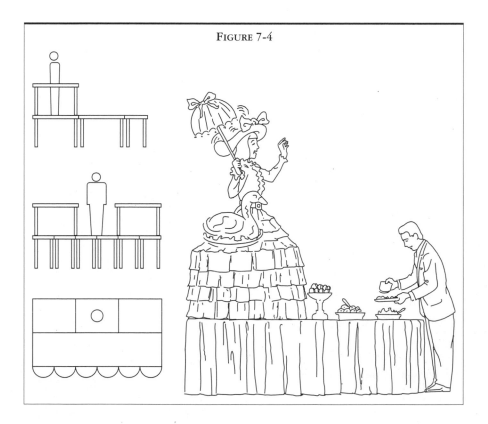

FIGURE 7-4

Reaction

Your guests may first wonder why there are no centerpieces for this elaborate catered event. However, once the glow-in-the-dark gifts are distributed the guests will applaud as they become the room decor and you produce magic at a fraction of the cost of traditional decor.

Bonus

Purchase white gloves for the servers and color them with glow-in-the-dark dye. As the lights go to black have the servers wave their hands above their heads and then clap them before producing the glow-in-the-dark gifts.

DESSERT PARADE

Effect

Your guests believe a unique dessert has been created for them as your team of servers parades the dessert to their tables.

Method

Use glow-in-the-dark swizzle sticks or other items to decorate the dessert trays. Play a lively march or theme music that reflects the style of the catered event as the servers march forward. Stage the servers so that they enter at the rear of the room and march through the tables holding the trays high above their heads. Lower the lights and use follow spotlights to sweep the room to create additional excitement. Prior to their entrance announce: "The chef has prepared a once in a lifetime dessert creation to celebrate this momentous occasion. Please welcome your servers!" The servers march (or dance) to each table and serve dessert.

Reaction

Your guests will respond with spontaneous applause followed by clapping rhythm to the music as your servers deliver dessert.

Bonus

At the conclusion of the dessert parade line the servers up in front of the stage and have them gesture to the left or right as the pastry chef appears for a brief bow. Make certain the pastry chef is dressed in all white with a traditional chef's hat so that he or she is easily recognized. This will cause an additional ovation and perhaps a standing one at that!

INCREDIBLE EDIBLE CENTERPIECE

Effect

Your guests will notice that their centerpiece is both beautiful and edible. The guests will see and smell as well as taste this delicious work of art.

Method

Engage a chocolatier to carve a centerpiece out of chocolate for your guests to enjoy. The carving may represent the symbol of the event or the logo of the organization sponsoring the program. Use a pin light to independently illuminate each sculpture. Make certain the sculpture is on a raised platform such as a gold or silver epergne. Include fresh fruit in your display to add color to your final design. One excellent subject is a large chocolate cornucopia filled with fresh red strawberries.

Reaction

Your guests will soon notice the work of art gracing their table and engage in lively conversation about its origin. Some guests will take photos and others may try and nibble!

ICE-COLD LOGO

Effect

As your guests arrive for the cocktail reception they observe an ice carver putting the finishing touches on an elaborate sculpture.

Method

Your caterer can refer a professional ice carver who will precarve from a large block of ice your organization's logo, image, name, or other important and valued symbol of your group. Place the carver on a raised platform and use rope and stanchion to provide ample working room and keep your guests from being hit by flying chips of ice. Make certain the ice carver completes his or her work of art at the very moment your main function is to begin. Upon completion stage several photos of your key leaders with the new work of art and then announce that the main function will begin.

Reaction

Your guests will crowd around the carver and begin intense discussions with one another about his or her art work. At the conclusion of his artistic effort they will erupt into applause and begin taking numerous photos.

Bonus

Ask the ice carver to use an electric chain saw as this creates noise and excitement. In addition, the use of flame (fire and ice) is another dramatic touch that your ice carver may wish to incorporate into the final design (such as a dragon breathing fire).

Selecting the Best Caterer

The best caterer is the organization best equipped with experience, knowledge, creativity, personnel, and resources (human and actual equipment) to achieve your goals and objec-

WAR STORY

A client once insisted on turning her organization's logo into a giant ice sculpture. After consulting with the ice carver the client was informed that it would not be appropriate to display this symbol in the center of a buffet table. The ninety-minute buffet plus the half-hour preparation time would cause severe melting, and according to the ice carver, the client would not be pleased by the results. Not only was she displeased she was terribly embarrassed when her organization's symbol, the letter I, rapidly transformed itself into a gigantic phallus. Her event became the talk of the social season for all the wrong reasons.

Lesson Learned

Listen carefully to the advice given by your catering experts. Only display ice sculptures in locations where they can be easily removed if they are damaged or severe melting occurs. Do not display any ice sculpture for longer than forty-five minutes and avoid using the letter I!

tives. In each community there may be several full-service off-premise caterers with excellent reputations. However, the list will rapidly be narrowed to one, two, or hopefully three by using the criteria listed in Figure 7-5. Event manager Paul Broughton of Raleigh, North Carolina, suggests that the following criteria are also important considerations for selecting the best caterer for your event. Broughton, a former catering professional who now plans and produces complete events, believes that selecting the best caterer is one of the most important decisions the event manager must make.

CATERING COORDINATION

The event manager must closely coordinate all event activities with the director of catering or other catering team leader. Within the catering team Figure 7-6 describes the responsibilities of each of the catering team members.

To ensure that you are effectively coordinating each element with your catering team make certain that you hold a series of telephone or in-person meetings to review the various elements that will be included in your event.

The first meeting should be used to review the proposal and answer any questions you may have about the food, beverage, equipment, or service and terms of payment. The next meeting will be held prior to signing the contract to negotiate any final terms

FIGURE 7-5
Criteria for Selecting a Caterer

1. Find out how many years the company has been in business and what size events they have catered.

2. Ensure caterer has health and occupancy permits (and all other necessary permits).

3. If serving alcohol, make sure caterer has on-premise and off-premise alcohol beverage permits.

4. If permits are in order, make sure caterer has liquor liability insurance.

5. Ask to see references and/or client letters.

6. Ask to see pictures of past events—look for professionalism and setup of kitchen/staging area.

7. Identify past and present events caterer has handled and find out maximum and minimum sizes.

8. Check to see if site meets ADA requirements and complies with laws.

9. Find out policies on client tastings.

10. Review printed materials—menu descriptions will tell about level of professionalism.

11. Ask to see design equipment and/or in-house rentals—look for innovation and cleanliness.

12. Leave messages with company receptionist—see how long it takes to return calls.

13. If on-premise, make sure any electronic or live music complies with BMI or ASCAP regulations.

14. Check for membership in professional organizations (i.e., NACE and ISES).

15. Find out where executive chef received training.

16. Find out how wait staff is attired for different levels of services.

17. Find out if servers are proficient in French service, modified French service, or plated service.

18. Find out deposit requirements and terms.

19. Review and analyze contracts and cancellation agreements.

20. Call the local party equipment rental company and find out about their working relationship with the caterer.

FIGURE 7-6
Catering Professionals

Title	Responsibility
Director of catering	Senior catering official coordinates sales and operations.
Catering manager	Coordinates individual catered events including sales and operations.
Banquet manager	Manages specific catered functions. Servers report to banquet manager.
Server	Individual responsible for serving the guests.
Bartender	Individual responsible for mixing, pouring, and serving alcoholic and nonalcoholic beverages.

such as the inclusion of a complimentary food tasting. Some caterers prefer that you attend a comparable event and taste similar items that will be served at your event. However, if your event is introducing new cuisine it is essential that you insist on a separate food tasting to ensure the quality of each item prior to serving your guests. In some instances there will be a charge for this service and you should confirm this prior to signing the contract. The final meeting should include a thorough review of all elements including the schedule, equipment, service levels, and to answer any final questions the caterer may have regarding delivery, utilities, or other important issues.

REVIEWING PROPOSALS

Most caterers will provide a complete proposal including the type of cuisine, number of servers, schedule, equipment rentals, payment terms, and other pertinent information. Figure 7-7 provides a guide to ensure that all important information is included in the catering proposal.

Negotiating with the caterer is an important step in the process of selecting the best caterer. In smaller Event Management markets where competition is not as great

---

FIGURE 7-7
Catering Proposal Checklist

1. History of the catering organization including other clients of similar size and scope they have served.

2. Letters of reference from other clients of similar size and scope.

3. Complete description of cuisine.

4. Complete description of style of service including the number of servers/bartenders that will be provided.

5. Complete description of equipment that will be provided by the caterer. Equipment may include tables, chairs, and serving utensils as well as other items. Make certain that each is described and that quantity is included.

6. Listing of additional services to be provided by the caterer such as floral, entertainment, or other special requirements.

7. Complete description of payment terms including date of guarantee, taxes, gratuities, deposits, balance payments, and percentage of overage provided by the caterer.

8. All schedule information concerning deliveries, setup, service, and removal of equipment through load-out.

9. Insurance, bonding, and other information pertinent to managing the risk of your event.

10. Any additional requirements including utilities such as water, electric power, and so on.

as larger markets negotiation may be more difficult. Still, regardless of size, there are traditional areas that may be negotiated. Figure 7-8 lists several of these areas.

The Final Step

The last meeting should be held in person. Often it is held in conjunction with the food tasting or final walk through. This important meeting is your final opportunity to review the critical details regarding the caterer's contribution to your event. Figure 7-9 lists the major points that must be covered during this meeting.

Figure 7-8
Negotiating Points

1. The payment terms. Ask to pay the lowest deposit in advance or to pay a series of smaller deposits spread evenly over a period of months. Even better, if your organization has a good credit record, ask to pay net thirty days after your event.

2. Ask for a discount for prepayment. You may receive up to a 5% discount if you prepay your entire bill in advance.

3. Ask for a discount if you are a not-for-profit organization. Although all not-for-profit organizations ask for this concession, you may be successful if you can convince the caterer that your guests may bring him or her additional new business. Offer to actively promote the presence of the caterer at the event to ensure high visibility.

4. Ask for a complimentary service. Some caterers will provide services ranging from a complimentary ice sculpture to a pre- or post-event reception.

5. Ask for a complimentary food tasting for yourself and your key decision makers. This should not take the form of an additional event, rather, it is a business activity for the purpose of inspecting the food presentation, taste, and other important elements of the event.

Figure 7-9
Finishing Touches for Successful Catered Events

1. Confirm the day, date, time, location, parking, and other critical information with the caterer.

2. Carefully coordinate all catering deliveries and access to the loading entrance with other vendors.

3. Review the times for the service and instruct the caterer regarding the other elements of the program and how he or she will interface with these aspects.

4. Review the caterer's alcohol management program. Ask the caterer if his or her staff has received training and how they will handle guests who are obviously inebriated.

5. Review all payment terms and any elements you are required to provide as part of your agreement.

COST SAVING MEASURES

Increasingly both clients and their event managers are concerned with cost. In some corporate circles it is not the actual cost but the perception of a high-priced event that is of greater concern. To avoid these concerns and lower your overall catering costs use the checklist shown in Figure 7-10.

Catering Trends

A trend is a pattern of behavior that is likely to be sustained over time. Although the event catering profession is susceptible to shifting tastes, and is certainly impacted by the state of the economy, several trends are emerging. These trends are well worth noting as they will most certainly influence many of the decisions you will make.

Nutritious food and beverage is a trend that will affect both perception and reality in the catering field. As the world's population ages (especially in the United States) guests will be more and more concerned with good health and will turn to nutritious foods as a primary means of promoting this life-style. Not only must the food perception be that of healthy presentation but the ingredients must also be carefully considered.

FIGURE 7-10
Controlling Catering Costs

1. Carefully analyze the meals that must be provided. Some meals may be taken by guests on their own such as at networking dinners where all guests pay for their individual bills. You may also wish to substitute concessions for some meal functions. An individually priced buffet line may be a good alternative for some meal functions.

2. Use buffets and boxed lunches instead of seated banquet service. Reducing labor cost may reduce expense.

3. Price food items by the lowest possible unit (cup, piece, or dozen) rather than by the tray or gallon. Order only the amount of food you will require based upon the history of your event.

4. Secure sponsors for meal functions. In a recent study we identified a major interest by sponsors in providing funding for meals that are related to educational programs.

5. Secure in-kind sponsorships from bottlers and others in the food and beverage industry.

6. Reduce or eliminate alcohol from your event. Many events are becoming beer and wine functions in place of full open bar affairs. This change is happening due to concerns about health but also because of the perception associated with heavy drinking and drunk driving.

7. Serve a signature drink to everyone. A signature drink is an original drink that your bar manager creates for consumption by the entire group. The first need of most guests at a catered function is to place a drink in their hands. Offer your signature drink at the entrance to your event and solve this need while reducing your budget by controlling consumption.

8. Allow the guests to serve themselves. This is especially popular with the children's events. Make Your Own Sundae bars and five-foot long submarine sandwich making are not only entertaining but also may result in cost savings.

Increasingly more and more individuals and their hosts will want to know the ingredients in their food and beverage to make wise decisions regarding menu selection. Therefore, caterers will want to make available the ingredients and may even wish to list these items in a menu or signs posted near the food items. Furthermore, caterers will also wish to continue the practice of promoting heart healthy menu items as offering these items will provide a popular alternative but also differentiate the caterer from competitors because of this attention for low cholesterol.

A second trend is the shift from open full liquor bars to increased emphasis on beer, wine, and nonalcoholic beverages. The changes in lifestyles have, along with concern for responsible drinking, driven this important shift. Even more importantly caterers are more cognizant than ever before of initiating and sustaining a thorough alcohol management program. Designated driver programs along with systems to prevent underage drinking are admirable initiatives that will grow in the future. As a result of this trend caterers have had to search for new revenue streams to replace the loss of alcohol sales.

The third trend relates to the second trend in that increasingly caterers are seeking additional revenue streams and some are even moving from strictly food and beverage operations into full Event Management services. This change comes with great challenge as well as potentially great opportunity. Historically caterers have been involved in all aspects of Event Management. Caterers, especially in the social life-cycle event market, have been responsible for providing or recommending the services of florists, musicians, decorators, invitation designers, and other allied professionals. Today's trend merely quantifies this historic business opportunity and repositions the caterer as an event manager who specializes in catering services. However, to fully take advantage of this trend, the catering professional must be willing to round out his or her education with a rigorous course of study in Event Management. In every profession, eventually, superior quality combined with good value can conquer fierce competition. Event Management is no different from other professions in this regard. If catering professionals are to expand their services to include those of Event Management they must be willing to acquire the new skills that will complement their existing talents to improve their quality and provide them with the tools to effectively compete in the event marketplace.

Therefore, these three trends—nutritious and healthy menus, reduction in alcohol service, and the expansion of the caterer's services to include those of an event manager— may be viewed as economic opportunities provided education and commitment to quality is consistently implemented.

Catering Future Force

As caterers assume increased responsibilities in the Event Management profession other members of the professional team will need to adjust their marketing and operations strategies to cope with this new phenomenon. Questions such as "Can and will caterers charge for Event Management services beyond the cost of food and service?" and "Will all future catered events place significant emphasis on food and beverage at the risk of ignoring other elements and producing a more balanced event?" are but two of numerous questions that will be raised.

Earlier, I stated that historically caterers have provided Event Management services. Now, the question becomes, "Will caterers further develop these services to reflect full depth and breadth of resources available within the Event Management industry?" If they choose to broaden their education their force within the industry can have substantial implications. The future of Event Management may include both good food and beverage as well as other equally excellent services managed by the caterer. This consolidation will be welcomed by some clients who desire one-stop shopping and rejected by others who may for a variety of reasons prefer to entrust their event to another event manager. Regardless, the future force in catering will include offering many diversified services carefully combined into a nutritious, filling, and satisfying buffet. At the center of this diversified services bountiful buffet may be Event Management.

MAIN EVENT

1. Determine the goals and objectives of the event and use catering resources to achieve these goals and objectives.

2. Use specific criteria to select the best catering professional resource.

3. Adjust catering service to time, type, age, and other variables of each event.

4. Ensure that catering logistics are identified well in advance to provide smooth operations.

5. Group history as well as external trends should be studied to provide state-of-the-art service, cuisine, and style.

NEXT ON THE AGENDA

The art and science of lighting, sound, audiovisual, and special effects are growing in importance with emerging technologies, lower costs, and improved quality. Chapter 8 provides an in-depth look at these technologies and demonstrates how they may be integrated with catering, entertainment, and other event resources.

Audiovisual, Lighting, Sound, Special Effects, and Video

The Event Management profession has seen perhaps the greatest paradigm shift in the live production sector of this industry. Live production is also what differentiates events from other entertainment or creative products. Although one may argue that television specials are billed as "special events" in most instances these live events were filmed or taped before a live audience. Productions ranging from the National Football League Super Bowl halftime show to the Three Tenors concert combine live production with various audiovisual, lighting, sound, special effects, and video resources to produce a well-crafted event that is ultimately viewed by millions via television. The modern event manager cannot ignore this major shift and must understand as well as implement these resources when appropriate.

Why = What

Earlier I described that prior to selecting the most effective resources for your event you must establish clear goals and objectives by asking why this event is necessary. Due to the myriad of new technology now offered, this is more important than ever before. The inexperienced event manager may decide to mix and match a wide array of new technology to impress his or her guests during the event. In fact, this mixture becomes a collage of inappropriate resources that results in confusion to the guests. An award-winning designer reportedly cautioned his young apprentices that "less is indeed more." The event manager must also use caution when selecting appropriate resources to support or enhance his or her event to make certain that each device is well integrated rather than extraneous. Figure 8-1 may be used as a primary coordination tool for selecting and engaging these resources.

Event Technology and Its Purposes

Whether the purpose of your event is to educate or entertain or perhaps both, the technology that you select will help you best achieve your goals and objectives.

In the conference event field you may select slide projectors, overhead projectors, a TelePrompter™, or perhaps one microphone to improve communications between the presenter and the participant. The entertainment field may require theatrical lighting and special effects such as fog, laser, or strobe lights. Other fields will require different technology, however, ultimately the purpose of the event will determine the final selection and coordination of the event technology.

Figure 8-2 provides a guide for general usage in selecting equipment for the event style and purpose.

Audiovisual

The term audiovisual was most likely coined in the 1950s as schools, and later businesses and then associations, used slide and overhead projectors for instructional pur-

---

FIGURE 8-1
Selecting the Appropriate Resources

1. Identify the purpose of event technology for your program. Will the event technology be used to attract attention, guests, or to improve communications?

2. Determine the size of the live audience. The technology you select for the audience will be determined by the number of guests.

3. Identify the age, culture, and learning style of your guests. Some guests are visual learners while others are more attuned to audio influences. Still other audiences, due to their age, may prefer the sound level larger or smaller.

4. Inspect the venue and inventory pre-existing light (natural and artificial), in-house audiovisual equipment, utilities, the experience of local technical labor, and any other elements that will interact with your event.

5. Sit in a guest's chair or stand in the guest's place and try to envision the event through his or her eyes and ears. Check for obstructed views and other distractions. Identify potential solutions to develop optimum enjoyment through the entire event.

Figure 8-2
Matching Technology to Style and Purpose

Style/Purpose	Technology
Conference: communicate	Audiovisual: video magnification
Conference: focus	Lighting: key lighting of lectern
Civic: attract attention	Special effect: fireworks
Education: build retention	Audiovisual: interactive CD
Entertainment: attract	Sound and lights: announce and chase
Exposition: educate	Video: product description
Festival: communicate	Sound: public address
Reunion: excite	Audiovisual: slide show of guests

---

poses. During the 1970s this technology expanded rapidly with more sophisticated audio tools as well as video enhancement due to the invention of video projection systems. Indeed, today there are dozens of audiovisual tools available for use by event managers. However, I will concentrate on those ten tools that are most often used in the production of civic, entertainment, expositions, festival, and conference events. These ten tools are readily available in most event markets or may be obtained from nearby larger markets.

Audiovisual projection is primarily divided into two projection fields: visual and audio. The tool and its power depend on the factors described in Figure 8-1. Audience size, distance, the age, and type of attendee are critical considerations when selecting one of the tools listed below. The right tool will make your task easier and more enjoyable for your guests and the improper tool will cause you frustration and irritate your guests. Therefore, when selecting one or more of the following tools for your event carefully refer to Figure 8-1 to check and balance your decision.

Digital images are rapidly replacing traditional photography in the Event Management production industry. Today's slide projector is rapidly being replaced by the notebook computer loaded with hundreds of slides and entire educational programs including music and video. Monitor industry publications such as *Event World* and *Special Events Magazine* to stay current with the latest technological advancements in the audiovisual field. Following are some audiovisual technologies in use today.

Microphone

Technology

The lectern microphone is perhaps the most common technology in use in conference events. Two primary types of microphones are available for use by event managers. The unidirectional microphone is ideal for the individual speaker and the omnidirectional microphone is designed for occasions when more than one person shares the lectern.

In addition to the lectern microphone the lavaliere or clip-on microphone (sometimes the names are used interchangeably) allows the presenter to be mobile and move around the stage or room. Although more expensive, the wireless hand-held or lavaliere microphone provides even greater freedom as no cable is attached. Using an FM transmitter and receiver the audio signal is patched directly into the audio system and results in producing high-quality sound.

Usage

When using the clip-on microphone placement of the microphone head is extremely important. The head should be as close to the mouth as possible. Therefore, it should be placed on the upper part of a man's necktie or coat lapel. Women should wear it high on the blouse or also in the upper part of the suit jacket lapel. It is wise to provide redundant wired microphones for wireless systems. I usually place a wired microphone with fifty feet of cable in the lectern to provide security for the speaker and make the transition from wireless to wired as smooth as possible.

OVERHEAD PROJECTOR

Technology

If the slide projector is the workhorse of the conference industry the overhead projector is the most often requested projection device for smaller meetings. One major benefit of the overhead projector is its ability to project slides in a fully illuminated venue. The slide projector, due to distance, requires that the area immediately surrounding the projection surface be darkened to provide a bright image. However, the overhead projector is typically only a few feet from the projection surface and the image is much brighter for most media. One advantage of the overhead projector is the ability to use markers to illustrate and underscore the comments of the lecturer.

Usage

One of the more unusual ways I have used the overhead projector was to provide suspense and excitement for an awards program. In advance of the program I retained a caricaturist to sketch portraits of the award recipients. The artist was given photographs of each winner and the rough sketches were approved by a family member or close friend of the honoree. The overhead projector was placed behind the stage and projected on a rear projection screen. The front of the screen was decorated to appear as white canvas surrounded by a gold-gilded frame. As the award presenter described each recipient's accomplishments the artist began to quickly sketch the portrait. The audience, both hearing and seeing the life of the person, began to recognize the identity of the honored person. When the name was finally announced the audience immediately responded with gasps of recognition followed by sustained applause for both the recipient and the artist.

Liquid Crystal Display Panel (LCD Panel)

Technology

The LCD panel is used in conjunction with a computer to project graphic text onto a screen. Rapidly replacing the traditional overhead transparencies, this technology allows the presenter to have maximum flexibility when preparing and showing slides.

Usage

The LCD panel may be used to present complex charts and graphs, text, graphics, and other images in a lively format similar to television production incorporating wipes, crawls, rolls, and other moving images. Make certain you have the proper cabling for the LCD panel as the Mac and PC use different attachments. With additional technology, it is possible to incorporate video and audio into your presentations to create an attention-grabbing program and liven up even the most tedious lectures. Be careful not to allow your content to become buried under too much technological wizardry. Content must supercede presentation to maintain the integrity of your message.

Projection Screens

Technology

Event managers use both rear and front projection screens for different reasons and different venues. A front projection screen generally provides brighter illumination; however, the rear projection screen provides the opportunity to hide the projection equipment from audience view. Typically two types of screens are used most often. The tripod screen is supported by a metal tripod and the fast fold screen is supported by a metal frame and may be either supported on legs or hung from above. Projection screens generally range in size from six feet high by eight feet wide to fifteen feet high by twenty feet wide. These screens accept slides produced in horizontal formats. In addition to the screen, most audiovisual suppliers will also provide a dress kit for the fast fold screen. This kit consists of a skirt, valance, and perhaps side drapes for masking. You may also wish to use other pipe and drape to run off to the side of the room to further mask the backstage area.

Usage

Screens may be used for laser, overhead, slide, or video projection. Typically screens are underutilized at conferences. Consider using the screen surface to project the names of your event's sponsor or other information in addition to the educational content of the conference. Avoid leaving screens blank by using a title slide to cover periods when no video or slides are required. In case of an emergency, to create an instant title slide without the expense of a slide projector, use the video camera to shoot the lectern sign that usually features the organization's logo or name. This shot will then be projected onto the screens as if it were a title slide.

Slide Projector

Technology

The 35-millimeter slide projector may be the most basic visual tool for the conference event field. Either used singly for lectures or in combination with dozens of others to create a dramatic and emotionally moving image this technology is truly the workhorse of the conference field. This equipment will require the correct lens for proper focus as well as a wired or remote control device to advance the slides. When used in combination with other projectors a dissolve unit is required to network all of the units and produce smooth transitions. The term 35-millimeter specifies the size of the slide that is projected by this equipment. Obviously one of the major considerations and perhaps the most common problem is the burned out lamp. Therefore, having a spare lamp or two is important to remember. Newer slide projectors have a spare lamp included and this allows for rapid recovery from a burned or dysfunctional lamp. A more powerful unit is entitled the Xenon slide projector due to the Xenon lamp inside. The Xenon lamp is much brighter than the standard 35-millimeter slide projector and allows—with proper lensing—the projector to be placed many more feet away from the projection surface.

Usage

In the conference event field the slide projector is used to illustrate lectures and provide other visual enhancements. One of the most effective uses is to project a slide on the front of a curtain or surface other than a screen. For the fiftieth anniversary of an association I projected a slide of the original founders of the organization signing the first articles of incorporation. This slide was front projected onto a translucent curtain known as a *scrim*. After the guests settled into their seats and the venue lights dimmed, the voices of the founders were heard. A few moments later lights from behind the scrim rose to reveal the original founders seated in the same pose as in the slide. The men, now in their nineties, rose to greet the audience and thunderous applause was heard throughout the room.

Another effective technique for slide projection involves using the slide to create a backdrop for a speaker or stage set. During a patriotic program I used a slide of the American flag rear projected onto a curtain to create a thirty-foot-long by ten-foot-high image at a fraction of the cost of renting, installing, and removing an actual flag.

Video Projector

Technology

This technology first enjoyed widespread usage introduced in the 1970s and has rapidly expanded to become a staple of many conferences and other events. The video projector may be used to show close-up video images of the speaker or entertainers or

WAR STORY

The success described with the U.S. flag encouraged me to use this technique on a larger scale. The opening ceremony of a prestigious military organization meeting in Baltimore allowed me to further experiment with rear slide projection. For this client we used a multiple image slide projection to open the program with a brief historical slide program about the writing of the "Star-Spangled Banner" in Baltimore. Six slide projectors were positioned behind the scrim curtain and a music sound track accompanied these stirring images as they moved across the screen.

However, during rehearsal I noticed that some of the slides with lighter images revealed the hot white lamp of the slide projector and interrupted the show with a series of bright flashing lights. After consultation with the slide show designer we decided to substitute some of the lighter slide images with darker ones to correct this problem. However, some fifteen years later I am still not satisfied with the result. This was an example of a great idea that was not effectively produced due to poor implementation.

Lesson Learned

Schedule a rehearsal using performance conditions as early as possible. This will allow you to spot any problems and correct them prior to final technical rehearsals. Confirm and verify that your ideas can be translated to actual production by sufficient testing.

others at a program or event. In addition, it can be used to project slide media or a prerecorded program such as a videotape of a new product or future destination that is being introduced. Increasingly it is used to project computer data and graphics. Miniaturization has changed this technology from larger cumbersome devices to manageable small carton-size equipment. The video projector may be used for either front or rear projection. Using two projectors (layered on top of one another) provides a brighter image plus provides you with a redundant unit in case of trouble. The projection distance will vary based on the size of the screen. However, for a fifteen by twenty foot screen plan on approximately twenty foot between the projector and the screen. For greater distances, high-powered projectors are available.

Usage

Use the video projector to show a welcome videotape describing the destination where the event is being held or to magnify the image of the speaker or other presenter. During one event I used a combination of pretaped and live video to create the impression of a live television production. A local newscaster was hired to pretape a "breaking news story" about our association president. Next, the tape cut to the president giving a "live" interview across town near a prominent monument. Then the tape cut to the president running to the meeting and seconds later the door to the ballroom opened as the president briskly walked into the room in person, followed by the press corps and, as she ascended the stage, the now live video followed her movements. Upon her arrival on stage she made an announcement to the assembled media and the program officially began.

COST SAVINGS

When renting audiovisual equipment remember that this business, like many in the meetings and conference field, is seasonal. Therefore, the prices for the equipment may be negotiable. The price for labor is typically not negotiable. When bidding audiovisual equipment make certain that you list every possible application and time required for labor so that the bidders may evaluate the total value of your event. Many if not most audiovisual rental firms will offer a 25 percent producers discount. You may be able to receive greater discounts on equipment by adjusting the dates of your event to reflect periods when equipment is more readily available.

Still another way to save money is to find multiple uses for your audiovisual equipment during the same twenty-four-hour period. Too often event managers use a video projector for one hour when in actuality the rental is factored on a twenty-four-hour period. Preplan the use of this equipment to maximize the value. For example, can the projector be moved to a different room instead of renting a separate piece of equipment?

Finally, look for ways to share costs on audiovisual equipment with other groups. Perhaps there is another organization meeting in the same venue at the same time as your organization. Can you co-rent equipment with them to save costs?

Lighting

When God said, "Let there be light" it may have been the first time in recorded history that a lighting cue was called. Since that fateful day lighting has come to symbolize safety, mood, atmosphere, and transition as well as time of day and location.

In almost every event environment lighting improves the atmosphere. It may be used to focus attention on the speaker and to enhance the look of decor and food as well as to dramatically change the mood from one scene to another.

Miniaturization has impacted the lighting field in major ways. Only a few years ago a lighting control system would require enough space to fill a small bedroom. Today the same system fits compactly on a card table. This major reduction in size has made lighting more flexible and available than ever before.

Figure 8-3 demonstrates how lighting may be used in a variety of event situations.

These applications are only the tip of the iceberg because many event managers combine different lighting effects much as a visual artist combines color and texture to create the desired effect. The following lighting technology is commonly used by event managers to achieve these desired effects.

CHASE LIGHTS OR ROPE LIGHTS

Technology

These miniature lights may be encased in clear or colored plastic flexible tubing or assembled on a string of electrical wire. They are a low wattage method for creating excitement and directing focus.

Usage

They may outline a new product or sign, edge a stage or arch, or be incorporated in ceilings to create a starlight effect.

DIMMER OR CONTROL BOARD

Technology

This instrument allows the lighting operator to fade, black out, and perform other lighting cues. Many, if not most, control boards are computer driven allowing the operator to store the cues in memory and then at the press of one button perform dozens of tasks.

FIGURE 8-3
Applications for Lighting

Activity	Lighting Application
1960s or space age	Ultraviolet light
Atmosphere	Lighting projections (gobos)
Centerpieces	Pin spots
Change of mood	Backdrop colorization
Dance floor	Moving lights
Entertainer	Follow spotlight
High-tech focus	Laser light show
Product reveal	Chaser lights
Space age effect	Fiber optic backdrop
Speaker at lectern	Key light for focus
Stage set	Set light and back light

Usage

The control board sends the electronic signal to the individual lighting instrument instructing it to perform on cue a specific effect. These cues may range from blackouts to slow fades to everything in between. Some control boards have a light organ built in that allows the lights to pulse to the beat of live or recorded music. Use the control board to also cue the house lights or make certain that the control board is placed near the house light control so that you may coordinate these two functions.

ELLIPSOIDAL SPOTLIGHT

Technology

The major difference between the ellipsoidal spotlight (also known as *leko*) and the par cam is the ability to selectively focus light and to use a template for projecting specific images.

Usage

Using shutters, the ellipsoidal spotlight allows the event manager to narrowly focus light to highlight specific areas in either a cylindrical, horizontal, or vertical format. Additionally, this instrument accepts a metal or glass template known as a *gobo*. The gobo uses a design that can be projected on a surface such as a curtain, wall, floor, or other area. These designs may be mixed and matched to create a variety of effects. Using a scrim curtain you can project an image such as a window and using a rear light source, an actor may appear to actually raise the window by adding a second gobo of an open window. Gobos may also be used to project text such as sponsor names. This is an inexpensive way to quickly add sponsor recognition to an event.

FIBER OPTIC DROP OR CURTAIN

Technology

Thousands of microthin fibers carry light from a central source and create changing colors or chase effects.

Usage

This relatively new technology provides a dramatic backdrop for a stage set and may also be used in a theme event to create the illusion of a galaxy of stars.

FOLLOW SPOTLIGHT

Technology

A focusable spotlight with the ability to add color through gels and manually operated, this spotlight can follow speakers, actors, or other persons as they perform.

Usage

Focus attention on a principal performer or on a prop or other important symbol using this technology. It is also used to create excitement as the spotlight bally's (rapidly moves left and right) through the audience onto the stage.

PIN SPOT

Technology

This small instrument is used to provide a narrow focused beam of light on a table centerpiece.

Usage

This low wattage instrument is extremely effective for lighting a specific area such as a centerpiece.

INTELLIGENT LIGHTING

Technology

Robotic lights are able to tilt, pan, turn, change color, change gobo patterns, change focus, and perform other maneuvers at the touch of a switch. One intelligent lighting unit may be able to replace a dozen other units due to the flexibility it offers. Although significantly more expensive than traditional lighting instruments such as par cams, these units are able to perform many more functions.

Usage

Intelligent lighting is most appropriate for large scale productions where high-tech lighting will support or enhance the production. I have used them for theme parties inserting the client's gobo in the units and then ballying the image throughout the room. I have also used them when I required a flexible system that could change the look of the event environment several times over a short period of time.

PAR CAM LIGHTING INSTRUMENT

Technology

If the slide projector is the workhorse of the audiovisual field the par cam performs that same function among the many instruments in the field of lighting. The par cam provides a broad floodlight and is used to fill a stage with light. This instrument is tra-ditionally used to flood large areas and provide color to create mood and atmosphere.

Usage

From lighting the front area of a stage, providing side fill light for a lectern, to cre-ating dramatic mood lighting for a backdrop, the par cam has many uses. Gels may be inserted to provide color. To create an effect similar to *Star Trek's,* "Beam me up Scotty" illusion, I used four par cams placed on the floor of each side of a platform. Adding fog, the lights projected up through the particulate matter and created a low cost but highly effective impression.

STROBE LIGHT

Technology

This rapidly flashing light creates the illusion of slow or fast motion when used with movement. It is available in a variety of sizes including small egg-shaped products that when used in combination with other instruments produce a starlight effect.

Usage

In a theatrical production strobe lights may be used to simulate slow motion. I have used strobe lights to create a space age effect in an entrance tunnel as well as egg-shaped strobes to decorate the exterior of a building.

Caution

Both chase lights and strobe lights may cause discomfort or even injury to guests with disabilities such as hearing loss or epilepsy. When using these devices post a sign at the entrance stating:

"The following special effects are used during this event: strobe light and chasing lights."

ULTRAVIOLET OR BLACK LIGHT

Technology

Popular during the 1960s, this technology has improved tremendously. Originally only available in a tube format, its major drawback was the limited throw distance. In recent years manufacturers have invented new technology that allows longer throw distance and focusable light to create fantastic new effects.

Usage

This technology may be used to create a dark and haunting atmosphere or a space age thrill. As the light excites the color in a sign the graphic will suddenly pop out at the audience. I have effectively used this technology to reveal new products by outlining the new item in colors that are sensitive to black light and then at the appointed time illuminating the appropriate instrument.

COST SAVINGS

The easiest way to save money on lighting equipment and labor is to select a venue that has lighting equipment permanently installed in its facility. Sometimes the venue will include in the rental fee the use of some or all lighting equipment. You may also wish to share the costs of equipment rentals with other groups in the same venue.

When required to rent lighting equipment make certain you solicit bids. When possible, ask the bidders to inspect the venue with you as they may be able to offer additional ideas you may not have thought of previously.

Finally, remember costs rapidly escalate when work is performed outside of normal business hours. Find out the time frame for straight time and work within this window. Sometimes this will require renting the venue on a weekday to prepare for a weekend event. Compare the labor cost savings to the rental charges and determine which is better. Carefully schedule labor to avoid overtime charges.

Sound

The level of complexity and purpose of the event determines the level of audio support that is required. In most event environments audio is used for simple, noncomplex productions. However, as the size of the audience increases or the complexity of the production rises, simple audio must be replaced by the services provided by a production sound company.

Sound is used for public address, entertainment, to project speakers, and to transmit sound from video or film as well as numerous other applications. Figure 8-4 describes some of these applications and the type of equipment that may be required.

CASSETTE PLAYER

Technology

This equipment is rapidly being replaced by the compact disk player or digital audio tape (DAT) machine. However, it is still a staple of many events. This machine accepts a 30-, 60-, 90-, or 120-minute cassette tape. Some machines feature automatic rewind, automatic cueing of sides, and automatic stop.

Usage

One way to use this machine is to place it near a live tropical bird such as a parrot. Use a voice-over expert to record the sound of a parrot's voice welcoming the guests to the party. Using an endless loop cassette tape the bird will repeatedly welcome the startled guests. You may also use this equipment to play walk-in, background, or walk-out music at the event.

COMPACT DISK PLAYER (CD PLAYER)

Technology

This technology produces high-quality audio and video signals and provides enduring quality. Unlike the audio cassette player the compact disk player allows for instant

Figure 8-4
Sound Equipment and Applications

Sound Equipment	Application
Audio console and rack	Full-sound production capability including playback and recording
Boom attachment	Television, film, recording, specific sound source, and large groups
Cassette player/recorder	Recording live sound
Compact disk player	Playback of instrumental music and other sound including effects
Delay speaker	Used to project sound to areas that are a greater distance from the original sound source. In a stage setting the delay speakers may be mounted halfway over the audience. The signal received by these speakers is delayed to avoid an echo-like quality.
Digital audio tape (DAT) machine	Synchronized music
Fill speaker	A speaker used to send sound signals to dead spots such as the front center of an audience.
Mixer	Used for blending sound sources through one central unit.
Omnidirectional microphone	Chorus
Perimeter zone microphone (PZM)	Chorus, singers, and piano
Reel to reel	Slide or audio synchronization
Speaker	Used for projecting sound to either a specific area or a wide distribution.
Speaker cluster	A group of speakers clustered together to project a wide distribution of sound.
Speaker tripod	A speaker mounted on a tripod
Stage or ear monitor	Playback from other instruments and vocalists
Unidirectional microphone	Solo speaker

cueing and random access to specific audio or video segments. Stills photos (slides) and data storage are also important usages of this technology.

Usage

Instrumental music and/or video/slides may be instantaneously retrieved with this technology. Use for background or specific audio musical cues as well as to project photos or video images. Ideal for instrumental music for background music, fanfares, or dancing.

Digital Audio Tape (DAT) Machine

Technology

The digital audio tape machine (DAT) provides digital quality audio and allows the operator to program the cues for easy access during the production. Make certain you have redundant tapes for these systems as sometimes the programming varies from machine to machine.

Usage

Live entertainment, video slide, or other programs that require high-quality audio with multiple cues should use a DAT system.

EQUALIZER

Technology

The range between treble and bass is equalized using this valuable technology.

Usage

A professional sound engineer is required for this task and he or she will carefully use either your prerecorded sound source or the live performance to equalize the sound to provide a full range of audio dynamics.

MIXER

Technology

This device is used to blend or mix different sound inputs or sources and transmit them into a central output. The number of inputs may vary from four to dozens.

Usage

Instrumental musicians and multiple vocalists as well as event programs that feature both live and recorded sound sources will require the services of a mixing unit.

PERIMETER ZONE MICROPHONE (PZM)

Technology

The perimeter zone microphone (PZM) is a flat microphone that picks up sounds in a 180-degree radius. It is used inside a piano, on the floor of a stage, to record choirs or large musical ensembles, and other applications where sound may originate from more than one point.

Usage

Place inside the piano lid, on the center of a table for a group discussion, or on the floor of a stage to record or broadcast sound from multiple sources.

SOUND CONSOLE OR RACK

Technology

This multicomponent system may feature a recorder, player (cassette and/or compact disk), equalizer, mixer, and other important technology.

Usage

The term "rack" originates from the way the equipment is stacked on racks in a vertical system.

STAGE OR EAR MONITOR

Technology

The stage monitor is used to monitor sounds from other instruments in a musical group including vocals as well as monitor the sound level as the audience experiences it. Increasingly popular among entertainers is the ear monitor. This small hearing-aid type device is custom fitted to the ear and allows for monitoring of sound as well as cueing and synchronizing when singing or performing to a prerecorded track.

Usage

Singers and musicians use stage monitors to communicate with one another and to review their sound as the audience hears it. Singers, television performers, and others use ear monitors to receive cues from the director and monitor their vocal performance.

WIRELESS MICROPHONE

Technology

Both a hand-held and a clip-on model are regularly used for conferences, meetings, and live entertainment as well as video production. The speaker may freely move before and among the audience using this equipment.

Usage

When conducting a presentation featuring audience questions and answers, the wireless microphone is ideal. It is also the instrument of choice for speakers who move randomly on the stage and among the audience. Remember to have redundant equipment in the form of a wired microphone in case the wireless one should fail.

SOUND OPPORTUNITIES

There are generally three periods when sound is utilized for most events. First, sound is utilized prior to the event to prepare certain audio products such as sound tracks or fanfares for the live performance. Second, sound is used during the actual event for broadcasting both to the live audience attending the event and to those listening by radio and television. Finally, sound production may include a postproduction session when the live sound recorded during the event is further processed to documentary, marketing, or other use.

Preproduction

The preproduction period generally occurs during the design, planning, and coordination phases. Preproduction may include the design and production of specific audio elements for the event. These elements will vary depending on the complexity of the event. Your task could be as simple as selecting appropriate instrumental music tracks or as complex as mixing an entire symphony orchestra to provide recorded accompaniment for a major mega-event such as the Olympic Games opening or closing ceremony. The preproduction period must be carefully planned as others may need to review the finished product before usage in the actual event. Therefore, allow sufficient time to identify the appropriate resources, produce the product, and receive feedback from your important event stakeholders. When budgeting this time I usually allow 25 to 50 percent more time than estimated to handle last minute changes and requests.

Production

During this period the event manager *coordinates* the live, broadcast, or recording of sound from the actual event. Depending on the size and complexity of the event, the event manager may wish to assign a specific person from his or her staff to monitor the sound production. In most cases a competent and capable sound technician will handle the myriad of details required for this function. However, in those circumstances when the event is new or highly specialized it is wise to have one person supervise the sound department to ensure that this element of production is consistent with your expectations. Too often event managers assign too low a budget for production sound. Do not fall victim to this error. Make certain that you have carefully budgeted for the level of quality required. One way to do this is to be certain that you have retained both a sound console operator as well as a stage sound technician. Speakers, actors, singers, musicians, and others who are using sound equipment will benefit from the knowledge that a qualified sound technician is nearby to help prevent or correct problems. A simple mistake such as failing to turn on the wireless microphone can be easily prevented by investing in a professional sound technician to monitor these important details.

Postproduction

Once the event has ended the sound responsibilities may continue. More and more events are being recorded for both documentary and marketing purposes. Therefore, during the design, planning, and coordination process of the event, careful attention must be paid as to how you may use the sound product after the live event has ended. Although the two most common uses are documentation and recording, it is also possible to use the sound portion of your event for communications as well as risk management purposes. For example, a well-edited sound version of your event may be an effective way to communicate with your volunteers. You may duplicate this program on cassette tapes and distribute them to your volunteers to enjoy during their drive time to and from work. Should your organization become involved in a lawsuit resulting from a risk management incident, the sound recording may provide evidence that you practiced a standard of care acceptable in your area. For example, a recording of the evacuation announcement may provide you with evidence that you conducted this important activity with a reasonable degree of care to prevent injury. Throughout the research and design process the event manager must carefully consider how he or she will later use the sound product created during the event.

SOUNDSCAPING

Olympic Games and Super Bowl sound designer Bob Estrin of Creative Event Technology in Orange County, California, may have been the first person of his generation to soundscape a room. The soundscaper works very much like the landscape artist or architect in that he or she designs specific areas of the event venue to reflect the form and function of the event theme. Mr. Estrin has used miniature speakers to transform a themed environment into a symphony of sound effects that subtly transport the guest into a total experience.

SOUND IDEAS

There are no limits to the possibilities for exciting sound production for your event. However, implementing these ideas requires careful planning and well-executed coordination.

Famous Voices

To attract the attention of an audience meeting in Houston, Texas, the home of the U.S. Space Program, I quickly lowered the houselights and played an audiotape of President John F. Kennedy describing the space program. As President Kennedy spoke we showed a video with sound effects of the launch of the space shuttle. Using surround-sound the entire room felt as though it were preparing to lift off. We carefully and selectively added one speaker at a time until the entire room thundered with sound. As the audio program concluded, a burst of fog appeared from stage left and the presiding officer entered the stage to greet the space age delegates.

Invisible Actors

The president of a corporation wanted to reward his senior staff with a series of bonuses. To dramatically introduce this announcement the president agreed to dress as Ebeneezer Scrooge and meet the ghosts of Christmas past, present, and future. However, due to budget constraints there were no funds to hire or wardrobe actors to play the ghosts. Once again, we solved the problem with prerecording the voice of one actor playing all three ghosts. When the ghosts appeared we used fog and simple lighting effects to create the illusion of a ghost. The president impersonating Scrooge spoke to this area of the stage and the ghost answered him. At the end of the ghostly visit the president agreed to distribute the bonuses to his senior staff.

Goof Proof Sound

Only a few weeks before a major convention the meeting planner changed the theme of the event to reflect an international program. To open the convention we selected an international children's choir that featured children from over fifty different countries wearing native costumes. The children ranged in age from five to seven years. Concerned that their voices would not be strong enough to fill the event venue, I arranged for them to be prerecorded so that they could sing to tracks and be certain that they were in full voice on the day of the show. As it turned out nearly half of the children had bad head colds; however, the audience only heard clear, beautiful tones prerecorded in a studio several days prior to the event.

The element of sound will be the technology that is noticed in most of your event. How many times have you attended an event and winced at the sound of screeching feedback pouring forth from the oversized speakers? I have often said that the only two things that most people have a strong opinion about at events are the temperature and the sound level. In most cases the temperature will be either too hot or too cold and the sound too loud (usually) and too soft (sometimes).

The event manager must recognize that today many individuals have high-quality stereophonic sound systems in their homes and automobiles. Because of this new sophistication, your guests are extremely discriminating when it comes to the quality of sound used at your event. Make certain that you determine in advance the level of sophistication of your listeners and then allocate your resources effectively to satisfy their needs, wants, and desires.

COST SAVINGS

Wireless products are significantly more expensive than wired ones. Unless the production requires wireless products avoid this costly equipment. In some cases you will still pay for wired equipment as you will want to have redundant equipment as described earlier.

Labor can be a major cost in installing heavy-duty sound equipment. Consult with your sound rental expert and determine if small units may be used to avoid the rental of lifts and riggers required for the larger equipment.

Carefully bid sound equipment to make certain that the experience of the operators and condition of the equipment will ensure you meet the goals and objectives of your event. For example, in the Washington, DC, area there are only three or four sound companies that have the capabilities to handle the large-scale sound requirements for major demonstrations and marches. Using an inferior company can incur much greater costs than selecting the most qualified and perhaps higher bidder.

Special Effects

It is interesting that most special effects reflect variations in the weather of the planet. Effects such as fog, rain, thunder, lightning, and even pyrotechnics (fireworks) immediately conjure images of dramatic changes in the climatic conditions. Weather is perhaps the most talked about subject in the world as so much depends on it, including one's mood, that it is natural that special effects have come to play an important role in the development of Event Management.

Event managers use special effects to attract attention, generate excitement, and sustain interest as well as startle, shock, and even amuse. The key to properly integrating special effects into your event scheme is to determine during the design process how special effects will support or enhance your event's goals and objectives. The most common error made by event managers when using special effects is to add too many different components and thereby confuse the guests. Instead, special effects should be viewed as a natural and necessary part of the entire event strategy.

Figure 8-5 lists the most common special effects used in Event Management. However, it is important to remember that some event technicians use the term special effects to also describe a variety of specialty lighting devices such as black or strobe lights.

BALLOON DROP

Technology

A bag suspended above the heads of the audience opens and releases hundreds of balloons.

Usage

Traditionally used on New Year's Eve as well as at the conclusion of U.S. political party conventions, this technology is always appropriate as a capstone or finale element

---

FIGURE 8-5
Special Effects and Their Applications

Effect	Application
Air-propelled confetti cannons	Shower of paper flutters over and on guests as part of finale of entertainment
Balloon drop	Hundreds of balloons drop onto the heads of the audience from a net or bag suspended above
Dry ice	Low-level fog for ground cover
Flash pot/box	Explosion
Flying	Aerial effects such as outer space or illusions
Fog	Ghost, magic, laser beam projection, explosion, and outer space
Hologram	Illusion, attraction, and communications
Laser	Communication, entertainment, focus attention, and reveal product
Pyrotechnics (indoor)	Reveal new product and finale of production
Pyrotechnics (outdoor)	Capture attention and finale of sport or other event
Wind machine	Blowing, billowing trees, flags, and other fabric

for a significant event. In some instances, prizes may be placed in the balloons or slips of paper announcing gifts.

Confetti Cannon

Technology

Air-propelled cannons range from small to huge and can propel large pieces of confetti over 100 feet.

Usage

A fitting conclusion to an important meeting or conference or an effective way to attract attention through the introduction of a new product.

Dry Ice

Technology

A fifty-gallon drum combined with dry ice, heat, and a blower will easily fog a large stage floor surface. This substance, unlike chemical fog, clings to the stage surface and creates the illusion of ground cover.

W A R   S T O R Y

The young balloon artist rushed to my side and shouted, "We are having a major technical malfunction." Translation: The balloons are stuck and will not fall on cue. Turning to the balloon artist I whispered, "Fix it." He scurried away to try to remedy the situation and I instructed my staff to find every broom in the building. Although the staff looked at me in disbelief, they fetched the brooms and I then instructed them to distribute one broom to each table of guests. With very little coaching one person from each table began swatting at the balloon bags and ultimately released all of the balloons. Although this event did not turn out the way we had planned the guests were very pleased and will long remember the night they helped the balloons drop.

Lesson Learned

Hire only experienced special effects technicians who have a proven track record with events similar in size, scope, and style to the one you are planning.

Usage

A remote moat, graveyard, or lagoon at a theme party as well as a snowy winter wonderland can be easily established with this effect.

Flash Pot

Technology

A small amount of gun powder and flash paper combined with an electric charge creates a flash followed by a small amount of smoke.

Usage

The appearance of a genie, ghost, or other magical moment is appropriate for this startling effect.

Flying

Technology

Individuals, props, or both can appear to float effortlessly over the stage and sometimes over the heads of the audience. The most established purveyor of this art form is the firm Flying by Foy based in Las Vegas, Nevada.

Usage

Appropriate for a space age illusion or theme incorporating magic. May be used to levitate individuals or new props being introduced to the audience.

Fog

Technology

Usually dispensed from a small box using a chemical ingredient and heat. Chemical fog rises and may set off smoke sensors. It is available in a variety of scents or in an odorless form.

Usage

From creating an eerie graveyard scene at a theme party to establishing a cone shape for a laser beam to highlight in producing a "beam me up Scotty" effect, fog has become an indispensable part of many events.

Hologram

Technology

A film image and light combine to create a 3D image.

Usage

May be used to depict a product or spokesperson in a trade show booth or onstage.

INDOOR PYROTECHNICS

Technology

Small devices that emit little smoke and create sparks, flame, or other indoor effects.

Usage

Over an ice rink at the conclusion of an opening ceremony a shower of sparks falls from the ceiling or on the front of a stage, or flames appear to leap from the footlights.

LASER

Technology

A high-powered light source cooled by either water or air. The water-cooled laser projects beams many hundreds of feet.

Usage

From creating a vertical laser cone to introduce the chief executive officer in a "beam me down Scotty" effect to creating a waving canopy over the heads of the audience, lasers can dynamically animate the activities of an event. Using graphics, the laser beams can create logos and animation to tell a story or set the tone for an event.

OUTDOOR PYROTECHNICS

Technology

Large shells ranging in size from three to twelve inches propel up into the night sky and burst creating patterns and other colorful effects.

Usage

Many professional sport events conclude with an aerial fireworks display and some organizations use fireworks as a way of celebrating the culmination of a historic meeting or holiday, such as Independence Day in the United States.

PYROTECHNIC SET PIECE

Technology

A large sign that is illuminated with pyrotechnics. Sometimes it includes moveable pieces that spin, rotate, rise, and fall.

Usage

To announce a new idea or product, celebrate a historic occasion or holiday. Sometimes used in combination with indoor or outdoor pyrotechnics.

WIND MACHINE

Technology

A large high-powered fan mounted on a secure floor base.

Usage

Use to blow curtains, flags, or other scenery or costumes to create the illusion of movement by wind.

COST SAVINGS

When using special effects there are usually ancillary costs such as site preparation and cleanup as well as additional security. Make certain you factor in all costs before you blast the confetti cannon and later realize that a clean-up fee of several hundred dollars must be paid to the janitorial staff.

Some lighting and production companies will include special effects devices in the total bid for equipment. Carefully consult with lighting and production vendors to determine what equipment they own and then include these items in your specifications.

Finally, only use special effects if they support the overall goals and objectives of the event. Special effects may be the first areas of a budget that can be trimmed unless the added value is justified.

Video

Due to the growth of television and the rapid acquisition of video camera recorders (VCRs) video has become an integral part of many if not most live events. Video is used to enhance the live image of the speaker or performer so that the persons seated in the far reaches of the venue may see his or her facial reactions. Video is also used to document the entire event for future use, such as for historical or marketing purposes, or both.

The expansion of this field has placed the video camera in the hands of large numbers of the public and as a result, guests are more sophisticated with regards to video production. Because of supply and demand, even editing equipment is now available to consumers allowing them to perform simple editing functions for home video features.

Figure 8-6 identifies the most common uses for video at an event and the types of equipment required for these purposes.

FIGURE 8-6
Video Uses and Typical Equipment

Usage	Equipment
Audience interaction event	Multiple cameras and video switcher
Complex special effects editing	On-line editing equipment
Corporate communications	Animated character
Image magnification	VHS or four-chip camera and projector
Multi-image communications	Video wall system
Simple cuts only editing	Off-line editing equipment
Video roll	Video player and projector

CHARACTER GENERATOR (CG)

Technology

An electronic device used to create titles and project text on the video image.

Usage

May be used to identify speakers, project messages to the audience, or create other communications through video production.

OFF-LINE EDITING

Technology

Primarily designed for simple edits such as cuts only. During off-line editing the video product is further refined prior to the more expensive on-line editing session.

Usage

Simple video products may be prepared during the off-line session or may be used to prepare the product for the on-line session.

ON-LINE EDITING

Technology

Sophisticated, complex special effects may be achieved using this equipment.

Usage

During on-line editing, complex digital effects are included to produce exciting transitions, sweeten the music, and add other technical elements to complete the production.

SWITCHER

Technology

Enables the video operator to electronically switch between two or more cameras and also cue prerecorded video products.

Usage

Complex event production that requires two or more cameras and use of prerecorded video products must be programmed through a switching system.

VIDEO ANIMATION

Technology

An operator uses a mechanical device similar to a finger puppet and creates a dancing, talking electronic figure video projected on a screen.

Usage

To establish a new image or character, interact with the main presenter at the meeting, improve corporate communications, or improve other communications. When Xerox introduced its new logo—the digitized X—I retained Interactive Personalities of Minneapolis, Minnesota, to create the animated character we named Chip. He immediately brought the new symbol to life for the guests and even endeared himself to them as they literally became friends during this conference.

VIDEO CAMERA

Technology

Consumer as well as broadcast-quality cameras are available for rental from most audiovisual production firms. The broadcast camera is a four-chip model that may record on Beta videotape, the highest quality available for editing. However, for simple events where editing will not be required, consumer equipment may be acceptable.

Usage

Either live coverage for video magnification or live and recorded for future usage, the video camera is the primary tool in video production. One drawback with regard to video production at live events is the presence of the video camera, tripod, and sometimes platform to elevate this equipment. This complex setup may interfere with the audience's view of the event's live performance. Bob Johnson of Corporate Video Communications has overcome this challenge with the invention of robotic cameras designed for event production. In the "Video Bob™" system each four-chip camera is placed on a thin metal rod and is operated electronically by one operator. This saves both labor and space. One experienced operator may be able to control up to eight different cameras simultaneously.

VIDEO PLAYER/RECORDER

Technology

Either $\frac{1}{2}$" VHS, $\frac{3}{4}$", or Beta tape may be played or recorded on this machine. Beta $\frac{3}{4}$" allow for sophisticated editing techniques.

Usage

This equipment is used to either record the event activities or play back prerecorded video products during the live event.

VIDEO WALL SYSTEM

Technology

May include as few as four or up to ten times that many video monitors that simultaneously project a video image. A separate processor allows the video signal to produce a variety of effects including geometric images to generate visual excitement.

Usage

A high-tech solution for spreading a corporate message or introducing a new idea or product. May also be used as a background for an event stage set.

COST SAVINGS

Contact a local university or college and determine if its radio, television, or film program can provide you with equipment for preproduction or postproduction. Significant savings may be available through using these facilities.

When shooting, keep in mind that the better you plan your shots the less time may be required in postproduction. Shoot with editing firmly in mind. Some video directors shoot in a style that requires very little postproduction by carefully matching shots and maintaining continuity.

Carefully plan your postproduction schedule. The majority of time should be devoted to off-line editing as this is at a lower cost. The more you can accomplish in off-line editing the greater overall savings.

Check with the postproduction editing facility to find out if you can use off-peak times to complete your project. Avoiding normal business hours may result in significant savings.

Retain an experienced crew that can handle multiple functions. For example, the shooter or camera person may also be able to coordinate the audio feed and this will eliminate additional labor costs.

Video crews can range from $750 to over $1,500 per day depending on the type and quantity of equipment and labor required. Always solicit bids for these services and ask to see a demonstration reel of the crews' work.

Use robotic cameras for simple meeting and conference event production and include an option (with the permission of the speakers and entertainers) to sell tapes to the attendees. By selling the tapes you may not only recover all video production costs but also generate additional net proceeds for your sponsoring organization.

Synergy

Carefully integrate audiovisual, lighting, sound, special effects, and video to ensure a smooth and seamless event. Avoid overproducing your event to merely demonstrate the latest high-tech wonders. Most production personnel will state that their work is designed to support and enhance, and never to dominate. In fact, these technologies should be so well incorporated into your event planning and coordination that they are invisible to your guests' eyes. However, as a result of their combined power, a positive enduring effect should result.

THE MAIN EVENT

1. Identify the goals and objectives of the event and use audiovisual, lighting, sound, special effects, and video production to accomplish these aims.

2. Match the level of production to the size and type of event.

3. Always solicit competitive bids and involve your production vendors in the planning and coordination process for your event.

4. Save costs by finding multiple uses for the same equipment during a twenty-four-hour period or sharing costs with other organizations holding their event in the same venue.

5. Eliminate production elements that do not support the goals and objectives of your event. Do not use equipment merely to demonstrate its usage, instead, carefully select each technology to accomplish the specific goals and objectives identified during the needs assessment and feasibility study (research and design process).

NEXT ON THE AGENDA

Deciding whether or not to use music and entertainment at your event can be the difference between captivating your audience and confusing them. From Dixieland bands to interactive media, Chapter 9 discusses major issues behind event entertainment.

Music and Entertainment

In earliest recorded history music and entertainment has been intrinsically linked to feasting. From King David of biblical days to today's modern banquets, balls, and other celebrations music and entertainment continues to play an important role in Event Management.

Although music historically is a form of entertainment for the purposes of this text we will use separate definitions to clearly differentiate between the specific and the general. Music is either the live or recorded medium used to establish and sustain the mood, animate the event (dancing), or provide transitions from one moment to the next.

Entertainment reflects those resources that provide either passive or active opportunities for your guests to become further connected to the goals and objectives of the event. Both music and entertainment may be used to attract, capture, and transform your guest.

The late Howard Lanin of Philadelphia, in addition to his role as a musical contractor, also functioned as one of the early event managers. During the early part of the twentieth century in the United States band leaders and music contractors such as Lanin were often called upon by their clients to provide additional services including the coordination of the entire event. Two essentials for many U.S. events were music and food and therefore, either the music contractor or the caterer and sometimes both provided Event Management services.

Entertainment producer Jack Morton, a legend in the Event Management field, is credited by his peers for transforming this casual relationship into a formal business opportunity. Morton, who got his start booking bands while still a student at The George Washington University in Washington, DC, pioneered in the development of music and entertainment for association and corporate meetings and conventions. Like Walt Disney, Mr. Morton later diversified his business interests to provide communications services for museums, sport events, and other organizations that required innovative approaches to convey their messages.

Today, largely due to the development of jet air travel in the 1950s, which allowed shorter stays, along with the rapid ascension of television as the primary communications medium, entertainment is briefer, louder, and too often filled with spectacle in place of pure talent. Morton once said that he defined great talent as "that which endures." Indeed, most critics and audience members would be hard pressed to identify even as few as five postmodern musicians or entertainers whose talent will be remembered and celebrated one century from now. This means that the task of event managers is increasingly difficult in this challenging environment.

The event manager must know how to assess the need for music and entertainment, identify the proper resources, coordinate these resources, and evaluate the impact of these efforts.

WAR STORY

Sometimes the best music is no music. One of the first events we produced was entitled National Mime Week. This event included a parade on Pennsylvania Avenue and featured the world famous Cardoza High School Marching Band. Over one hundred musicians marched down the avenue of the presidents and pantomimed playing their instruments. Hundreds of spectators scratched their heads wondering what was going on as the parade made its way toward the Corcoran Gallery of Art. Joan Mondale, wife of then Vice-president Walter Mondale, and an artist herself, welcomed the mimes and musicians and for the first time the band played "The Star-Spangled Banner." The combination of a mime parade followed by a live rendition of our national anthem brought goose bumps to all assembled.

Lesson Learned
Carefully consider how the music or entertainment will most benefit the event. Sometimes less is more.

The Need for Music and Entertainment

Although most events benefit from music and entertainment, not every event needs to incur this expense. The event manager must carefully assess the needs of his or her guests and determine whether or not music and entertainment is appropriate for each individual event. For example, the ground breaking of a historic battlefield site may require speeches, but it would be inappropriate to engage a Dixieland jazz band. Too often music and entertainment is engaged based upon the personal tastes and desires of the organizers with little regard for the appropriateness of the event or the interests of guests. To avoid making this mistake use the checklist in Figure 9-1 to conduct some preliminary research.

Identifying the Resources

Once you have conducted the research to identify the need, the next step is to identify the most appropriate and cost-effective resources for your event. Fortunately, in the postmodern entertainment era there have never been more choices.

In most communities literally dozens of resources are available for music and live entertainment. Figure 9-2 provides a brief list of many of the resources available for both professional and amateur music and entertainment.

Matching the best music and entertainment resource to the needs, wants, and desires as well as the goals and objectives of your event is a complex task. The first step is to comprehend the various musical and entertainment options that are available (see Figure 9-2). Although descriptions of music and entertainment are largely comprised of industry jargon and may vary according to location, the terms are considered standard

---

FIGURE 9-1
Determining the Need for Music and Entertainment

1. Carefully research the history of the event to determine if music and/or entertainment was used in the past.

2. Interview the event stakeholders through a formal focus group or informally to ascertain their individual and collective tastes.

3. Determine how music and/or entertainment will be used to further the goals of the event.

4. Analyze the event budget to determine available resources for music and/or entertainment.

5. Review the time frame for planning and production to determine if sufficient time is available for incorporating these elements into the event.

FIGURE 9-2
Thirty-Five Resources for Music and Entertainment

1. *Academy Directory,* a listing of television and film stars (see Appendix)

2. Actor's Equity Association, the union of professional stage actors and actresses

3. Agents who represent a variety of acts

4. American Federation of Musicians

5. American Federation of Television and Radio Artists, the union of television and radio artists

6. American Guild of Variety Artists, the union of live entertainment artists such as circus performers

7. Amusement parks and permanent attractions such as zoos

8. Arts advocacy societies and commissions

9. Bars, nightclubs, restaurants, and taverns

10. *Cavalcade of Acts and Attractions,* directory of live entertainment (see Appendix)

11. Churches

12. *Circus Report,* a magazine for circus enthusiasts

13. Clubs including fraternal organizations

14. Dance clubs, groups, and dance advocacy organizations

15. Educational institutions including public, private, primary, middle, and secondary schools as well as colleges and universities

16. *Event World,* the official magazine of the International Special Events Society

17. Fraternal organizations such as Shriners

18. Historical reenactment organizations

---

and customary in these fields. See Figure 9-3 for a list of music and entertainment terms. For further definitions, please refer to *The Official Dictionary of Event Management* (Van Nostrand Reinhold).

Music for Mood, Atmosphere, Animation, and Transitions

Music, according to veteran band leader Gene Donati of Washington, DC, is used to create the proper mood, sustain the atmosphere, and most importantly "animate" the room. According to Donati, "The music should begin before the doors open to draw

---

FIGURE 9-2

Thirty-Five Resources for Music and Entertainment *(continued)*

19. Institutions such as museums that may provide lecturers

20. Instrumental music organizations

21. Musical contractors

22. Native American organizations

23. Newspaper critics familiar with local arts organizations

24. Parks and recreation organizations that offer dance, music, and other arts programs

25. Producers of radio, television, or live entertainment programs

26. Radio disc jockeys familiar with local bands and who may provide DJ services

27. Religious organizations other than churches and synagogues

28. Schools, colleges, and university music and theater departments.

29. Screen Actors Guild, the union of film actors and actresses

30. Shopping centers that feature live music and entertainment

31. Synagogues

32. *Special Events Magazine* (see Appendix)

33. Theatrical organizations from professional to community or amateur groups

34. Travel agents familiar with local entertainment resources

35. Very Special Arts, an organization representing disabled people who are artists

36. Zoological parks

---

people into the room. Up-tempo songs should be used to energize this segment of the party." Donati and his colleagues not only conduct the musicians but in fact conduct the guests using music to animate their actions.

Alice Conway, a musician and instructor of Event Coordination at The George Washington University, recommends that event managers first try to identify the proper atmosphere their clients are trying to create and sustain. To do this she asks clients to close their eyes and describe what they envision their guests doing as they listen to the music. As clients describe the guests listening, dancing, applauding, and performing other activities Conway takes careful notes and then creates a sequence of music and entertainment to accomplish these goals.

Music may be used as a transition to create punctuation marks in the order of a program. One of the best examples is the awards event. Using music associated with the

FIGURE 9-3
Music and Entertainment Terms

Act: A self-contained, rehearsed performance of one or more persons.

Agent: An individual who represents various acts or artists and receives a commission from the buyer for coordinating the booking.

Amateur: A musician or entertainer who does not charge for their services usually due to lack of professional experience.

Arrangements: Musical compositions arranged for musicians.

Band: A group of musicians who perform contemporary music as in rock 'n' roll, jazz, or big band.

Booking: A firm commitment by a buyer of entertainment to hire an act or artist for a specific engagement.

Combo: A musical ensemble featuring combined instruments (usually piano, base, and drums).

Commission: The percentage received by the agent when booking an act or artist.

Conductor: An individual responsible for directing/conducting the rehearsal and performance by musicians.

Contractor: An individual or organization that contracts musicians and other entertainers. This person handles all of the agreements, payroll, taxes, and other employment tasks.

Cover song: A tune popularized by another artist performed by a different artist or group.

Doubler: A musician who plays two or more instruments during a performance.

Downbeat: The cue given by the conductor to the musicians to begin playing.

Drum roll: A rolling percussive sound used for announcements and to create a suspenseful atmosphere.

Drum riser: A small platform used to elevate the drummer above the other musicians.

Duo: An act with two persons. Also known as a double.

Fanfare: A musical interlude used to signal announcements of awards or introductions. Usually includes horns but not always.

Fife and drum corp: A small or larger musical ensemble featuring fifes and drums playing music from the eighteenth century.

Horn section: A group of musicians that specializes in wind instruments and is usually part of a larger ensemble.

Leader: An individual who organizes and conducts a musical or entertainment group.

Manager: An individual who provides management services to an artist, act, or several artists and acts. The manager normally handles all logistics including travel and negotiates on behalf of the artist or act. The manager is paid by the act or artist from fees that are earned through performing.

Marching band: A musical ensemble usually comprised of percussion, horns, woodwinds, and other instruments that play and march simultaneously.

Minimum: The minimum number of hours musicians must be paid.

Octet: A musical ensemble comprised of eight musicians.

Overture: The music performed before the actors or entertainers enter the stage. Also known as pre-show music.

Professional: A musician or entertainer paid for their services.

Quartet: A musical ensemble comprised of four persons.

Quintet: A musical ensemble comprised of five persons.

Road manager: The individual who travels with an act or artist and handles all logistical arrangements.

Sextet: A musical ensemble comprised of six persons.

Sideman/men: Musicians within a musical ensemble who accompany an artist.

Single: An act with one person.

Soloist: A single performer.

Stage manager: An individual who coordinates the technical elements for the act or artist, cues the performer, and provides other services to support the performance.

Stand: The music stand used to hold sheet music.

Top Forty: The top forty musical compositions/recordings selected by *Billboard* magazine. A top forty band is able to perform these selections.

Trio: A musical ensemble comprised of three persons.

Walk-in, walk-out music: Live or recorded music played at the start and end of an event as guests enter or leave the venue.

Walk music: Live or recorded music played as award presenters, speakers, and recipients enter or exit the stage area.

Windjammers: The slang name for circus musicians (mostly horn players).

presenters or award recipients helps the audience remain interested and focused on the program. Figure 9-4 lists typical tunes for awards programs and the appropriate way to implement them.

Use awards music to introduce the presenters by sequencing the music in the following manner. First cue the drummer to perform a drum roll. Next, have your off-stage announcer introduce the presenter using the following text:

"Ladies and gentlemen, please welcome the president of XYZ corporation, from New Orleans, Louisiana, Ms. Jane Smith!"

As the presenter's name is announced the remainder of the musicians should play a lively Dixieland jazz melody and conclude promptly when Ms. Smith reaches the microphone. This will help accelerate the action for the event and keep things running on time.

As Ms. Smith introduces the award recipient the musicians should begin to play immediately as the name is called. Because musicians need a warning before they begin to play I recommend you give the cue to play as the first name is announced so that as the surname is announced the tune has begun. Here is an example:

Ms. Smith: And now welcome our award winner, from New York City, Mr. (cue conductor) John Doe (music begins).

The music should continue until Mr. Doe reaches Ms. Smith and then conclude with a brief fanfare as the award is presented. A generic walk-off melody may be played as Mr. Doe exits the stage.

Properly sequenced and timed, music can ensure that your event runs on time. Even Ole Blue Eyes himself, Frank Sinatra, learned at the Grammy Awards that unless you sustain the interest of the audience, the music will abruptly change the mood, ending one segment and cueing another.

FIGURE 9-4
Awards Event Musical Selections

Presenter/Recipient	Musical Selection
Individual from California	"California Here I Come"
Individual from New York City	"New York, New York"
Sports-related award	Olympic Games theme
Championship award	Main theme from "Chariots of Fire"
Chapter of the year	Theme from "Rocky"
Person of the year	"Let a Winner Lead the Way"
Volunteer of the year	"Together" from "Gypsy"
Leadership award	"The Washington Post March"

```
            W A R   S T O R Y

As the award recipient from Texas droned and drawled on tearfully about how
much the award meant to him I noticed that some members of the audience were
starting to get restless and others were heading for the exits. Waiting for him
to draw a breath I warned the conductor to be ready to play "The Eyes of Texas"
to cue the Texan to leave the stage. As soon as he paused I gave the cue, the band
played a brisk and loud version of the Texas state song, and the tall Texan
remarked, "I guess that's my cue to go." It was, and fortunately he took it.

    Lesson Learned
    Warn the presenters that if they hear music, that is their cue to courteously
escort the recipient offstage before they can bore the audience. Another impor-
tant lesson is to provide the conductor with a half dozen extra tunes just in case
you need them for situations as outlined above. Music can be a lifesaver.
```

MUSICAL FORMULAS FOR SUCCESS

Veteran society band leader Lester Lanin of New York City recommends that event managers carefully consider the number and type of guests that will be attending the event
prior to the selection of musical performers. Lanin finds that while at one time both
opera and classical music were commonly used for social life-cycle events, today it is
not uncommon to incorporate contemporary music.

Cantor Arnold Saltzman of Adas Israel Synagogue in Washington, DC, cautions
individuals involved in religious events to work closely with their clergy to select appropriate music that is in accordance with the traditions and customs of the religious
denomination. As one example, a bride asked Saltzman for permission to use the theme
from Star Wars as the processional music. Since the event was a secular occasion there
were no policies set by the location. However, Saltzman correctly counseled the bride and
groom that if this music was used for the processional, the guests might be distracted
by this departure from tradition and the rest of the ceremony could suffer as a result.

Lanin recommends, as shown in Figure 9-5, the following staffing levels for musicians at specific events. While a few years ago a thirty-member orchestra might have
been standard fare, in today's cost-conscious times, Lanin's formulas are more likely to
be used.

Figure 9-5
Attendance and Minimum Musicians Required
as Recommended by Lester Lanin

Number of Guests	Minimum Number of Musicians
125	5-7
250	7
500	12
750	12 plus strings if budget allows
1,000	15-20

Electronic Music

Miniaturization in lighting and sound has also found its way into the orchestra. Today many modern musicians use electronic instruments to perform the sounds of dozens of instruments. It is not unusual today to see four musicians performing music that once required a 100-member symphony orchestra. However, there are liabilities that accompany this progress.

Managing Musicians

Musicians as well as other personnel require careful management to be able to deliver an optimum performance. Musical artists require the event manager to provide the support systems that allow them to do what they do best: deliver a quality musical performance. Figure 9-6 provides the most common considerations for effectively managing musicians.

Union Requirements

Whether contracting union musicians or other entertainers affiliated with labor unions it is important that the event manager carefully study union contracts and comply with the responsibilities that apply to the event sponsor. For example, union musicians must be compensated separately if their performance is audiotaped or videotaped. Failure to provide additional compensation can result in severe penalties for the event organizer. In addition, union members must be given a certain number of breaks during each performance or paid additionally for performing continuously without the prescribed number of breaks. Therefore, it is important that the event manager work closely with his or her music contractor when engaging union musicians. Certain union locals have established trust funds that will provide some money for musicians to perform for worthwhile causes at no cost to the sponsor. Check with your local American Federation of Musicians to determine if your event may qualify for this outstanding opportunity.

WAR STORY

A major corporation required dancing for 300 guests. I turned to the band leader and asked him to give the down beat and he asked me, "Who pulled the plug?" When I inquired further, I realized that all of his instruments were electronic. Someone had literally pulled the plug and the outlet could not be located. As a result the dancers stood in silence while we invested a great deal of time searching for the missing power source. The musicians stood on stage looking lost and helpless.

Lesson Learned

Find out if the musicians are somewhat or totally reliant on electronics to be able to perform. For a small group (under 100 guests) it is possible for some musical groups to perform without amplification. However, larger events will require amplification and therefore it is critical that the sound be continuous. Refer to Chapter 8 for additional information concerning this important element.

ELECTRONIC MUSIC

During the 1970s as recording quality improved, disc jockeys became popular at many events. Indeed, in some situations electronic or recorded music is more appropriate than live music for the following reasons.

First, electronic music may be easily controlled. Unlike live music it may be faded, stopped, started, and refocused through different speakers. Second, it is usually less expensive than the engagement of live musicians. Finally, and perhaps most importantly, for those events with space restrictions, electronic music solves important logistical problems.

Today disc jockeys provide not only music but entire party production services including lights, effects such as fog, and interactive games conducted by the disc jockeys. In addition to providing music for dancing and background atmosphere, electronic music may serve other purposes as well.

In lieu of using a live orchestra, many professional entertainers and industrial productions use pre-recorded tracks to supplement their live performances. When using these systems it is critical that the event manager use redundant equipment in case of failure. In other situations, live musicians actually play along with the recorded tracks creating a combination of live and recorded sound. Still in other situations, the orches-

---

FIGURE 9-6
Effective Management of Musicians

1. Provide clear, written instructions regarding date, time, and location.

2. Communicate a profile of the guests in order that appropriate music may be selected.

3. Provide an event schedule and supply the leader of the musical group with a summary of the musical activities.

4. Arrange for parking for the musicians and notify them of the authorized locations.

5. Identify and communicate to the musicians where equipment may be loaded into the venue.

6. Select and notify the musicians of a room where their cases may be stored during the performance.

7. Provide adequate dressing or break room.

8. Carefully adhere to required breaks.

9. Arrange for and provide food and beverage service if required by contract.

10. Assign a key contact person to serve as principle liaison to the leader of the musical group.

11. Identify adequate electric power.

12. Provide ample performance space as required by contract.

13. Adhere to schedule specified by contract.

14. Warn musicians if overtime is required.

15. Assist musicians with load-out/departure and offer thanks.

---

tra will perform some music live and actually pantomime to the pre-recorded sound in other numbers.

As discussed earlier, when music is synchronized to video or film separate rights must be negotiated and obtained. Usually these rights include a clause limiting the usage to certain mediums and time periods. Ultimately someone will pay for the use of privately-owned music each time it is used. Therefore the event manager must budget for this expense.

MUSIC LICENSING

In the early 1990s, the two major music licensing firms in the United States decided to enforce their rights to collect fees from sponsors of meetings, conventions, and expositions as well as other events. Prior to this date the American Society of Composers, Authors, and Publishers (ASCAP) and its competitor Broadcast Music International (BMI) collected fees from restaurants, nightclubs, hotels, and even roller skating rinks. However, perhaps recognizing the enormous possibility for revenue from the meetings, convention, exposition, and events industry, these organizations made it clear that they planned to require sponsors of these events to pay for the use of live or recorded music they licensed.

The first organization to sign a separate agreement with ASCAP and BMI was the International Association for Exposition Management (IAEM) and soon the American Society of Association Executives (ASAE) convened a task force to study this issue. As a member of this task force I asked both organizations to assign the responsibility for payment to either the musical contractors or the professional producers of these events. Both organizations rejected this request and today there continues to be acrimony regarding who pays what to whom and why.

The official sponsor or organizer of the event is the entity responsible for obtaining a license for the use of protected music from either or both ASCAP or BMI or other rights licensing organizations. The official sponsor or organizer is the entity that bears the financial responsibility for the event. The only exception to paying these fees is events that are small gatherings of individuals who are known to you. This usually means social life-cycle events such as weddings, bar and bas mitzvahs, birthday parties, and other events attended by family and friends.

ASCAP and BMI each have separate licensing agreements that require careful consideration by event managers. Both electronic and live music is covered in these agreements. According to ASCAP, the majority of popular music is licensed through its organization. However, most event managers obtain on behalf of their sponsors, agreements with both ASCAP and BMI for obvious reasons. Among these reasons is the problem associated with the live dance band and the guest who requests a tune from the band leader only to have the band leader decline because the rights are assigned to BMI and the license is with ASCAP.

For most events, the costs associated with music licensing are minimal, and the filing of the license agreement is merely another part of the long paper trail that is a natural part of Event Management. However, in the field of expositions, especially the larger ones that attract tens of thousands of persons, the costs can quickly mount. How are these fees assessed?

Both ASCAP and BMI assess fees based upon the daily attendance at each event. The fees are therefore charged daily and are factored using separate formulas for recorded and live music. If both recorded (electronic) and live music are used the costs are higher.

To enforce these licenses both ASCAP and BMI use spotters who frequently and randomly visit event venues and investigate organizations that are unlawfully using their licensed works. The penalties for this illegal activity are substantial.

Recent court cases concerning expositions have somewhat weakened the position of ASCAP and BMI to require that sponsors of expositions assume responsibility for their individual exhibitors with regards to the use of music. However, ASAE continues to investigate the entire music licensing issue with the major concerns relating to potential monopolies by ASCAP and BMI who control the majority of all musical composition.

What music is covered? Literally any musical work licensed by ASCAP and BMI and this includes "Happy Birthday." Even classical compositions may be covered if they have recently had a new arrangement authored.

Alternatives to paying music licensing fees are limited. First, the event manager may of course elect to not use music at all. Second, the event manager may commission an original work of music and purchase the song or selections for use at their event. Third, the event manager may purchase commercial music produced by a private firm. Commercial music may be obtained from recording studios or other private organizations and usually includes some sound-a-like tunes that are appropriate for use at awards programs and other events other than those where popular tunes may be requested. Still larger organizations may negotiate individually with ASCAP, BMI, or others and seek to create a separate agreement. In some cases, licensing fees may be waived. However, this is a rare occurrence.

In order to play you must pay. Failing to do so may injure your event sponsor and your responsibility. Therefore, it is the responsibility of the event organizer to fully comprehend the requirements for music licensing and allow sufficient planning and coordination time to attend to these important details.

WAR STORY

The late Irving Berlin, composer of "God Bless America," held tightly onto the rights for many of his most lucrative songs including what many consider America's second national anthem. When our firm produced the inaugural events for President and Mrs. Bush I conceived the idea of closing the productions at the Kennedy Center with having three separate orchestras perform "God Bless America." I contacted The Irving Berlin Music Company and asked that Mr. Berlin waive the rights in order that the song be played for the President and First Lady. "Are you kidding?" the business manager responded, "That's one of our best sellers. Absolutely not." And so The Irving Berlin Music Company was paid along with the other authors, composers, and publishers whose music we used and continue to use. Many years ago Berlin assigned all royalties from "God Bless America" to the Boy Scouts of America, so the public good was ultimately served.

Lesson Learned

Allow adequate time to negotiate the rights for important events. Budget to pay music licensing fees as in the majority of cases you will be required to pay.

Entertainment Options

In Figure 9-2 a variety of resources for music and entertainment is described. However, now it is time to consider entertainment as a separate resource. Figure 9-7 provides a list of the most commonly used entertainers for live events.

INEXPENSIVE OPTIONS FOR LIVE ENTERTAINMENT

The term amateur implies one who has not yet begun to charge for his or her services. However, the term literally means "what one does for love." Every community is filled with hundreds and perhaps thousands of individuals whose avocational interests include performing. From barbershop and sweet Adeline singing groups to entire community orchestras, with a little detective work you can identify lots of entertainment at low cost.

When using amateur performers make certain that you supplement their performance with those elements that will achieve the level of sophistication required for your event. This may mean the addition of professional costuming, lighting, or other elements. In some cases you will need to assign a professional producer to further develop the amateur performer's act to fit the needs of your event.

Amateur performers will require more time, both in advance and immediately preceding as well as during the production. Therefore, although you will save significant dollars by using nonprofessional performers, you must allocate additional resources and allow more time for this opportunity.

Professional performers may be obtained directly by contacting the performer or his or her manager, through agents, or by holding auditions. When contracting professional performers, first identify all of the tasks you wish the performers to handle during your event. List these tasks and then prioritize them so that if you find you can-

---

FIGURE 9-7
This Is Event Entertainment

Acrobats	Disk jockey	Limbo dancers	Pep band
Animal acts	Dixieland band	Magicians	Puppeteers
Balloon sculptors	Escape artists	Marching band	Robots
Ballroom dancers	Folk dancers	Marionettes	Singers
Bands	Fortune tellers	Mentalists	Spaceship
Cancan dancers	Horseshoes	Mimes	Sport games
Caricaturists	Humorists	Modern dancers	Square dancers
Carnival games	Hypnotists	Oompah band	Stilt walkers
Carnival rides	Illusionist	Opera singers	Tap dancers
Clowns	Japanese Koto musicians	Organ grinders	Tight wire walkers
Contortionists	Jazz band	Organists	Trapeze artists
Dancers	Jugglers	Palm readers	Ventriloquists

not afford everything you want you will be able to quickly identify the most important elements that must be preserved.

One way to save lots of money when using professional performers is to *block book* the act or artists with other organizations. Block booking entails contacting other organizations in your city or area that may also be able to use the services of the act or artists. By offering performers a series of engagements closely connected by time and location you may be able to save as much as 50 percent of the cost.

Another way to save is to work with acts that are routed annually through your area. Major music and entertainment groups that tour frequently may be able to add your date to their tour at nominal expense. To identify the routing for these groups, track them through publications such as *Variety, Billboard, Amusements Business,* and *Performance Magazine.*

Oftentimes performers will participate in additional events for the same basic fee. Therefore, determine well in advance what other activities such as book signings, media conferences, and hospitality events you want the performer to participate in and incorporate these into the agreement.

Travel expenses can often be a significant part of an act's cost, especially for those that require a large retinue of performers. To save money on travel, first determine if the act will travel coach versus first class. Next, contact the major airlines and seek sponsorships. Finally, although performers like to have flexibility, arrange the travel as far in advance as possible to take advantage of lower fares.

Whether contracting amateur or professional entertainers, the event manager is ultimately responsible for the final performance. To ensure the satisfaction of your client and guests, invite the client to attend the sound check or lighting rehearsal so that he or she can meet the performer in advance of the event. Furthermore, make certain that the performer mentions the name of the sponsoring organization during his or her act. To facilitate this, I write this information in large block letters on an index card and hand it to the performer during rehearsal. A second copy is given to the performer before he or she walks on stage for the final performance, just in case the first copy was misplaced or lost.

Carefully sourcing, contracting, and managing live entertainment will further ensure the financial and artistic success of your event. When you make the decision to include live entertainment as one of the important elements for your event you have assumed a considerable and complex responsibility. Make certain you devote the proper time and resources to effectively fulfill this important responsibility.

CELEBRITIES AND SPEAKERS

The professional speaker is a relatively new phenomenon. Only a few decades ago a speaker was a scholar, clergyman, or entertainer who received an honorarium. Today, the National Speakers Association in Tempe, Arizona, reports that its association represents over 3,000 individuals who earn some or all of their living by giving speeches, conducting seminars, or presenting workshops. Their topics may range from anthropology to zero-population growth. However, as members of this association they are committed to improving their performance on the public platform.

Previously, the professional speaker was an accomplished individual whose credits from another field produced demand for public appearances and speeches. Consequently individuals such as film and television stars, politicians, and leading religious figures delivered speeches to their devotees.

According to most futurists continuing education will be the major growth industry of the new millennium. As a result, there is greater demand than ever before for these sales trainers, motivators, and other experts in both content and performance.

When contracting a professional speaker for your event, first identify the needs, wants, and desires of your audience. Next, identify how you will use the speaker from a marketing perspective. Will the speaker's name or subject matter help increase attendance? Finally, and perhaps most importantly, determine what you expect to happen as a result of the speaker's appearance. The outcome of the event is paramount to every other decision.

Matching the speaker type to the outcome is the most important task facing the event manager who has decided to use a professional speaker. Although speaking fees may range from a few hundred dollars to tens of thousands of dollars the most important consideration is what value will be derived from this investment. For example, if the sales trainer's fee is $10,000 and there is the potential of generating $100,000 in sales as a result of his or her appearance the outcome is well worth the investment.

Figure 9-8 lists the most popular types of speakers and the audience locations that may benefit from their content.

FIGURE 9-8
Speakers and Their Audiences

The Speakers	Plenary or General Session	Luncheon	Spouse or Partner Program	Evening Banquet
Authors	X	X	X	X
Celebrities	X			
Futurists	X			X
News media	X	X		X
Humorists		X	X	X
Hypnotists				X
Magicians		X		X
Motivational	X	X	X	X
Psychologists	X	X	X	
Sales trainers	X	X		
Seminar leaders		X	X	
Workshop leaders		X	X	

In addition to professional speakers most organizations can provide you with outstanding lay speakers whose industry expertise qualifies them to speak to your audience. However, it is important to consider that the failure rate for lay speakers is extremely high. Therefore, plan to provide them with coaching or support equal to their stature on the program. For example, if the lay speaker is your plenary keynoter you may wish to provide a speech coach to assist the speaker with his or her talk. However, if the speaker is presenting a workshop it may be sufficient to work with him or her via telephone to fine tune his or her content and presentation techniques.

All speakers require an investment of time and time is money. To maximize your investment communicate clearly and often to the speakers what you want them to accomplish. Determine if they can perform other functions at your event (such as serving as emcee for the banquet) and perhaps author an article in advance for your newsletter or magazine. Finally, ask if there is a discount for multiple engagements in one day or week. You may be able to save substantial dollars by block booking your speaker as you would an entertainer.

Finding the appropriate speaker involves finding the right resources, auditioning the speaker either in person or using videotape, and then confirming your assumption by speaking directly with the speaker. Figure 9-9 provides you with a list of resources for locating the appropriate speaker for your event.

Negotiating with Celebrities and Speakers

Most personal appearances require some degree of negotiation prior to signing the contract. The success of the negotiation will ultimately depend on both parties' desire to complete the deal. The greater the desire from both parties the more quickly the deal will come to fruition.

Remember that you are in search of a win-win-win outcome. In this scenario the guest, the celebrity or speaker, and the event manager win because of hard work and persistence. Do your homework to determine the history of fees for celebrities or speakers. Also find out what other income they have generated from the sale of books, tapes, and other products. Next, explain to the celebrity, speaker, or their representative your

---

FIGURE 9-9
Finding the Right Speaker

Agents and bureaus that represent professional speakers
Churches
Colleges and universities
Corporate speakers bureaus
Industry speakers
National Speakers Association "Who's Who in Professional Speaking" (see Appendix)
Synagogues
Volunteer speakers bureaus

desire to book them. Describe in detail the role the celebrity or speaker will play at your event. Explain the outcome you desire from their involvement. Then, and only then, ask them to quote a fee. Tell them you would like to have a few days to consider this fee and then thank them for their time. At this point two things may happen. First, the celebrity or speaker or their representative may call you back and offer a better deal, or they may accept another engagement.

To prevent the latter you can ask the individual to put a tentative hold on this date for a specified period of time. A tentative hold implies that the individual will contact you prior to accepting another engagement on the same date as your engagement. If another client calls the celebrity or speaker he or she will tell the other client that he or she is tentatively holding the date for you and then will check with you first before accepting the other engagement.

After a few days call the speaker, celebrity, or their representative back and ask him or her to reserve a time to discuss the engagement with you when he or she will not be interrupted. During the discussion/negotiation offer other incentives in lieu of the full fee. For example, if you are providing video magnification, you could offer to provide the speaker with a professional video of his or her speech (estimated value of $3,000) or you could allow the speaker to sell books, tapes, and other products in advance, during, and after the engagement. Another valuable concession is to offer the speaker your mailing list or offer to promote his or her services to your guests. After determining the value of these concessions ask the speaker to work with you on the fee so that you may complete the contract. Once you make your request ask for his or her reaction. Tell the speaker to take his or her time to think about your offer but set up a time frame to complete the agreement. When the individual calls you back within the specified period of time, ask for his or her answer. Now you have the first news. It may not be the best news but it is sufficient for you to provide a counteroffer. Make certain you are prepared to offer a counteroffer such as shifting the date, shortening the responsibilities, or increasing the fee. Using these techniques, step by step, you and your negotiating partner will move closer to closure.

If for any reason you fail to reach closure, always thank your negotiating partners for their time and interest and tell them you will recommend their services to others but you are not able at this time to work with them. Don't be surprised if the other party calls you in a few days with a very attractive offer to use their services.

Contracting with Celebrities and Speakers

A letter of agreement, contract, or contract with rider must be prepared and/or executed by the event manager to engage the celebrity or speaker. In some cases, the celebrity or speaker will provide his or her own contract and in others the event manager will be responsible for drafting the agreement.

The rider is the attachment on the contract that spells out the special conditions under which the celebrity or speaker will perform. The rider may specify lighting, sound, transportation, food, beverage, and other conditions. To make certain you are only pro-

WAR STORY

The speaker entered the meeting room and delivered his entire speech. During his program he noticed that occasionally he received puzzled looks from his audience members. At the conclusion of his speech the audience applauded politely and then began to exit the meeting room. One person stayed behind and asked the speaker why there had been a change in the program and speaker. "What do you mean?" asked the speaker. The audience member explained that the topic and speaker that was advertised was different than that which the speaker delivered. Horrified, the speaker ran to the door of the meeting room and studied the sign stating that it was indeed a different topic and speaker. He then asked the audience member for the name of the organization and learned it was different from the one who contracted him. Then he asked the name of the hotel and confirmed it was the right franchise. Finally, he said, "This is Kansas City, isn't it"? "Yes," said the audience member, "Kansas City, Missouri." The speaker then gasped in horror as he had just delivered his *Kansas* speech in the hotel franchise located in Missouri.

Lesson Learned

Allow sufficient time to brief, coordinate, and monitor the activities of your speakers. Due to multiple engagements speakers can become confused. Event Managers are responsible for their speakers' appearances and must make the best effort to ensure they deliver quality speeches to the right audiences every time.

viding necessary items in the rider, contact previous clients and find out what they provided. In some instances, the rider may be used to incorporate everything including the kitchen sink. You cannot allow the celebrity or entertainers to use the rider as a tool to abuse your limited resources.

TRENDS IN MUSIC AND ENTERTAINMENT

The music and entertainment field has undergone tremendous change during the past several decades since Howard Lanin and Jack Morton first organized their orchestras. However, the changes in the last decade of the twentieth century have far surpassed all of the previous changes.

During this decade many musicians have been replaced by electronic instruments.

WAR STORY

The sudden ringing of the telephone awakened me from a sound sleep at 1 A.M. Sleepily I asked the caller, "What do you want?" The caller, a popular television star scheduled to appear in the major parade later that morning, announced, "I need butane for my hair rollers."

I groggily asked her to repeat the request and not being familiar with the art and science of hair rolling, I remained confused. However, the rider in her contract stated the following: "The producer will make every best effort to provide the equipment required by the celebrity to ensure a professional performance." I then decided that butane for her hair rollers must qualify. I quickly dressed, and three hours later had found a twenty-four hour grocery store, delivered the butane, and returned to bed to enjoy what would be two hours of sleep before the parade.

Lesson Learned

Make certain the rider is precise and specific with regard to what you will provide. List the times of your availability, the types of accommodation, and the menu items for food service if the celebrity or speaker is concerned about his or her meals. Do not leave anything to chance or you may find yourself chasing butane at 1 A.M.

The electronic synthesizer, the musical instrument digital interface (MIDI), and the development of additional computer software for composing have revolutionized the music field. Entertainment too has experienced great change. Perhaps the most significant change is the incorporation of technology such as video and computers within the context of a live performance. This blend of live and electronic media is known as interactive media.

Interactive Media

The interactivity inherent in this media is supplied by on-line users who provide both proactive and reactive techniques for event purposes. For example, a general session at an association meeting may require a vote be taken by the hundreds of delegates to settle an important issue. Instead of requiring a manual show of hands, a large screen flashes the command "Vote Now" and each delegate presses green for yes, red for no, or yellow for abstain. Their votes are electronically recorded, tallied, and in seconds the results are shown both numerically and graphically on the screen.

Another example of interactive media involves live performers interacting with electronic media. This engagement may be live action combined with pretape. In one such occasion I produced a film of a car racing down a track and suddenly the car came to a screeching halt. The film was shown using rear production on the back of a screen. The screen had a small door cut into the exact location where the driver would later emerge. When the car stopped the door opened and the president of the corporation walked right through the screen. This is but one of many examples of live and electronic media interacting with one another.

Perhaps in Event Management's education field, the potential for interactive media is the greatest. Using technologies such as CD-ROM, modems, and powerful personal computers tomorrow's event may look something like this. First, the guest enters the venue and is greeted by a robotic registrar who requests that the guest insert his or her credit card in the "Welcome" station. Upon reading the card the machine welcomes the guest to the meeting and issues a smart card that contains all of the critical information about the guest, including medical, to ensure a safe and productive visit. The same card may be used to gain access to his or her sleeping room.

Next, the guest reports to his or her first meeting and uses his or her smart card to receive a complimentary computer disk from the "Communications Center," a multistation machine that provides workspaces for telecommuting with the home office. The computer disk will be used to record the lecture to be delivered by the keynote speaker.

Finally, the guest is seated in an ergonomically correct chair, fastens his or her seat belt, and "experiences" the opening ceremony. His or her experience includes not only a visual and auditory presentation, but also such olfactory experiences as smell, taste, and touch. The visual images are delivered three-dimensionally as the guest wears glasses provided by a commercial sponsor. His or her chair moves hydraulically, controlled by dozens of levers and pumps as the visual images unfold on the ten-foot, high-definition screen. The audio portion of the program is enhanced with over 100 miniature speakers positioned throughout the venue to create a total surround-sound effect. At the conclusion of the opening ceremony the guest is invited to vote using his or her smart card to gain access to the ballot box. He or she will vote to select the topics the electronic speaker will address. Instead of merely receiving what the motivation speaker delivers, the guest will become an interactive learner selecting those topics that are most useful at this time. Once the selection has been made, the prerecorded speaker will instantly process the choices and provide state-of-the-industry knowledge that the guest most requires.

Have no fear. All of this new technology will not decrease the demand for in-person events. Instead, it will create even greater demand as individuals meet online and seek other opportunities and venues within which to interact in person. For example, asynchronous discussion groups such as one offered by The George Washington University Event Management Distance Learning Program encourage electronic discussants to meet in person for further inquiry. Individuals who participate in list servers or other bulletin board type communications technologies will discover new organizations and new groups where they want to affiliate in person to improve their skills or simply enhance their lives. These new technologies will serve as the catalyst for bigger and better events.

Virtual Reality

Perhaps one of the most startling and certainly most effective interactive media innovations is virtual reality. Since the early 1990s it has been used for entertainment and education as well as sales. As an entertainment device, it can be used to engage the guest in navigating through a virtual game. Wearing a large helmet the guest sees a virtual environment. Using movements from his or her hand, the guest can run, jump, and even fly through outer space. In education, virtual reality may be used to train pilots (for whom the technology was first developed) and other technicians such as surgeons to perform complicated maneuvers without risking human life. And in sales, virtual expositions are fast becoming effective methods for introducing buyers to the concept of virtual shopping.

Teleconferencing: Up-Link, Down-Link, and Fiber Optic

Increasingly, meetings and conferences as well as other event fields are being linked using both satellite and fiber optic technologies. In the case of video, the satellite technology is less expensive and more reliable. However, data transmission is more cost effective via fiber optic technology. This may change as economies of scale prevail in the telecommunications industry.

When assessing the need for a teleconferencing or data transmission component for your event, first determine what resources currently exist and then review the added value of using these technologies. If the added value provides significant advantages, then the added cost will be relative to the investment. However, some event managers succumb to these technologies as the latest bell and whistle to be used without careful thought regarding the need, the added value, and the return on the investment.

To select a firm to assist you with teleconferencing, first discuss your needs with the venue and find out what vendors they recommend. The venue is usually your best reference because the vendor they recommend has most likely transmitted or received communications successfully for a previous organization. In some instances, modern conference and congress centers have this technology in place and can purvey this service directly through their staff audiovisual or communications personnel.

Next, meet with those individuals who will provide this service or those who will submit bids. Provide them with a list of transmission dates, times, content, purpose, locations, and other pertinent data. Seek their recommendations for reducing costs and improving quality.

Finally, always put a contingency plan in place. Weather, power blackouts, and other unforeseen problems can affect your transmission or reception. Determine in advance how you will cover for an interruption in the signal. In some instances, it may be appropriate to ask the audience to adjourn and reconvene. In other cases, you may wish to have a local moderator lead a discussion and generate additional questions to be used when the teleconference continues. Regardless of what you decide, it is important to have an alternate plan or program firmly in place.

That's Edutainment!

The term "edutainment" may have been first coined during the early 1970s when a large number of corporations began to combine entertainment with education to motivate their human resources. Edutainment is simply the use of live or recorded entertainment to promote learning.

Edutainment productions may range from a group of actors that presents short skits about sales, customer service, or negotiation to an elaborate interactive multimedia program involving video, slides, teleconference, and live entertainment to motivate cus-

W A R   S T O R Y

The new cable television network was going to launch itself with three gala parties in New York City; Springfield, Missouri; and Dallas, Texas. In each city a video wall would project the first live telecast simultaneously. The feed for this telecast would come from a remote satellite truck. In Dallas, the truck was lost and later found. In New York City, winds of fifty knots interrupted the transmission and produced snow (ironically it was also snowing heavily in New York), and in Springfield, all was well. One out of three is not a good average when you only have one time to launch a network.

Lesson Learned

Prepare a backup prerecorded tape of the launch in case of interruption of the live transmission. In the case of the lost truck, know the twenty-four hour numbers of at least three remote satellite truck companies in case you need a last minute backup.

tomers to invest in a new product. When designing edutainment programs for your event, start with behavioral objectives in mind. Focus carefully on what you want to happen as a result of your edutainment activities.

Perhaps the best example of edutainment is the murder mystery phenomenon that became very popular during the mid-1980s. During this period, largely due to popular television programs such as "Murder She Wrote," murder mystery companies began popping up all over the United States as well as in other countries. In Harrogate, England, The Royal Swan Hotel (where Agatha Christie was mysteriously found after having been missing for several days) stages a popular murder mystery weekend. During the opening reception the guests witness a murder. The next morning a real coroner/medical examiner delivers the autopsy results as the "detectives" take exhaustive notes. By Sunday evening the mystery is solved and everyone goes home satisfied that they had participated in finding the murderer.

Corporations and associations in the United States as well as other organizations may use the murder mystery premise as a way of delivering important messages about sales, customer relations, membership development, ethics, and other principles. To use this medium as your message, first interview several murder mystery directors and select the one who will carefully customize his or her script to meet your goals and objectives. Next, make certain you see his or her troupe in performance before you make engagement plans. While a videotape is a convenient audition device, it is far better to see them in person and determine how they handle the important audience participation segments of their production.

Whether you use a murder mystery, a musical production, or a tightly scripted three-act play it is critical that the message be simple, repeated, and well produced. Too often event managers develop a complex message that requires too much explanation to make sense to the guests. In other instances, the message is used once and never repeated. This denies the guests the opportunity to review and have the message reinforced. Retention requires repetition. Finally, regardless of what budget is assigned to this production make certain it is produced with high-quality ingredients. The message will suffer if the packaging is not of sufficient quality.

The Event Manager as Producer

The modern event manager is both consultant and producer. He or she not only must research, design, and plan, but also must coordinate all of the event elements such as a producer does with a play, film, television show, or other theatrical presentation. While the music and entertainment will ultimately reflect the tastes of your clients and their guests, you must never allow your own taste to be compromised. Remember that your signature is part and parcel of every production. Your next opportunity to produce an event is directly tied to the one you produce today. Quality, and only quality, must prevail if you are to have the opportunity to produce future events. Therefore, see every Event Management opportunity as your personal and professional challenge to produce the very finest music and entertainment with the time and logistical and financial resources that may be allocated.

THE MAIN EVENT

1. Determine whether or not music and entertainment is appropriate for your event by developing profiles on the guests and studying the history of the event.

2. Use music to set the mood, create the atmosphere, signal a start or stop in the proceedings, underscore, captivate, and animate.

3. Electronic or recorded music may be used as a cost-savings measure; however, live music is preferable due to the overall aesthetics that it provides.

4. Music licensing is required for all events unless they are only attended by a small group of family and friends who are known to the host/sponsor.

5. Entertainers may come from professional agents or managers or through educational and community organizations.

NEXT ON THE AGENDA

The third major competency in Event Management is marketing. Event Marketing is one of the fastest growing fields in all of marketing and in the next chapter you will learn why and how you can benefit.

III

Marketing

Integrated Marketing

Advertising Age, the weekly tabloid that many in advertising consider the bible of their profession, has added a new feature to its editorial section in addition to the traditional mix of advertising, public relations, and promotions. The new section is entitled Events and Promotions. According to an editorial in *Advertising Age* the editors have decided that events are a critical component of marketing.

Traditionally marketing students have recognized that product, promotion, price, public relations, and location, or place, are critical components in the marketing process. Each of these five Ps of marketing is a catalyst for sales. Although marketing has become more sophisticated in the twentieth century, savvy event marketers recognize that marketing is ultimately is only a three-syllable word for sales.

The founder of *Parade* magazine, Red Motley, once wrote, "Nothing really happens until someone sells something." According to some marketing experts the most efficient and cost-effective way to make sales is through events. Whether you are selling a product, service, idea, or cause, an event allows you to use all of the senses to persuade the prospect to make an investment. The components of product, promotion, price, public relations, and place directly influence the desire and decision to make this investment. However, it is important to remember that a festival, fair, wedding, meeting, exposition, or other event is a legitimate product that also must be developed and sold.

Product

Successful salespeople have both expert product knowledge and effective sales skills. Expert product knowledge is essential in today's competitive environment. The expertise the salesperson demonstrates regarding the sponsorship package or other event component will differentiate this individual from the competition. More important than sales skills, demonstrated product expertise shows the client that he or she is making a purchase that has added value and helps to develop confidence as well as long-term loyalty.

Every event product combines history, quality, and value to produce a unique program. Even new events may draw from the experience or history of the organizers. This demonstration of consistent capability to produce similar events will influence prospective clients to recognize the overall quality of the event organization. Finally, every event product must convey not only perceived value, such as dollar for dollar, worth but also added value. The concept of added value is perhaps best described with the Cajun word "lagniappe." This term literally means "everything one deserves and a little bit more." The little bit more may mean providing the client with a home telephone number of the key contact person, developing a unique approach to achieving the event objectives, or perhaps simply spending additional time with the client to better understand his or her needs.

Promotion

You may have the best quality event product, but unless you have a strategic plan for promoting this product it will remain the best kept secret in the world. Even large, well-known mega-events such as the Super Bowl, Rose Parade, and Olympic Games require well-developed promotion strategies to achieve the success they require.

Figure 10-1 provides a systematic checklist to assist you with identifying and budgeting for your event promotion.

The promotion strategy you identify for your event requires a careful study of past or comparable efforts, expert guidance from individuals who have specific expertise in this field, and most importantly, setting benchmarks for specific measurement of your individual promotion activities.

There are a variety of ways to measure promotion efforts. First, you may measure

W A R   S T O R Y

The American Legion executive explained why our firm had won the contract to produce its opening ceremony. "You were the only firm that proposed having an actor descend from a thirty-foot-high rope." When I inquired further, he said, "The difference between your firm and others was that you really listened to us. You did not repeat what we had done in the past but instead took our history and then enhanced this with your creativity." Later I told my staff that if all it took was a long piece of rope we could win every client. However, in actuality, the real secret was listening, analyzing, and then using our creativity to achieve the client's goals.

Lesson Learned

Added value can be an illusive quality. Start by asking clients what hidden expectations they may have beyond the typical requirements for earning their business. Not only meet their expectations but exceed them to demonstrate added value. After the experience with the American Legion I placed a small plaque on each associate's desk. The plaque showed two large letters, EE. Exceed expectations. The term *special event* immediately conveys to the purchaser that you will deliver the extraordinary. Strive to do so by practicing EE.

FIGURE 10-1
Promotion Checklist

1. Identify all event elements that require promotion from the proposal through the final evaluation.

2. Develop strategies for allocating scarce event promotion resources with efficient methods.

3. Identify promotion partners to share costs.

4. Carefully target your promotion to those market segments that will support your event.

5. Measure and analyze your promotion efforts throughout the campaign to make corrections as required.

awareness by your target market. Anticipation of the event may be tantamount to ultimate participation. Next, you may measure actual attendance and the resulting investment. Finally, you may measure the post-event attitudes of the event promotional activity. Did the promotions you designed persuade the participants or guests to attend the event?

Promotion is the engine that drives the awareness of your event by others. Throughout event history legendary promoters such as Bill Veck, Joe Engel, and perhaps most importantly, P.T. Barnum realized that you must shamelessly promote your event product to attract the attention of the public.

Veck did this in major league baseball by hiring midgets as players. At the time of this stunt, there was no height requirements and Veck took advantage of this oversight to promote his Chicago team. Engel, a minor league baseball promoter in Chattanooga, Tennessee, staged a fake elephant hunt on the baseball diamond to generate capacity attendance for his losing team. And of course P.T. Barnum continually amused the public with his legendary promotions such as the smallest man (Tom Thumb) and the biggest mammal (Jumbo).

Most event marketers use a variety of media to promote their products. However, it is essential that event managers carefully select those media outlets that will precisely target the market segments that are appropriate for their events. Targeting promotion strategies is essential to ensure the alignment of the event's attributes with the needs, wants, and desires of potential attendees.

Price

Market research will help you determine price. Part of this market research will include conducting a competitive analysis study of other organizations offering similar event products. You may initially believe that your product is uniquely different from every other event. However, when you interview potential ticket buyers or guests you may be surprised to learn that they consider your event similar to many others. Therefore, you must carefully list all competing events and the prices being charged to help you determine the appropriate price for your event.

Typically two factors determine price. First, the event manager must determine the financial philosophy of the event. If the event is a not-for-profit venture, the organization may not be concerned with a large commercial yield from the event. Instead, the philosophical purpose of the event may be to generate overall awareness and support. However, if the event is a commercial venture, the goal is probably to generate the greatest potential net profit. Once the philosophy is clear, then the event manager will be able to determine price. The price must reflect the cost of all goods and services required to produce the event plus a margin of profit or retained earnings.

The second factor is the perceived competition from other similar events. If your event ticket costs $100 and does not offer the same *perceived value* as a similar event selling for $50, your prospective guests are more likely to select the latter event. Therefore, you must be price-competitive. Becoming price-competitive does not mean lowering your ticket price. Rather, it may require raising the perception of value (as discussed earlier) to justify the slightly higher price.

These two factors—the cost of doing business and the marketplace competition—certainly influence price. One third area that may also influence price is the general economic conditions, not only in your area, but also the region, your country, and increasingly the world. During times of recession, some events with lower ticket prices will flourish while other upscale event products may not be as successful. Keep a close eye on market economic indicators to make certain your price matches the purchasing power of your target market.

Public Relations

Advertising is what *you* say about your event whereas public relations is what *others* (or that perception) are saying about your event. Since many events require a second party endorsement or even review to encourage people to attend, public relations is significantly more valuable and effective than traditional advertising.

In the 1930s and 1940s public relations consisted primarily of press agents who worked diligently to convince the print media to devote editorial space to their clients. With the influence of leaders such as Edward Bernays the public relations effort soon became more complex and respected. Bernays recognized the psychological factors that govern a person's decision-making ability. Therefore, he advocated that public relations professionals first engage in research, including focus groups, to determine the values, attitudes, and lifestyles of their target markets and carefully match their messages to these important factors.

Today, in many event marketing campaigns, public relations is at least equal to and in many cases, even more important than traditional advertising. However, public relations involves much more than merely grinding out a short press release.

The effective event public relations campaign will involve research with event consumers as well as the media; the development of collateral materials such as media kits, fact sheets, and other tangibles; the organization and implementation of media conferences; the development of a speaker's bureau; and on-site media relations assistance at the event.

Event public relations helps create the overall impression that others will develop about your event. In that regard it is significantly more valuable than advertising because it implies greater credibility. For that reason the Public Relations Society of America, an organization that includes membership of professionals in the public relations profession, states that public relations exposure is more valuable financially than advertising. Figure 10-2 demonstrates the impact of this value.

Use the power of public relations to beat the drum loudly for your event. Carefully select those public relations tools that will most effectively and cost efficiently help you inform and persuade others to support your event.

Place

In real estate, location is everything. In event marketing, distribution of your product may be everything as well. The location of your event often determines the channels of distribution.

If your event is located in a rural area not only may it be difficult to promote the event due to limited media resources, but it may also be difficult for your target market to make the purchase due to logistical restraints. However, in a study I conducted in 1994, I discovered that rural events are growing in number and size in the United States. Therefore, despite these limitations, demand due to lack of competition and need for tourism dollars has overcome these obstacles.

The place where you locate your event ultimately will determine the marketing efforts you must exude to drive sales. For example, it has been shown that those events that are close to inexpensive, safe public transportation or those events that feature closed-in reasonably-priced parking will attract more guests than those that do not offer these amenities. Furthermore, those events that are connected to other nearby attractions or infrastructures (such as shopping malls) may also draw more attendees due to the time efficiency of the destination. For upscale events, the addition of valet parking may improve the chances of attracting guests to a new or nontraditional location.

The event manager must seriously consider place when designing the marketing program for the event. Place not only implies the taste or style of the event, it also, in large part, defines the type of individual that will be persuaded to invest in the event. In this regard, the event marketer must determine the place in the early stages through

---

FIGURE 10-2
The Value of Public Relations

$\frac{1}{2}$ Page Newspaper Advertisement
Cost = $5,000

Editorial about your event
in the same space as the advertisement
Value = $15,000

research and design. This is the perfect time to convene a focus group or conduct a survey to determine who is likely to attend your event when they are given a variety of location choices. Making certain you have thoughtfully analyzed this important issue will save you time and money throughout the entire event marketing process.

Internal vs. External Event Marketing

Event managers may use an event or a series of events as one of the marketing methods to promote external events, products or services such as shopping malls, tourism destinations, or attractions (such as amusement parks or zoos), or any entity that is appropriately promoted through events.

However, in most cases, event managers use marketing forces such as advertising, public relations, promotion, advertising specialties, stunts, and other techniques to promote individual events. These traditional marketing techniques should be used to inform, attract, persuade, sustain, and retain potential customers for your event.

Increasingly a blend of internal and external event marketing is being utilized to promote events. In some cases, event managers use miniature events as a means of promoting major events. The Atlanta Committee for the Olympic Games staged a parade to celebrate the decision by the International Olympic Committee to stage the games in Atlanta. The parade began the marketing process of identifying Atlanta as the city of the next Olympic Games. Other smaller events such as the torch run are used throughout the days preceding the opening ceremonies to promote this event.

On a smaller scale, fund-raising organizations such as the National Symphony Orchestra use smaller focus-type events (for example, receptions) to promote larger events (for example, the Symphony Ball or the annual Designer's Show House). These ancillary events serve to promote the larger event to different market segments and maintain excitement about the overall event product.

Therefore, both internal and external event marketing is an important strategy for your event. Figure 10-3 depicts how this process is used to market your event product.

Since resources are always limited for marketing it is important to carefully select those internal or external elements that will most effectively reach and influence your target market.

External Event Marketing

Using events to market products and services is increasing. As mentioned earlier, *Advertising Age* has declared that events are now critical in the total marketing effort. Therefore, although using an event marketing strategy may be more costly due to the addi-

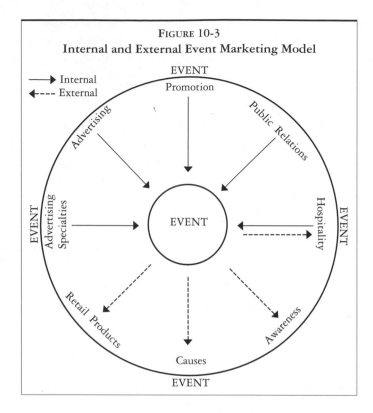

FIGURE 10-3
Internal and External Event Marketing Model

tional labor required, it must be seriously considered when promoting products and services.

RETAIL EVENTS

Our firm began by producing fashion shows, petting zoos, Santa Claus appearances, and other retail events. During the mid-to-late 1970s, regional mega-shopping centers opened throughout the United States and mall developers such as the Rouse Company and Homart recognized that they were the new main streets of America. To attract the appropriate target market, a series of events was developed and implemented to position the shopping mall as an attraction.

Using the fashion show as one example, the shopping mall management could satisfy the needs of both its internal and external customers. First, the store owners and managers could showcase their goods and services to a highly targeted audience in a cost-effective manner. Second, the external customer—the shopper himself or herself—would be held captive during the twenty- to thirty-minute production and then directed to visit each store for special discounts during the time immediately following the show.

WAR STORY

An attorney telephoned me to inquire whether I would be able to serve as an expert witness in a case involving an opera impresario who had failed to stage a production of a grand opera that had received a one million dollar sponsorship from a major corporation. After reviewing thousands of pages of documents I soon realized that although this conductor had some success with promoting the opera to his key constituents (opera fans) he could not apply these same promotion principles to a broader market segment. Therefore, along with his poor judgment in selecting marketing partners and counsel to support his efforts, his lack of experience resulted in poor ticket sales. As a direct result of this marketing mismanagement, the opera did not stage one performance. The sponsor initially lost one million dollars (until I testified on behalf of the sponsor and they settled for a larger amount).

Lesson Learned

When designing the marketing plan for your event product, make certain you select counsel that has direct experience promoting your type of event. A firm that has been successful in sports may not be able to transfer that experience to the arts and vice versa. In addition, test every seemingly good idea with marketing research to confirm there is a sufficient number of individuals who will not only anticipate but also participate financially in your event's success. One way to do this is to presell a limited number of tickets to test the willingness of your target market to financially support your event before proceeding with further development.

The fashion show is still a hugely successful event. One of the fastest growing segments of fashion shows is male fashions.

When producing retail events it is important to consider both the external and internal customer. The external customer will only be attracted and influenced to make purchases if you have the complete support of the internal customer. The typical retailer has little time to design, develop, and implement these events and therefore turns to a marketing director employed by the shopping mall to coordinate these activities.

According to the International Council of Shopping Centers, the trade association that educates and promotes the shopping center industry, many marketing directors are earning the Certified Marketing Director (CMD) designation to develop specialized knowledge of this increasingly complex and competitive profession.

Figure 10-4 lists several retail events that have proven successful and the market to whom they are best targeted.

Figure 10-4 provides a brief illustration of the types of events the event manager may organize on behalf of the retail organization. You will note that most of these events target women, as historically women have comprised the largest customer bases for retail businesses. However, these demographics are shifting as two-income families have emerged in the United States and now both men and women increasingly share the responsibilities and pleasures of shopping. Therefore, successful event managers will look for events that they may use to develop other markets with disposable income such as men, teenage boys, and even senior citizens.

Timing is everything when developing and producing the retail event. In order to allow the consumer to devote as much time as possible to spending money, the live event should be brief in duration (under twenty minutes) and offered frequently throughout the day to allow a variety of customers to experience the event activity. Obviously due to the increase in working adults, the middle-of-the-week day should be avoided so that the most consumers can witness the event. Finally, many retail events are tied directly to paydays. Find out what the pay period is from large organizations such as factories,

---

Figure 10-4
Retail Events and Their Target Markets

Event	Target Market
Arts and crafts shows	Women and senior citizens
Children's entertainer	Young children
Circus and petting zoo	Young families
Computer show	Men
Cooking demonstration/tasting	Women
Fashion show	Women and teenage girls
Fine art show	Women and men
Health fair	Senior citizens
Magician	Young boys
Model railroad show	Young boys and men
Puppeteer	Young children
Soap opera star appearance	Women and teenage girls
Sport celebrity appearance	Men and boys
Sport memorabilia festival	Men and teenage boys

government, or other sources of large numbers of consumers and then time your event to coincide with this window of time when there will be a large amount of expendable income available.

FAIRS AND FESTIVALS

Fairs, festivals, and other public events may also serve as temporary retail locations (TRLs). These events often contract space to vendors, craftspeople, and others to demonstrate and sell their products and services. However, like their permanent retail counterparts, to be successful they must be aggressively marketed through both internal and external event marketing efforts.

A media preview event is an excellent way to inform the media about the size, scope, and excitement being offered at your fair or festival. Designing a ribbon-cutting event featuring prominent local citizens along with celebrities is an important way to announce "open for business." Finally, a series of ongoing ancillary events held at other public venues such as sporting event halftime shows is an important form of external marketing to introduce and remind other market segments of your event's importance.

LAUNCHING NEW PRODUCTS

Perhaps one of the most important activities within the event marketing area is that of launching new products developed by corporations. Each year in the United States and other countries billions of dollars are invested in advertising to promote new products. Before these products are introduced to the general public they are usually showcased before retailers or dealers. Such as the launch of a new automobile, this type of event serves several constituent groups. First, the trade media may be invited to promote the product to others. Second, the general media (newspapers, radio, and television) may be invited to help make the general public aware of the new product benefits and features. Finally, and perhaps most importantly, the product launch must target those individuals who will either sell the item to others or purchase it themselves.

The organization and presentation of the product launch event may be one of the most important steps in the overall marketing effort. Whether introducing software such as Windows '95 or an attraction such as the Trump Taj Mahal Resort and Casino, great thought must be given to the goals, objectives, and desired outcomes to create a successful event.

Figure 10-5 provides a checklist for developing and producing consistently successful product launch events.

Sometimes lavish plans for product launch events have been foiled by circumstances beyond the control of the event manager. However, most circumstances can be easily controlled through close communication with other parties. Make certain that you contact the corporate communications or public relations department early in the process to identify their goals and incorporate them into your plans. Next, and equally impor-

---

FIGURE 10-5
Product Launch Marketing Checklist

1. Determine the goals and objectives of the product launch event.

2. Identify the target market(s).

3. Coordinate planning with sales promotion, public relations, human resource development, and other critical departments.

4. Conduct research to refine your general production plans.

5. Use creativity to introduce your product in a nontraditional yet attractive manner.

6. Use creativity to unveil a new product.

7. Identify who will speak, for what length of time, and why.

8. Identify ways to reach those individuals who could not attend the event (such as through a video program or satellite presentation).

9. Measure and analyze your results by how sales are affected.

10. Develop opportunities for added value the next time you produce a similar event.

---

tant, make certain that the vice-president or director of sales is closely involved in your planning as your activities will directly affect his or her efforts. Finally, ensure that senior management, including the chief executive and operating officers, understands, supports, and is committed to your success. However, despite all of this careful interaction with other stakeholders, sometimes old Murphy raises his devilish head.

Event Promotion Techniques

There are five typical or traditional techniques used to promote events. These techniques include advertising, public relations, cross promotions, street promotions, and stunts. Some events only use one of these techniques while others may use all of them to ensure that their message is received and acted upon by their target market.

ADVERTISING
Advertising includes print and electronic media, transportation media (such as bus and rail), advertising specialties (calendars, key rings, coffee mugs, and other products), and outdoor media (billboards). Larger events may use many of these media resources while smaller events may carefully target their message to one or two media.

Print advertising is not limited to only magazines and newspapers. It may also include membership directories, inserts in local newspapers, flyers (sometimes called

WAR STORY

One of the big automobile manufacturers hired a world class event manager to design the launch of its newest automobile at a dealer's show in Atlantic City, New Jersey. At the conclusion of an elaborate audiovisual program that included live dancers, the automobile was to rise on a hydraulic platform surrounded by fog, spin on a turn table, and as the music reached a crescendo, hundreds of snow white doves would be released from overhead and flutter to the four corners of the convention hall. During the rehearsal the theatrical lights located below the dove cages were not used to conserve energy. However, during the actual production for 5,000 audience members, the lights burned for one hour prior to revealing the automobile. When it was time to release the doves they, unfortunately, did not survive the heat from the lights, and dropped in huge thumps onto the top of the car, as the event manager yelled to the lighting director, "Quick, turn off the lights!"

Lesson Learned

Always have a contingency plan for corporate product launch events. Remember, you never have a second chance to make a first impression. Although spectacle is impressive, do not risk quality in deference to spectacle. Millions and sometimes billions of dollars are involved in the introduction of this new product and you must be certain that it happens flawlessly.

one sheets), posters, church and synagogue newsletters, brochures, and virtually any media that is printed. When analyzing your print advertising needs make certain that you test your advertising product in advance with a small distribution to test its effectiveness. Specialists in direct mail recommend that you use a *split test* approach. This requires that you mail one type of advertising printed matter to one group and a different type to another to test the best response from both types. Varying items such as the color of the ink, copy, type and weight of the paper, or other decisions may produce different results. Test your print advertising using focus groups to make certain your event product is well positioned for success.

Classic advertising terms such as *free, discount, now, sale,* and *new* may help you influence the consumer to invest in your event. Clever graphics, endorsements, testimonials, and other credibility-building devices will help differentiate your event product from others.

Electronic media includes radio, television, the Internet, and any form of advertising that involves electronic delivery. Radio advertising is typically used to remind the listener about the event, whereas television is used to build excitement. The Internet is an excellent means with which to reach upscale consumers and those who are interested in science, technology, and travel. Before you select electronic media as a means to advertise your event, examine all potential media outlets.

Within television media you may elect to broadly cast your event through major networks or instead narrowly cast by selecting a finely targeted cable station. For example, if you are promoting an arts-related event you may select a cable station with arts programming. These decisions may require the assistance of experts in media buying or from an advertising agency specializing in radio or television media.

Transportation media requires that you place your message on busses, subways, and other forms of transportation. Usually this media is aimed at a very wide market but has proven effective for circuses, fairs, festivals, and other events that require large attendance from diverse groups.

Advertising specialties are those items that are usually given away or offered as a premium, as an incentive to purchase a product or service. Advertising specialties include thousands of products; however, the most typical are calendars, refrigerator magnets, coffee mugs, writing instruments, and key chains. In recent years clothing has become popular as advertising specialties and some event organizers give away clothing to the media and other key constituent groups and sell the rest at souvenir stands. Once again, carefully research this purchase to ensure that the recipient values the item and will use it. Prolonged usage will serve as reminders about your event.

Outdoor advertising was, at one time, one of the major forms of advertising in America. However, during the late 1960s many billboards were banned in a "beautify America" campaign. Still, the outdoor billboard is an excellent way to reach large numbers of potential event participants for an extended period of time.

Regardless of what type of advertising media you select make certain that you first conduct market research followed by tests to determine actual response. Once you have found a medium that effectively reaches your target market, use repetition to build reinforcement and retention. Finally, measure all responses to develop history and determine in the future where your advertising dollar pulls best for each event.

PUBLIC RELATIONS

Public relations, discussed earlier, involves informing the media and your target market about your event and persuading them to support your programs. Public relations activities for your event may include designing, printing, and distributing media kits, producing public service announcements for radio and television, producing and distributing audio and video news releases, or even producing events. In fact, according to many public relations professions, events are the fastest growing segment of the public relations strategy.

The media kit is typically a presentation-type folder that contains a fact sheet, request for coverage notice, media releases, and even a public service announcement (either written or recorded). This kit is distributed well in advance of the event to the print and electronic media to inform them of opportunities for coverage. In smaller markets, some media outlets may print your media releases word for word, whereas in larger, more sophisticated markets, members of the media may use the kit for background information alone.

A public service announcement, or PSA, is a written or prerecorded audio or video announcement about your event. Broadcasters in the United States are required by federal law to provide a certain allotment of time for public service announcements. In some cases, the broadcaster may provide help, as a further public service, in producing these announcements. Oftentimes a local celebrity or even nationally prominent individual will participate at no charge to add credibility to your announcement.

The audio or video news release, while a relatively new phenomenon, is one of the most effective ways to distribute your event message. Audio news releases (ANR) and video news releases (VNR) require that you pretape a news story about your event and then by overnight mail or use of satellite transmission send the story to local stations that you want to air it as part of their news programming. Since news programs are often the most watched segments of television programming, this type of public relations has the potential of reaching a large, well-targeted audience in a credible and cost-effective manner.

Finally, events themselves often become major public relations vehicles. To promote the opening of a new shopping center, movie actress Teri Garr starred in a public service announcement to benefit The National Center for Missing and Exploited Children. Ms. Garr filmed the announcement in the mall. Later she appeared on "The Tonight Show" with Johnny Carson and described in detail her activities on behalf of the national center including the filming of the public service announcement in the mall. This *event-within-an-event* serves to further position you firmly in the minds of those in the target audience you are trying to reach.

Remember that the two chief goals of public relations are to inform and persuade. Therefore, using collateral materials, public service announcements, and audio and video news releases as well as smaller events are excellent ways to accomplish these two important goals of your overall marketing campaign.

CROSS PROMOTIONS

To allocate your market resources in the most efficient manner you must identify and incorporate marketing partners into your campaign. These organizations may actually contribute marketing dollars or may provide in-kind services such as providing celebrities, tagging their ads with your event date and time, or contributing other valuable components to your campaign.

When seeking marketing partners to develop a cross-promotional strategy, study the advertising and marketing activities of compatible businesses in your area. Determine which of these activities will benefit your event. Next, develop a proposal that clearly describes the resources that you can bring to the event. Finally, present the proposal to your prospective marketing partners and answer any questions they may pose.

Tagging advertising involves your marketing partner adding a line of copy to his or her regular advertising placements that promotes your event. It may read, "Official supporter of XYZ event" or "Meet us at XYZ event, date and time." Tag lines may appear in both print and electronic advertising.

Make certain you chronicle all marketing activities so that you can report to your partners after the event and describe in intricate detail those placements that were successful. Cross promotions and tie-in activities are sensational ways to reach a much larger market in a cost-effective manner.

STREET PROMOTIONS

This marketing activity requires that you literally take your message to the street. Street promotions may include the handing out of flyers by a clown in a high-traffic area, the appearance of a celebrity at a local mall, contests, or other promotional activities designed to draw high visibility to your event.

Before leafleting (handing out flyers) make certain that this is allowed by local code. You certainly don't want to generate negative publicity by having the clown arrested for causing a disturbance. A celebrity appearance can help generate significant publicity if it is handled properly. Carefully schedule the celebrity to include radio and television interviews, appearances at a local children's hospital or other public facility, and ceremonial events with local, state, provincial, or federal leaders. At each appearance make certain the celebrity is well informed about the event and carefully articulates your event message in a consistent manner. Contests and other promotional events also require analysis to ensure that they are within the bounds of the local code and that they are appropriate for your event. For instance, selling raffle tickets at a nonprofit event may require that you file legal forms.

STUNTS

During the early 1950s in the United States advertising agencies used stunts as an important method of breaking through the clutter of traditional print and electronic advertising. Today, stunts continue to be effective but must be carefully crafted to ensure that the integrity of the event is preserved.

A stunt involves an activity designed to generate media coverage and attendance by spectators to promote a specific event or series of events. Radio stations continue to rely heavily on stunts and will often provide remote broadcasts to cover stunts involving their on-air personalities. Stunts can be tied to charitable endeavors such as locking up prominent officials until enough donations are raised to cover their release. Other stunts may involve creating the world's largest pizza, cake, sandwich, or other product. Before you incorporate a stunt in your event marketing program it is important to analyze how the stunt will further your marketing objectives and to determine all associated costs. Finally, make certain you carefully chronicle all media coverage that results from the stunt, distribute bounce-back coupons to attendees, and track all responses resulting from the stunt.

THE INVITATION

Whether your invitation is a print or electronic advertisement, a flyer, or a formal engraved document, the copy that is composed, art that is created or selected, and paper that is chosen will greatly influence the response.

Figure 10-6 describes the central components of all effective invitations. Remember that an invitation is an official offer to the consumer or guest to participate in your event. Therefore, from a legal perspective it is important that you carefully choose your words to reflect the actual event you are promoting.

FIGURE 10-6
Central Components of an Effective Invitation

1. Name of host or event organizer

2. Date, time, and location

3. Dress requirements

4. Parking

5. RSVP

Additional components may include:

1. Purpose of the event

2. Names of honorary board or committee

3. Names of prominent speakers

4. Frequency or historic nature of the event (first annual, 100th anniversary celebration, or biannual event)

5. Limited supply of tickets

6. VIP status

Each of these components is designed to generate a specific response from the recipient. The most important response is to build anticipation toward acceptance followed by actual attendance.

Marketing Thrust

Noted corporate marketing expert Ira Westreich describes the word *event* as an acronym that represents **E**xtract **V**alue with **E**very **N**ew **T**hrust. The purpose of your event marketing campaign is to ensure that every decision you make provides greater value for the overall event outcome. To do this you must carefully match the objectives to the strategies, test all ideas using feedback from actual event consumers, and perhaps most importantly use creativity and innovation to differentiate your event product as a unique and valuable investment. By carefully integrating marketing activities such as advertising, public relations, cross promotions, street promotions, and stunts you will be able to build a strong campaign that will effectively promote your event to your target audience.

MAIN EVENT

1. Product, promotion, price, public relations, and place are integral ingredients in the event marketing process.

2. Both internal and external event marketing may be used to market your event. Internal event marketing means using advertising, promotion, and other marketing tools to inform and persuade others to support your event. External event marketing requires that the event itself be used to promote other products, services, or causes.

3. Event promotion techniques include advertising, public relations, cross promotions or tie-in activities, street promotions, and stunts. Some events use only one or two of these techniques whereas other events use all of them.

4. The invitation is the most important advertising vehicle for your event as it is the official offer. Test this invitation prior to distribution to make certain it is understandable and produces the desired response.

NEXT ON THE AGENDA

Researching, negotiating, acquiring, and servicing a sponsorship can be time consuming and labor intensive. Learn how to maximize your efforts and profits with a win-win-win relationship for you, your sponsor, and your stakeholders in Chapter 11.

Sponsorship

Without sponsorship many events would not be financially viable. Other events would not be able to provide the quality expected by event participants. Still other events would not be able to achieve their specified goals and objectives. Suffice it to say, sponsorship, more often than not, provides the grease that allows the event wheel to function smoothly.

Historically, sponsorship has its earliest modern origin in professional sport events. These events have always appealed to the widest demographics and were therefore perfect event products for sponsorship. Sponsorship is a uniquely American invention brought forth from the need of advertisers to reach certain markets, and the need of event organizers to identify additional funding to offset costs not covered by normal revenue streams such as ticket sales.

In recent times there has been a noticeable shift in sponsor dollars away from sport events and toward arts events. The reason for this shift is that sponsors are seeking more highly targeted upscale demographics and the arts' audience delivers that market segment. Therefore, those events that deliver the higher income demographics are predicted to best benefit from sponsorship dollars in the future.

Perhaps the best example of sport sponsorship is the 1984 Summer Olympic Games in Los Angeles, California. For the first time in the history of the modern Olympic

Games movement, sponsors were aggressively solicited as marketing partners for this unprecedented event. Offers were made, deals were cut, and the Los Angeles Olympic Organizing Committee received a net earnings of over 200 million dollars.

From fairs to festivals to hallmark events such as a world's fair, the role of the sponsor has earned a permanent place in the marketing lexicon of events. Figure 11-1 lists typical types of sponsors for a variety of events. Use this list as a guide to begin to identify sponsors for your event.

Sponsorship Needs Assessment

Although most events may benefit from sponsorship, not every event is appropriate for this component. Sponsorship is a commercial endeavor and is extremely time consuming. Therefore, unless you are prepared to enter into a commercial relationship with other parties and have the time resources to devote to this activity, you may instead wish to solicit donations.

Many event managers confuse sponsorship with benevolence. A fund-raising event where donors contribute without any expectation of commercial benefit is a benevolent activity. Sponsorship, on the other hand, is a commercial transaction in which two parties agree by way of an offer and acceptance. The offer generally involves marketing services provided by the event organizer in exchange for the sponsor's cash or in kind contribution to the event. The marketing services may range from advertising to banner displays to hospitality to a full-blown marketing plan involving public relations, advertising, and promotion.

As you can begin to see, these marketing services place new demands on the event

---

Figure 11-1
Events and Their Prospective Sponsors

Event	Prospective Sponsors
Fair	Bottler, grocer, automotive, and bank
Festival	Department store and record store
Sport	Athletic wear manufacturer, bottler, brewery, and hospital or health care facility
School program	Children's toy stores, children's clothing stores, and amusement park
Meeting/conference	Printer, bank, insurance broker, and associate member firms

organizer. Therefore, the event resources may need to be reallocated to handle this new demand. Not every event is able to do this.

Before you give the green light to soliciting sponsorships use the checklist in Figure 11-2 to determine if your event is appropriate for this activity.

The questions in Figure 11-2 can save many event organizations much wasted time, energy, and heartache. Examining the internal and external resources may be one of the most important aspects of this process.

Although sponsors may provide much needed funding for your event, to help you achieve the quality that is required, sponsors also require your own financial resources to meet their objectives. They may, for example, require that you commit a certain amount of marketing dollars. Second, they may require minimal or substantial hospitality services that may amount to hundreds or thousands of dollars per day. Finally, if you are going to retain these sponsors assign one or more individuals to monitor the activities, service these accounts, and develop long-term relationships. Yes, sponsors can provide needed funding; however, as in any commercial transaction they must also receive a fair return on their investment. You are responsible for orchestrating this return.

Your event may benefit from additional exposure through sponsorships. Earlier we discussed using tag lines in advertising as one way to inexpensively increase your exposure. Sponsors may also provide you with *shelf space* in their retail stores to promote your event through coupons. Your sponsors can also help you with the development of a public relations campaign or can supplement their own public relations efforts with your message. Some sponsors have celebrity athletes, television stars, and movie personalities on contract who they may wish to involve with your event.

Perhaps one of the most important reasons event organizers align themselves with commercial sponsors is the opportunity to achieve greater credibility for the event. Securing the sponsorship of AT&T, IBM, Coca-Cola, or other Fortune 500 firms immedi-

---

FIGURE 11-2
Sponsorship Needs Assessment Checklist

1. Does the event require an infusion of sponsor dollars to achieve the quality required?

2. Are there sufficient internal and external resources to support this activity?

3. Is commercial sponsorship appropriate for the nature of the event?

4. Are there sufficient prospects for sponsorship sales and is the timing appropriate to approach them?

5. Is this activity legal, ethical, and appropriate for the spirit of the event organization?

ately positions your event as a major player and may help your event organization secure additional funding from other sources.

Developing Sponsors

The competition by event organizers for sponsors is keen at every level. Whether your event is a local event or a national one you must first conduct a competitive analysis to identify all competing events and study their sponsorship history and present activities. Figure 11-3 offers several suggestions on how to identify appropriate sponsors for your event.

Once you have developed a list of prospective sponsors, the next step is to qualify them for solicitation. Do not waste your valuable resources by making endless presentations to sponsors who do not have the interest or resources to financially support your event. Instead, qualify your sponsors by contacting local organizations such as the Chamber of Commerce, Board of Trade, banks, and other centers of commerce to inquire about the financial viability of the prospective sponsor. Next, thoroughly review the sponsor's past marketing efforts to determine if the sponsor's overall marketing plans are conducive to sponsoring your event. Finally, talk to advertising and public relations executives and attempt to forecast where your prospective sponsor may put his or her marketing dollars in the future. Perhaps the logical place for investment is your event.

Selling Sponsorships

Always do your homework regarding the sponsor's needs, wants, and desires prior to attempting to sell a sponsorship. To make the sale, the sponsorship offer must be an

---

FIGURE 11-3
How to Identify Appropriate Sponsors

1. Determine the financial level of sponsorship you require. Not every sponsor can make a five or six figure decision.

2. Review trade journals such as *Advertising Age* and *Sponsorship Report* to track sponsor activities.

3. Review the local business tabloid in your area to search for prospective sponsors.

4. Network with advertising and public relations agency officials to find out if their clients have an interest in your event.

5. Conduct a focus group with prospective sponsors to solicit and later analyze their opinions and attitudes toward your event.

exact fit with the needs, expectations, goals, and objectives of the commercial sponsor. Customize the offer to achieve these goals and objectives prior to your presentation.

Constructing a successful proposal is equal parts of art and science. As an artist, you must design an attractive, enticing, and aesthetically pleasing product that the sponsor will want to purchase. Therefore, carefully describe the capability of your organization and past sponsors (if any), incorporate testimonials and references from leading individuals, and package the proposal in a professional design. Avoid being clever. Remember that the sponsor will be making a business decision and will prefer a serious business plan over hokeyness. The science part involves carefully identifying your target market and linking all sponsorship activities to sales or recognition that will benefit the sponsor. List the benefits and activities the sponsor will enjoy as a sponsor of your event. For example, the sponsor may be able to provide free samples of his or her product or service and conduct marketing research. He or she may be able to offer his or her product or service for sale and measure the results. Or the sponsor may benefit from public relations exposure. Regardless of the benefit or feature, detail each potential activity that may result from the sponsorship.

Include in the proposal sponsorship terms for payment and any requirements the sponsor may have in addition to these payments. In some events, the sponsor is allowed to provide an exhibit at his or her own cost. In other events, the exhibit is provided as part of the sponsorship costs. Describe any additional costs or services the sponsor is required to contribute to avoid any future surprises. Figure 11-4 summarizes the key elements in a winning sponsorship proposal.

FIGURE 11-4
How to Create a Winning Sponsorship Proposal

1. Describe the history of the event.

2. Include a capability statement about your organization's resources.

3. Incorporate testimonials and references from other sponsors.

4. Describe the benefits and features the sponsor will receive.

5. List all financial responsibilities the sponsor must accept.

6. Describe any additional responsibilities the sponsor must accept.

7. Describe how you will chronicle the sponsorship activity.

8. Include a time and date for acceptance of the offer.

9. Include a provision for renewal of the sponsorship.

10. Include an arbitration clause in case you and the sponsor disagree regarding the sponsorship activities.

One of the most effective ways to persuade sponsors to participate in your event is to organize a prospective sponsor preview program. During this program you and your staff describe the benefits and features of your sponsorship activities to a large number of prospective sponsors. You may wish to invite a couple of previous sponsors to provide in-person testimonials about the benefits of the sponsorship. You may also wish to presell one or two sponsors so that when you ask for a reaction from those in attendance, at least two from the group will respond favorably. Their favorable response may, and usually does, influence others. Avoid trying to hard sell during this program. Use this program to plant seeds that will be further cultivated during meetings with individual sponsors.

Overcoming Sponsor Objections

Most sponsors will want their sponsorship activities customized to achieve their specific goals and objectives. Therefore, they may have some preliminary objections after receiving your initial offer. Once you have presented the offer, ask them for their reaction on each benefit and feature. Listen carefully and list these comments. Make two lists. One list is for approvals—those items that they see the value in the sponsorship. The second list is for objections—those items that they cannot see the value at this time. Your goal is to move all of the items from list number two into list number one. To do this, ask sponsors what is required by their organization to overcome their objections on each point. In some cases, it may be additional exposure. In other cases, it may be the price of the sponsorship. To overcome these objections be prepared to provide them with the tools they need to make a positive decision. For example, if their objection is cost, you may be able to combine their sponsorship with others and lower their contribution. If their objection is limited exposure, you may be able to inexpensively reposition their involvement to provide them with greater and more sustained visibility. Handling objections is an integral part of the sponsorship sales process. Rehearse these discussions with your internal stakeholders to identify other common objections and be prepared to provide the solution your sponsors need to remove these barriers.

Negotiating Your Sponsorship

Almost every sponsorship will require intense negotiations to move it into fruition. Whenever possible conduct these negotiations in person with the decision maker. Assign a specific date and time for these negotiations and confirm that the sponsor is a viable prospect before entering into a serious negotiation. In most negotiations both parties desire a win-win-win outcome. In this type of negotiation you win as the event organizer, the sponsor wins as the event funding agent, and the stakeholders of your event win from your mutual efforts to secure these dollars.

Carefully analyze what your sponsor expects from the sponsorship prior to your negotiating session. Determine in advance what additional components you may be able to offer if required. Also, list those concessions that you cannot make. Finally, list these items that may require further approval from your board or others before you agree to them. Begin the negotiation by asking the prospective sponsor to list all of those items that are acceptable, bundle them, and have the sponsor approve them. Now you are prepared to focus on those items that require further resolution. Ask the sponsor to describe his or her concerns about each negotiation point and take careful notes. Look at your list of concessions and decide if any item you have listed will help resolve these concerns. If it is appropriate to offer a concession, do so and ask the sponsor for his or her approval. Once the sponsor has approved, then ask him or her to provide you with an additional service, usually at modest additional cost to the sponsor, to balance his or her end of the negotiation. If the sponsor is unable to provide you with an additional service or product, determine if you are able to proceed to the next point.

Do not be afraid to walk away. In some cases, the concession that the sponsor will ask for may sacrifice the credibility or reputation of your event. In other cases, the sponsor will want a concession that may undermine the financial viability of your event. Do not concede your reputation or the financial success of the event. Instead, thank the sponsor for his or her time, offer to work with him or her in the future under different circumstances, and leave the room as quickly as possible. In some instances, event organizers have reported that this approach has forced the prospective sponsor to reexamine his or her position. It is not unusual to have the sponsor call the event organizer the next day and offer a greater concession to save the sponsorship.

Closing the Sponsorship Sale

You must always *ask for the order* when presenting your sponsorship proposal. State at least three times that you want to develop a positive relationship with the sponsor. Start your discussions by stating that your desired outcome is to ensure that the sponsor understands all of the benefits and features of your event and will desire to become a sponsor.

Throughout your presentation ask for feedback from the sponsor and build upon the sponsor's positive reactions by telling him or her that you are pleased that he or she recognizes the value of your event product. Finally, at the conclusion of your presentation ask the sponsor for his or her overall impression and state once again that you would like his or her business.

Unfortunately, these techniques may not be enough to get a clear answer. In some cases, you may have to say something like, "So, can we count on you to sponsor our event?" Sometimes you need to secure the answer to this question in order to plan your next step in sponsorship negotiations or to decide to move forward with the next sponsor. The word "ask" is the most powerful three letter word in sponsorship sales. Unless you "ask" you will never know. Remember to ask early, often, and before leaving to confirm the sponsorship sale.

Servicing Sponsorship Sales

Once the sponsor has accepted your offer, the next task is to service this sale in order to retain his or her support in the future. One of the most common reasons sponsors fail to renew their sponsorship is due to poor communications. In part one of this book we discussed in great detail the importance of open and continuous communications. Make certain that you develop methods for implementing positive communications with your sponsors. Some event organizers use newsletters to update their sponsors while others provide regular briefings. Still others offer their sponsors marketing seminars to help them with designing their booth or targeting their product or service to event guests. It is wise to assign one or more persons on your staff to service all sponsorships and communicate regularly with your sponsors to make certain they remain informed, excited, and committed to your event activities.

Another reason some sponsorships go sour is due to the inability of the event organizers to deliver what they promise. If you promise that the sponsor's banner will be suspended on the main stage above the head of the performing artist, first you must confirm with the artist that this is acceptable. It is unacceptable to later renege on your commitment to the sponsor. It is always best to underpromise and overdeliver with stating the benefits of sponsorship. Exceeding the sponsor's expectations is how you turn a one-year sponsorship into a five-year plan with options to renew forever.

Every sponsor has a hidden agenda. It can be as simple as the chairman of the board wanting to meet his or her favorite celebrity or as complex as the sales manager's bonus and promotion decision resting on this particular sponsorship activity. Ask the sponsor's representative what else you need to know about the needs of his or her organization as you design the sponsorship measurement system. For example, if the sponsor's representative is in the public relations department, his or her interest may be in seeing lots of ink and television time devoted to the name of the sponsor. Therefore, you will want to carefully measure these outcomes to assist your sponsor. Remember that you may sign a sponsorship agreement with a large corporation or organization, but the day-to-day management of this agreement is between people. Find out what these people desire and try to provide them with these outcomes.

Although communications between you and your sponsors is critical to your success, perhaps even more important are the internal communications between the event manager and his or her operations personnel. You must first confirm that your personnel will be able to support sponsorship activities at the level required by the individual sponsors. Determine if you have sufficient internal resources to satisfy the requirements both in contract as well as implied to ensure the well-being of your sponsor's investment. For example, if your sponsor wants a hospitality setup arranged at the last minute, do you have a catering operation that can handle this request? One way to ensure that the sponsors' needs are handled expeditiously is to create a written system of orders, changes, and other instructions that clearly communicate those activities required by your sponsors. Prior to distribution of these forms, have the sponsor's representative sign one copy. Then have the event's representative initial approval before forwarding it to the appropriate department or team leader.

Evaluating Sponsorships

To secure multiple year sponsorships it is important that you develop and implement a system for measuring the sponsor's activities. First, decide what needs to be evaluated and why. The answers to these questions typically may be found in the goals and objectives of the sponsorship agreement.

To collect this data, conduct sponsorship evaluations that are comprehensive in scope. You may wish to interview the sponsors, your own staff, the sponsor's target market, and others to solicit a wide range of opinions regarding the effectiveness of the sponsorship. Furthermore, you may wish to include in the event survey-specific questions about the sponsor's participation. Finally, ask the sponsor for tracking information regarding sales that have resulted from the sponsor's participation in your event.

You may measure the sponsor's public relations benefits by measuring the number of minutes of television and/or radio time as well as the number of inches and columns of print media that was devoted to the sponsor's products or name. List the comparable value using the 3 to 1 ratio provided by the Public Relations Society of America (see Chapter 10).

Ask the sponsor how he or she would like to see the data you have measured presented. Some may prefer an elaborate in-person presentation using video clips and slides while others will prefer a simple summary of the goals, objectives, and outcomes that were achieved. Make certain that you present this information in a manner that is useful to the sponsor and that you take the time to professionally prepare this presentation to adequately address the sponsor's needs. All future sponsorship activities will come from this important activity.

Timing is Everything

The process for identifying, soliciting, negotiating, securing, servicing, and evaluating sponsorships is a complex one. However, as is true with most things, timing is every-

---

Figure 11-5
Typical Time Line for Major Sponsorship Activities

18 months in advance: Conduct needs assessment and research
16 months in advance: Identify prospective sponsors
14 months in advance: Develop and present proposals
12 months in advance: Negotiate proposals and sign agreements
9 months in advance: Implement sponsorship operations plan
6 months in advance: Audit sponsor's changes and additions
4 months in advance: Review changes and additions with staff
2 months in advance: Meet with sponsor to provide update on event progress
1 month in advance: Begin sponsor public relations campaign
1 month after event: Meet with sponsor to provide analysis of results

---

thing. Allow a minimum of twelve to eighteen months to formulate and consummate a successful sponsorship program. Figure 11-5 provides a typical time line for the various stages described above.

Some event organizers have come to see sponsorship as the goose with the golden egg. However, while specific benefits come from individual sponsorships, every event must individually audit their own needs, the resources available, and the benefits they may offer, prior to engaging in this time-consuming and expense-laden activity. When developing sponsorship activities always start small and year-by-year, or event-by-event, build your base of sponsors from your ability to consistently deliver high-quality and successful events. This is the best way to make sure your goose avoids a rotten egg in favor of a golden one for your event organization.

MAIN EVENT

1. Conduct a comprehensive needs assessment to determine if your event is appropriate for sponsorship.

2. Audit the internal and external resources of your event organization to identify the viability of proceeding with sponsorship activities.

3. Use trade journals, newspapers, and networking to identify prospective sponsors.

4. Qualify all sponsors through in-depth research.

5. Sell your sponsorship through careful customization that reflects the prospect's needs, wants, desires, goals, and objectives.

6. Ensure you have operations support to service the sponsorships that you sell.

7. Provide a plan for evaluating every sponsorship in a comprehensive manner.

8. Seek multiple year sponsorships by consistently providing high-quality events and meeting the sponsor's goals and objectives.

NEXT ON THE AGENDA

Cause related marketing is one of the fastest growing activities for corporations and other organizations that wish to develop strong loyalty with their consumers. The role of fund-raising and Event Management historically has been a close and beneficial one. In Chapter 12 you will learn how to use the new trend of cause related marketing to identify support for your fund-raising event activities.

Cause Related Events

Increasingly sponsors are more interested in becoming involved in a new phenomena entitled *cause related marketing*. This provides sponsors with the added value of demonstrating that they are good corporate citizens. As more and more groups form around specific causes such as the environment, children's concerns, peace, crime prevention, and other important issues, sponsors are looking for natural linkages that will strengthen the loyalty that they desire from their consumers.

The National Society of Fund Raising Executives (NSFRE) has a library of materials related to event fund-raising activities. Event fund-raising is one of the fastest growing segments of the fund-raising profession. Events are not only used to generate new dollars for not-for-profit organizations but they are also used to identify new potential major donors as well as reward past and present contributors. Major authors in this field including Gerald Plessner and Jerry Panas recognize that cause related events provide a win-win-win opportunity for event organizers, the organizations they represent, and the donors who contribute to these events.

Linking a well-known cause to your event can generate greater support from both the media and the general public. Using the event to emotionalize your cause can convert casual contributors into major donors. Although events are a labor-intensive alternative to direct mail solicitation, for significant events such as campaign kick-offs or other major events, they are highly effective.

Organizations such as United Way, the Nature Conservancy, and others have successfully used events as a way to generate awareness about their activities to a broader constituency. Because events are usually visual and often spectacular in size and scope, the media may find the combination of a unique event linked to a good cause irresistible. Although there are exceptions to this rule, generally, the media in smaller to mid-sized markets is more likely to cover your event if it is linked to a good cause.

Nancy Lynner, of the Smithsonian Institution's Office of Special Events and Conference Services, has had extensive experience coordinating events to reward, recognize, and nurture donors and prospects. According to Lynner, "These events allow the staff to stay in close touch with our supporters. They also serve as educational opportunities for us to inform our donors about the important activities they are helping to fund."

Other development professionals recognize that events serve as ideal vehicles to probe donors to learn about their interests and use this knowledge to design programs that they may wish to fund in the future. Tom Peters and Robert Waterman, coauthors of *In Search of Excellence,* interviewed a bank official who explained that most great deals do not happen in the bank. Rather, they occur on the golf course. In a relaxed setting, people are generally more open and willing to share their private agendas and allow development officials to learn important information that can be used to further their cause.

Most of the giving in the United States of America is by individual donors. When was the last time you met a corporation or a foundation at a charitable event? Instead, you may have been introduced to the corporation's representative. In fact, individuals make the decision to attend events, RSVP, sit in the chairs, fill out the pledge cards, and authorize checks. Events are perfectly suited for individual donors because they surround them with multisensory environments that may positively influence their desire to contribute.

The new role of events in fund-raising therefore is actually a refinement of the historic mission of philanthropy. Through events, individuals may receive sufficient information to make a decision to support a worthwhile cause. Additionally, through events, those who have been supportive in the past may see the fruits of their giving and elect to increase their contribution. The transformation of a first-time donor into a lifelong donor (or perpetual giver through planned giving programs) may be one of the most important justifications for using events as an intregal part of the fund-raising or cause awareness process.

Major Donor Development

The wooing of major donors is one of the most complex and yet effective activities in fund-raising. Jerry Panas, an expert in the field of major donor solicitation, believes that the approach to a major donor is equal to the ratio of success. Working with Panas on the Greater Nashville, Tennessee YMCA Capital Campaign I realized how valuable the kick-off event can be to develop this important approach.

Julie Sistrunk, director of special events for the YMCA, and Panas conceived a spring event that would recognize longtime volunteers as well as announce those major gifts and pledges that were received. Panas and Sistrunk called upon me to design and coordinate the event.

Panas urged me to use drama and theater to tell the story of the YMCA. Sistrunk suggested that we use as many existing resources as possible to not only save money but showcase the YMCA programs. Finally, both Panas and Sistrunk said that it was important that this event demonstrate the energy and innovation that was driving the new capital campaign.

Figure 12-1 is a scenario of this successful event. It demonstrates how to effectively achieve the goals and objectives of a cause related event using limited resources.

FIGURE 12-1
Scenario of a Successful Cause Related Event

Why? To recognize volunteers, announce major gifts, and motivate others to participate in the campaign.
Who? Prospective donors and volunteers.
When? May, Friday evening.
Where? Opryland Hotel, Tennessee Ballroom.
What? A seated banquet attended by 500 persons.
How? Use existing resources where possible to dramatically and theatrically tell the dynamic story of the YMCA of Greater Nashville.

Research: Audit the existing resources of the YMCA to identify individuals, photographs, groups, slides, and other components for the program.
Design: Present Sistrunk and Panas with a preliminary plan for the program. The plan incorporated the following elements in this sequence.

Theme: Celebration!

1.   Upon arrival guests were served YMCA Power Punch (in lieu of alcohol). During the pre-event reception they toured several exhibits displayed by various branches of the YMCA.

2.   As the doors to the ballroom opened, thirty YMCA participants ranging in age from five to eighty-five formed an honor guard at the entry door. Each participant wore a YMCA tee shirt with the celebration logo. The thirty individuals greeted each guest with "Thank you!" and applauded them as they entered the room. Recorded march tempo music was played through the sound system. Gobos were projected on the four walls with the phrase "Thank You!"

3.   The simple set consisted of a center rear projection screen on the ballroom stage with a slide of celebration logo displayed. During the needs assessment the "where" stage revealed that a permanent stage was included in the ballroom. This physical structure provided many additional permanent theatrical possibilities. Two standing lecterns were used left and right of the screen and each displayed the celebration logo. Simple balloon bouquets were used behind each lectern to create a colorful backdrop.

4.   Once all of the guests had entered and been seated, the house lights dimmed rapidly and the award-winning Tennessee State University Marching Band entered the rear of the ballroom. The drum major leading the band wore the typical large fur hat that covered much of his face. The band quickly marched to the front of the stage and the off-stage announcer spoke, "Ladies and gentleman, please rise for our national anthem." The drum major gave the downbeat and the band performed the anthem as 500 guests joined in singing. A slide of the American flag was projected on the screen.

5.   At the conclusion of the anthem the announcer spoke once more. "Ladies and gentlemen, please welcome our celebration band leader, Mr. Lee Barfield!" Barfield was the chairman of the capital campaign. As he turned to accept the applause from the surprised audience the band quickly exited.

6.   Barfield then stepped on stage and asked the audience to remain standing for the invocation. One dozen adorable

(Figure continued on next page)

FIGURE 12-1
Scenario of a Successful Cause Related Event *(continued)*

preschoolers (who previously had greeted the guests at the entrance) entered the stage and sang a simple invocation. These children were participants in YMCA sponsored day-care programs.

7. Following the invocation Barfield invited the guests to enjoy their salad and entree. During the entree a previously produced video of YMCA programs was shown.

8. Following the video, Barfield returned to the stage and introduced several leaders of the campaign who announced major gifts. These brief speeches set the tone for what would follow.

9. Barfield followed these speeches with the introduction of a multiprojector slide show entitled "A Place for Us." This show, produced by audiovisual specialist Will Reynolds, depicted desolate poverty and the faces of sad children, and then transformed into brighter images of YMCA branches and participants benefiting from YMCA programs. As each branch was shown, hundreds of people applauded for their neighborhood "Y." Throughout the program, the face of an African-American teenager was shown benefiting from YMCA programs.

10. As the program ended with thunderous applause a small spotlight rose on the lectern on the opposite side of the stage from where Barfield had been standing. At this lectern, the African-American teenager, Donald, was smiling as he greeted the audience. "Hello, my name is Donald and thanks to the YMCA I am here to share my story with you."

11. Donald told of growing up in stark poverty and being rescued by his YMCA through programs ranging from mentoring, to tutoring, to helping satisfy his spiritual needs. To prepare Donald for this presentation a YMCA staff member and myself spent many hours coaching him to enable him to write and perform his brief talk so that he would feel comfortable and deliver it in a way where he would feel successful about the outcome.

12. At the end of his talk Donald invited the audience to meet some other friends who have also benefited from the Y's many programs. He turned to his right to face the screen and with the audience watched a second slide program featuring audio taped interviews with individuals ranging from new immigrants to the Mayor of Nashville. These miniature stories told, in the first person, about the many different types of successes achieved by the YMCA helped the audience to further understand the broad reach of this cause.

13. At the end of this slide program Donald spoke again and invited the audience to meet a few more people who have benefited from the "Y."

14. A follow spotlight picked out of the darkened ballroom an eighty-five-year-old man standing in the front row as he described that he had been a member of the downtown YMCA for over fifty years and that his swimming exercise and the fellowship that surrounds it had enriched his life. He thundered, "Thank You, YMCA!" The follow spot then swept a few feet to the left as a teenage boy said, "The YMCA youth programs enable me to develop my body and my mind. Thank You, YMCA!" Finally, the spotlight once more moved to the left and illuminated a small child, a girl, standing on a small box. She whispered into the microphone, "The YMCA helps me with school work and is where I meet my friends. Thank you, YMCA!"

15. Donald thanked his friends for sharing their stories and thanked the audience for their support of the YMCA. His presentation was followed by a sustained, cheering, tearful standing ovation by 500 important supporters of the YMCA of Greater Nashville.

16. Barfield thanked Donald for his contribution and reminded the audience that thanks to their support of the YMCA there will always be a place for Donald and thousands of others. Once again the lights dimmed and a brief version of "A Place for Us" was seen on the screen featuring happy faces enjoying YMCA activities. As the final slide faded, gobos throughout the room projected the YMCA logos on the walls and the Tennessee State University Marching Band began playing in the reception area as the guests exited more determined to support this important cause.

Resources required: Slides or photographs provided by the YMCA. Eight ellipsoidal spotlights for gobos. Programming and production of slides by Mr. Reynolds. Volunteer talent provided by the Tennessee State University Marching Band, preschool children, YMCA participants, and speakers.

Outcome: Several million dollars in major gifts and other contributions was received as a direct result of this event. According to Panas, Sistrunk, and others the YMCA leaders were still talking about that magical night for many years when the cause was embraced by all. There is little magic to this effort. Effective Event Management ensured that the goals and objectives would be met using scarce resources allocated in the most efficient manner.

Communications Vehicle

The YMCA event is an excellent example of how the event manager can use live and recorded speakers, theatrical staging, slide production, and music to communicate an important or several important messages. When using events as a communications vehicle for your cause it is important to remember that different individuals receive messages through different senses.

Using both auditory and visual communication is wise when trying to reinforce your message to your audience in a short period of time. Furthermore, you may wish to use the tactile sense to further impress your audience at your event. Getting your audience involved in the actual activities (for example, experiencing what the beneficiaries experienced through their largess) is much more effective than simply telling them about the importance of the cause. The old maxim is true that if you tell me I know, show me and I remember, but *involve* me and I understand.

Integrating your message in a consistent fashion throughout the event is an important way to reinforce the message for the cause. This will require that you identify a strong logo or image, use it consistently, and incorporate it in lectern signs, programs, advertisements, and other visually significant locations. Also important is that the slogan be used over and over again until the listener becomes familiar with the language.

Trends in Cause Related Events

Three significant trends have emerged in cause related event management and marketing. Master event marketers such as "We Are The World" and "Hands Across America" organizer Ken Kragen recognized in the early 1980s that events must be thoroughly integrated in the campaign strategic plan from kick-off through final wrap-up. Next, all events must be used at some level to identify and nurture major donors. Lastly, a series of inclusive gatherings with shorter planning cycles enable cause related event manager-marketers to quickly react to external variables that may influence the decision to give.

Integration

When planning the cause related strategic plan, use the event process as a tool for communication, research, and other important activities that cannot be achieved solely through a mail or other traditional program. Compare the cost of researching, designing, planning, coordinating, and evaluating an event to that of direct mail and other forms of solicitation or image building. Once you have compared costs, then design whether to use events as a primary or secondary method to achieve your goals and objectives.

Developing Major Donors

If you use an event as the major strategy in your cause related program, it is important to note that a greater yield will come from the identification and nurturing of major donors than from actual donations during these events. Each event should be seen as a first step toward winning long-term contributions and each donor should have an individual profile established that allows you to carefully nurture them for future development activities.

Each event should include, where possible, a few new prospective donors who will meet established donors and perhaps be influenced to support your cause by this direct contact. This mix of established donors and prospective donors enables some to serve as mentors to the others and in so doing deepen their commitment to your cause.

Inclusive Gatherings with Short Planning Cycles

Earlier we discussed the important relationship of time, space, and tempo. Nowhere is this more important than with cause related events. Too often inexperienced event managers do not allow sufficient time to develop a major fund-raising event and subsequently fail. Instead of using your imagination to plan a spectacular event, why not instead produce a well-targeted, mini-event to begin to define and nurture your key constituent donor base?

These smaller, inclusive gatherings of qualified individuals are ultimately much more effective than a broad, open-to-the-public event that may include more disinterested or unqualified individuals than those with major donor potential. A shorter planning cycle or the beginning of a new campaign should begin with small, intimate, inclusive events of carefully qualified prospects. On these small successes you will build many future major campaigns.

Cause Related Events as Major Marketing Phenomena

Millions of copies of "We Are the World" were sold as a direct result of this event and the celebrities who donated their time and talent. In fact, this event was so successful that many other artists replicated this idea with other collections to benefit important causes. You can use your event as a catalyst to sell products ranging from recordings to calendars and ultimately benefit your cause substantially more than through ticket sales alone.

When developing your event idea, try to identify a product whose demand will be broad and can be branded by your event. Successfully marketing and distributing a winning product as a spin-off of your cause related event can mean millions more in dollars and visibility for your important cause.

The combination of a well-produced event coupled with a product (or series of products) in great demand can be the winning formula for long-term success for your organization. The passive income generated by these products can not only liquidate the costs of your event but also produce a significant stream of revenue for the future.

Perhaps one day the National Society of Fund Raising Executives and other similar organizations will be able to expand their limited collection of books dealing with cause related event management and marketing into a major resource that will support this growing field. As I told another speaker at a recent fund-raising day luncheon, "The potential for good through cause related event management and marketing is boundless. Not only do event managers influence those who attend but in fact this influence is echoed many times in many ways as those in attendance touch others." I encourage you to use this potential to the fullest extent to support the many worthwhile causes that may benefit from your talents.

MAIN EVENT

1. Cause related events are rapidly growing due to the winning formula of linking a well-known and well-respected cause with a popular and successful event.

2. Developing major donors is one of the most important missions of cause related event management and marketing.

3. Cause related events initially are communication vehicles used to inform current and future donors about the value of your cause and the need for their support.

4. All cause related events should be well integrated from kick-off through wrap-up to ensure a maximum return on the investment of time and other resources.

5. Start small. Use smaller, more inclusive events to identify major donors and develop these individuals for future roles in your cause related event program.

NEXT ON THE AGENDA

The legal, ethical, and risk management issues faced by event managers are part and parcel of every decision you will make. In Part Four you will explore each of these areas and learn why they are interrelated to ensure the consistent success of your events.

PART IV

Legal, Ethical, and Risk Management

CHAPTER 13

Contracts, Permits, and Licenses

Most modern events have the potential for negligent activity that can lead to long and costly litigation. As the number of professionally managed events has increased, so has the concern for risk management and other legal and ethical issues.

During the mid-1970s in the United States, many events were held to celebrate the 200th anniversary of American independence. During this period most events were organized by amateurs. As a result of lack of understanding or training in risk management, there was a corresponding interest by the legal profession in bringing litigation against negligent event managers. This relationship continues today with one notable difference. Event managers are becoming smarter with regard to legal, ethical, and risk management issues.

The Convention Liaison Council publishes a newsletter edited by attorney Jeffrey King that addresses legal issues in the meetings and conference field. The International Events Group has published an entire volume entitled *The Legal Guide to Sponsorship* that covers most of the legal issues related to this complex subject. Seminars, workshops, and courses are being offered throughout the United States covering recent developments in the areas of legal, ethical, and risk management issues relating to Event Management. Perhaps the best evidence of this change has been the development of alternative dispute resolution (ADR) programs to avoid lengthy and expensive litigation. Indeed, the paradigm has dramatically shifted from an environment governed by ignorance to one where education and proactive measures may reduce the level of risk and the resulting cost to event organizers.

Contracts, Permits, and Licenses

Most public events in the United States as well as other countries require some type of official permission to be held. The larger the event in terms of attendance or technical complexity, the more official oversight that is usually required.

Official review may come from either local (town, city, county), state or province, or federal agencies. There are numerous reasons why your event must comply with existing laws and regulations. The four primary reasons are to protect your legal interests, to abide by ethical practices, to ensure the safety and security of your event stakeholders, and overall to protect your financial investment.

PROTECTING YOUR LEGAL INTERESTS

Preparing proper contracts, researching the permits and licenses that are required, and complying with other legal requirements helps ensure that your event may proceed without undue interruption. Contracts or agreements may range from a simple letter or memorandum of understanding to complex multipage documents with lengthy riders (attachments). The event manager should utilize the services of competent legal counsel to review all standard agreements, such as hotel contracts, to ensure validity prior to execution. Furthermore, when writing new agreements, local legal counsel must make certain the contract conforms to the code of the jurisdiction where it is written and executed (usually where the event takes place). Lawyers are admitted to the state bar in the United States and must be experts on the state code (laws). Therefore, it is important to use an attorney who is admitted to the state bar where your event is being held or where, in the case of litigation, the case may be tried.

The majority of permits and licenses will be issued by local agencies. However, some state, provincial, or federal authorities may also issue licenses for your event. Therefore it is wise for the event manager to carefully audit past and similar events to identify the customary permits and licenses that are required for the event.

The permitting and licensing process may require weeks or even months to accomplish so the event manager must carefully research each jurisdiction where he or she will produce the event and meet these time requirements. The cost for permits and licenses is typically nominal. However, some larger events or events that pose high risk (such as grand prix auto racing) may require the posting of expensive bonds.

Figure 13-1 lists the major reasons why you must convince your event stakeholders of the importance of legal compliance and the need to obtain all necessary permits and licenses.

HONORING ETHICAL PRACTICES

One of the primary definitions of a profession is adherence to a code of ethical conduct. As Event Management has emerged as a modern profession a code of ethics has been developed by the International Special Events Society (see Appendix) and many other related industry organizations such as Meeting Professionals International have separate but similar codes. The code of ethics is different from the moral law of biblical times and is certainly different from the legal code voted by governing bodies.

A code of ethics reflects what is standard and customary in both a profession and geographic area. In that sense it is somewhat elastic in that it is applied in different degrees as needed for different circumstances. For example, when a hotelier offers an event manager a complimentary lunch at the first meeting should this be construed as a bribe by the event manager and therefore refused? Attorney Jeffrey King, an expert in the field of event legal procedures, states that he advises his event manager clients to always pay for their lunch when meeting with the hotelier for the first time. "This immediately lets the hotelier know that the relationship is equal and represents a business transaction," according to King. It also sets an ethical standard for future discussions and the building of a relationship.

Although many professional societies including ISES enforce their code of ethics

---

FIGURE 13-1

Compliance: Five Reasons Why You Must Plan, Prepare, and Provide This Assurance

1. Many events are legally required to obtain certain permits and licenses to officially conduct the event. Failure to do so may result in fines, penalties, interest, or cancellation of the event.

2. You have a fiduciary responsibility to your event stakeholders to plan, prepare, and provide evidence of compliance. Avoiding compliance can have dire economic consequences for your event.

3. You have an ethical responsibility (as stated by various industry code of ethics) to comply with all official regulations and provide written agreements.

4. Although an oral agreement may be binding, the written agreement usually takes precedence. Written agreements provide all parties with a clear understanding of the terms, conditions, and other important factors governing the event.

5. One of the primary ultimate responsibilities of the event manager is to provide a safe environment in which to conduct the event.

with a grievance procedure, in most cases it is up to the event manager to determine using the code of ethics as a guide for what is and is not appropriate ethical behavior. Robert Sivek of The Meeting House Companies, Inc. suggests that event managers use the front page of the newspaper rule. "Ask yourself if you would like to wake up and see your decision or action plastered across the front page of the newspaper," says Sivek. This may quickly determine whether or not your proposed action is one that is acceptable, not only to you but to others in your events community. Ethics are covered in detail in Chapter 15.

ENSURING THE SAFETY AND SECURITY OF EVENT STAKEHOLDERS

A *safe event environment* implies that it is free from hazard. A *secure environment* is one that is protected from future harm. The event manager is responsible for constructing this environment and sustaining it during the course of the event. Do not transfer this responsibility to others. The event manager either extends the invitation or coordinates the event at the invitation of others. You have both a legal and ethical responsibility to your event stakeholders to design and maintain a safe and secure event environment.

PROTECTING YOUR FINANCIAL INVESTMENT

The legal, ethical, and safety-security aspects of your event can dramatically impact upon your bottom line. Therefore, every decision you make that is proactive may reduce your risk of unforeseen financial impacts. Practicing thorough legal, ethical, and risk management proactive measures may actually help your event produce greater revenues over expenses.

Although not every contingency can be anticipated, the more adept you are at strategically planning preemptive measures to prevent these contingencies the better your balance sheet may look at the end of the event. Lapses in legal, ethical, and risk management judgment may cause not only loss of property, life, and money, but loss of your event's good name as well.

Key Components of an
Event Management Agreement/Contract

The Event Management contract reflects the understanding and agreement between two or more parties regarding their mutual interests as specified in the agreement. A binding contract must contain the following key components.

PARTIES

The names of the parties must be clearly identified. The agreement must be described as being between these parties, and the names that are used in the agreement must be defined. Typical Event Management agreements are between the event manager and his or her client or the event manager and his or her vendor.

WAR STORY

The event manager received a call from the bride the day after the wedding to advise her of a terrible incident. After the beautiful wedding two guests, a husband and wife, left the reception and proceeded to their automobile that was parked in a nearby parking garage. The husband was severely inebriated. He and his wife began to argue. Finally, as he entered the garage he stormed away and said that he was going to walk home. He lifted his leg over the garage rail assuming he was on the ground floor and fell ten stories to his death. When the bride learned of this terrible occurrence she called the man's wife to offer condolences but her call was refused. Instead she heard from the woman's attorney in the form of a subpoena deposing her for pretrial testimony. Because the bride issued the invitation, she was implicated in the litigation.

Lesson Learned

The event manager must audit every aspect of the event to ensure a safe and secure environment is present before, during, and after the event. Those who issue the invitation may be responsible for contributing to the negligence that caused the accident. Those who coordinate the event may be accused of gross negligence if it can be shown that they willingly ignored standard and customary safety procedures. In the case of the deceased wedding guest, the event manager would be asked if she had an alcohol management program in place to encourage responsible drinking or whether the bartenders contributed to his accident by continuing to serve him after he was obviously too intoxicated to drive.

OFFER

The offer is the service or product tendered by one party to another. The event manager may offer consulting services to a client or a vendor may offer products to an event manager.

CONSIDERATION

This clause defines what one party will provide the other upon acceptance of the offer.

ACCEPTANCE

When both parties accept the offer they execute (sign) the agreement confirming that they understand and agree to comply with the terms and conditions of the agreement.

OTHER COMPONENTS

Although the key components are the two or more parties, the offer, consideration, and acceptance, usually Event Management agreements include many other clauses or components. The most typical clauses are listed next.

Terms

This clause defines how and when the funds will be paid to the person extending the offer. If the event manager offers consulting services he or she may request a deposit in the amount of the first and last month's retainer and then require that the client submit monthly payments in a certain amount on a certain date each month. These terms define the financial conditions under which the agreement is valid.

Cancellation

Events are always subject to cancellation. Therefore, it is important to legally provide for this contingency with a detailed cancellation clause. Usually the cancellation clause defines under what circumstances either party may cancel, how notification must be provided (usually in writing), and what penalties may be required in the event of cancellation.

Force Majeure (Act of God)

The force majeure clause allows both parties to agree on what circumstances beyond their control the event may be canceled without penalty to either party. The force majeure clause must always be specified to reflect the most common or predictable occurrences. These may include hurricanes, earthquakes, floods, volcanic eruption, tornadoes, famine, war, or other disasters.

Arbitration

It is common practice to include in Event Management agreements a clause that allows both parties to use arbitration in place of a legal judgment when they fail to agree. The use of arbitration may save the parties substantial costs over traditional litigation.

Billing

Because many events involve entertainers or are theatrical events in and of themselves, the agreement must define how the entertainers will be listed in advertising and in the program. Usually a percentage is used, such as one hundred percent, to describe the size of their name in relation to other text in the title.

Time Is of the Essence

This clause instructs both parties that the agreement is only valid if it is signed within a prescribed period of time. Usually this clause is inserted to protect the offerer from loss of income due to late execution by the purchaser.

Assignment

As individuals have shorter and shorter tenures with individual organizations it is more important than ever that agreements contain clauses indicating that the contract may not be assigned to other parties. For example, if Mary Smith leaves XYZ company, the agreement is between XYZ company and the offerer and may not be transferred to Ms. Smith's successor who may or may not honor the agreement as an individual. Therefore, Mary Smith has executed the agreement on behalf of XYZ company.

Insurance

Often agreements will detail the type and limits of insurance that must be in force by both parties as well as a requirement that each party coinsure the other. Some agreements will require copies of certificates of insurance naming the other party as additional insured in advance of the event date.

Hold Harmless and Indemnification

In the event of negligence by either party the negligent party agrees to hold the other party as harmless and to defend them (indemnify) against harm.

Reputation

The production of an event is a reflection of the personal tastes of the event organization and sponsors. Therefore, some event managers include a specific clause that recognizes the importance of the purchaser's reputation and states that the event manager will use his or her best efforts to protect and preserve the reputation during the management of the event.

The Complete Agreement

Typically this is the final clause and states that the agreement constitutes the full understanding of both parties. Figure 13-2 demonstrates how these clauses are used in a typical event management consulting agreement.

RIDER

The rider is an attachment to the main agreement and usually lists those important ingredients that support the main contract. These ingredients may include sound equipment and labor, lighting equipment and labor, food, beverage, transportation, and housing for artists/entertainers, or other important financial considerations other than the artist's fee. The rider should be attached to the main agreement and the rider should be separately initialed or signed to signify acceptance by both parties.

CHANGES TO THE AGREEMENT

Most agreements will require negotiation prior to execution and the result of these executions will be changes. If only two or three nonsubstantial changes are made you may

FIGURE 13-2
Event Management Sample Consulting Agreement

Agreement

This agreement is between Jane Smith Productions (otherwise known as Event Manager) and ABC Corporation (otherwise known as purchaser).

Event Manager agrees to provide the following services:

1. 50 hours of research regarding XYZ Festival.

2. 40 hours of design regarding XYZ Festival.

3. 30 hours of planning regarding XYZ Festival.

4. 20 hours of coordination regarding XYZ Festival.

5. 10 hours of evaluation regarding XYZ Festival.

A total of 150 hours of consulting time will be provided by Event Manager.

Purchaser agrees to provide:

1. A total fee in the amount of $7,500.

Terms:

The purchaser agrees to provide a nonrefundable deposit in the amount of seven hundred and fifty dollars (U.S.) ($750.00) to officially retain the services of Event Manager. The purchaser furthermore agrees to provide monthly payments in the amount of seven hundred and fifty dollars (U.S.) ($750.00) on or before the fifteenth day of each month commencing August 15, 1996, until the balance has been paid in full.

Cancellation:

In the event of cancellation notice must be received in writing. Should purchaser cancel ninety days or earlier prior to event Event Manager shall be entitled to retain all funds paid as of this date. Should purchaser cancel less than ninety days prior to event the Event Manager shall receive full payment as specified in the agreement above.

Force Majeure:

This agreement is automatically null and void if event is canceled due to act of God including hurricane, earthquake, flood, volcanic eruption, tornado, famine, or war. In the event of cancellation due to act of God neither party shall be liable for any further payments.

Insurance:

Both parties shall maintain in full force one million dollars per occurrence comprehensive general liability insurance. Each party shall name the other as additional insured for the duration of the event. Both parties shall provide a certificate of insurance demonstrating evidence of additional insured status prior to the start of the event.

Hold Harmless and Indemnification:

Both parties agree that if either party is negligent they will defend the nonnegligent party and hold them harmless against future action.

(Figure continued on next page)

FIGURE 13-2
Event Management Sample Consulting Agreement *(continued)*

Arbitration:

Both parties agree that if a dispute arises concerning this agreement a professional arbitrator certified by the American Arbitration Association or the alternative dispute resolution process through the Conventional Liaison Council will be used in place of normal litigation.

Reputation:

Both parties agree to use their best efforts to preserve and protect each other's reputation during the conduct of this event. The Event Manager recognizes that the purchaser has over time developed good standing in the business and general community and will use the best efforts available to protect and preserve this reputation from harm.

Billing:

The Event Manager shall be listed in the official program of the event with the following text in type the same size and style of the body copy.

This event managed by Jane Smith Productions.

The Event Manager shall be listed in the official program with other staff in the following manner with text in type the same size and style of the body copy.

Jane Smith, Event Manager

Time Is of the Essence:

This agreement must be executed by July 15, 1996. After this date this agreement must be considered null and void and a new agreement must be created.

Assignment:

This agreement may not be assigned to others. The persons executing this agreement have the full authority to sign this agreement on behalf of the organizations they represent.

The Full Agreement:

The agreement and any riders attached represent the full understanding between both parties. Any amendments to this agreement must be approved in writing and separately attached to this agreement.

Execution:

The signatures below confirm complete understanding and compliance with the terms and conditions described in this agreement.

_____   _____

ABC Corporation, Purchaser   Date

_____   _____

Jane Smith, Event Manager   Date choose to initial and date each change prior to returning the agreement for execution by the other party. Your initial and date signifies your acceptance of the change but does not obligate you to fulfill the entire agreement until you have affixed your signature. If there are substantial changes (such as in the date, time, venue, or fees) or more than three changes it is best to create a new agreement.

TERMS AND SEQUENCE OF EXECUTION

First, and foremost, always require that the purchaser sign the agreement first prior to affixing your signature. Once both signatures are affixed the agreement becomes official. If you sign the agreement first and then forward it to the other party, and they make changes and sign it, you may be somewhat obligated for those changes. It is always wise to request the purchaser's signature before affixing your own.

Second, never use facsimiles. Should you be forced to litigate the agreement the court will seek the "best copy" and that is usually an original. You may use a facsimile for an interim memorandum of understanding, but binding, official agreements must be originals.

Third, take the time to sign the agreement in person. Explain to the purchaser that the terms implied in the agreement are only as valid as the integrity of the persons signing the document. Offer your hand in friendship as you jointly execute this agreement.

Other Agreements

In addition to the main event consulting agreement, the event manager may be required to prepare and execute other types of agreements. Samples of these agreements may be found in the Appendix. Figure 13-3 lists typical event management agreements.

These agreements along with many others may be required to ensure the professional operation of your event. To identify all of the agreements that may be required check with other event organizers and local officials as well as your vendors to determine the critical documents that must be executed prior to the start of your event.

PERMITS

Permits are issued by local, state, provincial, or federal government agencies and allow you to conduct certain activities at your event. Figure 13-4 details the typical permits that may be required for your event.

Allow sufficient time to obtain your permit. A permit may only be issued after you have submitted the appropriate documentation and have paid a fee. Determine well in advance what type of documentation is required by the issuing agency and how funds are accepted.

Remember that permits are not automatically issued. A permit reflects that an agency is permitting your event organization to conduct certain activities provided you conform to the regulations they have established. Make certain you are able to com-

FIGURE 13-3
Typical Event Management Agreements

Consulting Agreement
Where one party (usually the event manager) agrees to provide consulting services for another party.

Employment Agreement
Where the employee agrees to specific terms for employment.

Exhibitor Contract
An agreement between an individual exhibitor and the sponsor of an exposition to lease space for a specific booth at the exposition.

Hotel Contract
An agreement between the hotel and the organization holding an event to provide rooms and function space as well as other services (food and beverage) for a specific event or series of events.

Noncompete Agreement
Where an employee agrees not to compete within a specific jurisdiction or marketplace for a specified period of time following the termination of employment.

Purchase Order
An order to a vendor to provide services or products.

Sponsorship Agreement
A contract between the sponsor and the event organizer where the organizer agrees to provide specific marketing services to the sponsor for a prescribed fee and/or other consideration.

Vendor Agreement
An agreement between the vendor and the event manager or client to provide specific services or products for the event.

FIGURE 13-4
Typical Event Management Permits and Where to Obtain Them

Permit	Source
Bingo	Lottery or gaming department
Food handling	Health department
Lottery	Lottery or gaming department
Occupancy	Fire department
Parking	Transportation and parking department
Parks usage	Park department
Public assembly	Public safety and police department
Pyrotechnics	Fire department
Sales tax	Revenue or tax collector's office
Sign and banners	Zoning department
Street closing	Transportation and parking department

ply with these regulations prior to applying for the permit. If you are denied a permit you may consider appealing your case. In some cases, event managers have sued the agency to obtain permission to successfully conduct their event. However, since most event managers rely on the goodwill of the local agencies to successfully conduct the event, litigation should be the absolute final resort.

LICENSING

The license is granted either by a private organization (as in music licensing) or public entity to officially allow you to conduct a specific activity. The difference between a permit and a license may be slight in some jurisdictions. Usually the requirements for obtaining a license are much more stringent and require due diligence (evidence of worthiness) prior to issuance.

Figure 13-5 lists the most common licenses required for events and their sources.

Additional licenses may be required for your event. To determine what licenses are required make certain that you examine the event's history, check with organizers of similar events, and confirm and verify with the appropriate agencies that issue these licenses.

One of your best sources of information will be your vendors. Audit your vendors, especially in the technology field, and determine if licenses are required (as in the case of laser projection) or if the event manager must secure the license.

For many events both permits and licenses must be secured. The larger the event, the more likely the number of permits and licenses will increase. Remember that licenses and permits are the government's way of establishing a barrier to entry to protect their interests. Work closely with these agencies to understand their procedures, time frames, and inspection policies. A close working relationship with the agencies that issue licenses and permits for your event will help ensure the success of your overall event operation.

CONTRACTS, PERMITS, AND LICENSES: A SYNERGISTIC RELATIONSHIP

Professional event managers understand, and use to their advantage, the synergy between a well-written and executed contract and the acquisition of proper permits and licenses. All three instruments are essential for the professional operation of modern events.

FIGURE 13-5
Typical Event Management Licenses and Where to Obtain Them

Permit	Source
Alcohol	Alcohol Beverage Control
Business	Economic development/Recorder
Food	Health department
Music	American Society of Composers, Authors, and Publishers or Broadcast Music International
Pyrotechnics	Alcohol, Tobacco, and Firearms, Fire Department

When developing an agreement determine in advance who is responsible for obtaining and paying for specific permits and licenses and incorporate this language into the agreement. Unless you have specified who is responsible for obtaining and paying for permits and licenses, this can lead to an interruption of your event and conflicts among the various stakeholders.

Therefore, carefully conduct your research during the planning stage to identify all necessary permits and licenses and determine who will be responsible for coordinating this process. Include this information in your master event consulting agreement as well as your vendor agreements.

Since permits and licenses are unavoidable in most event situations it behooves the event manager to practice the maxim that an ounce of prevention (or risk management) is worth a pound of cure. Use the planning phase to examine potential permit processes and then use the coordination stage to link these two important steps within the Event Management process.

Contracts, permits, and licenses have legal, ethical, and risk management ramifications. To ensure that these impacts are positive, event managers must understand their importance and work diligently to communicate with the required agencies as well as prepare and execute valid agreements.

MAIN EVENT

1. Event agreements include one or more parties, an offer, consideration, and acceptance.

2. Additional clauses in event management agreements may include cancellation, force majeure, time is of the essence, assignment, reputation, the complete agreement, and other issues deemed important to both parties.

3. Event managers must obtain permits to properly conduct their events. Allow sufficient time to conduct research, obtain, and pay for these permits.

4. Event managers must obtain licenses for food, music, business, and other operations. Determine who is responsible for obtaining and paying for these permits.

5. The contract should specify who will obtain and pay for permits and licenses. Do your homework regarding permits and licenses prior to creating and executing the contract.

NEXT ON THE AGENDA

Permits and licenses begin the process of risk assessment and management; however, this process must ultimately include all of the event stakeholders. In Chapter 14 you will learn how to conduct an effective risk assessment for your event and practice risk management procedures to reduce, control, transfer, or avoid these risks.

Risk Management Procedures

"Hundreds of people burned to death in tent during graduation ceremony in India," shouted the headlines. Whenever human beings assemble for the purposes of celebration, education, marketing, or reunion there is an increased risk of loss of life or property. This has sadly been proven many times as similar newspaper headlines have reported the accidents that have occurred at events.

With these increased injuries, thefts, and other misfortunes there is of course increased expense. The increased expense may stem from two sources. First, and foremost, is the loss of revenue directly resulting from the occurrence. The second is the increase in insurance premiums when the underwriter is forced to pay large settlements as a result of negligence. Perhaps the most profound loss is the loss of business opportunity that results from the bad publicity attached to these tragedies. After all, who wants to visit an event where the tent periodically collapses and injures people or where too many incidents of food poisoning have been reported?

Alexander Berlonghi, an expert in the field of risk assessment and risk management, has devised a method for attempting to identify and contain the many risks associated with events. Berlonghi describes this activity as the risk assessment process and the first step is to hold a risk assessment meeting. Following is a step-by-step guide to holding your risk assessment meeting. I suggest you use it for each of your events—it could be an event, if not a lifesaver.

Organizing the Risk Assessment Meeting

The first question when organizing the risk assessment meeting is: "Who should attend?" Ideally all key event stakeholders should be involved in this meeting and you may wish to use a written survey to audit their opinions regarding risks associated with your event. However, for practical purposes you must first identify those event team leaders who can bring you the best information from which to manage present and future risks associated with your events. Figure 14-1 provides a list of event team leaders who should be included in the risk assessment meeting.

BEFORE THE MEETING

Once you have identified the participants for your risk assessment meeting it is time to put them to work, before the meeting. Assigning prework helps the meeting participants focus on the seriousness of the risk assessment meeting and will most likely improve the efficiency of the actual meeting itself. Figure 14-2 demonstrates a typical risk assessment meeting announcement that you may customize for your own use.

Make sure you follow up with the meeting participants to ensure that everyone returns their list to you and that you understand the risks they have identified as important to their area. Once you have received 100 percent of the participants' responses it is time to compile a master listing of all risks that have been identified. You may either list these risks in alphabetical order or subdivide them by event area.

The final step in preparing for the risk assessment meeting is to prepare a detailed agenda that may be used to conduct the meeting. Prior to the meeting circulate the agenda and seek feedback from the participants. Figure 14-3 provides a sample agenda and premeeting announcement that you may customize for your event risk assessment meeting.

FIGURE 14-1
Risk Assessment Meeting Potential Participants

Admissions manager	Electrician	Parking specialist
Advertising manager	Entertainment specialist	Police liaison for event
Animal handler	Fire department liaison	Public relations manager
Box office manager	Food and beverage manager	Pyrotechnic specialist
Broadcast manager	Hotel security director	Security director for event
Catering manager	Insurance broker	Sound specialist
Comptroller	Laser specialist	Special effects specialist
Computer or data processing manager	Lighting specialist	Transportation specialist
	Office manager	

FIGURE 14-2
Risk Assessment Meeting Announcement

TO: Event Risk Assessment Team
FR: Event Manager
SUBJECT: Meeting Announcement and Instructions
DATE: August 15, 1996
ACTION REQUIRED: Return your list of potential risks by July 15, 1996.

A risk assessment meeting will be held on July 20, 1996, at 1 P.M. for the purpose of identifying and managing the major risks associated with this event. Prior to this meeting you should audit your own area and prepare a comprehensive list of risks associated with your event responsibilities.

Interview the team members in your area and ask them to assist you in this important task of identifying potential risks. These risks may involve potential injuries, loss of life or property, or other risks that you may identify.

Submit this risk to me by close of business on July 15, 1996. Thank you for your contribution to this important process.

FIGURE 14-3
Event Risk Assessment Meeting Sample Agenda/Announcement

TO: Event Team Leaders
FR: Event Manager
SUBJECT: Event Risk Assessment Meeting Agenda
DATE: July 15, 1996
ACTION REQUIRED: Review the enclosed agenda and return to me by July 18, 1996
                       with your comments.

Tentative Agenda

   I.   Welcome and introductions
   II.   Explanation of purposes, Event Manager
   III.   Comprehensive risk review, all participants
   IV.   Additional risks not covered in listing, all participants
   V.   Recommendations for risk management, all participants
   VI.   Economic impacts of risk management, all participants, Comptroller
   VII.   Post meeting work assignment, Event Manager
   VIII. Adjournment

CONDUCTING THE MEETING

After the agenda has been distributed, corrected, and approved it is time to actually convene the risk assessment meeting. Use a hollow square seating design and prepare tent cards for each participant listing his or her name and event area of responsibility. A flip chart displayed on an easel stand should list the agenda for the meeting and the subsequent pages should list the risks previously identified by the meeting participants. In addition, participants should receive a typed copy of the agenda and the comprehensive list of risks along with any other collateral material that will help them make the important decisions that will be required during the meeting.

As the event manager you are also the facilitator for this meeting. Your job is to facilitate the participation of all participants. To do this, first welcome the participants and explain that the meeting will only be successful if they actively participate by offering their expert opinions and engaging in a lively discussion concerning recommendations for reducing or alleviating the risks that have been identified.

After you have set the tone for the meeting, review the list of risks and ask the meeting participants to study them for a few moments and identify any gaps. What risks have been overlooked?

The next stage of the meeting is to begin discussions on how to reduce, control, transfer, or eliminate the risks that have been identified. This is a good time to ask the participants to form small groups that represent cross-disciplinary task forces. For example, you may ask the admissions, box office, and comptroller team members to work on reducing the risk of theft from the box office or eliminating the risk of gate crashing. Allow fifteen to thirty minutes for this activity.

When you reconvene the group ask them to feedback their recommendations to the entire group and try to seek consensus from the group members. Do not rush this process. During these discussions important concerns may be expressed and you must make sure you address and attempt to satisfy these concerns before moving on to the next stage.

Every risk decision will have corresponding financial impacts. This is a good time to use a Likert Scale to rate the importance of each risk in terms of the overall event. For example, you may use the following rating system to identify those risks that should receive the greatest consideration when considering the financial impacts to your event.

With the number one representing least concern and the number five representing most concern, ask each participant to assign a number to each risk. For example, theft from the box office might rate a five while rain in July may receive a one. Once you have reached consensus on the level of importance of each risk, you may concentrate your discussions on those that the group deems most important.

DOCUMENTING THE MEETING'S RECOMMENDATIONS

The final stage of the risk assessment meeting is to carefully document your recommendations and assign postmeeting work groups to continue to address the important issues covered in the meeting. Assign one person as a scribe during the meeting and ask them to prepare review notes from this meeting to be circulated within three business days. The review notes should reflect the substance and content of the discussions during the meeting and list the recommendations the group has agreed to pursue as a result of this meeting.

From convocation to commencement, the university or college event manager is responsible for coordinating dozens of events. Blending tradition with highly detailed logistical planning requires careful planning and sensitivity. *(Photo courtesy of The George Washington University)*

The meeting or conference event may require a standing lectern and skirted table or elaborate staging. The modern event manager must carefully assess the needs for this event and satisfy the participant's expectations by providing proper equipment.
(Photo courtesy of J. Gerard Smith)

An arts and crafts show may be coordinated by the event manager as an independent event, or it may be used to attract customers to a preexisting retail operation such as a retail shopping center. These shows may attract upscale guests that will provide investment for the local area. *(Photo courtesy of J. Gerard Smith)*

Festivals are often designed for the entire family and, in recent years, children's activities have been developed to allow mom and dad to have an additional reason for participating in the event. Savvy event managers carefully match demographics and psychographics with the activities that are offered to ensure a good fit. *(Photo courtesy of J. Gerard Smith)*

Strolling or street performers (also known as sight acts) not only provide decor, but can distract and entertain guests as they wait on lines for an activity, such as registration. *(Photo courtesy of J. Gerard Smith)*

Musicians, representing a specific region, often provide the central theme for an event in both sight and sound. *(Photo courtesy of J. Gerard Smith)*

Modern tenting provides a four-walled environment that will sustain the impact of an event. *(Photo courtesy of J. Gerard Smith)*

Defining an event with themed entertainment will provide an educational as well as cultural aspect to your celebration. *(Photo courtesy of J. Gerard Smith)*

One of the oldest events in human history is the parade or procession. The inclusion of colorful matching units provides a moving pageant of splendor.
(Photo courtesy of J. Gerard Smith)

The modern half-time show or spectacle is one more example of how sport has become total entertainment and further demonstrates the important role the event manager must play in this activity. *(Photo courtesy of J. Gerard Smith)*

Creating a dramatic stage set featuring the central logo of MTV™ enables the event manager to create interest while also conveying an important message to the audience members. *(Design by XYZ, photo courtesy of The Photographer's Gallery, Washington, D.C.)*

Stage sets must carefully consider the sight lines of the audience members. In some cases, the stage set must be enhanced with video projection to allow full visibility by the audience members. *(Photo courtesy of J. Gerard Smith)*

The 1984 Olympic Games in Los Angeles were a major paradigm shift in event production. Elaborate technology was utilized to create a world class spectacle and many modern day event management pioneers began their career with this event.

(Photo courtesy of Image Engineering)

Interactive entertainment creates interest and focus to make the event experience memorable. *(Photo courtesy of The Photographer's Gallery, Washington, D.C.)*

The work groups are responsible for conducting additional research to identify ways in which to better manage the risks that were discussed at perhaps lower cost to the event. Their work may include interviewing external experts or further brainstorming with their fellow event stakeholders to seek better solutions.

The review notes also serve an important purpose of preserving the history of this meeting. Should there be an incident at your event that requires evidence that you conducted risk assessment and management procedures to attempt to prevent this occurrence, these review notes may serve as valuable proof documenting your proactive stance.

Safety Meeting and Other Considerations

Before you allow your vendors to install the various event elements you must conduct a brief safety meeting to alert all event stakeholders to the standards your organization has established with regards to safety. Notify the event stakeholders in writing and explain that this meeting is required for participation in the event. Usually this meeting is held prior to installation and is conducted by the event manager.

Survey the event stakeholders to find out if they have particular expertise in event safety. You may wish to call upon this expertise during the safety meeting.

Use a checklist or written agenda distributed to each participant at the meeting to remain focused on the goals and objectives of the meeting. Detail your expectations of minimum safety requirements for the event. These may include taping or ramping of exposed cables, grounding of all electric power, keeping the work areas cleared of debris, nonsmoking policies, and other important issues.

Ask those assembled if they have been trained in the Heimlich (choking) maneuver or CPR (cardiopulmonary resuscitation) during the past three years. Ask those who have been trained to serve as first responders for the event if someone requires this level of response. The event manager should be trained in both the Heimlich maneuver and CPR and prepared to use these techniques to sustain or save lives if required.

Make certain you ask each person to sign in when they attend the meeting. This will provide you with a record of those persons who participated and may be helpful if there is a later claim against the event.

Conclude the meeting by reminding all participants that the overall goal of this event is zero percent tolerance of unsafe working conditions.

Inspections

Prior to opening the doors to admit your guests to your event, conduct a final inspection. Walk the entire event site and note any last minute corrections that must be made to ensure the safety of your guests. These walk-throughs are best conducted by a team that includes your client, key vendors, key event team leaders, and when possible police, fire, and other officials.

During this walk-through use an instant camera and/or video to record corrections you have made and post caution signs where appropriate to notify your guests of risks.

Figure 14-4 lists those areas that must be reviewed when conducting the walk-through prior to admitting your guests to your event.

These are but a few of the areas that must be inspected prior to opening the doors to admit your guests. You may wish to prepare a checklist to systematically inspect each area or simply use a small pad of paper and note those areas that must be corrected prior to the event. The walk-through should be conducted between one and two hours prior to the official start time of the event. This will afford you the time to make those minor corrections that are required.

WAR STORY

During the opening of the Trump Taj Mahal thousands of guests were exposed to numerous risks ranging from electric to vehicular. Many of the guests who participated in the grand opening were senior citizens with impaired vision. We posted hundreds of caution signs on top of electric cables, ramps, stairs, exposed rails, electric poles, and other areas with which guests could come into contact. In addition, each of our staff members was given an instant camera so that they could record slips, falls, and other accidents.

Lesson Learned

Perhaps as a result of the publicity Mr. Trump received as one of the world's richest men, many guests attempted to sue him for negligence at the event. To my knowledge none of these cases was ever fully litigated due to the excellent risk management procedures implemented for this event. For example, our staff took many photos of individuals falling (sometimes purposely) on top of ramps with big bright caution signs displayed warning them of the potential hazard. To reduce litigation and protect your guests, risk-proof your event site using caution signs and other proactive measures.

FIGURE 14-4
Final Walk-through Inspection List

Accreditation systems are in working order
Admissions personnel is in place
Air walls are in working order in case of evacuation
Bar personnel has received alcohol management training
Doors are unlocked from inside venue in case of evacuation
Edge of stage is marked with safety tape to mark edge
Electric boxes are labeled with caution signs
Electric cables are grounded
Electric cables traversing public areas are taped or ramped
Elevators are working
Light level is sufficient for safe ingress and egress
Lighting has been properly secured with safety chains
Metal detectors are in place and operational for VIP appearances
Ramps are in place for the disabled
Security personnel is posted
Signs are visible and well secured
Staging has chair and handrails
Stairs have handrails and individual steps are marked with safety tape to highlight edge
Ushering personnel is in place

Documentation and Due Diligence

Each of the steps listed above demonstrates to officials, and perhaps one day a jury, that you have attempted to do what a reasonable person would expect under similar circumstances to ensure the safety of your guests. This is the minimum expectation of a judge and jury should you have an incident at your event that will require litigation to resolve. Therefore, documenting your risk assessment, management, and prevention steps may assist you in demonstrating that you have practiced due diligence for your event. The goal is to achieve or exceed the standard of care normally associated with an event of your size and type. The steps listed above will help you move rapidly toward this goal.

Obtaining Insurance

Insurance is used by event managers to transfer the risk to a third party—the insurance underwriter. Many venues require that the event manager or event organization maintain in full force a minimum of one million dollars per occurrence of comprehensive general liability insurance. Some municipalities also require similar limits of insurance for events to be held in their jurisdiction. Events that are more complex and pose greater risks may be required to have higher limits of insurance.

Identifying a properly qualified insurance broker is an important first step in receiving expert advice regarding the types of insurance that may be required for your event. After checking with the venue and municipality to determine the level of insurance required, you will need a well-trained specialty insurance broker to further advise you on available coverage.

A specialty insurance broker is an individual whose insurance products and services are specifically relevant for the Event Management profession. For example, large firms such as Marsh and McLennan or K & K provide products for clients ranging from the Super Bowl to local parades and festivals. They are experienced experts in providing advice and counsel for the unique risks associated with events.

IDENTIFYING THE APPROPRIATE PREMIUM

After you have contacted two or more specialty insurance brokers and determined the type of insurance products that may be required for your event, you will request quotes from each of the brokers. The brokers will ask you to complete a detailed form listing the history of the event, specific hazards that may be involved such as pyrotechnics, and other critical information. The broker will then submit this information to several underwriters and present you with a quote for coverage.

The most cost-effective premium is an annual policy known as comprehensive general liability insurance. Some event managers pay as little as $2,000 annually to provide coverage for a variety of risks for which the event manager may be liable. Other event managers pay their premiums on a per event basis. Your insurance broker will help you decide what the best system is for your event or events.

Figure 14-5 lists the typical insurance products associated with events.

Your client or others involved with your event may ask that they be named as an additional insured on your policy. The term *additional insured* means that if, for any rea-

---

FIGURE 14-5
Typical Event Management Insurance Policies

Automotive liability	Earthquake	Life
Board of directors liability	Errors and omissions	Nonappearance
Business interruption	Fire	Office contents
Cancellation	Flood	Officers
Comprehensive general liability	Health	Rain
Disability	Hurricane	Worker's compensation
	Key Person	

son, there is an incident, your insurance policy will also cover claims against those listed as additionally insured. Before agreeing to name the other party or parties as additional insured, check with your insurance broker to find out if there is an additional charge or if this is appropriate. You may also want to ask the other parties to name you as additional insured on their policies.

EXCLUSIONS

Every insurance policy will list certain hazards that are excluded from coverage. Make certain that you check with your broker and carefully review your policy to make sure there are no gaps in coverage for your event. For example, if your event is using pyrotechnics and they are specifically excluded from your current coverage you may wish to purchase additional coverage to protect your event.

PREEXISTING COVERAGE

Before purchasing any coverage, audit your existing coverage to check for gaps regarding your event. Your event organization may already have in force specific coverage related to the risks associated with your event. Once you have conducted this audit, your specialty insurance broker can advise you with regard to additional coverage for your event.

Managing the Risk: Everyone's Responsibility

The field of event risk management has grown so rapidly that there is emerging a specialization within the profession for risk experts such as Berlonghi and others. Larger events such as the Pope's visit to Colorado may require the expertise of a risk manager such as Berlonghi to manage this complex event from a risk perspective. However, for most events, the event manager is also the risk manager.

As the risk manager you must assemble a risk management team that will assist you in identifying and managing the risks to improve your event operations. You must communicate to all event stakeholders that event risk management is everyone's responsibility.

MAIN EVENT

1. Increased injuries and losses have focused attention to the event profession and required more stringent risk management policies and procedures.

2. As a direct result to these increases in incidents, costs have risen. Practicing effective risk management is good business as it helps contain costs.

3. The event manager must organize a risk assessment meeting as one of the first steps in identifying and man-aging all risks associated with the upcoming events.

4. All key event stakeholders should attend this meeting and complete prework listing the potential risks asso-ciated with their area.

5. The event manager should facilitate the risk management meeting and seek full participation from each of the stakeholders.

6. The results of this meeting should be carefully documented in review notes and incorporated into policies and procedures.

7. Prior to opening the doors to your event, the official walk-through with a camera must be conducted to pro-vide a final inspection and to contain or remove additional risks.

8. A safety meeting should be scheduled and conducted prior to installation of the event elements.

9. The event manager must conduct an insurance audit to determine the levels of existing coverage and poten-tial risk, and identify gaps that must be closed with additional insurance products.

10. A specialty insurance broker should be contacted to provide specialized expertise regarding the types of insur-ance that may be required for your event.

NEXT ON THE AGENDA

Event Management ethics is an overriding concern throughout this new profession. Understanding the difference between the Mosaic code, the code of laws, and personal and professional ethics will provide the event manager with a solid framework within which to make sound ethical decisions as you will discover in Chapter 15.

CHAPTER *15*

Ethics

Is it ethical to take credit for an event you produced while working for another company? What about giving your business card to a prospective client at an event where you are working for another event manager? Should you accept a gift from a vendor who is trying to solicit future business from your firm or should the gift be given to the firm for whom you work? If you bring new business to a vendor should you receive a kick-back, commission, or referral fee? These questions and many more are rapidly emerging as Event Management develops into a full-fledged modern profession.

Professional ethics are standards of conduct that are acceptable to the majority of persons within a given profession. All modern professions set and enforce these standards to protect the profession from discredit by individuals who do not seek this higher ground. Medicine, law, accounting, and other established professions developed ethical standards in response to problems within their professions that, had they gone uncorrected, would have either slowed the growth of the profession or perhaps destroyed the credibility these professionals had worked long and hard to establish.

Distinguishing between Moral, Legal, and Ethical Codes

It is important to note that although there is an implied relationship between morals, laws, and ethics there is also a wide variance in terms of definition. Many laws derive from the ancient Mosaic code (the Ten Commandments); however, the moral code is typically a personal set of values that is developed by each individual and requires self-enforcement. The legal code, by contrast, is a series of legislative decisions that are enforceable by local, state, provincial, or federal law. Therefore, these laws are legally binding and developed for the greater good of all society. The code of ethics is markedly different from the moral and legal code.

A code of ethics or professional conduct is a dynamic set of guidelines for behavior within a profession. In a study by Kathleen Sigfried of The George Washington University, Ms. Sigfried compared to the International Special Events Society (ISES) Code of Ethics to two other professional societies within the travel and tourism industry. Ms. Sigfried noted that the ISES code of ethics—the newest one developed among the three—included a provision for extending the same conduct required for clients to vendors as well. The ISES code was the only one to include this provision. She concluded that this was because Event Management is a new profession, event managers sought to build long-term relationships with their suppliers and therefore proper ethical conduct was essential.

Regardless of the origins or the content of a code of ethics, enforcement is essential to ensure that it is evenly applied to all members of the profession. In most professional organizations ethical disputes are held in strictest confidence and only the opposing parties and the impartial panel that responds to their complaints are privy to this information.

Typically the process for resolving ethical disputes involves arbitration between the parties by an arbitrator selected by the professional association hearing the complaint. Obviously it is hoped that a resolution can be achieved without further discussion. However, if both parties insist on presenting their versions of the issue or issues then the organization hearing the complaint may convene a hearing before the ethics panel. The ethics panel may decide after hearing the complaint to sanction the offending party by censorship or in extreme cases revoke membership in the organization. Each professional organization uses different policies and procedures to adjudicate these ethical matters. What is most important is that the teeth of the organization are present if required to back up the words and values contained within the ethics statement. Furthermore, employers may incorporate the same teeth, as allowed by state, provincial, and federal law, in their employment agreements to ensure they are able to enforce the precepts contained in their mission, values, and beliefs statement.

Nearly fifty years ago my father opened his small hardware store in Dallas, Texas. Instead of hanging a grand opening banner or blowing up balloons he sat down and composed a simple but profound message to his customers. The message was then transformed into elegant calligraphy and displayed just inside the front door of his store where it greeted customers for over forty years. As I write these lines that same message faces me and it reads:

Once upon a time, I met a stranger . . . not so many years ago . . . in a distant city. When he learned that he knew my grandfather, the stranger looked at me and said, "You have a good

name." He went on to explain that my grandfather held the respect and esteem of his fellow
businessmen, his customer bestowed their confidence upon him, and his compassion and service
for others was an inspiration to all. It is the hope of this business that we will so conduct our
affairs that someday, somewhere one of our descendants will meet a stranger who will say,
"You have a good name."
—MAX B. GOLDBLATT (1911-1995)

Ethical decisions are abundant in a new emerging profession such as Event Management. Therefore, the event manager must recognize the guidelines for these decisions and the implications for exercising poor judgment. Ethical issues such as whether
to accept gifts from vendors, distribute business cards at an event organized by another
event manager, claim credit for an event you only partially produced, or use others' ideas
in another context are only the tip of the Event Management ethical iceberg. As the
profession develops the issues will grow in number. However, to provide a system for
addressing these issues the event manager should develop a mission or vision statement
such as the one authored by my father and then develop specific practices to support
this overall philosophy. For example, you may decide only to receive gifts with value
that is under a certain dollar amount or to refuse all gifts. You may elect to always give
credit to others when using even partial components of their ideas. These are but two
of numerous examples of policies and practices you may develop to consistently guide
your thinking with regards to the many emerging ethical issues in Event Management.

The ISES Code of Ethics

The code of ethics for ISES is shown in Figure 15-1. It was created in 1986 by a group
of Event Management professionals who used models from the certified public
accounting, legal, and medical professions as a conceptual framework to build their own
unique code. I was a member of this committee and remember the many heated discussions about what elements should or should not be included. Many of the original
tenets in the ISES code of ethics sprang forth from problems in the profession. For example, many agreements were made using only the verbal process. Therefore, one of the
first issues was the importance of issuing agreements in writing in order to provide a
clear understanding for all parties. Today this may appear to be a rather simple matter; however, when the profession was first developing, it was common to use verbal
agreements and as a result there was much derision between clients and event managers.

Because event managers rely heavily on subcontractors or vendors to service their
events and consider these individuals their true professional partners, members of the
original ISES ethics committee insisted that all tenets in the code of ethics extend with
the same weight and force to these contractors as well as to their clients. This single
action further defined the important role of the event manager in this emerging modern profession. By adopting this ethical provision, the Event Management profession

---

FIGURE 15-1
ISES Code of Ethics

Each member of ISES shall agree to adhere to the following:

1. Provide to all persons truthful and accurate information with respect to the professional performance of duties.

2. Maintain the highest standards of personal conduct to bring credit to the special events industry.

3. Promote and encourage the highest level of ethics within the profession.

4. Recognize and discharge by responsibility, to uphold all laws and regulations relating to ISES policies and activities.

5. Strive for excellence in all aspects of the industry.

6. Use only legal and ethical means in all industry activities.

7. Protect the public against fraud and unfair practices, and attempt to eliminate from ISES all practices which bring discredit to the profession.

8. Use a written contract clearly stating all charges, services, products, and other essential information.

9. Demonstrate respect for every professional within the industry by clearly stating and consistently performing at or above the standards acceptable to the industry.

10. Make a commitment to increase professional growth and knowledge by attending educational programs recommended, but not limited to, those prescribed by ISES.

11. Contribute knowledge to professional meetings and journals to raise the consciousness of the industry.

12. Maintain the highest standards of safety, sanitation, and any other responsibilities.

13. When providing services or products, maintain in full force adequate or appropriate insurance.

14. Cooperate with professional colleagues, suppliers, and employees to provide the highest quality service.

15. Extend these same professional commitments to all those persons supervised or employed.

16. Subscribe to the ISES Principles of Professional Conduct and Ethics and to abide by the ISES Bylaws.

---

declared that the event manager has a dual responsibility to not only conduct himself or herself ethically when dealing with clients but also when dealing with vendors. In fact, the event manager must treat both parties with equal measures of respect and maintain standards of high ethical conduct uniformly.

Gray Areas

In our increasingly global business community it is important for the event manager to understand that ethical conduct that is acceptable in Boston may not be appropriate for Brunei. The event manager must identify the customs and traditions in each community where he or she is planning or coordinating an event and determine how to best interpret the ethical code. While a code of ethics is usually created to set standards for a profession, it is also a reflection of the individual who acts on behalf of the profession. As an event manager, your own integrity is a priceless commodity that may not be sacrificed at any price to accommodate the ethics of a destination where you are producing your event. Often this is a difficult and challenging issue as event managers increasingly operate global businesses and produce events throughout the world.

WAR STORY

Saturday afternoon just before I was to board the air shuttle to produce an event in a northeastern city I telephoned my contact in that city and asked if there was anything else I should bring. "Five hundred dollars cash," she stated firmly and without emotion. Although I was used to bringing small amounts of cash for gratuities I was shocked and confused at the request for an amount of this size. "Why do we need so much money?" I asked. "To pay the fire inspector, the police lieutenant, and anyone else who may require a gratuity," she replied. I drew a deep breath and explained that it was not my policy to provide these payments. In fact, I flatly refused to tender these payments. My local contact explained, "The event is taking place in less than five hours. These officials have already granted the written approvals we requested. However, they will be on site tonight and it is the local custom to provide them with a gratuity to thank them for their help." I further explained that if I was to provide these payments the local officials might expect the same largess in the future. Therefore, I could not start this process.

I also realized that time was of the essence and that 200 people would be gravely inconvenienced (not to mention the dozens of vendors) if the event was suddenly interrupted because a local official was uncooperative. In search of the greater good I proposed that I provide my local contact with a check made payable to their company for $500 and that they would be responsible for any gratuities as they felt were needed. Although I would have preferred not to have engaged in this process, when in Rome one sometimes must do as the Romans do or risk ruin. However, let us not forget that Rome eventually fell according to historians due to the absence of a strong moral fiber among their citizens.

Lesson Learned

Try to identify in advance what local customs prevail with regard to gratuities and other sensitive issues. There is no such thing as a black-and-white ethical decision. Most decisions require weighing your own sense of integrity with the greater good (in this case the success of the event). The consequences can be disastrous if you do not carefully research and plan your conduct well in advance.

The Three-Way Tests

I recommend using the three-way test to determine if you are making an ethical decision that is appropriate and in accordance with your profession's code of ethical conduct. This three-way test is not foolproof. However, it uses old-fashioned logic to identify whether or not you are able to live with your ethical decision.

Now let us apply this three-way test to some of the examples provided at the beginning of this chapter. Using the three-way test does not guarantee instant, foolproof answers. However, it will help you in terms of forecasting the ramifications of your decisions.

A common ethical dilemma faced by event managers is that which concerns the vendors to your event. When the event manager employs a musician, a clown, or other entertainer and later discovers that they have freely distributed their business cards and perhaps even brochures to the event manager's clients and guests often there is anger and resentment from both parties. Should the entertainers have distributed their cards?

That depends. First, if the event manager clearly stated in writing that the entertainer was forbidden from promoting himself or herself during the event the answer would be more obvious. Second, if the event manager has noticed that the entertainer was distributing cards and asked him or her to cease and the entertainer continued, this would also be easy to identify as a breach of professional ethics. But what happens if neither of these scenarios took place? There was no written notification and the event manager only learned after the event that this self-promotion was taking place. In this case the entertainer would have difficulty applying the three-way test effectively. However, by contrast, if the entertainer flagrantly abused his or her privilege as a vendor to this event by ignoring the admonitions or warnings of the event manager he or she would have difficulty passing the three-way test.

Another common scenario involves receiving gifts either in cash or products from individuals who refer business to you. The most common question is at what point does a gift become a bribe? In the war story described previously the gift was not given to receive permission to hold the event. Nor was the gift distributed due to a threat of event interruption. Rather, it was given because it was the tradition and custom of this city to show appreciation to local officials. One may also believe (as I did and still do) that these gifts are improper and should be made illegal.

When you receive a gift from a vendor should you accept it? Should you offer gifts

---

FIGURE 15-2

The Three-Way Test Rules for Ethical Decision Making

1. Would I want to read about it in tomorrow's newspaper headlines?

2. Would I want my grandmother to know?

3. Can I look proudly at myself in the mirror after I make this decision?

to clients in advance of receiving their business? This is a common practice in the hotel industry where hotel salespeople regularly lavishly entertain future customers with amenities ranging from free airline tickets to rooms and meals as well as entertainment. Is there a quid pro quo (implied duty) when these gifts are accepted?

The American Medical Association (AMA) issued new policies regarding the sponsorship of certain events by corporations due to the concern with the implications of undue influence among doctors and their patients. Prior to these new guidelines pharmaceutical firms would provide physicians with lavish trips, gifts, and other perks with the hope that they would select their products for use by the physicians' patients. Today this is no longer allowed by the AMA. Corporations may still contribute to medical events but their support must follow stringent guidelines and usually incorporates educational activities.

Event Management, closely linked to the hospitality industry, recognizes the importance of providing gifts or demonstrations of hospitality to future clients. Conversely, event managers may more often than not be on the receiving end of such largess themselves from hotels or others who want their business.

The ethical dilemma is whether or not these gifts are appropriate methods of soliciting business. What happens when one accepts a gift? Is there an implied duty when the gift is accepted? Using the three-way test then becomes difficult to establish one answer for each circumstance. However, if the event manager establishes specific limits for gift receipts (as in under $25.00 per vendor annually) then the three-way test becomes a firm assessment tool to determine whether or not a breach of ethics has taken place.

The end result of these two examples of ethical decision making is that a set of guidelines would have greatly eased this arduous process. This is why companies compose and publish mission statements and establish policies, procedures, and practices for accepting gifts from vendors or giving gifts to prospective or current clients.

A few years ago, Johnson & Johnson Company was saddled with the horrific consequences of handling the Tylenol® tampering incident. They were well prepared, however, because their mission statement clearly stated that they must first and foremost provide the public with safe products. To fulfill this ethical mandate they pulled all Tylenol® products from the shelves, investigated the incident, and then developed the most stringent tamper-proof system henceforth available for over-the-counter medications or other products for that matter. Because they had clearly defined their mission and it included their core values as a company, Johnson & Johnson Company knew exactly how to act when a decision of great magnitude was required.

Proactivity

The best method for resolving ethical disputes is to avoid them whenever possible. Carefully reviewing the ISES code and using these principles proactively will eliminate almost all possibility of infraction. However, Figure 15-3 examines typical violations of the code and proactive measures that could have been taken to avoid this infraction.

Creating Your Own Mission, Values, and Core Beliefs Statement

You do not need to be a Fortune 100 company to establish a mission and values statement for your event organization. Furthermore, the smaller your organization, the easier it is to reach consensus regarding your core beliefs. Figure 15-4 provides you with a checklist for this important process.

The process for creating your own mission, values, and core beliefs statement can become one of the most valuable times in your professional career. As these core beliefs will guide your day-to-day decision making, the process should not be entered into half-heartedly or rushed. You may wish to invite a critical friend from a noncompetitive company to assist you with the process and provide you with objective input. Another critical friend may be an attorney or accountant who may advise you on the types of tests that may be applied to your statement.

When preparing the final draft of your statement it is wise to use strong, direct language that is easy for others to understand. The sample shown in Figure 15-5 provides you with a framework from which you may craft your final version.

Dividing the statement into three distinct parts—mission, values, and core beliefs—is a logical and understandable way to present your final version so that others can readily use it to develop their perception of your organization. A wise public relations practitioner reportedly once said "perception is reality" and indeed it is. Before a client will invest $10,000 with your Event Management firm he or she must first like you (a subjective decision), respect you (an analytical decision), and trust you (an evaluative deci-

---

FIGURE 15-3
Typical Violations of ISES Code and Proactive Measures

1. **Accepting expensive gifts:** Ban or set a limit on gifts.

2. **Confusion regarding a change in an agreement:** Put all agreements (and changes) in writing and have both parties initial acceptance.

3. **Improper promotion of your services:** Seek written authority while working for another event manager.

4. **Claiming credit for an event you produced while working for another firm:** Clearly disclose the circumstances concerning the production of the event.

5. **Submitting photos of an event as an example of your work:** Clearly disclose that you helped produce your specific contributions to this event.

FIGURE 15-4
Developing the Mission, Values, and Core Beliefs Statement

1. Interview the founders, officers, and other key people in your event organization.

2. Interview the external stakeholders in your organization and ask them how your organization is currently perceived as an ethically-sound operation.

3. Determine if there are any gaps between the perceptions of the external stakeholders and the internal leaders and seek to close them through discussion.

4. Review similar organizations and use their policies and procedures for ethical decisions as a model.

5. Prepare a first draft of your statement and circulate it to all stakeholders for input.

6. Refine the statement after receiving input from the stakeholders.

7. Seek ways to reduce the number of words to the minimum amount necessary to communicate the intent of the statement. Avoid lengthy mission statements.

8. Identify how the statement will be communicated and to whom.

9. Set a regular time each year to review the statement make necessary revisions.

10. Proudly distribute the statement to the stakeholders and display the statement for all future stakeholders (vendors and clients) to see and appreciate.

FIGURE 15-5
Framework for the Mission, Values, and Core Beliefs Statement

Mission

The mission of this organization is to consistently provide the highest quality Event Management services to our clients and to treat all those we deal with in a fair and honorable manner.

Values

We value integrity, honesty, and fairness and will use these core values in the fulfillment of our mission.

Core Beliefs

We believe:

1. All people deserve to be treated with respect, honesty, and courtesy.

2. Accurate, honest representation of our work is mandatory.

3. Original creative ideas are the property of the individual or organization responsible for this creation until such time as they are sold or leased to others.

4. Quality is essential for consistent success.

5. The ISES Code of Ethics and Principles of Professional Conduct is the acceptable standard of behavior within the Event Management profession.

sion based on the prior two decisions). To raise your integrity quotient, thoughtfully develop your mission, values, and core beliefs and then use them with the three-way test to not only improve your standing in Event Management but to raise the overall image of this emerging profession.

MAIN EVENT

1. The moral, legal, and ethical codes have different origins but many linkages.
2. A code of ethics is usually developed by a profession as it matures to protect the profession from unethical practices.

3. There are no black-and-white ethical answers. Rather, ethics is subject to the culture, tradition, and principles of the community where the decision is being made.

4. Event managers must never sacrifice their personal and professional integrity for the benefit of others whose ethics may be in conflict with the profession of Event Management.

5. To be effective, ethics must be enforceable by the profession.

NEXT ON THE AGENDA

Learning is a continuous process that is essential for professional advancement and long-term career as well as financial success. In Chapter 16 you will discover how to remain competitive, set professional goals, and benefit from on-line education as well as professional certification programs to validate your abilities.

Epilogue

Event Management is a process combining the five phases of research, design, planning, coordination, and evaluation. The event manager may enter the process during any single phase; however, he or she must thoroughly understand each of the phases and their relationship to one another to be effective.

Education too is a process, and similar to Event Management, it is a continuous one that requires that those engaged in the process demonstrate both rigor and persistence. The reward for this rigorous process is obvious.

Whether full-time or part-time, event managers are more educated and skilled than the general population. The skills required for managing people and technology, administration of agreements, financial instruments, and other organizational requirements as well as the creativity needed to compete in a global marketplace are no longer acquired through the school of hard knocks. For literally hundreds of years this was the only school available to event managers. In fact, I was a product of this school and as a result estimate that I lost over one million dollars in potential revenue (earnings) and ten years of my life. Had I been able to avail myself of professional training such as that now being offered by universities and colleges throughout the world I would have earned more money earlier and cut my learning curve completely in half. Learning through trial and error is not only the most expensive way to learn it is also the most dangerous.

As an expert witness in litigation involving Event Management negligence the majority of cases involves individuals who have decent values but no formal training in research, design, planning, coordination, or evaluation of events. These same individuals would have greatly benefited (and perhaps still be in business) if they had availed themselves of a professional program of Event Management education.

Getting Started in the Profession

Individuals who wish to enter this profession frequently E-mail or telephone me from the four corners of the earth and ask the age-old question "How do I get started?" My answer is simple. Develop a plan for learning about this profession that includes formal skill training as well as practicums or internships. These same individuals often bemoan the fact that other Event Management businesses will not open their doors to them as volunteers so they can readily receive professional experience. I remind them that every business by its nature must be suspicious of individuals who, without credentials, wish to explore this fun and fascinating profession. Perhaps the individual is dishonest and is instead seeking to steal the ideas, and even clients, of the very business where he or she is working. Therefore, the shortest route between exploring and succeeding in this profession is affiliation with a well-known school or university where you can immediately enjoy the credibility required to identify worthwhile internships while receiving formal training.

Certainly certification is one of the most important symbols of growth and possible maturity in any profession. The International Special Events Society (ISES) formulated the first certification program for the Event Management industry in an effort to provide evidence of competence for the most qualified practitioners. The Convention Liaison Council developed one of the early certification programs in the meetings industry. Their certified meeting professional program has designated over two thousand individuals as CMPs.

Programs such as The ISES Conference for Professional Development (CPD), The Special Event, sponsored by Mirimar Publishing of Malibu, California, and The Sponsorship Seminar sponsored by the International Events Group of Chicago, Illinois, have experienced rapid growth during the past few years. These programs and many others have grown during the past decade to provide extremely focused in-depth education for an increasingly sophisticated event manager. In other professions, including public relations, there is a direct correlation between certification and compensation. Professionals who have worked to attain certification in their field of expertise are perceived by the majority of prospective employers to be more qualified than those who do not have this designation. In fact, in the more established professions such as medicine, law, and accounting, certification or licensing is required to be able to practice in the profession. Event Management will sooner, rather than later, follow the same course due to the complex nature of this discipline and the enormous responsibility event managers assume when producing public events.

The International Special Events Society has identified no less than twenty-two disciplines within their membership, and this circle is rapidly expanding. It is very difficult to identify the total annual dollars invested in special events. To do this would require statistical information from a variety of sources, including international sport events, private celebrations, party merchandise sales, meetings and conventions, corporate events, retail events, weddings, bar and bas mitzvahs, fairs, festivals, expositions, and more. Suffice it to say, the marketplace is large enough to support and sustain your endeavor. If you are currently working in one special events area, there are many directions in which you can expand. If you are just entering the profession of special events, there is a lucrative market awaiting you on many fronts.

Many schools and universities throughout the United States, Great Britain, Australia, and New Zealand offer both academic courses that lead to degrees and professional programs that result in certificates of completion. The average length of study for a professional certificate is about one year and usually involves a minimum of core required courses and elective subjects. My research has identified that the average number of courses required for a certificate in the United States is seven. When researching these programs request permission to observe one of the classes in session and interview graduates to determine their perspectives. It is unwise to ask questions about placement of graduates as in the ever-changing U.S. economy it is unlikely a graduate will find placement immediately or even stay in that position for a long period of time. Instead, ask the directors of the programs you are interested in about the types of jobs their students are involved in and perhaps what they earn. This will give you a good indication if this program can match your own career expectations.

Continuing Education for Experienced Professionals

Doctors, lawyers, and accountants are required for purposes of recertification and licensure to participate in a prescribed number of hours of continuing education annually. This requirement further assures the public that these professionals will be familiar with the latest developments in their professions.

Event managers currently have no such requirement unless they are certified by the International Special Events Society. Without this requirement, most event managers are not highly motivated to engage in professional continuing education. However, perhaps the following reasons for establishing annual continuing education goals or targets will enable you to see the value of this important process. First, the more you *learn* the more you *earn*. In all U.S. professions, those individuals with higher degrees and more education earn more annually. You will absolutely improve your earnings with continuing Event Management education. Second, remaining competitive is one of the important trends in Event Management. One of the best ways to remain competitive is to find ways to reduce costs, improve productivity, develop more efficient marketing strategies, and improve the overall quality of your product. As you know, trial and error is a slow, costly, and cumbersome way to accomplish these important goals. In fact, while you are learning through years of trial and error, your competition may be receiving the same information in one weekend at a conference. Continuing Event Management education will keep your saw sharp and make it easier and profitable for you to compete in today's and tomorrow's marketplace. Finally, developing portable skills is perhaps one of the most important career development strategies you can employ. This portability will enable you to easily move between fields such as corporate and reunion events so that if you experience a period of decline, your skills may be effectively employed in other areas of the economy.

WAR STORY

Weekly, students who wish to enroll in professional education in Event Management enter my office. Lately I have noticed a trend emerging. This trend involves somewhat older professionals in their mid-fifties and late fifties who, although somewhat nervous at first, soon articulately and, I might add, passionately describe their desires. One woman who has been a corporate meeting planner for nearly twenty years told me, "I want to have more control over my professional future and the only way to do that is to prove to my employer that I am serious and able to excel through Event Management education." Another woman with over fifteen years experience as an association meeting planner stated, "I am determined to remain competitive and grow in my career. Who knows, one day I may operate my own Event Management consulting practice." A man in his late forties and a government meeting planner said, "Although my colleagues don't take what I do very seriously, I do. I am convinced that this is a valuable and important profession. Through continuing education I can prove it." Perhaps the most heartening example of this late career commitment to Event Management continuing education was from a woman I will call Janet. Janet explained to me that she had been an elementary school teacher for over twenty

The experienced Event Management professional who engages in continuing professional education is one who is leading from a position of strength. That strength comes from knowledge. Remember, unless you are the lead dog in any profession the view is always the same. The way to step to the head of the pack is through the discipline of developing a system for learning.

Your system may involve attending annual conferences and workshops, writing articles for industry publications, or giving speeches for other professionals. Each of these learning experiences will contribute to your professional growth as each requires research, preparation, analysis, and evaluation. To further motivate you to engage in continuing education you may wish to set your sights on professional certification.

CERTIFICATION

Certification in the United States is a process for confirming that a professional has achieved specific standards set by a professional organization. Usually that professional

W A R   S T O R Y *(continued)*

years and, during that time, planned and coordinated many school events. I asked her what her goals were and she shook her head and replied, "I don't know. I am over fifty and can't imagine finding employment in Event Management." I explained that, to the contrary, individuals with maturity and training were in high demand. A few weeks later following one of her weekend Event Management courses she rushed up to me and said, "I tried to reach you last week to tell you about my new job. I am a meetings assistant for a large association. One of the primary reasons they hired me was because of my commitment to education in the Event Management profession. They were impressed that at my age I was willing and disciplined to enroll and succeed in these courses." And there are hundreds and perhaps thousands of others just like Janet who will find fulfillment through proper training in this profession.

Lesson Learned

You are never too old to succeed. My father logged onto the Internet at eighty-three and enrolled and graduated from computer school at eighty-four. In fact, the surest way to age is by accepting ignorance over knowledge.

organization represents a specific industry. For example, the Convention Liaison Council (CLC) represents over two dozen individual organizations in the meetings and exposition industry and provides a certification program entitled Certified Meeting Professional. The International Association for Exposition Management represents individuals who manage trade shows and other expositions and administrates the Certified Exposition Manager certification program. In the Event Management profession the International Special Events Society administers the Certified Special Events Professional (CSEP) program.

Certification is not usually related to licensing although in some instances the words are used interchangeably. Instead, certification is a voluntary program administered by a private organization such as an association. Most meeting, exposition, and Event Management certification programs require that candidates meet certain criteria such as a prescribed number of years of professional experience and demonstration of competency through some sort of assessment methodology. Most certification programs in the meeting, exposition, and Event Management professions require additional continuing education for recertification that usually occurs every five years after initial certification.

The CSEP certification program requires that candidates enroll and use specific study materials provided by the organization. These materials include *The Dictionary of Event Management* (Van Nostrand Reinhold, 1996) and a self-study guide. In order to sit for a two-part examination each candidate must earn a minimum of thirty-five points through a variety of professional activities including education, service, and experience. Once the candidate has earned sufficient points he or she is declared ready to sit for the examination. The CSEP exam involves three parts. Part one is 100 multiple-choice questions that test the candidate's knowledge of terms defined in *The Dictionary of Event Management.* Part two involves a case study/essay that describes a theoretical event. The candidate is required through an essay to describe, list, analyze, and evaluate the research, design, planning, coordination, and evaluation process for the case.

The final step in completing the certification process is the development and submission of a professional portfolio representing an actual event produced by the candidate during the past two years. In addition to documenting the various event elements including needs assessment, organization, financial administration, risk management, and others, a series of learning reflections must be composed to document what the candidate learned during this Event Management process. The portfolio requirement concludes with a statement by the candidate regarding his or her career goals and a plan for continuing education to achieve these goals.

The examination and portfolio are reviewed and graded by three trained examiners who are randomly selected from the ISES certification committee. Usually the candidates are notified of their outcome within sixty days of completing the exam.

As of the date of publication of this text, there are thirty-five CSEPs throughout the world. Although there are literally thousands of individuals who claim to be event managers, less than fifty throughout the world have been certified by their peers as special event professionals. As the process for certification becomes more widely known, the number of candidates will most likely increase as will the number of those who are certified. However, due to the rigor required for certification, only a small percentage of individuals who are involved in the Event Management profession will achieve this designation and earn the right to use the initials CSEP with their name.

WHO ARE THE CSEPS AND WHAT DOES IT MEAN?

During a focus group comprised of nine CSEPs it was determined that the median number of years each person had in the Event Management profession was fifteen. Furthermore, the median age was forty. When asked what certification meant to their businesses or careers it was the consensus of the group that although there have been no direct monetary rewards, the self-esteem and self-confidence that resulted from certification enabled them to be more successful. One CSEP stated, "I did receive one piece of business as a result of the CSEP. However, it was two years after I earned the designation."

All of the CSEPs concurred that as the number of certified persons grows and knowledge about the value of certification increases and multiplies, the monetary worth of certification will increase as well. Several CSEPs stated that by actively promoting the CSEP designation to their clients they are able to differentiate themselves from others who have not earned the designation.

When asked what the minimum number of years of experience should be required to sit for the CSEP exam (following a healthy discussion regarding the importance of the quality of the experience) the majority of those present said that five years should be required. "It takes five years to really experience many of the common problems and issues that can undermine you in this industry," stated one CSEP.

Several CSEPs remarked that since professional educational programs are relatively new in this profession, it is possible that these students may be able to sit for the exam earlier following extensive internships in the profession. However, once again, the majority of the group stated that maturity along with experience and education are essential for certification.

Later I interviewed sixteen individuals who have the ability to employ Event Management professionals. Each person agreed that certification definitely gives an individual the advantage over someone who is not certified. They added, however, that certification was most useful to select a candidate for an entry-level position. Furthermore, they noted that persons who are certified in Event Management may require less training and supervision than those who are not. This represents a significant cost savings to most, if not all, Event Management organizations.

In a related study of certification, Professor Carol Hills of Boston University (the first person to receive the master's degree in public relations in the United States) told me, "Students should not be able to be accredited immediately after receiving their bachelor's degree in public relations. It requires many years of professional work experience to be able to earn the right to be accredited in public relations." The accredited in public relations (APR) designation is awarded by the Public Relations Society of America. Professor Hills has been a keen observer of the development of the profession of public relations over the past half century and her cautionary statement should be heeded by those who seek instant certification without sufficient maturity and professional experience.

Certification is not a terminal degree. Unlike a doctorate—the terminal degree in higher education—certification only reflects the judgment of the certification body at the time the candidate was granted the designation. Certified individuals must demonstrate through continuing education that they are life-long learners to be able to retain their status as certified professionals. Participation in conferences, higher education, and other programs recognized by the certification body is required for recertification. Figure 16-1 provides you with important guidelines for becoming certified.

FIGURE 16-1
Guidelines for Becoming Certified

1. Determine the certification you wish to earn and why it is personally and professionally important to you and to your clients or employer.

2. Review all relevant certification programs and interview individuals who have earned the designation to determine their views.

3. Thoroughly review all information regarding the steps to final certification and recertification and set a logical and reasonable time frame for completing this process.

4. Give up something. Certification takes a lot of time. You may have to forego another activity during the months you are preparing for certification.

5. Make certain you are studying the proper materials. Most well-developed certification programs provide specific materials to assist your preparation. Use only the materials that have been approved by the certification body.

6. Form or participate in a study group. This will help maintain your interest and make the process more fun. It will also allow you to network professionally.

7. Set aside a specific amount of time each week for self-study. Make certain you rigidly adhere to this schedule and are not interrupted during this time.

8. Prepare for the exam by carefully reviewing as much information as is possible. Use practice tests to develop your self-confidence. For example, the CSEP self-study program includes several practice tests.

9. On the day of the exam, begin by trying to relax through deep breathing and remind yourself that you are well prepared for this exam. Then, if allowed by the certification body, write down important items that you may have difficulty remembering later.

10. Answer the easiest questions first. Then go back and answer all of the questions saving the most difficult for last. Make certain you answer all of the questions even if you do not know the answers. Go back and check all of your answers to determine if you need to make any changes and if you have answered every question.

HIGHER EDUCATION

It is well known that a person with a master's degree earns more than those with a bachelor's or associate's degree. Only a few universities throughout the world in 1995 offered courses or majors in Event Management or related fields. Northeastern University in Tahlequah, Oklahoma, may have been the first institution of higher education to offer the bachelor's degree in meetings and destination management, and The George Washington University is the first university to offer the Master's of Tourism Administration with a concentration in Event Management. Although the number of universities and colleges offering this curriculum is limited, this too, like the profession itself is rapidly changing and growing. In a search using the TRINET list server, a database comprised of scholars and researchers in the travel, tourism, and hospitality field, over two dozen new higher education programs were identified in Minnesota, California, Great Britain, Australia, New Zealand, Canada, and other destinations.

Students often inquire as to whether a master's degree or a certificate is more desirable, as there is considerable cost and time differences between the two programs. I advise them to audit their employers or prospective clients and ask them to share their attitudes about each program. In some organizations the master's degree is required for advancement, whereas in others it is not deemed important. Before applying for admission to a master's program it is critical that the student carefully investigate the perceived value of a degree or certificate prior to making a final commitment.

On-Line and Other Emerging Resources

The rapid expansion of the Internet required the editors of *The Dictionary of Event Management* to include dozens of terms specifically used in this technology to enable modern event managers to navigate the net effectively. This is but one example of how the Internet is becoming an important instrument in the arsenal of tools available for continuing Event Management education.

In a recent search of the World Wide Web (WWW) I was able to identify over 300 sites using the key words "Event Management." These sites or web pages included educational programs, calendars listing individual events, and advertisements for event consulting practices among many other services.

When using the Internet to search for Event Management resources be careful not to narrow your subject area to a limited field of inquiry such as "events and education" as you may not be able to find the full scope of materials that is available under a wider listing such as "special events" or "Event Management." Do use related fields such as "meetings and conferences," "expositions," and other subject headings.

Shmuel Ben-Gad, a subject specialist at the Gelman Library of The George Washington University, has created a finding aid for Event Management scholars. Using this finding aid to search the catalog of monographs and serials in the library system individuals can quickly identify dozens of resources specific to Event Management.

This same library is the repository of the world's first Event Management and Marketing Archives. In this special collection are the manuscripts of luminaries such as Jack Morton, Barnett Lipton, Frank Supovitz, and others. You can also see the world's first indoor flying spaceship, colorful air and wind tubes used in major events, and other marvels of professional Event Management. Perhaps even more importantly, professionals may study through videotapes, audiotapes, and actual production manuals the systems used by successful event managers to produce many of the world's most memorable and entertaining events.

However, you do not need to live in or even visit Washington, DC, to use these materials. Using your personal computer you can identify many of these records through interlibrary searches, and for a nominal fee, the Gelman Library will make video, audio, or manuscript copies available to you.

Other universities also have special collections and important materials in related fields. The University of Nevada at Las Vegas Harrah School of Hotel Management as well as the Conrad Hilton School of Hotel at the University of Houston have extensive materials that will support your Event Management interests.

In addition to these resources you will find a variety of periodicals, books in print, and other resources including World Wide Web sites for Event Management in Appendix 2. The fastest and most efficient way to use your time is to log on to one of these databases and review the many electronic resources available in Event Management.

Self-Study

By now if you have not been convinced of the need for continuing education to maintain your competitive position in the Event Management field you will probably never be (or at least until you lose your job, your chance for a job promotion, or a client). For those who are now ready, willing, and able to join the education consider the following opportunity for self-study. First, always use your experienced professional Event Management colleagues as your trusted advisors. Prior to making any significant business or career decisions consult with your *brain trust* and seek several opinions. Second, consider formalizing these advisors with an *Advisory Panel* that meets annually to review your progress. Perhaps you arrange lunch or dinner and provide your advisors with a brief synopsis of your goals for the past year, record of achievement, and then ask for their feedback. Third, read a wide range of Event Management literature on a weekly basis. In addition, review general and specialized business periodicals such as *The Wall Street Journal* and *Advertising Age*. These periodicals will expand your world view of your profession and place your profession in a context with the larger economic and business environment. Finally, give yourself an annual report card. Set specific goals for attending continuing education programs, reading books, and engaging in other life-long learning pursuits. At the end of the year review your progress and, if you have achieved your goals, reward yourself, and if you have exceeded your goals . . . well then, celebrate!

You are a member of a profession worth celebrating. Your professional journey may be just beginning or well established; however, your future through continual learning ensures that both you and the profession will enjoy many years of prosperity and success.

During your journey through this book you have experienced both theories and facts, both war stories and lessons learned, and both humor and seriousness. The journey you take throughout your Event Management professional career in many ways parallels the journey you have taken through these pages. I invite you to return to this book from time to time to compare your professional journey with the blueprint I have provided you and compare and contrast your experiences. Furthermore, I invite you to write to me at the address found in Appendix 1 and tell me about your discoveries. With your permission I may share your successes with other readers in the future.

Now as you turn to the Appendix to unlock additional resources for Event Management education, allow me to remind you of Aunt Gert's early admonition to me those many years ago. *Be careful what you wish for, because it might come true.* Although I never questioned Aunt Gert's authority or wisdom, I might add that your chances are much improved, certainly better than mine or others of ages past, because of the growth and expansion of this emerging profession now known as Event Management. I am also certain that your dedication and pursuit of knowledge in Event Management will ensure that your wishes do come true. And to that, in the tradition of celebration, I raise my glass with you and say, "Cheers!"

Organizations and Resources

The following event management related organizations and resources can help propel your career success.

1. Do your homework and contact listed associations via e-mail and request information about their educational and networking programs and resources.

2. Join a primary organization based upon your field of interest. For example, if you are interested in the broad category of Event Management, The International Special Events Society should be your first choice. However, if your selection is narrowly confined to expositions, you will want to join the International Association for Exposition Management. The primary organization will be where you devote the majority of your time and energy while the secondary organization is one whose resources and programs can further assist you in developing your career.

3. Set a three to five year goal that includes committee involvement, board leadership, and ultimately serving as one of the officers of the organization's local chapter or national organization. In many industries, the most successful individuals are those who are also the leaders within their industry's professional organizations.

4. Once you have set your goal, annually keep track of how you are doing. Continually remind those who are more established in the organization of your career goals and seek their help in making sure you are advancing properly within the leadership of the organization.

In summary, do not merely join and expect success. Success comes naturally from your investment of time and talent.

Definitions

Professional trade association-A national or international organization whose purpose is to actively promote the industry that its members are active within.

Professional society-A national or international organization that provides research and educational services for its members and the general public.

Regional association-An organization whose members are located in one regional location.

Key

N = Networking opportunities for *Event Managers* with other Event Managers

E = Educational opportunities for *Event Managers*

C = The organization includes local or state chapters.

Affiliated organizations = The organization has official or unofficial relationships with organizations with mutual industry interests.

Event Management Related Organizations

American Society of Association Executives (ASAE)
1575 I Street, N.W.
Washington, DC 20005-1168
(202) 626-ASAE
A professional trade association whose members are executives in professional, trade, and civic associations as well as those who provide services and products for this industry. The Meetings and Exposition Section is specifically comprised of event managers.

E, N, Allied associations throughout the United States and Europe

Association of Conference and Events Directors International (ACEDI)
Colorado State University, Tiley House
Fort Collins, CO 80523-8037
(303) 491-5151
A professional trade association whose members operate conferences and events at universities and colleges.
E, N

Association for Convention Operations
Management
1819 Peachtree Street, N.W., Suite 712
Atlanta, GA 30309
(404) 351-3220
A professional trade association whose
members are employed as convention
service managers and other conference
positions.
E, N

Association of Bridal Consultants (ABC)
200 Chestnutland Road
New Milford, CT 06776-2521
(203) 355-0464
E, N

Association of Convention Marketing
Executives
1819 Peachtree Street, N.E., Suite 712
Atlanta, GA 30309
(404) 355-2400
A professional trade association whose
members are professional convention
marketing executives.
E, N

Association of International Meeting
Planners (AIMP)
1811 Monroe Street
Dearborne, MI 48124
(313) 563-0360
A professional trade association whose
members organize international meetings.
E, N

Casino and Theme Party Operators
Association
2120 G.S. Highland Drive
Las Vegas, NV 89102
(702) 385-2963
A professional trade association whose
members specialize in casino and theme
events.
N

Convention Liaison Council (CLC)
1575 I Street, N.W., Suite 1190
Washington, DC 20005

(202) 626-ASAE
An organization whose members are
associations representing various fields in
the convention industry. The CLC
administers the Certified Meeting
Professional (CMP) designation.
E

Council of Engineering and Scientific
Society Executives
P.O. Box 12215
Research Triangle Park, NC 27709-2215
(919) 549-8141
A professional society whose members
organize meetings in the engineering and
scientific industries.

Council of Protocol Executives (COPE)
101 West 12th Street, Suite PHH
New York, NY 10011
(212) 633-6934
A professional society whose members are
primarily engaged as experts in protocol.
E, N

Foundation for International Meetings
(FILM)
2111 Wilson Boulevard, Suite 350
Arlington, VA 22201-3058
(703) 908-0707
A professional association whose members
specialize in organizing international
meetings.
E, N

Dr. Joe Goldblatt, CSEP
The George Washington University
Event Management Program
School of Business and Public Management
2100 Pennsylvania Ave., N.W.
Suite 250
Washington, DC 20037-3202
(202) 785-9623
Email: drevent@gwis2.circ.gwu.edu

Healthcare Convention and Exhibitors
Association
5775 Peachtree-Dunwood Road, #500-G
Atlanta, GA 30342
(404) 252-3663

A professional trade association whose members are exhibitors and others in the healthcare industry.
E, N

Hospitality Sales and Marketing Association International (HSMAI)
1300 L Street, N.W., Suite 800
Washington, DC 20005
(202) 789-0089
A professional trade association whose members are professional sales people in the hotel, convention center, and hospitality industry and those who provide services and products for this industry. HSMAI sponsors a conference entitled "Affordable Meetings." This conference provides low cost resources for event managers in the convention industry.
E, N, C

International Congress and Convention Association
The International Meetings Association
Entrada 121
1096 EB Amsterdam, The Netherlands
Int+ 31 20 690 1171
A professional trade association whose members are travel agents, congress centers, professional congress organizers and others involved in the organization and servicing of international meetings.
E, N

Insurance Conference Planners Association
2810 Woodbine Drive
North Vancouver, British Columbia, V7R 2R9, Canada
(604) 988-2054
A professional association whose members are planners of conferences in the insurance industry.
E, N

International Association of Fairs and Expositions (IAFE)
P.O. Box 985
Springfield, MO 65801
(417) 862-5771

A professional trade association whose members organize and manage fairs and expositions.
E, N

International Association for Exposition Management
5001 LBJ Freeway, Suite 350
Dallas, TX 75244
(214) 458-8002
A professional trade association whose members manage trade and public expositions and provide services and products for this industry.
E, N, C

International Association of Amusement Parks and Attractions (IAAPA)
1448 Duke Street
Alexandria, VA 22314
(703) 836-4800
A professional trade association whose members own, manage, market, and consult in the amusement park and attraction industry and provide services and products for this industry.
E, N

International Association of Auditorium Managers
4225 W. Airport Freeway, Suite 590
Irving, TX 75062
(214) 255-8020
The professional trade association whose members own, manage, operate, market, consult or supply services and products for arenas, auditoriums, stadiums, and other venues.
E, N, C

International Association of Conference Centers
243 North Lindbergh Boulevard
St. Louis, MO 63141
(314) 993-8575
The professional trade association whose members own, operate, manage, market, consult, and supply goods and services for conference centers.
E, N

International Association of Conventions
and Visitors Bureaus (IACVB)
2000 L Street, N.W., Suite 702
Washington, DC 20036-4990
(202) 296-7888
The professional trade association whose
members manage and market convention
and visitor's bureaus for individual
destinations and supply goods and services
for these bureaus.

International Association of Professional
Congress Organizers (IAPCO)
40 Rue Washington
B-1050 Brussels, Belgium
Int+ 32 26 40 7105
The professional trade association whose
members are professional congress
organizers.
E, N

International Council of Shopping Centers
(ICSC)
665 Fifth Avenue
New York, NY 10022
(212) 421-8181
The professional trade association whose
members own, operate, manage, market,
and supply goods and services for shopping
centers. ICSC administers the Certified
Marketing Director (CMD) exam and
designation. This program includes
competencies relating to shopping center
promotion including special event
management.
E, N, C

International Exhibitors Association (IEA)
5501 Backlick Road, Suite 105
Springfield, VA 22151
(703) 941-3725
The professional trade association whose
members exhibit at international meetings.

International Federation of Festival
Organizations
4230 Stansbury Ave, No. 105
Sherman Oaks, CA 91423
(818) 789-7569

A professional trade association whose
members organize festivals.
E, N

International Festivals and Events
Association (IFEA)
P.O. Box 2950
Port Angeles, WA 98362-0336
(800) 432-4304
A professional trade association whose
members own, operate, manage, market,
and supply goods and services for festivals
and events. IFEA in conjunction with
Purdue University administers the
Certified Festival Executive (CFE)
designation/certification.
E, N, C

International Institute of Convention
Management
9200 Bayard Place
Fairfax, VA 22032
(703) 978-6287
The professional trade association whose
members are active in managing
conventions.
E

International Special Events Society (ISES)
9202 North Meridian Street, Suite 200
Indianapolis, IN 46260-1810
(800) 688-ISES
The only umbrella organization
representing all aspects of the special
events industry.
E, N, C

Meeting Professionals International (MPI)
1950 Stemmons Freeway, Suite 5018
Dallas, TX 75207-3109
(214) 712-7700
The professional trade association whose
members include corporate, association,
and other meeting planners as well as those
who provide goods and services for
meeting planners.
E, N, C

National Restaurant Association (NRA)
1200 17th Street, N.W.

Washington, DC 20036-3097
(202) 331-5900
The professional trade association whose members own, operate, manage, market, consult, or supply goods and services to the restaurant industry.
E, N, C

National Association of Catering Executives (NACE)
60 Revere Drive, Suite 500
Northbrook, IL 60062
(708) 480-9080
The professional trade association whose members provide on- and off-premise catering services as well as goods and services for the catering industry.
E, N, C

National Society of Fundraising Executives (NSFRE)
1101 Kings Street, Suite 3000
Alexandria, VA 22314
(703) 684-0410
The professional trade association whose members are employed in development, fund-raising, or consulting in the philanthropic field and provide goods and services for this profession.
E, N, C

National Association of Reunion Planners
P.O. Box 21127
Tampa, FL 33622-1127
(800) 654-2776
The professional trade association for persons who professionally organize reunions.
E, N

National Ballroom and Entertainment Association (NBEA)
2799 Locust Road
Decorah, IA 52101-7600
(319) 382-3871
The professional trade association whose members provide or organize entertainment.

National Bridal Service (NBS)
3122 W. Cary Street

Richmond, VA 23221
(804) 355-6945
The professional trade association whose members consult in the bridal industry.

National Coalition of Black Meeting Planners (NCBMP)
8630 Fenton Street, Suite 328
Silver Spring, MD 20910
(202) 628-3952
The professional trade association whose members are black meeting planners or those who provide goods and services for meeting planners.
E, N

National Institute of Off-Premise Catering
2355 North Clark
Chicago, IL 60614
(312) 525-6800
An organization comprised of professionals who provide education and related services for professional caterers.
E, N

Northwest Festivals Association
49 Beaverbrook Crescent
St. Albert, Alberta T8N 2L4, Canada
(403) 458-3900
A regional professional trade association for persons involved in organizing and operating festivals.
E, N

Professional Convention Management Association (PCMA)
100 Vestavia Office Park, Suite 220
Birmingham, AL 35216
(205) 823-7262
The professional trade association whose members plan and manage meetings and supply goods and services for meeting planners.
E, N, C

Public Relations Society of America (PRSA)
33 Irvin Place

New York, NY 10003
(212) 995-2230
The professional trade association whose members are involved in public relations activities or supply goods and services for this profession.
E, N, C

Religious Conference Management Association (RCMA)
One RCA Dome, Suite 120
Indianapolis, IN 46225
(317) 632-1888
A professional trade association whose members are professional meeting planners for religious organizations and those who provide goods and services for this industry.
E, N

Society of Corporate Meeting Professionals (SCMP)
1819 Peachtree Road, N.E., Suite 620
Atlanta, GA 30309
(404) 355-9932
The professional trade association whose members are involved in corporate meeting planning and supply goods and services for this industry.
E, N

Society of Government Meeting Planners (SGMP)
219 East Main Street
Mechanicsburg, PA 17055
(717) 795-7467
The professional trade association whose members are involved in planning government meetings and those who

supply goods and services for this industry.
E, N, C

Society of Incentive Travel Executives (SITE)
21 West 38th Street, 10th Floor
New York, NY 10018-5584
(212) 575-0910
The professional trade association whose members organize incentive activities and supply goods and services for this industry.
E, N, C

Society of Travel Agents in Government (STAG)
6935 Wisconsin Avenue, Suite 200
Bethesda, MD 20815
(301) 654-8595
The professional trade association for travel professionals involved in government and those who supply goods or services for this industry.

Stage Managers Association
225 West 14th Street
New York, NY 10011
(212) 691-5633
The professional trade association whose members are theatrical stage managers. Many professional stage managers work in the Event Management profession.
E, N

Western Fairs Association
1776 Tribute Road, Suite 210
Sacramento, CA 95815-4410
(916) 927-3100
A regional association whose members organize and manage fairs.
E, N

Miscellaneous Organizations and Resources

Air Transport Association of America
1301 Pennsylvania Avenue, N.W., Suite 1100
Washington, DC 20004-1707
(202) 626-4218
The professional trade association whose

members are active in the air transport industry.

Actor's Equity Association (AEA)
165 West 46th Street
New York, NY 10036

(212) 869-8530
The professional union representing professional actors, actresses, and stage managers working in live theater.

American Federation of Musicians of the United States and Canada (AF of M)
1501 Broadway, Suite 600
New York, NY 10036
(212) 869-1330
The professional union representing musicians.

American Federation of Television and Radio Artists (AFTRA)
260 Madison Avenue
New York, NY 10016
(212) 532-0800
The professional union representing television and radio performers.

American Floral Marketing Council
1601 Duke Street
Alexandria, VA 22314-3406
(703) 836-8700

American Guild of Variety Artists (AGVA)
184 Fifth Avenue, Sixth Floor
New York, NY 10036
(212) 675-1003
The professional union representing performers in nightclubs, cabarets, circuses, and other variety venues.

American Hotel and Motel Association (AH&MA)
1201 New York Avenue, N.W., Suite 1100
Washington, DC 20005-3931
(202) 289-3111
The professional trade association representing owners, managers, marketers of hotels and motels and those who provide services and products for this industry. (Allied Organizations)

American Institute of Floral Designers
720 Light Street
Baltimore, MD 21230
(410) 752-3318

The professional trade association whose members represent floral designers and those who provide products and services for this industry.

American Pyrotechnics Association (APA)
P.O. Box 213
Chestertown, MD 21620
(410) 778-6825
The professional trade association representing manufacturers, designers, and producers of professional fireworks.

American Rental Association
1900 19th Street
Moline, IL 61265
(309) 764-2475
The professional trade association whose members own and operate rental stores including party rental stores.
C

American Society for Training and Development (ASTD)
P.O. Box 1567
Merrifield, VA 22116-9812
(703) 683-8100
The professional trade association whose members are trainers and those who provide services and products for this industry.
C

American Society of Composers, Authors and Publishers (ASCAP)
One Lincoln Plaza
New York, NY 10023
(212) 621-6000
A licensing organization for live and electronic music.

Broadcast Music International (BMI)
10 Music Square East
Nashville, TN 37203
(615) 401-2000

Communications and Media Management Association (CMMA)
P.O. Box 227

Wheaton, IL 60189
(708) 653-2772
A professional trade association for professionals in the communications industry.

Exhibit Designers and Producers Association (EDPA)
611 East Wells Street
Milwaukee, WI 53202
(414) 276-3372
A professional trade association whose members design and produce exhibits for expositions.

Exposition Service Contractors Association (ESCA)
400 South Houston Street, Suite 210
Dallas, TX 75202
(214) 742-9217
A professional trade association whose members provide services for expositions.

International Communications Industries Association (ICIA)
3150 Spring Street
Fairfax, VA 22031
(703) 273-7200
The professional trade association whose members provide communications services.

International Group of Agencies and Bureaus (IGAB)
6845 Parkdale Place, Suite A
Indianapolis, IN 46254-5605
(317) 297-0872
The professional trade association whose members own, operate, and manage professional speakers bureaus.

International Platform Association (IPA)
P.O. Box 250
Winnetka, IL 60093
(708) 446-4321
The professional trade association whose members are professional speakers or organizations that represent professional speakers.

National Association of Balloon Artists
1205 West Forsyth Street
Jacksonville, FL 32204
(904) 354-7271
The professional trade association whose members provide balloon products and services.

National Limousine Association
1300 L Street, N.W., Suite 1050
Washington, DC 20005
(202) 682-1426
The professional trade association for persons who own, manage, market, and supply goods and services to the limousine industry.

National Speakers Association (NSA)
1500 South Priest Drive
Tempe, AZ 85281
(602) 968-2552
The professional trade association whose members are professional speakers and those who provide services and products for the professional speaking industry.
C

North American Association of Ventriloquists (NAAV)
P.O. Box 420
Littleton, CO 80160
(303) 798-6830
The professional trade association for individuals involved in ventriloquism.

Pyrotechnics Guild International (PGI)
(410) 560-0513
An organization comprised of individuals engaged in fireworks (pyrotechnics).

Screen Actors Guild (SAG)
5757 Wilshire Boulevard
Los Angeles, CA 90036
(213) 954-1600
The professional trade union for actors, actresses, and others in the film and television industry.
C

Society of American Florists (SAF)
1601 Duke Street
Alexandria, VA 22314-3406
(703) 836-8700
The professional trade association for florists and those who provide goods and services for the floral industry.

Special Events Office of the Military District of Washington
Fort Lesley J. McNair
4th and P Streets, S.W.
Washington, DC 20319-5058
(202) 475-1399

The organization responsible for providing military units such as bands, color guards, and others for special events in the Washington, DC metropolitan area.

Travel Industry Association of America
1100 New York Avenue, N.W.
Washington, D.C. 20005
(202) 408-8422
The professional trade association whose members promote, market, research, and provide information about the travel industry.

Internet Addresses

Cities and Convention and Visitors Bureaus

CITY NET
A comprehensive guide to communities all over the world.
http://www.city.net

INTERNATIONAL ASSOCIATION OF CONVENTION AND VISITORS BUREAUS
http://www.acvb.org

USA CITYLINK PROJECT
A directory of US city sites on the web listed by state. Focuses on two types of cities—tourism sites and sites whose mission is to support their local community.
http://www.neosoft.com/citylink—check

General

BIG BOOK
Directory of addresses of any business in the United States, as well as maps and restaurant reviews.
http://www.bigbook.com

BLUEDOT INTERACTIVE
Software to create extensions for physical trade shows on the World Wide Web.
http://www.expocity.com/tappi

CNN FINANCIAL NETWORK "BE YOUR OWN TRAVEL AGENT"
This links to ways to make your own travel reservations on the web. Hotel, airlines, frequent flyer tips, technology, etc.
http://CNNfn.com/resources/links/travel.html

EXPOGUIDE
Listing of tradeshows. Allows searches by alphabetical order, by date and by location, and keyword searches. About 4800 shows.
http://www.expoguide.com

THE GEORGE WASHINGTON UNIVERSITY EVENT MANAGEMENT PROGRAM
The gateway to distance learning opportunities for Event Management students. A live interactive discussion group of Event Management hot topics. A source for information on the latest Event Management research from The George Washington University.
http://uol.com/gwu/esi/em

THE GEORGE WASHINGTON UNIVERSITY INSTITUTE OF INTERNATIONAL TOURISM STUDIES
The home page for information regarding graduate and professional programs in tourism studies. The International Institute of Tourism Studies was the first to offer the master's degree in tourism in the United States.
http://gwis.circ.gwu.edu/~iits

MEETINGS INDUSTRY MALL
Professional connections for meeting planners and suppliers.
http://www.mim.com

THE MEETING AND EVENT PLANNING CENTER
http://eventplanner.com/mainmenu.htm

MEETING PAGES AND MEETING MAPS
A dynamic way to post visual summaries of your meetings on the World Wide Web.
http://www.pgc.com/pgc/home-stuff/meeting-maps-page-00.html

MEETING PLANNER'S ORGANIZER
Software that will guide you through the meeting planning process.
http://www.bravopubs.com/MPO.htm

Hotels and Alternative Venues

ALL THE HOTELS ON THE WEB
http://www.digimark.net/dundas/hotels/

DIRECTORY OF ALL HOTELS ONLINE
http://hotel.com

"THE GUIDE TO CAMPUS, NON-PROFIT & RETREAT MEETING FACILITIES"
A site that lets planners search by geographic location for a selection of less customary venues. Free. Over 500 sites listed.
http://www.theguide.com.

On-Line Publications

BIZTRAVEL
On-line magazine for the business traveler from e-publishers.
http://www.biztravel.com/guide

CORPORATE TRAVEL COORDINATORS OF AMERICA, INC.
On-line version of directory for hundreds of hotels in the United States and worldwide.
http://styx.ios.com/corp-hotels/

NEWSPAGE
A clipping service creating virtual news pages for the travel, hospitality, and gaming industry.
http://www.newspage.com/NEWSPAGE/cgi-bin/walk.cgi/NEWSPAGE/info/d19/

SUCCESSFUL MEETINGS
The electronic version of the magazine.
http://www.successmtgs.com

THE ULTIMATE GUIDE TO SPORT EVENT MANAGEMENT AND MARKETING
by Graham, Goldblatt, and Delpy. Handbook containing important information to stage a successful sport event.
http://www.marketingtools.com/mpower/f95sm.htm

Professional Associations/Listservers

AMERICAN SOCIETY OF ASSOCIATION EXECUTIVES
The membership organization for the association management profession.
http://www.asaenet.org

AMERICAN TRAVEL ASSOCIATION
Carriers that are members of the American Travel Association.
http://www.air-transport.org/ata/home.htm

HOSPITALITY NET
Internet homepage for the global hospitality industry. Provides a global communication platform for professionals and students, as well as vendors.
http://www.xxlink.nl/hospitalitynet/home.htm

HOTELNET
For hospitality professionals in lodging management and hotel food service. HotelNet provides a platform for discussing hospitality industry issues; provides relevant electronic information to hoteliers. Access by Telnet:hotelnet.com. Cost is $30 for three months. For more information, contact steve.adams@hotelnet.com.

IAEMNET
Available through the International Association for Exposition Management. For more information, IAEM may be reached at (214) 712-7742.

INFO-TEC TRAVEL
A moderated internetwork mailing list dedicated to the exchange of information about information technology in travel and tourism. To subscribe, send an e-mail to Majordomo@igc.apc.org leaving the subject line blank. In the body of the message, type "subscribe to info-tec travel."

INTERNATIONAL SPECIAL EVENTS SOCIETY
The homepage for the International Special Events Society, the only international association serving the events industry.
http://www.NDGphoenix.com/ises.html (This site will soon become http://ises.com.)

MPINet

Available through Meeting Professionals International on Compuserve. An excellent method for planners and suppliers to network, get education on-line via the message sections and library. Conduct real-time conversations, have meetings. For more information, MPI may be reached at (214) 712-7700.

Tradeshow Listserver

The Tourism and Convention Department at the University of Nevada, Las Vegas operates an e-mail tradeshow listserver. Simply send a message to listproc@nevada.edu leaving the subject line blank. In the body of the message, type "subscribe trade show (your name)."

Virtual PCMA

A private broadcast network that delivers news, education courses, and the ability to interactively plan meetings. Similar to a cable television network, except the television is replaced with a personal computer. For more information, call the Professional Convention Management Association at (205) 823-7262.

Speakers

New Market Ventures Online Speakers Directory
http://www.newmarket-forum.com

Transportation

"Airlines of the Web"
http://haas.berkeley.edu/~seidel/airline.html

Amtrak
Information about Amtrak's rail service.
http://www.amtrak.com

Miscellaneous

www.tsnn.com

Event Resources
www.eventresource.com
Who's Who in Event Management

References

Professional speaker Charles "Tremendous" Jones has been widely quoted as having originated the simple philosophy that many years from now most of us will be exactly the same person we are today except for two things: the books we read and the people we meet along the way.

I encourage you to develop the rigor of reading one new book per week and surveying other written resources daily, such as magazines and newsletters. This will help ensure that you stay current in your profession, plus provide you with many new ideas to accelerate the growth of your career.

I am often asked, "Where do you get all of your ideas?" The questioner assumed that I reach into pandora's fabled box and divine new wonders of creation. Usually I reply to this question by stating, "Plato, Aristotle, Shakespeare, Keats, Browning, Hemingway, Dickinson, Stein, Eyre, Barrett, Seurat, Beethoven, Bach, Brahms, Picasso, Vermeer, and other renowned writers, painters, and composers."

The following resources have guided my career and will further ensure your professional success.

Books Specifically for Event Managers

Adcock, E., Buono, D., McGee, B. (1995). *Premium, Incentive, & Travel Buyers.* New Providence: The Salesman's Guide.

American Society of Association Executives (1984). *Association Education Handbook: A Guide to Planning and Conduction Quality Educational Programs.* Washington, DC: ASAE.

American Society of Association Executives (1982). *Association Meeting Trends.* Washington, DC: ASAE.

American Society of Association Executives. *Guidelines for Effective Association Conventions and Meetings* (Vols. I and II). Washington, DC: ASAE.

American Society of Association Executives (1985). *Fundamentals of Association Management: Conventions.* Washington, DC: ASAE.

ANA Event Marketing Committee (1995). *Event Marketing: A Management Guide.* New York: Association of National Advertisers.

Astroff, M.T., Abbey, J.R., (1995). *Convention Sales and Services* (4th ed.). Cranbury, NJ: Waterbury Press.

Baghot, R., Nuttall, G. (1990). *Sponsorship, Endorsements and Merchandising: A Practical Guide.* London: Waterlow.

Bagley, N.F. (1994). *Reunions for Fun-Loving Families.* St. Paul, MN: Brighton Publications, Inc.

Baldridge, L. (1993). *Letitia Baldridge's New Complete Guide to Executive Manners.* New York: Rawson Associates, Maxwell Macmillian International.

Batterberry, A.R. (1976). *Bloomingdale's Book of Entertaining.* New York: Random House.

Bergen, M.T. (1988). *How to Have Fun at Work: The Complete Employee Services/Recreation Handbook.* Crete, IL: Abbott, Langer & Associates.

Bergin, R., Hempel, E. (1990). *Sponsorship and the Arts: A Practical Guide to Corporate Sponsorship of the Performing and Visual Arts.* Evanston, IL: Entertainment Resource Group.

Berlonghi, A.E. (1990). *The Special Event Risk Management Manual.* Dana Point, CA: Alexander Berlonghi.

Bowan, J. (1992). *Family Reunions: A Guide to Planning, Organizing and Holding Family Reunions.* Carson, CA: Akila Publishers.

Brashich, C. (1990). *World Manual for Group and Incentive Travel.* Livingston, NJ: Networld, Inc.

Brenland, C. (1995). *Wild Planet: 1,001 Extraordinary Events for the Inspired Traveler.* Detroit, MI: Visible Ink Press.

Brody, M., Pachter, B. (1994). *Business Etiquette.* Burr Ridge, IL: Irwin Professional Publishing.

Brown, B.E., Ninkovich, T. (1992). *Family Reunion Handbook: A Guide for Reunion Planners.* San Francisco, CA: Reunion Research.

Brown, R., Marsden, M. (1994). *The Cultures of Celebrations.* Bowling Green, OH: Bowling Green State University Popular Press.

Catherwood, D.W., Van Kirk, R.L. (1992). *The Complete Guide to Special Event Management: Business Insights, Financial Advice, and Successful Strategies from Ernst & Young, Advisors to the Olympics, the Emmy Awards and the PGA Tour.* New York: John Wiley & Sons.

Charsley, S.R. (1992). *Wedding Cakes and Cultural History.* New York: Routledge.

Church, B.R., Bultman, B.E. (1987). *The Joys of Entertaining.* New York: Abbeville Press, Inc.

Church, B.R., Harrison, L.R. (1993). *Weddings Southern Style.* New York: Abbeville Press Publishers, Inc.

Colby, L.H. (ed.) (1994). *A Working Guide to Effective Meetings and Conventions* (6th ed.). Washington, DC: The Convention Liaison Council.

Cole, H., (1993). *Jumping the Broom: The African-American Wedding Planner.* New York: Henry Holt.

Convention Liaison Council (1994). *The Convention Liaison Manual* (6th ed.). Washington, DC: Convention Liaison Council and the Joint Industry Council (1993). *International Meetings Industry Glossary* (5th ed.). Washington, DC: Author.

Dance, J. (1994). *How to Get The Most Out of Sales Meetings.* Lincolnwood, IL: NTC Business Books.

Deal, T.E., Kennedy, A.A. (1982). *Corporate Cultures: The Rites and Ritual of Corporate Life.* Reading, MA: Addison-Wesley Publishing Company, Inc.

Delacorte, T., Kimsey, J., Halas, S. (1981). *How to Get Free Press: A Do-It-Yourself Guide to Promote Your Interests, Organizations or Business.* San Francisco, CA: Harbor.

Devney, DC (1990). *Organizing Special Events and Conferences: A Practical Guide for Busy Volunteers and Staff.* Sarasota, FL: Pineapple Press.

Dlugosch, S.E. (1980). *Folding Table Napkins: A New Look at a Traditional Craft* (9th ed.). St. Paul, MN: Brighton Publications, Inc.

Dlugosch, S.E. (1989). *Wedding Hints and Reminders.* St. Paul, MN: Brighton Publications, Inc.

Dlugosch, S.E. (1990). *Table Setting Guide.* St. Paul, MN: Brighton Publications, Inc.

Dlugosch, S.E. (1991). *Tabletop Vignettes.* St. Paul, MN: Brighton Publications, Inc.

Dlugosch, S.E. (1993). *Wedding Plans: 50 Unique Themes for the Wedding of Your Dreams* (3rd ed.). St. Paul, MN: Brighton Publications, Inc.

Dunkins, M., Gray-Miott, J. (1994). *The Perfect Choice: Wedding & Reception Sites: The Perfect Choice.* Silver Spring, MD: Gray, McPherson and Associates.

Finkel, C.L. (1991). *Powerhouse Conferences: Eliminating Audience Boredom.* East Lansing, MI: Educational Institute of American Hotel & Motel Association.

Flanagan, J. (1993). *Successful Fund Raising: A Complete Handbook for Volunteers and Professionals.* Chicago: Contemporary Books, Inc.

Foster, J.S. (1991). *Business Insurance for Independent Planners.* Atlanta, GA: John S. Foster, Esq. Law Offices.

Foster, J.S. (1991). *Choosing a Business Form: What's Best For You?* Atlanta, GA: John S. Foster, Esq. Law Offices.

Foster, J.S. (1991). *Independent Planner Checklists.* Atlanta, GA: John S. Foster, Esq. Law Offices.

Foster, J.S. (1992). *Sample Contract Clauses for Independent Planners.* Atlanta, GA: John S. Foster, Esq. Law Offices.

Foster, J.S. (1995). *Hotel Law: What Hoteliers Need to Know About Legal Affairs Management.* Atlanta, GA: John S. Foster, Esq. Law Offices.

Foster, J.S. (1995). *Independent Meeting Planners and the Law.* Atlanta, GA: John S. Foster, Esq. Law Offices.

Foster, J.S. (1995). *Meeting & Facility Contracts.* Atlanta, GA: John S. Foster, Esq. Law Offices.

Foster, J.S. (1995). *Meetings & Liability.* Atlanta, GA: John S. Foster, Esq. Law Offices.

Freedman, H.A., Smith, K.F. (1991). *Black Tie Optional: The Ultimate Guide to Planning and Producing Successful Special Events.* Rockville, MD: Fund Raising Institute.

Frechtling, Douglas. *Tourism Forecasting.* Washington, DC: Butterworth Heinman.

Fulmer, D., Eddy, N. (1990). *A Gentleman's Guide to Toasting.* Lynchburg, TN: Oxmoor House.

Gartell, R.B. (1994). *Destination Marketing for Convention and Visitor Bureaus* (2nd ed.). Dubuque, IA: Kendall/Hunt Publishing Co.

Getz, D. (1991). *Festivals, Special Events, and Tourism.*

Giblin, J.C. (1983). *Firework, Picnics and Flags: The Story of the Fourth of July Symbols.* Boston: Houghton Mifflin Company.

Gilbert, E. (1989). *The Complete Wedding Planner: Helpful Choices for the Bride and Groom* (Revised ed.). Hollywood, FL: F. Fell.

Global Media Commission Staff (1988). *Sponsorship: Its Role and Effect.* New York: International Advertising Association.

Goldblatt, Joe Jeff. (1995). *The Ultimate Party Handbook.* Chevy Chase, MD: The Goldblatt Company, Inc.

Goldblatt, J., McKibben, C. (1996). *The Dictionary of Event Management.* New York: Van Nostrand Reinhold.

Graham, S., Goldblatt, J.J., Delpy, L. (1995). *The Ultimate Guide to Sport Event Management and Marketing.* Chicago, IL: Irwin Professional Publishing.

Greier, T. (1986). *Make Your Events Special: How to Produce Successful Special Events for Nonprofit Organizations.* New York: Folkworks.

Hall, C.M. (1992). *Hallmark Tourist Events: Impacts, Management and Planning.* New York: Halstead Press.

Hall, S.J. (1992). *Ethics in Hospitality Management: A Book of Readings.* East Lansing, MI: Educational Institute of the American Hotel & Motel Association.

Hansen, B. (1995). *Off-Premise Catering Management.* New York: John Wiley & Sons, Inc.

Harris, A.L. (1988). *Special Events: Planning for Success.* Washington, DC: Council for Advancement and Support of Education.

Heath, A. (1995). *Windows on the World: Multicultural Festivals for Schools and Libraries.* Metuchen, NJ: Scarecrow Press.

Hildreth, R.A. (1990). *The Essentials of Meeting Management.* Englewood Cliffs, NJ: Prentice Hall.

Hoffman, L.J. (1992). *The Reunion Planner: The Step-by-Step Guide Designed to Make Your Reunion a Social and Financial Success.* Los Angeles: Goodman Lauren Publishing.

Howe, J.T. (1993). *The International Travel Resource for International Meeting and Congress Professionals.* Dallas, TX: Meeting Professionals International.

Howe, J.T., Schaffer, H.M. (1992). *Keeping in Step with Music Licensing.* Dallas, TX: Meeting Professionals International.

Howe, T.H. (1996). *U.S. Meetings and Taxes* (3rd ed. - available January 15, 1996). Dallas, TX: Meeting Professionals International.

Hoyle, L.H., Dorf, DC, Jones, T.J.A. (1989). *Managing Conventions and Group Business.* East Lansing, MI: Educational Institute of the American Hotel & Motel Association.

International Association of Business Communicators (1990). *Special Events Marketing (IABC Communication Bank Series).* San Francisco, CA.

International Events Group (1995). *Evaluation: How to Help Sponsors Measure Return on Investment.* Chicago, IL: International Events Group.

International Events Group (1995). *Media Sponsorship: Structuring Deals with Newspaper, Magazine, Radio and TV Sponsors.* Chicago, IL: International Events Group.

International Special Events Society (1993). *ISES Gold.* Indianapolis, IN: ISES.

Jarrow, J., Park, C. (1992). *Accessible Meetings and Conventions.* Columbus, OH: Association on Higher Education and Disability.

Jewell, D. (1978). *Public Assembly Facilities: Planning and Management.* New York: John Wiley & Sons, Inc.

Jolles, R.L. (1993). *How to Run Seminars and Workshops: Presentation Skills for Consultants, Trainers and Teachers.* New York: John Wiley & Sons, Inc.

Jones, J. (1984). *Meeting Management: A Professional Approach.* Stamford, CT: Bayard Publications, Inc.

Jones, J.E., Phypers, C. (1985). *Incentive Travel: The Professional Way.* Stamford, CT: Bayard Publications, Inc.

Jones, P., Pizman, A. (1993). *The International Hospitality Industry: Organizational and Operational Issues.* London: Pitman Publishing.

Kahan, N.W. (1990). *Entertaining for Business: A Complete Guide to Creating Special Events with Style and a Personal Touch.* New York: C.N. Potter.

Kaiser, T.A. (1995). *Mining Group Gold: How to Cash in on the Collaborative Brain Power of a Group.* Burr Ridge, IL: Irwin Professional Publishing, Inc.

Karasik, P. (1992). *How to Make It Big in the Seminar Business.* New York: McGraw Hill.

Keegan, P.B. (1990). *Fundraising for Non-Profits.* New York: Harper Perennial.

Kring, R. (1993). *Party Creations: A Book to Theme Event Design.* Denver, CO: Clear Creek Publishing.

Krueger, C. (1993). *Dream Weddings Do Come True: How to Plan a Stress-Free Wedding.* St. Paul, MN: Brighton Publications, Inc.

Kurdle, A.E., Sandler, M. (1995). *Public Relations for Hospitality Managers.* New York: John Wiley & Sons, Inc.

Levi-Strauss, C. (1990). *The Origin of Table Manners, Vol. 3: Mythologies.* Chicago: University of Chicago Press.

Levitan, J. (1994). *Proven Ways to Generate Thousands of Hidden Dollars From Your Trade Show, Conference and Convention.* Vernon Hill, IL: Conference and Exhibition Publisher.

Levy, O., Davidson, A. (1991). *Party Planner.* New York: Langson Press.

Lewis, C.L. (1992). *How to Plan, Produce, and Stage Special Events.* Chicago, IL: Evergreen Press.

Liebold, L.C. (1986). *Fireworks, Brass Bands, and Elephants: Promotional Events with Flair for Libraries and Other Nonprofit Organizations.* Phoenix, AZ: Orynx Press.

Lindsay, D.J. (1994). *Bravo Meeting Planner's Organizer: A Step-by-Step Road Map to Planning a Successful Meeting or Event.* Portland, OR: Bravo Publications, Inc.

Lippincott, C. (1994). *Meetings: Do's, Don'ts and Donuts: The Complete Handbook for Successful Meetings.* Pittsburgh, PA: Lighthouse Point Press.

Mack, W.P., Connell, W. (1980). *Naval Ceremonies, Customs and Traditions* (5th ed.). Annapolis, MD: Naval Institute Press.

Mackenzie, J.K. (1989). *It's Show Time!: How to Plan and Hold Successful Sales Meetings.* Homewood, IL: Dow Jones-Irwin.

Malouf, D. (1988). *How to Create and Deliver a Dynamic Presentation.* Australia: Simon and Schuster.

Manning, F.E. (1983). *The Celebration of Society: Perspectives on Contemporary Cultural Performance.* Bowling Green, OH: Bowling Green University Popular Press.

Marsh, V. (1994). *Paper-Cutting Stories for Holidays and Special Events.* Fort Atkinson, WI: Alleyside Press.

Martin, E.L. (1992). *Festival Sponsorship Legal Issues.* Port Angeles, WA: International Festivals Association.

Masciangelio, W.R., Ninkovich, T. (1991). *Military Reunion Handbook: A Guide for Reunion Planners.* San Francisco, CA: Reunion Research.

McGinnis, C. (1994). *202 Tips Even the Best Business Travelers May Not Know.* Chicago, IL: Irwin Professional Publishing.

McIntosh, R.W., Goeldener, C.R. (1990). *Tourism Principles, Practices and Philosophies* (6th ed.). New York: John Wiley & Sons, Inc.

McKinzie, H. (1992). *Reunions: How to Plan Yours.* Los Angeles: McKinzie Publishing Company.

McMahon, T. (1990). *Big Meetings, Big Results.* Lincolnwood, IL: NTC Publishing Group.

Meeting Professionals International and Canadian Council and the Governments of Canada, The Department of Human Resources Development (1994). *Meeting Manager Standards.* Dallas, TX.

Meeting Professionals International and Canadian Council and the Government of Canada, The Department of Human Resources Development (1994). *Meeting Coordinator Standards.* Dallas, TX.

Miller Brewing Company. *Good Times. A Guide to Responsible Event Planning.* Milwaukee, WI.

Miller, S. (1991). *How to Get the Most Out of Trade Shows.* Federal Way, WA: The Adventure.

Montgomery, R.J., Strick, S.K. (1995). *Meetings, Conventions, and Expositions: An Introduction to the Industry.* New York: Van Nostrand Reinhold.

Morrisey, G.C. (1995). *Morrisey on Planning (Vol. I-III).* San Francisco, CA: Jossey-Bass.

Morton, A., Prosser, A., Spangler, S. (1991). *Great Special Events and Activities.* State College, PA: Venture Publishing.

Morton, J. (1985). *Jack Morton (Who's He?) Story.* New York: Vantage Press.

Morton, J. (1993). *The Poor Man's Philosopher.* Washington, DC.

Mothershead, A.B. (1982). *Dining Customs Around the World: With Occasional Recipes.* Garrett Park, MD: Garrett Park Press.

Museum of Fine Arts (1992). *Wedding Planner.* New York: Rizzoli International Publications, Inc.

National Association of Broadcasters (1991). *A Broadcaster's Guide to Special Events and Sponsorship Risk Management.* Washington, DC.

Neel, S.M., Wray, R. (1995). *Saying "I Do": The Wedding CeremoNew York: The Complete Guide to a Perfect Wedding.* Colorado Springs, CO: Meriwether Publishing.

Neuhoff, V. (1987). *Scientists in Conference: The Congress Organizer's Handbook: The Congress Visitor's Companion.* Weinheim, Germany: VCH.

Newman, P.J., Lynch, A.F. (1983). *Behind Closed Doors: A Guide to Successful Meetings.* New York: Prentice Hall.

Nichols, B. (1989). *Professional Meeting Management* (2nd ed.). Birmingham, AL: Professional Convention Management Association.

Ninkovich, T. (1991). *Reunion Handbook: A Guide for School and Military Reunions* (2nd ed.). San Francisco, CA: Reunion Research.

Norris, D.M., Loften, J.F. & Associates (1995). *Winning with Diversity: A Practical Handbook for Creating Inclusive Meetings, Events and Organizations.* Washington, DC: Foundations of Meeting Planners.

International, Professional Convention Management Association, Association of Association Executives, International Association of Convention and Visitor's Bureaus and International Association of Exposition Management.

Oldenwald, S.B. (1993). *Global Training: How to Design a Program for the Multinational Corporation.* Chicago, IL: Irwin Professional Publishing.

Packham, J. (1993). *Wedding Parties and Showers: Planning Memorable Celebrations.* New York: Sterling Publishing Company.

Petersen, K. (1992). *Historical Celebrations: A Handbook for Organizers of Diamond Jubilees, Centennials, and Other Community Anniversaries* (3rd ed.). Bosie, ID: Idaho State Historical Society.

Plessner, G.M. (1980). *The Encyclopedia of Fund Raising: Testimonial Dinner and Luncheon Management Manual.* Arcadia, CA: Fund Raisers, Inc.

Plessner, G.M. (1980). *The Encyclopedia of Fund Raising: Golf Tournament Management Manual.* Arcadia, CA: Fund Raisers, Inc.

Plessner, G.M. (1986). *The Encyclopedia of Fund Raising: Charity Auction Management Manual.* Arcadia, CA: Fund Raisers, Inc.

Post, E. (1991). *Emily Post's Complete Book of Wedding Etiquette,* (Revised Ed.). New York: HarperCollins Publishers.

Powers, T., Powers, J.M. (1991). *Food Service Operations: Planning and Control.* Melbourne, Australia: Krieger Publishing Company.

Price, C.H. (1989). *The AMA Guide for Meeting and Event Planners.* Arlington, VA: Educational Services Institute.

Professional Convention Management Association (1985). *Professional Meeting Management.* Birmingham, AL.

Quain, B. (1993). *Selling Your Services to the Meetings Market.* Dallas, TX: Meeting Professionals International.

Ramsborg, G.C. (1993). *Objectives to Outcomes: Your Contract with the Learner.* Birmingham, AL: Professional Convention Management Association.

Reed, M.H. (1989). *IEG Legal Guide to Sponsorship.* Chicago, IL: International Events Group.

Reynolds, R., Louie, E., Addeo, E. (1992). *The Art of the Party: Design Ideas for Successful Entertaining.* New York: Viking Studio Books.

Rutherford, D.G. (1990). *Introduction to the Conventions, Expositions, and Meetings Industry.* New York: Van Nostrand Reinhold.

Scannell, E.E., Newstrom, J.W. (1991). *Still More Games Trainers Play.* New York: McGraw Hill.

Scannell, E.E., Newstrom, J.W. (1994). *Even More Games Trainers Play.* New York: McGraw Hill.

Schindler-Rainman, E., Cole, J. (1988). *Taking Your Meetings Out of the Doldrums* (Revised ed.). San Diego, CA: University Associates.

Schmader, S.W., Jackson, R. (1990). *Special Events: Inside & Out: A "How-to" Approach to Event Production, Marketing, and Sponsorship.* Champaign, IL: Sagamore Publishing.

Schreibner, A.L., Lenson, B. (1994). *Lifestyle and Event Marketing: Building the New Customer Partnership.* New York: McGraw-Hill.

Shaw, M. (1990). *Convention Sales: A Book of Readings.* East Lansing, MI: Educational Institute of the American Hotel & Motel Association.

Sheerin, M. (1984). *How to Raise Top Dollars from Special Events*. Hartsdale, NY: Public Service Materials Center.

Shenson, H.L. (1990). *How to Develop and Promote Successful Seminars and Workshops: A Definite Guide to Creating and Marketing Seminars, Classes and Conferences*. New York: John Wiley & Sons, Inc.

Shock, P.J., Stefanelli, J.M. (1992). *Hotel Catering: A Handbook for Sales and Operations*. New York: John Wiley & Sons, Inc.

Simerly, R. (1990). *Planning and Marketing Conferences and Workshops: Tips, Tools, and Techniques*. San Francisco, CA: Jossey-Bass.

Simerly, R.G. (1993). *Strategic Financial Management for Conferences, Workshops, and Meetings*. San Francisco, CA: Jossey-Bass.

Sinclair, M.T., Stabler, M.J. (1991). *The Tourism Industry: An International Analysis*. Oxon, United Kingdom: C.A.B. International.

Siposs, A.J. (1991). *How to Develop and Conduct Successful Seminars: Practical Guide for Entrepreneurs and Managers*. International Business Handbooks Series.

Smith, L.J. (1989). *Tourism Analysis: A Handbook*. Harlow, England: Longman Scientific & Technical.

Soares, E.J. (1991). *Promotional Feats: The Role of Planned Events in the Marketing Communications Mix*. New York: Quorum Books.

Society of Incentive Travel Executives (1990). *The Incentive Travel Case Study Book*. New York.

Sokolosky, V. (1990). *Corporate Protocol: A Brief Case for Business Etiquette*. Dallas, TX: Valerie and Company.

Sokolosky, V. (1994). *The Fine Art of Business Entertaining*. Dallas, TX: Valerie and Company.

South Australia Department of Tourism (1982). *Planning Festivals and Special Events*. Adelaide, Australia.

Sowden, C.L. (1990). *Wedding Occasions: 101 New Party Themes for Wedding Showers, Rehearsal Dinners, Engagement Parties, and More*. St. Paul, MN: Brighton Publications, Inc.

Sowden, C.L. (1992). *An Anniversary to Remember: Years One to Seventy-Five*. St. Paul, MN: Brighton Publications, Inc.

Stern, L. (1995). *Stage Management* (5th ed.). Boston, MA: Allyn and Bacon.

Stewart, M. (1987). *Weddings*. New York: C.N. Potter.

Stewart, M. (1988). *The Wedding Planner*. New York: C.N. Potter.

Strick, S. (1995). *Meetings and Conventions*. New York: Van Nostrand Reinhold.

Surbeck, L. (1991). *Creating Special Events: The Ultimate Guide to Producing Successful Events*. Louisville, KY: Master Publications.

Swartz, O.D. (1988). *Service Etiquette* (4th ed.). Annapolis, MD: Naval Institute Press.

Talbot, R. (1990). *Meeting Management: Practical Advice for Both New and Experienced Managers Based on an Expert's Twenty Years in the "Wonderful Wacky World" of Meeting Planning*. McLean, VA: EPM Publications.

Tepper, B. (1993). *Incentive Travel: The Complete Guide.* San Francisco, CA: Dendrobium Books.

The 3M Meeting and Management Team with Jeannine Drew (1994). *Mastering Meetings: Discovering the Hidden Potential of Effective Business Meetings.* New York: McGraw-Hill.

The Reunion Network (1992). *Class Reunions: Lesson #1 A Planner's Guide.* Hollywood, FL: The Reunion Network.

The Reunion Network (1992). *Survival Guide for Military Reunion Planners.* Hollywood, FL: The Reunion Network.

Thomsett, M.C. (1991). *The Little Black Book of Business Etiquette.* New York: American Management Association.

Torrence, S.R. (1991). *How to Run Scientific and Technical Meetings.* New York: Van Nostrand Reinhold.

Turner, V. (1982). *Celebration: Studies in Festivity and Ritual.* Washington, DC: Smithsonian Institution.

Von Bornstedt, M., Prytz, U. (1981). *Folding Table Napkins.* New York: Sterling Publishing Company, Inc.

Washington, G., Applewood Books Staff (1989). *George Washington's Rules of Civility and Decent Behavior in Company and Conversation.* Mount Vernon, VA: Applewood Books.

Weirich, M.L. (1992). *Meetings and Conventions Management.* Albany, NY: Delmar Publishers.

Weissinger, S.S. (1992). *A Guide to Successful Meeting Planning.* New York: John Wiley & Sons, Inc.

Wiersma, E.A. (1991). *Creative Event Development: A Guide to Strategic Success in the World of Special Events.* Indianapolis, IN: Elisabeth A. Wiersma.

Wilkinson, D. *A Guide to Effective Event Management and Marketing.* Willowdale, Ontario: The Event Management and Marketing Institute.

Williams, W. (1994). *User Friendly Fundraising: A Step-by-Step Guide to Profitable Special Events.* Alexander, NC: World Comm.; Associated Publishers.

Wilson, J., Undall, L. (1982). *Folk Festivals: A Handbook for Organization and Management.* Knoxville, TN: University of Tennessee Press.

Wisdom, E.J. (1992). *Family Reunion Organizer.* Nashville, TN: Post Oak Publications.

Witkowski, D. (1994). *How to Haunt a House.* New York: Random House.

Wolf, T. (1983). *Presenting Performances: A Handbook for Sponsors.* New York: American Council of the Arts.

Wolfson, S.M. (1986). *The Meeting Planner's Guide to Logistics and Arrangements.* Kansas City: Institute for Meeting and Conference Management.

Wolfson, S.M. (1991). *Meeting Planner's Workbook: Write Your Own Hotel Contract.* Kansas City: Institute for Meeting and Conference Management.

Wolfson, S.M. (1995). *The Meeting Planner's Complete Guide to Negotiating: You Can Get What You Want.* Kansas City: Institute for Meeting and Conference Management.

Wright, R.R. (1988). *The Meeting Spectrum: An Advanced Guide for Meeting Professionals.* San Diego, CA: Rockwood Enterprises.

General Interest Business Books for Event Managers

American Society of Association Executives (1985). *Achieving Goals.* Washington, DC.

Axtell, R.E. (1990). *The Do's and Taboos of Hosting International Visitors.* New York: John Wiley & Sons, Inc.

Axtell, R.E. (1994). *The Do's and Taboos of International Trade: A Small Business.*

Axtell, R.E. (1993). *Do's and Taboos Around the World* (3rd ed.). New York.

Axtell, R.E. (1991). *Gestures: The Do's and Taboos of Body Language Around the World.*

Baker, D.B. (1992). *Power Quotes: 4,000 Trenchant Soundbites on Leadership & Liberty, Treason & Triumph, Sacrifice & Scandal, Risk & Rebellion, Weakness & War and Other Affairs Politiques.* Detroit, MI: Visible Ink Press.

Bartlett, J. (1994). *Familiar Quotations: A Collection of Passages, Phrases and Proverbs Traced to Their Sources in Ancient and Modern Literature,* (14th ed.). Cutchogue, NY: Buccaneer Books.

Davidson, J.P., Fay, G.-A. (1991). *Selling to the Giants: A Key to Become a Key Supplier to Large Corporations.* New York: McGraw Hill.

Harris, T.L. (1991). *The Marketer's Guide to Public Relations: How Today's Top Companies Are Using the New PR to Gain a Competitive Edge.* New York: John Wiley & Sons, Inc.

Goldsmith, C.S., Waigand, A.H. (1990). *Building Profits with Group Travel.* San Francisco, CA: Dendrobium Books.

Humes, J.C. (1993). *More Podium Humor: Using Wit and Humor in Every Speech You Make.* New York: Harper Perennial.

Kawasaki, G. (1991). *Selling the Dream: How to Promote Your Product, Company or Ideas—and Make a Difference—Using Everyday Evangelism.* HarperCollins Publishers.

Anthropological and Folklore Resources of Interest to Event Managers

Baron, R., Spitzer, N.R. (1992). *Public Folklore.* Washington, DC: Smithsonian Institution Press.

Browne, R.B. (1980). *Rituals and Ceremonies in Popular Culture.* Bowling Green, OH: Bowling Green University Popular Press.

Cannadine, D., Price, S. (1993). *Rituals of Royalty: Power and Ceremonial in Traditional Societies.* New York: Cambridge University Press.

Jensen, V. (1992). *Where People Gather: Carving a Totem Pole.* Vancouver, British Columbia: Douglas & McIntyre.

Johnston, W.M. (1991). *Celebrations: The Cult of Anniversaries in Europe and the United States Today.* New Brunswick, NJ: Transaction Publishers.

St. Aubyn, L. (1995). *Rituals of Everyday Life: Special Ways of Marking Important Events in Your Life.* Buffalo, NY: General Distribution Services, Inc.

Visser, M. (1986). *Much Depends on Dinner: The Extraordinary History and Mythology, Allure and Obsessions, Peril and Taboos, of an Ordinary Meal.* Toronto, Ontario: McClelland and Stewart.

Visser, M. (1991). *The Rituals of Dinner: The Origins, Evolution, Eccentricities and Meaning of Table Manners.* New York: Grove Weinfeld.

4

Periodicals

To remain current in the overwhelming amount of event management literature that crosses my desk each month, I quickly prioritize publications into three stacks. The first stack represents information I am currently in need of and I set aside a specific time each day to review this material. The second stack goes in my travel bag and is read when I have time during travel or other down time. The third stack is filed under the topic of the article so that when I need the information I am able to quickly retrieve it.

The periodicals with an asterisk are specifically edited for event managers. The other periodicals are of general interest to event managers.

Advertising Age. Weekly by Bill Publications, Chicago, IL.

*_Agenda New York._ Annually by Agenda USA, Inc., 686 Third Avenue, New York, 10017 (800) 523-1233.

Amusements Business. Weekly, by Box 24970, Nashville, TN 37202; (615) 321-4250.

Association and Society Manager. 825 South Barrington Avenue, Los Angeles, CA 90049.

Association Management. Monthly, by the American Society of Association Executives, 1575 I Street NW, Washington, DC 20005; (202) 626-2740.

*_Association Meetings._ Bimonthly, by Adams/Laux Publishing Company, 63 Great Road, Maynard, MA 01754; (508) 897-5552.

Association Trends. Weekly, by Association Trends, 7910 Woodmont Avenue, #1150, Bethesda, MD 20814; (301) 652-8666.

Backstage. Weekly, by BPI Communications, 1515 Broadway, 17th Floor, New York, NY 10036; (212) 764-7300.

Billboard. Published by Billboard Publications, New York, NY.

Business Travel News. Approximately biweekly, by CMP Publications, Inc., 600 Community Drive, Manhasset, NY 11030; (516) 562-5000.

Business TV and Video Guide. Bimonthly, by Business TV Inc., TeleSpan's Business TV, c/o TeleSpan Publishing Corporation, P.O. Box 6250, Altadena, CA 91003; (818) 797-5482.

City Business. Weekly, by Stuart Chamblin, Publisher, 5500 Wayzata Boulevard, #800, Minneapolis, MN 55416; (612) 591-2701.

Conference and Association World. Bimonthly, by ACE International, Riverside House, High Street, Huntingdon, Cambridgeshire PE18 6SG, England; (0480) 457595; international 011 44 1480 457595.

Conference and Exhibitions International. Monthly, by International Trade Publications Ltd., Queensway House, 2 Queensway, Redhill, Surrey RH1 1QS, England; (0737) 768611; International, 011 44 1737 768611.

Conference & Incentive Management. Bimonthly, by CIM Verlag fur Conference, Incentive & Travel management GmBH, Nordkanalstrasse 36, D-20097 Hamburg, Germany; International; 40 237 1405.

Convene. Ten times a year, by Professional Convention Management Association, 100 Vestavia Office Park, Suite 220, Birmingham, AL 35216-9970; (205) 978-4911.

Conventions and Expositions. Bimonthly, by Conventions and Expositions Section of the American Society of Association Executives, 15751 Street, NW, Washington, DC 20005; (202) 626-2769.

Corporate and Incentive Travel. Monthly, by Coastal Communications Corporation, 488 Madison Avenue, New York, NY 10022; (212) 888-1500.

Corporate Meetings and Incentives. Bimonthly, The Laux Company, 63 Great Road, Maynard, MA 01754; (508) 897-5552.

Corporate Travel. Monthly, by Miller Freeman Inc., 1515 Broadway, New York, NY 10036; (212) 626-2501.

Delegates. Monthly, by Audrey Brindsley, Premier House, 10 Greycoat Place, London SW1P 1SB, England; 0712228866.

Entertainment Marketing Letter. Twelve times a year, by EPM Communications, Inc., 488 East 18th Street, Brooklyn, NY 11226-6702; (718) 469-9330.

Events Magazine. Monthly. 1080 N. Delaware Street, Suite 1700, Philadelphia, PA 19125; (215) 426-7800.

Event Solutions. Monthly, by Virgo Publishing Inc. Phoenix, AZ; (602) 990-1101.

Events USA. Suite 301, 386 Park Ave. South, New York, NY 10016; (212) 684-2222.

Event World. Quarterly. International Special Events Society. Indianapolis, IN.

*Events. Bimonthly, by April Harris, Published by Harris Communications, Madison, AL.

*Festival Management & Event Tourism. Quarterly, by Cognizant Communication Corp., 3 Hartsdale Road, Elmsford, NY 10523-3701.

Hollywood Reporter. Weekly, by 5055 Wilshire Boulevard, Los Angeles, CA 90036-4396; (213) 525-2000.

Hospitality Research Journal. Three times a year, by the Council on Hotel Restaurant and Institutional Education, 1200 17th St., NW, Washington, DC 20036-3097; (202) 331-5990.

IEG Sponsorship Report. Weekly, by The International Events Group, (IEG), 640 North Lasalle, Suite 600, Chicago, IL 60610; (312) 944-1727.

In-Tents. Biannually, by the Industrial Fabrics Association (IFAI), 345 Cedar Street, Suite 800, St. Paul, MN 55101-1088; (612) 222-1366.

*Incentive. Monthly, by Bill Communications Inc., 855 Park Avenue South, New York, NY 10010; (212) 592-6200.

*Insurance Conference Planner. Bimonthly, by The Laux Company, 63 Great Road, Maynard, MA 01754; (508) 897-5552.

Journal of Travel Research. Quarterly, by the Travel and Tourism Research Association and the Business Research Division, University of Colorado at Boulder, Boulder, CO 80309-0420.

*Konferensevarlden. Monthly, P.O. Box 515, S-611 10 Nykoping, Sweden Int+ 46 155 21 98 15.

*Legal Information Review. Quarterly, by Convention Liaison Council, 1575 I Street, NW, #1200, Washington, DC 20005; (202) 626-2764.

Lighting Dimensions. Nine times a year, by Entertainment Technology Communications Corporation, 32 W. 18th Street, New York, NY 10011-4612; (212) 229-2965.

Marketing Review. By Hospitality Sales and Marketing Association International, 1400 K Street, N.W. Suite 810, Washington, DC 20005.

*Medical Meetings. Eight times a year, by The Adams/Laux Company, Inc., 63 Great Road, Maynard, MA 01754; (508) 897-5552.

*Meeting Manager. 3719 Roosevelt Road, Middletown, OH 45044-6593.

*Meeting Manager, The. Monthly, by Meeting Professionals International, 1950 Stemmons Freeway, Suite 5018, Dallas, TX 75207-3109; (214) 712-7700.

*Meeting News. Monthly, by Gralla Publications, 1515 Broadway, New York, NY 10036; (212) 869-1300.

*Meeting Planners Alert. 126 Harvard Street, Brookline, MA 02146

*Meetings and Conventions. Monthly, by Reed Travel Group, 500 Plaza Drive, Secaucus, NJ 07096; (201) 902-1700; subscription service: P.O. Box 5870, Cherry Hill, NJ 08034.

Museum Premiers & Exhibitions, Special Events. Annual, by Information Services, St. Louis, MO.

Performance Magazine. Weekly, by 1101 University Drive, Suite 108, Fort Worth, TX 76107-3000; (817) 338-9444.

Public Relations Journal. 845 Third Avenue, New York, NY 10022.

*Religious Conference Manager. Five times a year, by The Laux Company, Inc., 63 Great Road, Maynard, MA 01754; (508) 897-5552.

Rental Management. American Rental Association, 1900 19th Street, Moline, IL 61265; (800) 334-2177; (309) 764-2475.

Research Alert. Twenty-four times a year, by EPM Communications, Inc., 488 East 18th Street, Brooklyn, NY 11226-6702; (718) 469-9330.

Sales and Marketing Management. Fifteen times a year, by Bill Communications, 355 Park Avenue South, 5th Floor, New York, NY 10010-1706; (212) 592-6200.

Show Business News. Weekly, by 1501 Broadway, 29th Floor, New York, NY 10036; (212) 354-7600.

*Special Events Forum. Six times annually, by Dave Nelson, 1973 Schrader Drive, San Jose, CA 95124.

*Special Events Magazine. Monthly, by Miramar Publishing Company, Malibu, CA; (800) 543-4116.

*Stress Free Planning of Special Events. Quarterly, by Patty Sachs. Published by Patty Sachs, Minneapolis, MN.

*Successful Meetings. Thirteen times a year, by Bill Communications, 355 Park Avenue South, New York, NY 10010; (212) 592-6403.

Tent Rental Report. By the Tent Rental Division of the Industrial Fabrics Association International, 345 Cedar Street, #800, St. Paul, MN 55101; (612) 222-2508.

*The Reunion Network News. By The Reunion Network, 2450 Hollywood Boulevard, Suite 301, Hollywood, FL 33020; (800) 775-1945.

TLL The Licensing Letter. Twelve times a year, by EPM Communications, Inc., 488 East 18th Street, Brooklyn, NY 11226-6702; (718) 469-9330.

*Trade Show and Exhibit Manager. Bimonthly, by Goldstein and Associates, Inc., 1150 Yale Street, #12, Santa Monica, CA 90403; (310) 828-1309.

*Tradeshow Week. Weekly, by Tradeshow Week, 12233 West Olympic Boulevard, #236, Los Angeles, CA 90064; (310) 826-5696.

Training and Development Journal. Monthly, by American Society for Training and Development, 1640 King Street, Alexandria, VA 22313; (703) 683-8100.

Training. Monthly, by Lakewood Publications, 50 South Ninth Street, Minneapolis, MN 55402; (612) 333-0471.

U.S. Association Executive (USAE). Weekly, by Custom NEWS, Inc., 4341 Montgomery Avenue, Bethesda, MD 20814; (301) 951-1881.

Variety. Weekly, by Cahners Publishing Company, 249 West 17th Street, New York, NY 10011; (212) 645-0067.

World's Fair. Quarterly, by World's Fair, Inc., P.O. Box 339, Corte Madera, CA 94976-0339; (415) 924-6035.

Youth Markets Alert. Twelve times a year, by EPM Communications, Inc., 488 East 18th Street, Brooklyn, NY 11226-6702; (718) 469-9330.

5

Directories

Directories are an invaluable resource for event managers. Many libraries stock directories in the reference section, however, for day to day use, you will want to own your own copy for quick reference. The directories listed below with an asterisk are specifically for event managers usage and the others are for general business use.

*1995 World Party Map: The Original Global Guide to Special Events (1994). Published by Goodland and Grande. A list of major events.

*Academy Players Directory. Published by Academy of Motion Picture Arts and Sciences, 8949 Wilshire Boulevard, Beverly Hills, CA 90211. A listing of hundreds of television and film stars and their contact telephone numbers.

*AFTRA/SAG Talent Directory. Published by American Federation of Television and Radio Artists/Screen Actors Guild, 1108 17th Avenue South, P.O. Box 121087, Nashville, TN 37212; (615) 327-2944. A listing of local performers in the Nashville, Tennessee area.

*Agenda Washington: Special Events Resource Directory (1995). Published by Agenda Washington. A listing of special event resources in the Washington, DC area.

America's Meeting Places (1984). Published by Facts on File. A listing of event venues.

ASAE Convention Themes. Published by American Society of Association Executives, 1575 Eye Street, N.W., Washington, DC 20005. A list and description of successful convention themes.

Auditorium/Arena/Stadium Guide. Published by Amusement Business/Single Copy Department, Box 24970, Nashville, TN 37202. A listing of venues for events.

Banquet Guide (1995). Published by Banquet Guide, 8948 S.W. Barbour Boulevard, Suite 132, Portland, OR 97219.

Cavalcade of Acts and Attractions. Published by Amusement Business/Single A Copy Department, Box 24970, Nashville, TN 37202. A listing of live acts for events ranging from musical performers to circus attractions.

Chase's Annual Events: Special Days, Weeks, and Months (Annually). Published by Contemporary Books, Inc., 180 North Michigan Avenue, Chicago, IL 60601. A listing of thousands of annual events.

CHRIE Member Directory and Resource Guide. Published by Council on Hotel, Restaurant and Institutional Education, 1200 17th Street, N.W., Washington, DC 20036; (202) 331-5990. A listing of scholars and others involved in the hotel and restaurant education field.

Circus and Carnival Booking Guide. Published by Amusement Business/Single Copy Department, Box 24970, Nashville, TN 37202. A listing of circuses and carnivals.

Culinary & Hospitality Industry Publications Services. Published by C.H.I.P.S., 1307 Golden Bear Lane, Kingwood, TX 77339; (713) 359-2270. A listing of books specifically selected for the hospitality industry.

Directory of City Policy Officials. Published by National League of Cities, 1301 Pennsylvania Avenue, N.W., Washington, DC 20004; (202) 626-3150. A listing of individuals including event managers who work for municipal governments.

From Day to Day: A Calendar of Notable Birthdays and Events (1990). Published by Scarecrow Press. A list of significant birthdays and other events.

Golden California Special Events 1994. Published by the California Trade and Commerce Agency, Division of Tourism. A listing of California events occurring in 1994.

Here Comes the Guide, Hawaii (1994-1995). Published by Hopscotch Press, 1563 Solano Avenue, Suite 135, Berkeley, CA 94707. A listing of venues for events for Weddings in Hawaii. (510) 525-3379.

Here Comes the Guide, Northern California (1993-1994). Published by Hopscotch Press, 1563 Solano Avenue, Suite 135, Berkeley, CA 94707; (510) 525-3379. A listing of venues for events for weddings in Northern California.

Hospitality, Travel and Tourism Catalog. Published by Delmar Publishers, P.O. Box 15015, Albany, NY 12212-5015; (518) 464-3500.

IEG Guide to Sponsorship Agencies. Published by International Events Group, 640 North Lasalle, Suite 600, Chicago, IL 60610; (312) 944-1727. A listing of sponsorship agencies.

IEG Directory of Sponsorship Marketing. Published by International Events Group, 640 North Lasalle, Suite 600, Chicago, IL 60610; (312) 944-1727. A listing of individuals and organizations involved in sponsorship marketing.

International Handbook. Published by International Exhibitors Association, 5501 Backlick Road, Suite 105, Springfield, VA 22151; (703) 941-3725. A listing of international exhibitors.

Locations, etc: The Directory of Locations and Services for Special Events (1992). Published by Innovative Productions. A listing of event locations.

Morris Costumes. Published by Morris Costumes, 3108 Monroe Road, Charlotte, NC 28205; (704) 333-4653. An annual catalog of inexpensive costumes for events.

MPI Membership Directory. Annually published by Meeting Professionals International. A listing of over 10,000 individuals involved in meeting planning and related services.

Party Resource (1994-1995). Published by Directories of America, Inc., 14770 Biscayne Boulevard, North Miami Beach, FL 33181; (305) 949-4948. A listing of local resources for events.

Perfect Places - Northern California (2nd ed.). Published by Hopscotch Press, 1563 Solano Avenue, Suite 135, Berkeley, CA 94707. A listing of event venues in California.

Protocol Directory. Published by Protocol Directory, Inc. 101 West 12th Street, Suite PH-H, New York, NY 10011. A listing of resources for protocol throughout the world.

RCRA *Membership Directory.* Published by Resort and Commercial Recreation Association, P.O. Box 1208, New Port Richey, FL 34656-1208; (813) 845-7373. A listing of members and resources for resorts and commercial recreation.

Sites & Insights: The Special Event Location & Resource Directory. Published by Site Network, 550 Orange Avenue, Suite 132, Long Beach, CA 90802.

Sourcebook (annually). Published by Bill Communications, Inc., *Successful Meetings,* 355 Park Avenue South, New York, NY 10010; (212) 592-6403. A listing of resources for meeting planners.

State Municipal League Directory. Published by The National League of Cities, 1301 Pennsylvania Avenue, N.W., Washington, DC 20004; (202) 626-3000.

Tent Rental Directory (1993-1994). Published by the Tent Rental Division of the Industrial Fabrics Association International, 345 Cedar Street, Suite 800, St. Paul, MN 55101-1088; (800) 225-4324. A listing of resources for tent firms.

The Almanac of Anniversaries (1992). By Kim Long. Published by ABC-CLIO. A listing of anniversary events.

The ASAE Meetings and Expositions Section Networking Directory (Annually). Published by American Society of Association Executives, 1575 Eye Street, N.W., Washington, DC 20005-1168; (202) 626-2748. A listing of meeting and exposition managers.

The Beverly Hills International Party Planner. Published by Jan Roberts Publications, 139 South Beverly Drive, Suite 312, Beverly Hills, CA 90212. A listing of resources for events in various cities.

The Events Register. Published by Marilou Stannard Doyle, P.O. Box 98, Hastings-on-Hudson, NY 10706-0098. A listing of event resources.

The Garden Tourist: A Guide to Garden Tours, Garden Days, Shows and Special Events (1995). Published by Garden Tourist Press. A listing of events specifically related to garden tours.

The Government Contracts Reference Book (1992). Published by The George Washington University, National Law Center, Government Contracts Program, Suite 250, 2100 Pennsylvania Avenue, N.W., Washington, DC 20037-3202. A guide to obtaining government events contracts.

The Guide to Campus and Non-Profit Meeting Facilities. Published by AMARC. A listing of venues on campus for event managers.

The Management Sourcebook. Published by the American Rental Association, Rental Management, 1900 19th Street, Moline, IL 61265-4198; (800) 334-2177. A listing of rental resources.

The Meetings Mart. Published by *Corporate Meetings & Incentives,* The Laux Company, 63 Great Road, Maynard, MA 01754; (508) 897-5552. A listing of meeting planning resources.

The Original British Theatre Directory (1990). Published by Richmond House Publishing Company Limited, 1 Richmond Mews, London W1V 5AG; (01) 437-9556. A listing of equipment rental for events in Great Britain.

The Tradeshow Week Data Book (1985). Published by Tradeshow Week, New York, NY, in cooperation with the Trade Show Bureau. A listing of annual data from The Tradeshow Bureau concerning expositions.

Tradeshow and Convention Guide. Published by Amusement Business/Single Copy Department, Box 24970, Nashville, TN 37202. A listing of venues and resources for events.

Unique Meeting Places in Greater Washington (1988). By Elise Ford. Published by EPM. A listing of unusual venues for events in Washington, DC.

Who's Who in Association Management. ASAE Membership Directory. Published by American Society of Association Executives, 1575 Eye Street, N.W., Washington, DC 20005; (202) 731-8825. A listing of association executives (including meeting planners) and their suppliers.

Who's Who in Professional Speaking (1994-1995). Published by National Speakers Association, 4747 North Seventh Street, Phoenix, AZ 85014. A listing of over 3,000 professional speakers.

Who's Who in Religious Conference Management (1994-1995). Published by Religious Conference Management Association, Inc., One RCA Dome, Suite 120, Indianapolis,

IN 46225; (317) 632-1888. A listing of professional meeting planners employed by religious organizations and their suppliers.

Your Special Event Planning Guide. By Patty Sachs. Published by Your Special Event, Inc., 2809 Wayzata Boulevard, Minneapolis, MN 55404; (612) 377-9525. A listing of special event resources and ideas.

Audio and Video Resources

Many of the major event management organizations such as the International Special Events Society (ISES) maintain extensive audio recordings of seminars held at their annual conferences. These audio tapes may be purchased directly from the organization.

The Gelman Library of The George Washington University maintains a complete set of all audio recordings from ISES conferences. These recordings may be used within the confines of the library media resources division.

Additionally, The Gelman Library maintains an extensive video collection containing footage of corporate, association, civic, retail, and other types of events including large scale programs such as Super Bowl half-time shows and the opening and closing ceremonies of the Olympic Games, the Goodwill Games, and the Olympic Festival. These video tapes may also be viewed within the confines of the library and with permission of the copyright holder, may be duplicated for scholarly or professional use. To receive a complete listing of these resources, contact The Gelman Library Media Resources Division, at (202) 994-1000.

Although the resources of The Gelman Library and the Event Management and Marketing Archives are too numerous to list (in fact each collection has its own finding aid listing dozens of resources), I have a few personal favorites.

First, review the 1988 Super Bowl Half-time Spectacular produced by Radio City Music Hall Productions. This event is a masterful depiction of logistics, both mechanical and human.

Next, view the Goodwill Games opening ceremonies in Russia. The use of cards by thousands of spectators was so impressive that the television newscaster reporting the games stated that "this was the most memorable moment."

Finally, review the opening ceremonies for the 1984 Olympic Games in Los Angeles, California. This video depicts the transformation of the opening ceremonies from a one dimensional live event into a multi-dimensional production staged for both a live audience as well as hundreds of millions of television viewers. As a result of this production, the format of the Olympic Games' opening and closing ceremonies shifted to include more spectacular effects.

In addition to these resources, I recommend the following video products for scholarly and professional use:

Political Money for Senate Candidates (1989). Produced by Purdue University Public Affairs Video Archives, West Lafayette, IN. Subject matter deals with raising funds for U.S. senate candidates.

A Matter of Judgement, Conflicts of Interest in the Workplace. A brief vignette entitled "Special Events Director" dealing with the subject of event managers who receive gifts from hotels and other vendors and the consequences that may follow. This is an excellent way to begin an in-depth discussion of ethics in event management. Ethics Resource Center, Barr Media Group, Irwindale, CA.

Successful Special Events with Virgil Ecton, *CFRE*. A lecture by Virgil Ectorn, CFRE of the United Negro College Fund dealing with brainstorming, budgeting, operations, and other factors for helping ensure the success of special events for fund raising purposes. National Society of Fundraising Executives, Alexandria, VA.

The Event Marketing Process (1988). Produced by Petit Communications, Don Mills, Ontario, Canada. A description of the various competencies involved in event marketing.

Software

Using the software listed below may save you time and money. However, remember that part of your investment is the learning curve that must be mastered, and this may require a considerable investment of time. Carefully compare software prior to investment to ensure that you are maximizing your scarce resources with the most efficient software solutions available for your Event Management practice.

Software is typically divided into four categories. First, software is available for word processing. Second, software is available for financial and data analysis. Third, software is available for publishing, such as the development of diagrams and site plans. Finally, software is available for compiling extensive data bases. Whenever possible, try and obtain a software product that combines as many of these functions as possible. In some instances, you may wish to purchase a standard product and customize the functions to solve your individual event management business challenges.

Advanced Solutions International, Inc. Special event planning/management package, Alexandria, VA; (703) 765-6380.

ALERT Computer Systems. Rental management package, Colordao Springs, CO; (800) 530-8050; (719) 634-7755.

AlphaSoft, Inc. Rental management package, Minneapolis, MN; (800) 969-SOFT; (612) 561-7375.

Automation Plus. Rental management package, Ft. Lauderdale, FL; (305) 587-1501.

Business Computer Solutions. Special event planning/management package, Columbia, MD; (301) 596-5005.

Catermate. Catering package, the Event Management Software Co., Indianapolis, IN; (317) 875-5271.

Codesmiths, Inc. (Printing). Tent supplier management, Champaign, IL; (217) 352-5510.

Computer Ease. Rental management package, Novato, CA; (800) 338-0686.

Creative Business Services. Rental management package, Manchester, MO; (314) 227-5190.

Culinary Software Services. Catering package, Boulder, CO; (800) 447-1466; (303) 447-3334.

ErgoSoft, Inc. Special event planning/management package, Columbia, MD; (800) 346-9484; (410) 381-5599.

EventMaker Pro. Special events management software, Compagne Associates, Nashua, NH; (800) 582-3489.

I *Do, The Ultimate Wedding Planner.* Touchsoft, Malpetus, CA; (800) 887-8960; (408) 956-0884. (Windows)

InScribe, Inc. Calligraphy/printing package, Cambridge, MA; (800) 346-3461; (617) 868-5743.

International Hospitality and Tourism Database CD-ROM, The Guide to Industry and Academic Resources. The consortium of Hospitality Research Information Systems, available through MPI, Dallas, TX; (214) 712-7742.

MeetingPRO. Peopleware, Inc., Copyright 1987.

Microchips, Inc. Function space management, St. Louis, MO; (800) 373-0693; (314) 645-2800.

Mom 'N' Pops Software. A shareware company offering party and event planning programs, Springhill, FL; (352) 688-9108.

MPI Net. The first global communications network for the meeting industry, Dallas, TX; (214)712-7742.

Operation Management System. Rental management package, Stockton, CA; (800) 767-0280.

Parsons Technology. A large-sized company with software for both PC's and Macs, Hiawatha, IA; (800) 679-0670.

Peopleware, Inc. Registration package, Bellevue, WA; (800) 869-7166; (206) 454-6444.

Quality Software Products. Rental management package, Arvada, CO; (303) 273-9633.

QuickSilver Software. Catering package, Sussex, WI; (800) 999-DYNE.

R.E.N.T.S. Computer Systems. Rental management package, Sioux Falls, SD; (800) 369-RENT; (605) 338-1800.

RE: Event (a component of The Raiser's Edge for Windows). Manufactured by Blackbaud, Inc. Helps planners organize and manage their events, Charleston, SC; (800) 443-9441.

ROOMER3 Demo. 1986-1993 by Henry M. Hufnagel. All rights reserved. Portions 1982-1990 Microsoft Corp. All rights reserved.

Smart-N-Easy Wedding Planner. Automated Systems; (800) 588-6972; (201) 812-1428. (DOS).

Social Software. Calligraphy/printing package, New York; (212) 956-2707.

Solutions by Computer, Inc. Rental management package, Springfield, MA; (800) 950-2221; (413) 737-0499.

Synergy Software International. Catering package, Arlington, VA; (800) 522-6210; (703) 522-6200.

Terrapin Systems. Special event planning/management package, Silver Springs, MD; (301) 933-5599.

The Event Edge. The ultimate event planning tool, ErgoSoft, Inc., Simpsonville, MD; (800) 346-9484.

The Event Management System Version 5.3. Dean Evans & Associates, Englewood, CO; (303) 773-3264.

The Wedding Planner. Ninga Software, Calgary, AB, Canada; (800) 656-4642; (403) 383-2772. (DOS, Windows).

The Woodward Group. Rental management package, Glendora, CA; (818) 335-6045.

Unique Business Systems. Rental management package, Santa Monica, CA; (800) 669-4827.

Wedding Workshop. MicroPrecision Software, Santa Clara, CA; (800) 688-9337; (408) 358-8250. (Windows, Macintosh).

Zea Software. Calligraphy/printing package, Alexandria, VA; (703) 379-8201.

Sample Client Agreement

The client agreement must be reviewed by a local attorney, as each state requires individual language to conform with the code. However, the following template provides the event manager with the conceptual framework for the basic client agreement.

Client Agreement

Account number: XYZ-1

This agreement is between ABC Event Management Company (hereafter referred to as EVENT MANAGER) and XYZ Firm (hereafter referred to as CLIENT).

I. EVENT MANAGER *agrees to provide:*

1. Research, design, planning, coordination, and evaluation of the event entitled "The Night of a Thousand Stars."

2. Research that will commence with the joint execution of this agreement.

3. A professional event that will begin on July 15, 1996 at 8 P.M. central time in the city of Kansas City, Kansas and conclude on the same date at 11:00 P.M. central time.

4. A comprehensive evaluation including financial and attitudes and opinions will be submitted to CLIENT by August 15, 1996 at 5:00 P.M. central time.

5. Comprehensive general liability insurance with one million dollars' limit per occurrence naming CLIENT as additional insured for the period of the event.

II. CLIENT agrees to provide:

1. One individual as principal contact, decision maker for the EVENT MANAGER.

2. General liability insurance with one million dollars' limit per occurrence naming EVENT MANAGER as additional insured for the period of the event.

3. Decisions in a timely manner as required by the final approved production schedule.

4. Ten (10) volunteers to coordinate registration and guest relations during the event from 7:00 P.M. central time to 11:00 P.M. central time.

III. INVESTMENT

The EVENT MANAGER will receive a fee for professional services in the amount of $10,000 exactly. The EVENT MANAGER will receive fees for all direct expenses approved by CLIENT.

IV. TERMS

The CLIENT agrees to provide the following payments to the EVENT MANAGER as compensation for the services described above.

June 30, 1996:	25% of fee ($2,500) plus 50% of direct expenses.
July 15, 1996:	65% of fee ($6,500) plus balance of pre-approved direct expenses.
August 15, 1996:	10% of fee plus any additional charges approved by client plus the balance of all approved direct expenses.

V. CANCELLATION

Should the EVENT MANAGER cancel his or her services for any reason other than acts of God, the client shall receive a refund of all prepaid fees less any costs expended on behalf of the event. Should the CLIENT cancel his or her event, the following payments shall be due:

Cancellation more than 120 days prior to event date: 25% of professional fee and 50% deposit of all direct expenses.

Cancellation less than 120 days prior to event date: 50% of professional fee and 50% deposit of all direct expenses.

Cancellation less than 60 days prior to event date: 75% of professional fee and 100% of all direct expenses.

Cancellation less than 30 days prior to event date: 100% of professional fee and 100% of all direct expenses.

VI. FORCE MAJEURE

This agreement is automatically cancelled if the event is interrupted due to acts of God, including, but not limited to, hurricanes, tornadoes, strikes, war, volcanic eruption, earthquakes, or pestilence.

VII. ARBITRATION

The American Arbitration Association is designated as the official body for arbitrating any disputes resulting from this agreement.

VIII. HOLD HARMLESS and INDEMNIFICATION

The EVENT MANAGER and CLIENT agree to hold one another harmless from negligence caused by either party and mutually indemnify one another.

IX. TIME IS OF THE ESSENCE

The services and related costs described in this agreement are guaranteed through 5:00 P.M. central time March 15, 1996. After this date, these services and related costs must be renegotiated.

X. THE FULL AGREEMENT

This agreement and any attachments constitutes the full agreement. Any changes, additions, or deletions to this agreement must be approved in writing by both parties.

XI. ACCEPTANCE

The parties whose signatures are affixed below agree to accept the terms and conditions stated within this agreement.

_____   _____

CLIENT   DATE

_____   _____

EVENT MANAGER   DATE

Note: Sign both copies and return one signed original to the Event Manager.

Sample Vendor Agreement

Account Number: DEF-1

This agreement is between ABC Event Management Company (hereafter referred to as EVENT MANAGER) and DEF firm (hereafter referred to as VENDOR).

I. EVENT DATE: July 15, 1996

II. EVENT ARRIVAL TIME: 7:30 P.M. central time.

III. EVENT START TIME: 8:00 P.M. central time.

IV. EVENT STOP TIME: 11:00 P.M. central time.

V. VENDOR shall provide:

1. Three (3) magicians performing walk around magic suitable for young children ages 5 to 12 years. Magicians shall wear black tuxedoes.

2. Eight (8) member top forty band entitled "Starlight" wearing matching black tuxedoes.

3. Balloon drop of 500 nine inch silver mylar balloons. Rigging to be complete by 2:00 P.M. central time and drop to occur between 10:00 P.M. and 11:00 P.M. central time.

4. Comprehensive general liability insurance with one million dollars limit per occurrence naming EVENT MANAGER as additional insured or period of event.

5. Refrain from distributing promotion literature at event and direct any and all inquiries for future business resulting from event to EVENT MANAGER.

VI. EVENT MANAGER *shall provide:*

1. Complimentary parking for VENDOR and his or her personnel.

2. Two dressing rooms.

3. One lift for rigging balloon drop. Lift to be available from 12:00 P.M. to 2:00 P.M. central time.

4. On-site event coordinator to liaison with VENDOR.

VII. FEES
EVENT MANAGER shall pay the following fees to VENDOR:

1.	Magicians,	$1,000
2.	Band,	$3,000
3.	Balloon drop,	$1,500
	Total:	$5,500

VIII. TERMS
EVENT MANAGER shall pay a VENDOR 50% deposit ($2,750) upon execution of agreement, and the balance net thirty days of event date.

IX. CANCELLATION
If the VENDOR cancels for any reason, he or she forfeits all funds received or due and shall promptly repay EVENT MANAGER any funds advanced for this event. If the EVENT MANAGER cancels for any reason, he or she must provide the following payments to VENDOR:

Cancellation before 120 days of event date:	No fees due.
Cancellation up to 90 days of event date:	15% of total fee.
Cancellation of up to 60 days of event date:	25% of total fee.
Cancellation of up to 30 days of event date:	50% of total fee.
Cancellation less than thirty days prior to event date:	75% of total fee.

X. FORCE MAJEURE

This agreement is automatically cancelled if the event is interrupted due to acts of God, including, but not limited to, hurricanes, tornadoes, strikes, war, volcanic eruption, earthquakes, or pestilence.

XI. ARBITRATION

In the event of disagreement pertaining to this agreement, the parties agree to submit to mandatory nonbinding arbitration. The American Arbitration Association is designated as the official body for arbitrating any disputes resulting from this agreement.

XII. HOLD HARMLESS AND INDEMNIFICATION

The EVENT MANAGER and VENDOR agree to hold one another harmless from negligence caused by that party and to mutually indemnify one another.

XIII. TIME IS OF THE ESSENCE

The services and related costs described in this agreement are guaranteed through 5:00 P.M. central time March 15, 1996. After this date these services and related costs must be renegotiated.

XIV. THE FULL AGREEMENT

This agreement and attachments contain the final and entire agreement between the parties, and neither they nor their agents shall be bound by any terms, statements, or representations, oral or written, not contained herein.

XV. ACCEPTANCE

The parties whose signatures are affixed below agree to accept the terms and conditions stated within this agreement.

_____   _____
CLIENT   DATE

_____   _____
EVENT MANAGER   DATE

Note: Sign both copies and return to Event Manager. A fully executed original will be provided once signed by the Event Manager.

10

Sample Incident Report

Note: The incident report should be completed as soon as possible after the incident has occurred. Copies of this form should be easily accessible to all event personnel.

1. Name of event: _____

2. Name of venue:_____

3. Report of incident: (check one) _____Injury _____Theft _____Lost Person
    _____Lost Property _____Violent activity _____Other _____
    Describe _____.

4. Location of incident: _____.

5. Date and time of incident: _____.

6. Date and time of report:_____.

7. Exact location of incident: _____
    _____.

8. Complainant: _____
    _____.

9. Sex/Race of complainant: _____.

10. Complainant address: ———————————————————————
    _____.

11. Complainant city, state, zip code: _____
    _____.

12. Complainant telephone contact: (Home) _____
    (Office) _____ (Fax) _____

13. Additional means to contact complainants/reporting persons:
    _____
    _____.

14. Illness/Injury received: _____
    _____.

15. Description of illness/injury: _____
    _____.

16. _____ Admitted for treatment

17. _____ Released
    Property code: (V) vehicle from which theft occurred (S) Stolen (R) Recovered (L) Lost (I) Impounded (E) Evidence (F) Found (O) Other

18. _____

Code	Items	ID#	Value Estimated by Complainant	Purchase Date	Value Estimated by Reporter
Example: **S**	**Purse**	12/31/96	$100	12/15/96	$75
_____	_____	_____	_____	_____	_____
_____	_____	_____	_____	_____	_____
_____	_____	_____	_____	_____	_____

19. Description of automobile:
    Year: _____ Make: _____ Model: _____
    Color: _____ Body: _____ Tag/State/Year: _____
    Vehicle Identification Number: _____

20. Suspect description:

   Race: _____

   Sex: _____

   Age: _____

   Height: _____

   Weight: _____

   Eye color: _____

   Hair color: _____

   Complexion: _____

   Scars: _____

   Hat: _____

   Coat: _____

   Jacket: _____

   Pants: _____

   Shirt: _____

22. Narrative. Describe and state the action taken by the Event Manager:

   _____

   _____

   _____

23. Reporting person: _____

24. Status:

   _____ Open

   _____ Closed (List date and if closed by arrest list arrest

               number): _____

25. Internal review: (Describe supervisor's findings below):

   _____

   _____

   _____

Sample Purchase Order

Note: To control payments, the purchase order must be issued to vendors prior to authorization of purchase. The purchase order is not an invoice, rather, it is an official order to the vendor to provide your event organization with specific goods and services. The vendor's invoice will serve as the agreement and therefore must be carefully inspected to ensure that it meets the specifications of the purchase order.

Purchase Order

Tracking Number: XYZ-1

    I. Event Name: _____

   II. Event Date: _____

  III. Vendor Name: _____

  IV. Vendor Address:_____

   V. City, State, Zip:_____

  VI. Vendor Telephone:_____

VII.   Vendor facsimile: _____

VIII.

Quantity	Item Description	Cost per Unit	Total Cost
Example:			
32	Black derbies	$1.00	$32.00
10	Red garters	$.50	$5.00
100	Red bandanas	$3.00	$300.00
Subtotal:			$337.00

IX.   Applicable taxes (if tax exempt attach appropriate documentation):

Tax exempt

X.   Total amount authorized for this purchase: $337.00

XI.   Terms: Net thirty days upon receipt of invoice.

XII.   Delivery date and time: _____

XIII.   Delivery address: _____

XIV.   Delivery contact person (receiving agent): _____

XV.   Telephone number at delivery site: _____

XVI.   Note to vendor. No substitutions or changes may be made to this order without the written consent of the purchaser.

XVII.   Name of Event Management Organization _____
Address _____
Telephone _____

XVIII.   _____
Authorized Signature

Sample Event Evaluation Form

Note

First determine what you are going to measure as the evaluation methodology must support these goals. Next, test the evaluation using a small sample to ensure that it is valid and reliable. Finally, always attempt to collect the highest percentage of responses using a variety of techniques to increase response.

Help Us Improve This Event

Instructions

Please take a few minutes and complete this brief evaluation form. Your comments will result in improved activities and services for this event. **Return your completed form to the collection box located at the exit of this event. Thank you!**

PART ONE

Instructions
Check the appropriate response.

1. Gender:
   _____Male   _____Female

2. Age: (Check one)
   _____18-24   _____25-30   _____31-35   _____36-40
   _____41-45   _____46-50   _____51-55   _____56-60
   _____61-65   _____Over 65

3. Annual household income: (Check one)
   _____$30,000-$49,000   _____$50,000-$59,000
   _____$60,000-$69,000   _____$70,000-$79,000
   _____$80,000-$89,000   _____$90,000-$99,000
   _____$100,000 and above

4. How did you discover this event?
   _____Newspaper   _____TV   _____Radio   Other_____
   Describe: _____

PART TWO

Instructions
Circle the number that best reflects your current opinion.

Scale: 1 = Poor   2 = Fair   3 = No Opinion   4 = Good   5 = Excellent

5. Promotion and advertising for event.
   1   2   3   4   5

6. Availability of tickets.
   1   2   3   4   5

7. Parking accessibility.
   1   2   3   4   5

8. Cleanliness of event site.
   1   2   3   4   5

9. Friendliness of event staff and volunteers.
   1   2   3   4   5

10. On site information and directional signs.
    1   2   3   4   5

11. Number of restrooms.

    1   2   3   4   5

12. Quality of food and beverage.

    1   2   3   4   5

13. Selection of food and beverage.

    1   2   3   4   5

14. Price/value of food and beverage.

    1   2   3   4   5

15. Price/value of entire cost of event.

    1   2   3   4   5

16. Safety and security of event site.

    1   2   3   4   5

PART THREE

Instructions

Check the most appropriate answer.

17. Will you attend next year?

    _____Yes   _____No

    (If you answered *no*, please explain why): _____

    _____

18. Will you tell others about this event in a favorable manner?

    _____Yes   _____No

19. If you answered yes to the question above, how many other people will you most likely tell? (Check one)

    _____1-2   _____3-4   _____5-7   _____8-9   _____Over 10

20. List any other suggestions for improving this event below.

    _____

    _____

    _____

    _____

Important! Return this survey to the collection box at the exit of the event. Thank you!

Index